Peace and Conflict in Inter-Group Relations

Peace and Conflict in Inter-Group Relations

The Role of Economic Inequality

Agnes Katalin Koós

LEXINGTON BOOKS
Lanham • Boulder • New York • London

Published by Lexington Books
An imprint of The Rowman & Littlefield Publishing Group, Inc.
4501 Forbes Boulevard, Suite 200, Lanham, Maryland 20706
www.rowman.com

16 Carlisle Street, London W1D 3BT, United Kingdom

British Library Cataloguing in Publication Information Available

Library of Congress Cataloging-in-Publication Data

Koós, Agnes K.
Peace and conflict in inter-group relations : the role of economic inequality / Agnes Katalin Koós.
pages cm
Includes bibliographical references and index.
ISBN 978-1-4985-0288-7 (cloth : alk. paper)—ISBN 978-1-4985-0289-4 (electronic)
1. Social conflict. 2. Minorities. 3. Income distribution. 4. Equality. I. Title.
HM1121.K677 2014
303.6–dc23

2014035577

∞™ The paper used in this publication meets the minimum requirements of American National Standard for Information Sciences—Permanence of Paper for Printed Library Materials, ANSI/NISO Z39.48-1992.

Printed in the United States of America

Contents

List of Tables

List of Figures

List of Acronyms

ACHPR	African Commission on Human and Peoples' Rights
CONIS	Conflict database of the University of Heidelberg (previously KOSIMO)
DPI	Database of Political Institutions (by a World Bank Research Group)
DSH	Demographic and Health Surveys (of USAID)
EPR	Ethnic Power Relations (dataset)
FSI	Failed States Index[1] (database of the Fund for Peace)
GPI	Global Peace Index (database of the Vision for Humanity)
ILO	International Labour Organization
IPD	Institutional Profiles Database (by the French Government)
ISSP	International Social Survey Programme
IWGIA	International Work Group for Indigenous Affairs
MAR	Minorities at Risk (database of CIDCM)
MICS	Multiple Indicator Cluster Surveys (of UNICEF)
MRG	Minority Rights Groups International
Norris	Pippa Norris's Democracy Indicators (datasets)
OECD	Organization for Economic Co-operations and Development
OSCE	Organization for Security and Co-operation in Europe
PRIO	Peace Research Institute Oslo (Norway)
QOG	Quality of Government (dataset, University of Gothenburg, Sweden)
SOWIP	State of the World's Indigenous Peoples (UN-DESA publication series)

UCDP	Uppsala Conflict Data Program
UN WDI	World Development Indicators (UN database)
UNESCO DME	UNESCO's Deprivation and Marginalization in Education dataset
WDM	World Directory of Minorities (of MRG)
WVS	World Values Survey series

NOTE

1. In May 2014 the measure series' name was changed into "Fragile States Index."

Acknowledgments

This book would not have been possible without the work of so many researchers developing the datasets on which my analyses rely. My primary gratitude goes to the creators of the Minorities at Risk, Ethnic Power Relations, and Quality of Government datasets, but the list of researchers whom I owe thanks for indispensable information is much longer, and includes the authors of a large number of surveys and scholarly publications from both the academic and the policy-making world.

Peace and Conflict was originally conceived as a doctoral dissertation, and I am indebted to Simon Fraser University (SFU), an institution that offered me an inspiring and challenging intellectual environment. I thank my professors for their help and advice, and I gratefully acknowledge receipt of several scholarships from SFU during my doctoral program there.

Besides that of SFU, and of the external reviewer of my dissertation, the book benefitted from the trust and support, as well as from the constructive criticism of a number of scholars who selected previous versions of certain chapters for conferences and publication. Nothing can eclipse, though, the merits of Lexington Books in venturing into the publication of a work with so little chance for bestselling, but that they trusted to be useful for the scholarly community.

And thanks to the person who gave me both advice and support, encouragement and criticism, and so often proofread and edited my drafts, yes, he is my Significant Other.

Chapter 1

Introduction and Roadmap to the Book

A PROBLEM FROM THE DARK SIDE OF DIVERSITY

Liberal democracy assumes that large groups of humans are unitary and cohesive enough so that all segments of the population, including the least advantaged, feel part of it, and accept rule in name of the majority as legitimate. Though the expectation of unity and cohesion has often proved deceptive in practice, the ideology that primarily fuels it has withstood several centuries. For nationalism, unity and cohesion are both fact and moral ideal; thus, a self-governing *demos* has to be a linguistically and culturally unitary ethnic group, and the only viable—and legitimate—form of polity is the sovereign nation-state.

The first salient European counterexample actually predated the formation of this nationalistic ideal. The cantons of Switzerland came together in a viable—and expanding, rather than disintegrating—state despite multiple cleavages along ethnic, linguistic, and religious lines. More generally, but maybe less obviously, the necessity of homogenization has been negated by the everyday life of hundreds of communal groups living side by side for decades, sometimes for centuries, with other ethnic, racial, linguistic, religious, tribal, regional groups, without any significant violent episode between them.[1] Yet, intergroup conflict happens—it happens as interstate and intrastate war, it happens as armed conflict, as intercommunal violence, as group rivalry for resources, as discriminative practices, as segregation, and more recently, increasingly often, it happens as political struggle carried out within the frames of democratic politics.

The relations among communal groups are at the very core of all political thinking. On the one hand, wars—either inter- or intrastate wars—are the most destructive phenomena that political scientists may aspire to avert or contain with their advice. On the other hand, the existence of multiple ethnic, racial, religious, linguistic, and cultural groups within the boundaries of a state raises uncomfortable questions about the fundamentals of our approach to the state, its governance, its sovereignty, and its legitimacy criteria.

Today, more than a quarter of the world's population live in states that are not "their" nation-state, in which they do not belong to the most numerous ethnicity providing the plurality or majority of that state. The indigenous populations (or first settlers of any area) are minorities everywhere, except in Bolivia, and most of the time very poor and sometimes severely oppressed. Outside Europe, not even the more numerous second settlers (such as the Hindus, Malays, Arabs, and Bantus) had much say in determining the boundaries of the state in which they have had to live. All African and South/Southeast Asian boundaries were traced by the European colonial great powers, without much regard for ethnic and other communal lines. In North America, the French and Spanish early colonizers had to succumb to the weapons and money of new waves of English-speaking immigrants.

By the twenty-first century, the Herderian congruence of ethnicity and polity, or of the ethnie and its fatherland, turned out to be an ideal that cannot be meaningfully pursued. Yet, the political imagination is still fettered by the normative implications of the concept. Maybe most importantly, democracy is imagined as based on one *demos* in one state; we have trouble imagining—let alone designing, as in the case of the European Union—multiple *demoi* within multilevel polities. Other normative implications concern things such as sovereignty and nation-building. In the last decades, it turned out that sovereignty can be "pooled," as in the European Union; it can be "morally lost," as in Indonesia, Serbia, and Sudan; and it also can be, less dramatically, "devolved," as in the United Kingdom. We have also learned to look with suspicion at the nation-building exercises of Third World rulers such as the Myanmar junta, but cannot deny the advantages of having (at least) a generally spoken *lingua franca* in a state, and we tend to think that a handful of common values are necessary for the practice of good governance.

Central to all these considerations is our understanding about what makes people with different communal features peacefully coexist and cooperate toward mutual benefits, versus aim at separation, to sever ties and define others as enemy rather than partner. We have a number of theories trying to explain the grip of communal identities on our minds, but also have a number of theories indicating that even the most cherished parochial identities, such as ethnicity and religion, are subject to change. Conquered peoples and victors came together in new nations; new religions were born and acquired millions of followers—sometimes losing them again, as in the process of Reformation and Counter-Reformation.

When are people ready to include "others" in an extended sense of "we," and when do they refuse to accept "others" as equally valuable human beings with equal entitlements to economic, social, and political resources? When are they ready to make concessions for peace, learn languages, tolerate rituals, and when do they expect the other party only to compromise? Is there anything like peaceful integration of minorities or are all minorities doomed to irredentism with their centrifugal aspirations curbed only by force?

For the external observer—and large-N studies cannot help adopting a distant stance to their cases—all of the abovementioned phenomena of tolerance versus intolerance, expanding versus contracting we-consciousness, and integration versus segregation, can be boiled down to the simple opposition between peaceful coexistence and conflict, as these are the manifest, behavioral consequences of all psychic events.[2] Because of a further methodological limitation of observational studies, which are much less equipped to answer causal claims than experimental studies, the prudent formulation of my research question is: "When do we have peace and when do we have conflict?" Yet to the extent to which regression models allow for deterministic claims, I would like to discover the ways in which violent conflict can be avoided.

As a matter of fact, most political science research on this subject thus far has been aimed at explaining the occurrence of conflict, and mainly of violent conflict between groups. Only one widely known paper targeted the explanation of intergroup peace, yet, in small communities that are both minorities in a democratic state (Fearon and Laitin 1996). I think that the fascinatingly wide gamut of relationship patterns among communal groups defined by ethnic, tribal, racial, linguistic, caste, and religious group markers can be conceived as on a scale from active, cooperative peace to implacable violence. I also believe that this variation can be studied as a social fact, and other social facts may be sought to explain it. This does not mean that I expect the same basic factors to account for the whole variation in all details; however, there are a few general factors of which impacts come through beyond the confusing influences of more specific determinants such as the groups' cultural distance, the number of minorities in a state, and even the strategies favored by the group leaders in any particular historical moment. The main issue of interest is what induces a move toward the violent end of the scale, as opposed to moves toward its peaceful and cooperating end.

Conflict mediation and resolution has become a booming specialized field in the last decades, a development helped by the increasing authority of the international community to intervene in warring and war-threatened areas. At its highest levels, this is related to constitutional design practices, that is, to changing the rules of the game in which the communal groups must interact. Much less spectacularly, considerations of communal coexistence have driven the decisions of urban planners for a long period in terms of segregation versus integration, suburbanization, slum redevelopment, and housing policies.

There is, then, a dense practice committed, at least partly, in the name of political science, aimed at fixing intergroup relations, but we cannot say that we have a coherent theory of intercommunal relations. There is also some axiological tension in the field on basic issues such as state sovereignty versus human rights, achieving peace versus achieving justice,[3] universalism versus multiculturalism, and fostering integration versus fostering autonomy. Despite the importance of these ethical issues, this book strives to stay as close to the facts as possible, and does not aim at passing judgments. I hope that more clear-sightedness in the factual domain may help us solve our ethical puzzles.

This introductory chapter offers an overview of the topics and methods covered in the two theoretical and four empirical chapters of the work. The basic design is the simplest possible: I forward some hypotheses about intergroup relations, and attempt to support them with cross-national large-N data. Presentation of the explanatory model in Chapter 3 is preceded by a chapter contextualizing the main research hypothesis and its corollaries. I assume that intergroup hostility is a multicausal phenomenon, and advocate the effect of a cause relatively neglected and sometimes prejudiced in the political science literature—that of economic inequality. Early supporters of this effect were criticized as believers of the myth of "EI-PC nexus" (Lichbach 1989), where the "EI-PC nexus" stands for the belief that "economic inequality breeds political conflict." I will often use this handy label to refer to the causal effect defended by me, though Lichbach's account did not make the distinctions that I make between types of economic inequality, on the one hand, and types of social conflict, on the other. This book is focused on the nexus between intergroup (horizontal) economic inequality and communal conflicts; concerns with interindividual (vertical) economic inequality and noncommunal social conflicts are addressed as contrasts and context of the main causal link to study. Presentation of the empirical support needed three distinct chapters (5 through 7), because my analyses involve three distinct datasets. As an additional feature, one of the three datasets, the result of a prolonged data collection effort bringing about a number of new measures necessary for my project, is depicted in a separate chapter, the fourth.

CONTEXTUALIZING THE INQUIRY (CHAPTER 2)

Researchers may gain inspiration from either reality or literature, from observed anomalies and from emerging new patterns, from discussion with colleagues and from science fiction—to name a few. My interest in intercommunal affairs was clearly overdetermined. I have lived in four countries, and belonged to the ethnolinguistic majority in only one. I have been spared any personal experience of bloody conflict and persecution, but struggled with exhausting language lessons, frustration because of weak language performance, occasional discrimination because of language performance, and yes, partook in group frustration when a majority breached our collective rights. I also had to witness as our previously peaceful neighbors in Yugoslavia started killing each other, and the growing xenophobia in the postcommunist Eastern Europe. My belief in the EI-PC nexus has probably been inspired by the fate of Roma in Eastern Europe, but during my studies of the extended literature on intergroup relations, I found several pieces of information reinforcing this belief.

Chapter 2 gives an overview of the evidence that encouraged my assumptions about the causal effect of intergroup economic inequality, as found both in the scholarly literature and in the directly observable social world. The latter is substantiated with two case examples relating to the hardships of Black Cubans and diasporic Chinese, aside from those of Roma. Most of the chapter, however, deals with the scholarship, because the literature on the relationships among communal groups is scattered across several fields and subfields of social science. It consists of discourses embedded in different disciplinary contexts that resist synthesizing into a well-outlined consistent theory. On the contrary, they rely on different notions of group, in which the salience of features and behavioral patterns is highly variable. For instance, while psychology tends to be interested in processes of group formation and a wide gamut of intergroup relations, political science focuses on groups outlined by ascriptive characteristics, and almost exclusively on violent conflict. My objects of study are the groups relevant to political science, large, "imaginary," going much beyond the face-to-face relationships, and based on socially inherited features, from which exit is not impossible, but comes at a price. That is, I focus on communal groups defined by ethnic, tribal, racial, linguistic, caste, and religious group markers. Yet, on the flipside, my perspective on the relationships among groups follows the diachronic approach of social psychology, and involves intergroup inequality concerns specific to some brands of sociology and development economics. Four areas of study have contributed to the understanding of communal group dynamics informing this work.

One is the social psychology of intergroup relations. This field is clearly dominated by two paradigms, which have kept their influence for decades: those of Allport (1954; 1979) and Tajfel (1974). I will focus on formulating the implications of these paradigms for my topic, while relying on more recent publications about the relations between communal groups (such as

Hogg 2006) and diversity issues (such as Moghaddam, Taylor, and Wright 2003). Social psychology contributes several essential claims to the explanation of intergroup hostility. First, in the spirit of Allport's paradigm, disappearance of prejudice hinges on the frequency of interpersonal contacts within conditions of equality. Second, as derivable from the Tajfel theses (and supported by the so-called functional school of Sherif, as well), in-group favoritism may be overcome only with the effacement of the group markers (such as when two groups ally themselves in a common enterprise) or their sinking into irrelevance (such as the loss of interest in each other's religion in secular developed states). The existence or perception of unfairness and inequality hardens group boundaries, and in "ranked" societies, where the life trajectories of people from different communal groups systematically end at different hierarchy levels, specific group ideology construction and social strategies have been revealed.[4]

The second field of interest is cross-national political science research, targeting the explanation of violent conflicts. This research surged after the end of the Cold War, focused on ethnic or ethnicized civil wars, and was prompted by the observation that after the WWII, internal wars have become more frequent than interstate wars. The dependent variable for this research typically comes from data collection projects such as the Correlates of War Intrastate War data, and the Uppsala Conflict Data Project (UCDP-PRIO[5]), which classify armed conflicts according to their strength, but generally collapse communal and noncommunal conflicts. There are an impressive number of case studies belonging to this brand of literature, but its most typical achievements are the quantitative "epidemiological" type studies, for instance, quantitative works by James Fearon, David Laitin, Jose Garcia Montalvo, Marta Reynal-Querol, Paul Collier, and Anke Hoeffler. The large-N methodology has a number of positive consequences, as the authors refer to each other's work, sum up previous results, and continually test each other's hypotheses and findings. The field seems to be geared toward bringing about a common paradigm for explaining violent conflict. Most explanations allow for multicausality, in which the country's development level, certain features of its institutional structure, as well as the communal group structure and history, together with the opportunities of the minority groups to mobilize, all have an impact on the occurrence of group conflicts. On the controversial side, the utilitarian explanations informing the regression models, which are often rooted in distinctly individualist rational choice outlooks, tend to collide with more communitarian-holistic perspectives.

The third brand of literature referred to in Chapter 2 studies nations, nationalism, and minority-majority relationships in nation-states. A still-persisting schism between constructivist approaches promoting a civic nationalist tradition, and perennialist-primoridalist ones promoting ethnocultural nationalism, emerged as early as the eighteenth century. The latter was preponderant in Europe in the nineteenth century, while the twentieth, mainly its second half, was more typified by a modernist-constructivist take. Work by Modernists such as Bendix (1964), functionalists such as Deutsch (1953) and Haas (1986), and also by constructivists such as Anderson (1983) and Gellner (1983, 1999) situated nation-formation as a historical process paralleling the evolution of capitalism, and it was typically qualitative, theoretical, interdisciplinary, and case study based. The other important focus of this problem area, at least of its share within political science, has been the implications of communal heterogeneity. At the heart of this inquiry are the minority-majority relations turned violent, though interest is not confined to them. On the contrary, if we want to distinguish between the second brand of literature defined above, and the third kind, then it is the latter's broader, sociological outlook, which does not sacrifice detail and complexity for the elegance of the hypothesis, to be called upon. For instance, the Minorities at Risk (MAR) project also aims at finding the causes of ethnopolitical violent conflict. Yet the dataset is much richer than a collection of a number of potential explanatory factors, and it allows researchers to address questions other than "Why and when do they fight each other with violent means?" There are, indeed, meaningful and important alternative questions asked about the minority-majority relationships that do not involve intergroup violence. For instance, there are the questions of whether diversity lowers social capital and the provision of common goods (Alesina and La Ferrara 2000, Baldwin and Huber 2010), or whether it jeopardizes the country's economic performance (Collier 2001, Montalvo and Reynald-Querol 2005). Three relatively recent books that have importantly contributed to the expansion of my theoretical horizon about communal coexistence—Chua 2002, Meerman 2009, and Stewart 2008—can be classified with this literature.

The fourth area of interest is that of policies. There are a large number of state actions or nonactions, at all hierarchy levels, which affect the coexistence of communal groups. The pertinent literature clusters around four main issues:

(i) Constitutional designs that prevent deadly ethnic conflicts. The two main perspectives can be labeled as "integrationist" (Horowitz) and "power sharing" (Lijphart). The big divide between these opposite recommendations seems to lie in their assumptions about the nature of ethnic identity and its relationships with other identity forms. The main tools to regulate intergroup relations are the definition of the state as national or multiethnic, official languages, state secularism, federalism, pillarization, decentralization, the electoral system, and cultural-educational policies.

(ii) Opposition to, versus support for, political mobilizing along communal lines, which involves concerns with the politics of identity, intersectionality, and affirmative action. Closest to my topic, it has witnessed a serious controversy about the role of ethnic parties, about whether these exacerbate intergroup cleavages or help to solve social malfunctions? A rational choice tradition going back to Rabushka and Shepsle (1972) tends to blame ethnic parties for intergroup hostility and violence, while newer research, such as that of Ishiyama (2009), indicates the lack of evidence for these claims.

(iii) The institutions and policies pertinent to majority-minority relationship can be said to pursue one of three ideals—though mixed solutions are also possible. The basic policy ideals to choose from are assimilation (e.g., France), civic patriotism (e.g., the United States), and multiculturalism (e.g., Canada). In general, ethnocultural assimilation is not regarded as a legitimate political goal any longer, and civic patriotisms have long been accused of false universalism, imposing assimilation to a dominant (such as white Anglo-Saxon) culture. Multiculturalism seems to be the intuitively most appealing ideal, but some skepticism can be raised with regard to a diverse population's ability to self-govern, that is, about the compatibility of democracy and diversity. (These concerns have received momentum with regard to the "ever closer union" of the European peoples.)

(iv) Defending the vulnerable groups against discrimination and abuse is a debated issue. According to generally accepted norms, a legitimate state cannot discriminate against any group in any of its functions and services. It is less consensual whether the state should intervene to protect the victims against discrimination by other groups. Advanced welfare states tend to implement laws targeting equal hiring practices, and they may intervene to prevent housing segregation. Effective antihate speech legislation is often opposed in the name of free speech, but there are such laws in place in several countries. More radical solutions are intended to redress the negative conditions attached to the definition of certain groups in order to crush the prejudice that leads to discrimination.

Chapter 2 addresses all of these fields of study in a quest for answers regarding the determinants of intergroup relations, particularly of minority-majority relations. The lessons are presented in Chapter 3, which synthetizes the causes of intercommunal relations in one explanatory model, specifies the hypotheses, and reveals the research design of the project.

HYPOTHESES AND RESEARCH DESIGN (CHAPTER 3)

Political science's cross-national studies focused on the causes of intrastate violent conflicts tend to come together in a common paradigm that allows for the effect of several determinants and is dominated by a methodology relying on multiple regression. My own inquiry has been designed to be compatible with this research tradition, and the methodology of empirical support for claims does closely follow the technique of regression modeling. From this perspective, my main contribution to the existing literature is to provide evidence of the statistically and substantially significant effect of intergroup economic inequality on intergroup hostility and violence.

Yet, the theorization that led me to believe in this effect, referred to as the EI-PC nexus by Lichbach (1989), does not completely fit the mold of the preponderantly utilitarian reasoning with which other determinants of the intrastate conflict have been hypothesized and subsequently—in general—supported.

First, I do not think that it is possible to explain the occurrence of violence on its own, independently of the explanation of intergroup relations in general. In my vision, violence is the end point of a sinuously evolving relationship, which is influenced by both the interaction between groups and certain external circumstances, such as the country's developmental level and international embedment. On the implementation side, this assumption has led to increased concern with the explanatory variables that convey information about the groups and their history, and also with the dependent variables that measure specifically intercommunal, rather than more generally social, tensions.

Second, I believe, and hope, that not all intergroup disputes, and not all conflictual relations lead to violence, as some intergroup issues may be solved in relatively peaceful ways within the limits of everyday politics. That is, certain social constellations inescapably breed intergroup discord, expressed in words and action, but often, the accumulating tension and hostility can be diverted from discharging into violence. On the implementation side, this has led to a two-stage analysis of the data. In my group-level analyses, I used the MAR dataset's "grievance" measures as indicators of a low-to-intermediate hostility level, while high level of hostility was measured with indexes based on the occurrence of a conflict in the CONIS (Conflict Information System; its previous name was Cosimo or Kosimo),[6] and UCDP-PRIO datasets.

Third, I believe in the consequentiality of group consciousness for interpreting the social world, passing judgments on it, and getting involved in political action. My main objection against some individualist utilitarian explanations is not that people are not egoist, but that they tend to be "collective egoist." That is, people do not make their choices exclusively along a cost-benefit analysis of what is good for them personally. Cost-benefit balances set in terms of "we," and "our loss and our gain," as opposed to "my loss and my gain," govern a great proportion of social choices. This "we" may be a family, an institution, a country, or, obviously, a communal group. On the implementation side, my basic explanatory model of intergroup hostility takes group consciousness into account as an important, though mediating factor of intergroup hostility.[7]

Group inequality is the main explanatory variable, the effect of which I intend to support in this work. I argue that difference, or otherness, which is not related to status inequality, is much less likely to become a socially salient group marker than a difference or otherness coupled with status inequality. Gender is salient, claim the feminists, because it is a hierarchy. Why did skin color become socially and politically consequential, while eye color and body height did not (except, maybe, in Rwanda)? Alternatively, why is religion an important group marker in Syria, while it is not in the United States any longer? After Chapter 2 revealed a number of theoretical arguments on behalf of the effect of inequality, Chapter 3 works on fine-tuning these ideas, for instance, addressing the issue of types of group inequality. Groups may be unequal along several dimensions besides the economic, such as political, social, cultural, and legal. Legal inequality has died out in its first meaning as state-sanctioned slavery, but practically, as a social disadvantage[8] and as a result of criminal activity, it is not extinct yet.

The effect of political inequality on intergroup conflict has received substantial support lately due to the work of successive teams headed by Cederman, who created a dataset called Ethnic Power Relations (EPR), and explored the consequences of political inequality on intergroup relations in a number of well-known papers. Since this side of the story is so well documented, originally I did not intend to use the Cederman power status variables in my own regressions, but planned to trace back the effect of political inequality onto the institutions that may empower minorities, such as democracy, proportional representation, and regional autonomy. However, in the group-level regression models, the group-level inequality variables performed much more convincingly than the country-level institutional variables, and I decided to report models that include an ordinal political power scale owed to the EPR project, as well.

My main hypothesis is related to the effect of economic inequality. I would refrain from speculating about the comparative importance of types of inequality to intergroup relations. Economic and political inequalities, in the ways in which they are measured in my models, seem to have quasi-equal effect on grievances and conflict. Unfortunately, I am not able to rigorously account for any other type of inequality. The social disadvantages are not completely absent from my dataset, but they are captured along their manifestation in the two measured dimensions, for instance, the condition of Dalits in India as economic disadvantage, and of Haratins in Mauritania as both economic and political disadvantage. In general, ethnic and linguistic minorities are culturally seriously disadvantaged, but cannot universally be coded as such, since there are a few exceptions.[9] In a number of models, I included MAR's measures of cultural restrictions on minorities in order to account for cultural disadvantages. Yet I have made a case in this book for not equating *de facto* inequality with the state-operating plurality's deliberate discriminative policies. This is of utmost importance in the case of economic inequality. Theorists around the MAR project tend to measure group economic disadvantages with a variable expressing state repression ("economic discrimination"). I claim that horizontal economic inequality engendered by any cause leads to deteriorating intergroup relations, though state intervention may exacerbate the cleavages.

My theory about intergroup relations is summarized in a flowchart in Chapter 3, which highlights the categories of determinants that must be taken into consideration. It also illustrates my assumption that the step from low-to-medium intensity hostility to violent conflict is conditioned and not necessary. The groups of determinants included in the model are: intergroup economic inequality, group consciousness (which, operationalized for tests, becomes a cluster of group characteristics and features of the country's group structure), development level, international influences, and the country's institutional structure.

I developed my hypotheses about the effect of diverse factors with regard to this flowchart, while also answering the need to include in regression models all explanatory variables advocated in the literature thus far. For example, we know that—or there is an emerging consensus about the fact that—a country's political institutions have an effect on the probability of violent conflict. Yet different authors single out different features of this complex. Gurr's (1993) focus is on state repressiveness, which means that democracy lowers the possibility of violence, while Reynal-Querol (2005) claims that it is only the inclusive democratic practices the effect of which is significant. Fearon and Laitin (2003) look at government effectiveness as an impediment to violence,[10] while Cederman et al. focus on participation in governing and classify ethnic groups as being in power versus excluded from power. That is, the explanatory model defines clusters of variables; it does not lead to unambiguous predictor choices. It makes possible, however, to have the hypotheses conveniently presented along six clusters of determinants:

(i) intergroup (horizontal) economic inequality,
(ii) group features and the country's group structure,
(iii) the country's development or modernization level,

(iv) international environment,
(v) the country's institutional system, and
(vi) opportunity for insurrection.

The single most important hypothesis to my project is the first. I claim that intergroup economic inequality increases intergroup hostility and the likelihood of violent conflict, and in all three empirical chapters, with three different datasets, and three different measurements of the intergroup inequality, the regression models aim to demonstrate this effect.

Group and group structure features must be controlled for, and there are a large number of features of interest. The size, or possibly more correctly, the proportion of a group is supposed to increase the probability of conflict (Garcia-Montalvo and Reynal-Querol 2005, Posner 2004), while fractionalization has turned out to have a curvilinear effect (as first hypothesized by Horowitz). Group concentration has an impact on both autonomy demands and the opportunity to organize. The strongest effect in this group may be expected from the history of the groups: past violent episodes make present and future violence more likely. There are no theoretically salient conflicting standpoints in the literature about the impact of distance on the group markers (e.g., language, ethnicity, race, and caste), nor have strong effects been found previously, and I have also refrained from forwarding hypotheses with regard to these.

The effect of development levels and modernization is a complex issue, which involves the "foundational debate" of the nationalism and ethnicity studies between perennialist (or primordialist) standpoints and modernist (or constructivist) theories.[11] Other connections between development and communal relations may be traced through industrialization and urbanization toward increasing diversity and waning group concentration, standardized dialects, and declining importance of tribes. Further, there are some phenomena associated with, but probably not caused by, modernization. Ethnic and linguistic fractionalization is much higher in the Third World than in the developed countries, and the proportion of pluralities is much larger in Europe than in Africa, for instance. Subsequently, while it is difficult to attribute any unique pattern to the effect of development as such, it is absolutely necessary to control for development levels in our models. Empirical work tends to show that violence is lower in more developed countries, and this is what I included among my hypotheses, as well.

Two arguments in the literature are at variance with this claim, but both are confined to some special conditions. Too rapid economic growth that destabilizes the traditional rural social systems before replacing them with new forms of social and political control may lead to more violence, as claimed by Huntington (1968) and Scott (1976), for instance.[12] Importation of free market arrangements by developing countries with unresolved ethnic tensions, mainly in the presence of an economically advantaged minority, is also detrimental to social peace, as claimed by Chua (2002).

Chua's argument is more appropriately addressed within the frames of the category of predictors containing features of the international environment. The effects of globalization can be studied, relatively meticulously, due to the existence of a tripartite measure accounting for three different aspects of globalization: economic, social, and political.[13] We have reasons to hypothesize that a socially and politically more internationalized country is less likely to experience severe communal intolerance and sustained hostility grounded in parochial affiliations. The effect of economic globalization, on the other side, may be taken as antagonistic, to do justice to Chua, and also because there is evidence that in countries adopting the Washington-consensus type economic openness, economic inequality has grown.[14] Yet the most typical independent variables belonging to this cluster of international effects refer to foreign support to warring parties. As most of the literature, I also assume that foreign support to minority groups contributes to their increased political activism, though not necessarily only to violent activism.

The country's institutional system is another complex of factors that emerges in all explanations of social violence, but different features of it may be, and have been, selected as explanatory principles by different authors. As for the formal political institutions, the explanations focus on two dimensions: "inclusiveness" and "repressiveness." Inclusiveness is easier to conceptualize. In an inclusive political regime, minorities are neither discriminated against nor oppressed, and can improve their lot through political activity in peaceful democratic ways, so do not have to turn to violence in pursuit of their group goals. The concept may be variously operationalized as a lack of political discrimination (as in MAR), as the corollary of a proportional representation electoral system (Reynal-Querol 2005), or as inclusion of the ethnic group in power (Cederman et al.), while "simple" democracy is obviously a baseline condition for peaceful interest protection of any kind. The real challenge here is adequately capturing all dimensions of the groups' political inclusion: their representation in the national legislature, executive, and judiciary, and also degrees of group autonomy, both territorial and functional.

The effect of state repressiveness, on the other hand, is more controversial, and there are inherent issues with its conceptualization and operationalization. A *prima facie* interpretation is that a strong state able to retaliate for law breaking deters lawbreakers. A diverging opinion is that state terror invites a fight for freedom, and people rebel against autocrats in the name of freedom, as such. A third claim is that when certain groups suffer in a society, and fail to obtain a remedy in peaceful ways, they rebel against the power in place even if it is perceived as being strong. All three assumptions may be supported with theoretical and empirical arguments, and the possibility of designing an *experimentum crucis* is deeply reduced by some level-of-analysis problems. Democracy is a country-level variable, and a country may be generally democratic while some groups are and feel excluded from power. Exertion of repressiveness may also target certain communal groups specifically; thus, the relationship between state repressiveness and inter-group hostility may look different on different levels of analysis.

Taking into consideration the availability of measurements, as well, I formulated and tested hypotheses claiming that inclusiveness reduces the likelihood of violent conflict by offering alternate ways to minorities to promote their group goals, while government effectiveness tends to deter violence.

The last cluster of explanatory variables to be considered is what I labeled the "opportunity for insurrection" cluster, and has most famously been advocated by Fearon and Laitin (2003). Strictly speaking, it is about a cost-benefit balance of insurrection. Factors that increase the price of conducting armed insurgencies against the power in place, such as a strong and effective state apparatus, are taken for reducing the incentives of the "political entrepreneurs" to initiate violence, while a number of other factors, such as large rural areas, and large proportion of unemployed young males, reduce the costs and increase the incentives of the "political entrepreneurs" to embark on a violent course. While there is no doubt that these cost-benefit balances contribute to the absence or presence of violent conflict, there are disputes about who count as the subjects involved in decision-making, and to what extent these balances influence them. Obviously, the possibility of a "cheap" insurrection is more attractive to political entrepreneurs than to communal groups, whose objective is to get remedies for their plight and naturally prefer peaceful means when available at all. If aggrieved groups take the decision, rather than Machiavellian elites, we should find grievances having more effect on choices, than the "opportunity for insurrection" variables. Subsequently, my expectations with regard to the determinants belonging to this group do not differ from those of Fearon and Laitin (2003) with regard to the significance and the direction of these effects; but I think that they are weaker than the effect of the factors expressing the status of communal groups within their county, and affecting the formulation of grievances.

The basic research design underlying this work is simple and straightforward. It banks on putting all of the abovementioned explanatory variables in cross-national multivariate regression models so that we study the statistical and substantive importance of the coefficients. The implementation, however, has become much more complicated.

First, there has been no readily available dataset that would contain all the explanatory and dependent variables involved in the project. I endeavored to make the best use of the best available data collection, the MAR, which contains 283 minority groups, but I have built up a larger dataset containing more than 700 minority groups for more comprehensive group-level analyses. The template for this extension has been provided by the EPR dataset, which also includes measures of political inequality, and of past intergroup conflict.

Second, intergroup relations can be studied on two levels of analysis: on the level of individual units and on the level of the whole of which they are parts, in this case, at the country level. The fact that most data for the cross-national study of group relations are available only for minority-majority relations, and are missing for the horizontal minority-minority relations, emphasize the importance of a country-level approach. Majorities or pluralities may use the whole state to shape their relationship with the minorities. Subsequently, there is a third dataset explored in this work, a dataset formulated on the country level.

Third, my explanation of the occurrence of violent conflict involves at least two stages. I contend that communal groups are not doomed to hate and fight each other. Intergroup hostility, including minority-majority hostility, emerges in specific and specifiable circumstances, which also influence its intensity. When groups become aware of reasons to be angry with the out-group, which in the case of minorities means that they formulate grievances, they must choose a course of action, which, in the utilitarian tradition, should be the one that is most likely to fix the problem at the smallest cost to the group. Their basic choice is between peaceful and violent political activity. In order to address the gradual unfolding of the events, I have first built models that explain the emergence of grievances, and second, models that explain the occurrence of violence on the basis of grievances. To harmonize my models with the ones commonly used in the cross-national study of violent conflict, I have also tested a third type of regression model, which traces violence back to the causes of grievance. (These are labeled "omnibus" models in the empirical chapters.)

Fourth, the number of dependent variables further multiplied because of practical reasons. I needed to use different sets of dependent variables for the analyses at different levels. As for the group-level dataset, grievances of the minority groups are dependably measured by MAR, but along three different dimensions: economic, political, and cultural. My group-level measure for violent conflict is an adaptation of conflict data from CONIS and UCDP-PRIO, and I was confronted with the dilemma of whether to use a simple binary measure of presence/absence of violence, or try to incorporate information about the intensity of the conflict from my sources. I chose both, which obviously led to more dependent variables and more models to run and report. As for the country-level dataset, I had conflict indicators from different sources for different timespans; I also experimented with measurements that distinguished between communal and noncommunal social conflict.

Fifth, because of the pervasiveness of missing data I had to resort to a technique of multiple imputations. This method is recommended to correct for possible biases caused by list-wise deletion in regression models.[15] I used the method in Chapter 7 with my country-level dataset to make up for missing data on some control variables, primarily the measure of the proportion of unemployed young males, and in Chapter 6 with the MAR data, here, with the intent to extend several variables available only for the 282 MAR groups to all 727 minority groups included in my larger group-level sample. Since I opted for reporting results from both the original dataset and the imputed data, the application of the method involved an extension of the respective chapters.

These five design-related features contributed to the analytic work becoming more complex and considerably longer than most regression-based quantitative research projects in political science. In addition, I have had to face the challenge, quite typical for the social sciences, that important explanatory variables to be used are highly associated with each other, reducing each other's regression coefficients and significance measures.[16] This made me experiment with a number of parallel measurements. Further, in the regression models run on group-level datasets, I still needed a few country-level variables, such as democracy, proportional representation, and government effectiveness. The conservative way to deal with such cases is to build multilevel models, and attempts to address this need brought about an additional number of regression models. Finally, the definition of minority group, and the delimitation of the groups included in analyses, have not always been clear-cut and straightforward. I chose to build the regression models in each chapter with the same groups or group clusters, such as historical minorities in Chapter 5, and historical minorities and also new immigrants and small pluralities in Chapter 6. Some additional data presentation, however, such as frequencies and bivariate relationships, has been extended onto most groups included in the datasets.

DATA (CHAPTER 4, PARTS OF CHAPTERS 6 AND 7)

The analyses presented in chapters 5 through 7 rely on an extensive data collection work comprising of two group-level and a country-level dataset. My main contribution was compiling data: I copied together data from various sources in the same spreadsheet. Yet occasionally, I merged, split, and recoded variables, calculated percentages and averages, and did small-scale imputation with interpolation or regression values. All changes that I made to preexisting measurements are accurately documented. On the one hand, each dataset comes with a codebook; and on the other hand, each of them has a "data collection" version, as different from the "operational" version. I call "operational" the datasheets that include only information that can be fed into SPSS software, and have been effectively fed into it—these are what the literature refers to as replication data, as well. The data collection sheet contains comments related to certain variables and variable values, and the input ("raw material") variables from which a more synthetic measure, or a measure more suitable for analyses, was calculated. For instance, data on internally displaced persons was averaged across a number of measurements, and then made proportional to the size of the country's population—the data collection sheet includes six "internally displaced" variables, while the operational or replication data include only one, a calculated version. Beyond compiled and cleaned data, the datasets contain two variables, technically variable groups, which are essentially new contributions to the previously available measurements.

First, I created a group-level measure of intergroup economic inequality, relying on official statistics and scientific survey data as raw material. After defining the communal groups of interest in each country, I looked for data that typified their comparative economic standing. My preference has been for official statistics, such as disaggregated income data, data on household net worth, and disaggregated educational statistics. Practically, though, most of my primary data came from two large-sample cross-national survey projects, carried out by USAID and by UNICEF, called the Demographic Health Survey (DHS) and Multiple Indicator Cluster Survey (MICS) series, respectively. In addition, I collected demographic data from scientific opinion surveys relying on nationally representative sampling, such as the International Social Survey Programme (ISSP), the World Value Surveys (WVS), and certain regional barometers, including the Afrobarometer, and the Asian Barometer, for instance. All of this information characterizing the comparative economic standing of the groups came in different units of measurement. Most helpfully, MICS classified respondents on a "Wealth Quintile" ordinal scale, that is, the respondents were assigned to one of five wealth categories based on their empirically observed possessions (land, house, animals, bonds, and shares). In countries in which MICS has also recorded the ethnic or other communal belonging of importance—unfortunately, this has not happened in every case—it was very simple to calculate the Wealth Quintile Index (WQI) value for each group. The group's position on the WQI became my main intergroup inequality measure (named INEQ_1).[17]

Since there was a large number of countries for which the raw material characterizing the groups' comparative position has been available in diverging kinds of measurements only, I had to work out conversion rules between the WQI and these later. For instance, as the WVS use a 10-point scale to classify the income of the respondents, this had to be collapsed for "translation." For converting the group educational achievement, or life expectancy, into WQI, I used the cases where both measurements were available, as Rosetta Stone. I have to admit that this work could not be done by applying very strict rules because of crosscutting complexities. For instance, the same educational (mainly female education) levels tend to be associated with higher wealth levels in Muslim, than in Christian populations. Ultimately, though, the whole "data collection dataset" is made available for public scrutiny. It displays both the "raw material" data point and the subsequently assigned WQI value. Further validity tests of my inequality data consist of comparing these variables to anything similar in the literature. Unfortunately, there are only three similar measures, and because of specific issues, none of them can be taken for a perfect standard. On the group level, MAR has a variable intended to measure the minority's economic disadvantage brought about by the majority's hostile activity, called "economic discrimination" (ECDIS). Though not meant to be a measure of intergroup economic inequality, as such, it captures much of it. Across 282 common cases, MAR's ECDIS variable is correlated with my INEQ_1 at –0.452, and with my INEQ_2, at 0.440. Other measures of inequality exist on the country level only, and I had to calculate the standard deviation of my INEQ_1 values for each country in order to compare my variable with those. Obviously, this collection of standard errors is not a perfect conversion of the information contained in the group-level indicator, but still results in considerable, statistically significant correlation coefficients with the two comparable measures.[18]

My second variable is a measure of group autonomy, to be added to the cluster of political institutions characterizing each country. It makes use of a number of decentralization indicators included in the Database of Political Institutions and Quality of Government datasets. Four existing decentralization measures were averaged into a single decentralization index measure. The less formalized part of the work was to examine to what extent each country's administrative subdivisions follow the settlement patterns of the communal groups. Once this congruence was classified on a 5-point ordinal scale, I could multiply it with the decentralization index, obtaining a measurement of the extent to which countries allow for self-governance of their regionally concentrated minorities. The only data source against which I may test my measures is, again, the MAR.[19] MAR has dedicated group-level variables for both group concentration and group autonomy—but for 283 groups only, not for 727 eligible groups. Across the 282 common cases, MAR's group autonomy dummy is correlated with my corresponding measure (the interaction term of decentralization and settlement patterns) at 0.377.[20]

The dependent variables used in-group-level analyses are specially modified versions of preexisting indicators. A triad of economic, political, and cultural grievances was imported from MAR, and left unchanged for the 282 MAR groups. Since MAR's selection criterion is to include minorities whose coexistence with their majorities is problematic, all other groups in my extended sample were assigned the "no-grievance" value by default, with a handful of exceptions, thoroughly documented in the codebook.[21] The indicators of conflict have been imported from the CONIS and UCDP-PRIO datasets. These two complement each other in the sense that all severely violent conflicts recorded in UCDP-PRIO are mentioned in CONIS, but the latter has a large number of lower-intensity conflicts, as well, and classifies conflicts on a 5-point ordinal scale. For each communal group in my dataset, I examined whether they have been involved in any conflict recorded in these datasets between 2005 and 2010. I considered only intergroup conflicts, and those fought between the state plurality and a minority group. After identifying the conflicts, three measures were formulated, a dummy and two interval variables.[22]

I named my group-level datasets EPR_MAR_EXT and MAR_EPR_MI. The names intend to make it clear that they rely on the EPR and MAR datasets,[23] though they include additional groups as well. These come from my third basic source, the World Directory of Minorities published and maintained by the Minority Rights Group International (MRG). This Non-governmental Organization (NGO) has collected and disseminated the largest quantity of information concerning minorities, but their knowledge is available in discursive, encyclopedia-like format only, not as a formalized database. During the preparation of my EPR_MAR_EXT dataset, the template of countries and groups included in EPR was completed with groups and countries listed in the world directory. The quantitative thresholds set by MAR were obeyed: I included only countries above 500,000 people and groups above 100,000 people or 1 percent of the population. Though the application of this rule led to dropping a few small groups from EPR, I had to add many more, and assign values to them on two basic EPR variables. The task was implemented with the help of MRG data.

Since this group-level dataset, the EPR_MAR_EXT is the most complex of the three, its creation and main features are presented in detail in a dedicated chapter, the fourth, while the analyses conducted with it are summarized in Chapter 5. Chapter 6 contains both a brief description of the features of MAR_EPR_MI, and the presentation of the analyses, and the same is true of Chapter 7, dealing with the country-level dataset. The latter concatenates well-known standard measures of development, political institutions, and country globalization level taken from United Nations-affiliated sources and scholarly compilations (such as the Quality of Government data, for instance), with data obtained from think tanks of increasing prestige and reputation, particularly the Vision for Humanity (creator of the Global Peace Index (GPI) series) and Fund for Peace (creator of the Failed States Index[24] (FSI) series).

DATA ANALYSIS (CHAPTERS 5, 6, AND 7)

The apex of this research project has been to run regression models that confirm or refute the effect of my zealously advocated main explanatory variable in the presence of a number of other variables. From the perspective of this testing, all other variables are probably rightly labeled "controls" —my intergroup inequality measures have had to prove their potential by competing against the influence of other predictors. From the perspective of an accumulating knowledge base about the evolution of intergroup hostility, and occurrence of violence, however, the other variables are codeterminants, or copredictors, and we cannot have a more important research task than accounting for them all so that we maximize the explanatory power of our models. Since I believe that intergroup relations are multicausal phenomena, and even overdetermined by a very large number of copredictors, I have pursued including in models all variables promoted in the literature, unenthusiastically accepting the associated risk of collinearity.

The results of the regression analyses are summarized in the concluding chapter. Yet, I cannot help reporting, here too, that the impact of intergroup economic inequality has been corroborated by data, on both group level and country level, and by using any of the three applicable measures: my own INEQ series, MAR's ECDIS variable, and the Fund for Peace's "Uneven Development" index. The strength of the effect is subject to interpretation, and practically hinges on comparisons with the effect of other predictors in the same models. As a general pattern, the impact of horizontal economic inequality appears stronger on grievances than on violent conflict, and stronger at the country level than at the group level. Wherever possible, I endeavored to report standardized coefficients from ordinary least squares models, for an immediate glimpse at the strength of each coefficient.[25]

The other predictor to which I have paid special attention is group autonomy, mainly as measured with my own variable. Evidently, I am interested in the effect of all indicators of political inequality, measuring either the fact of, or the potential for it, but a measure that can distinguish between the Horowitzian and Lijphartian projects has been of particular concern to me. I have had to realize that even if the effect of intergroup economic inequality garners serious scholarly support, the chances of deliberate political intervention engaged in easing group inequalities are not encouraging. Compared to this difficult task of closing economic gaps, changing the political institutions to reduce the probability of intercommunal conflict is a more promising path. Yet, here the highly controversial issue of integrationism versus power sharing still ensnares us. I would say that my analyses do justice to Lijphart; however, my data and methods have not been ideal for securing strong support for his proposal.

Even if the regression models were the most important analytical task to achieve, some simpler analyses, such as frequencies, group means, and correlations, have provided valuable, and sometimes surprising, background information on communal group issues and our ways to study it.

First, my EPR_MAR_EXT dataset, which contains data about communal groups in 155 countries, collectively comprising 97.5 percent of the world's population, allows for estimates of the minority and immigrant populations worldwide, and depending on the definition of minority, this share may reach more than 45 percent of the overall population included in the dataset.[26] Some basic trends typifying their condition, such as being poorer and politically less empowered than their majorities (or pluralities) may also be mapped. Closer analysis sheds light on the ambivalence of development's effect on minority populations; it cannot be sustained that modernization has improved their position relative to their pluralities.

A different type of secondary benefit from my research is related to the possibility of comparing data across different datasets, for instance, the group feature estimates given in MAR and EPR.[27] MAR, which contains 283 cases, can be contextualized in EPR_MAR_EXT, which contains 727 comparable groups, and we may get a better understanding of what is commonly referred to as its selection bias.

I have also had the opportunity to run a few comparative analyses about the causes of peaceful protest activities, as compared to the causes of violent rebellions, based on the MAR data, and to compare the causes of communal conflict with the causes of noncommunal social conflict, based on data borrowed from the Institutional Profiles Database (IPD), supported by the French government and included among the sources of the World Bank Institute's worldwide governance indicators. This opportunity contributed to a better outlining of the effect of types of inequality: as expected, horizontal economic inequality has a great role in shaping intercommunal conflict, while vertical economic inequality (Gini) is a predictor of noncommunal social conflict.

*

I would like to conclude this introduction by addressing a few questions that certainly arise with regard to any research project, and which concern three essential features of the work: the importance of the research question, the novelty of the approach, and the feasibility of a conclusive answer.

Minority issues have been an underresearched field within academia, and general awareness of the size of minority population worldwide, as well as of their special needs and problems, is minimal. Since nonmajorities are almost half of the world's population, we may imagine a research infrastructure approaching the size of that of women's studies to be a fair share for minority studies. Like in women's studies, the interest in relations between in-groups and out-groups should not be confined to explaining violent, militarized conflicts. In-group biases and intergroup hostility bring about much more social injustice and human suffering than that expressed in the number of battle deaths from organized violence.

This book's approach is relatively novel in political science quantitative research because it endeavors to apply a psychology- and sociology-inspired perspective about the gradual and step-wise unfolding of hostility in intergroup relations. Gurr and his colleagues also tend to see intergroup relations as processes, but they do not share the belief in the effect of horizontal inequality, as such. The role of intergroup inequality in shaping intergroup relations has been strongly promoted by theorists outside the political science domain, particularly the authors of the Stewart (2008) volume. The first well-known political science paper expressly referring to this theory of horizontal inequalities was published in November 2011. Yet, the authors of this paper, Cederman and colleagues, have not had the empirical tools to test the theory on a truly comprehensive worldwide sample. I managed to obtain reasonably useful measurements of intergroup (horizontal) economic inequality on both group level and country level for more than 95 percent of the world's population, and to build regression models, with all expectable control variables, which support the effect of horizontal inequality.

This is also an answer to the feasibility question. A large number of previous trials to support the effect of economic inequality on violent conflict failed because they lacked good quality data. Reliable factual information on economic inequality is more difficult to obtain than information on other economic facts (e.g., growth rates and economic globalization). However, conceptual issues—not distinguishing between vertical and horizontal inequality, and looking at the effect of vertical (interindividual or interhousehold) inequality, rather than at the effect of horizontal (intergroup) inequality—have also contributed to the weak performance of economic inequality in previous regression models. Wide-scale data collection on intergroup economic inequality was unimaginable before the publication of the DHS and MICS survey series. Official statistics fall much too short from providing these data in most countries, and the opinion poll-type scholarly surveys typically under-sample minorities, while in countries with smaller minority groups, the number of minority respondents might be unusably small even if they were correctly, that is, proportionally, sampled. As for the country-level measurements, the Fund for Peace's initiative of publishing their FSI has also been conditioned on technical and scientific advances, in this case, on the evolution and improvement of content analytic work.

Thus, as a final word to this chapter, I owe deeply felt thanks to the creators of all of my data sources and I hope that I made good use of their work.

NOTES

1. As Fearon and Laitin (1996) emphatically claimed, intergroup peace is a more general pattern than communal conflict.

2. Before the spread of scientific opinion polls, and the development of the content analytic tools capable to analyze enormous amounts of raw material in order to tap into the common psyche, a positivistic epistemology expected social sciences to rely on manifest behavior only. Though the reservations toward opinion poll and content analysis-based research have substantially subsided, a preference toward "hard," statistical or experimental data is still in existence.

3. The common normative ideal of the profession has always been intrastate peace, except for the case of unequal groups. When subordinate groups face dominant groups, the ideal of immutable peace is challenged and it may be surpassed by the ideal of emancipation.

4. Advantaged groups tend to elaborate self-legitimating mythologies, as exposed by Mary Jackman (1996), for instance. Stephen Wright has highlighted an armory of conflict-avoiding strategies on the side of the disadvantaged groups (e.g., Wright and Taylor 2003). Yet, other authors highlight that in certain circumstances the conflict-avoiding strategies collapse and give way to violent clashes (Hogg 2006).

5. The Uppsala Conflict Data Program (UCDP) data have been merged with the Peace Research Institute Oslo (PRIO) data.

6. "Conflict Information System," previously COSIMO or KOSIMO, a project of the University of Heidelberg, http://www.hiik.de/en/kosimo/kosimo2.html.

7. Because we lack measurements of group consciousness, it could not be included among the regression predictors. Yet the models feature a number of measurable objective facts that may plausibly be assumed to affect group consciousness, most notably the measures of intergroup inequality, and of past intergroup conflicts.

8. The legal environment may affect intergroup equality in several ways, not only by allowing for slavery. For instance, in the United States, laws on school segregation have enormous effect on racial relations. Unfortunately, the trend is a reversal of the last century's minority-friendly laws. As Hannah-Jones 2014 summarizes: "In recent years, a new term, apartheid schools—meaning schools whose white population is 1 percent or less . . . —has entered the scholarly lexicon. . . . In districts released from desegregation orders between 1990 and 2011, 53 percent of black students now attend . . . schools in which at least nine out of 10 students [are] racial minorities."

9. For instance, English-speaking (minority) Indian citizens are more advantaged in a globalizing world than the Hindi-speaking (plurality) Indian citizens; and Sunni Syrians may count on substantial external support from other Sunnis against an Alewite state power.

10. They also consider factors such as an economy with a large proportion of unemployed young males, and spread-out rural population, which may be conceptualized as institutional variables in the larger sense of the word.

11. The most optimistic Modernists (Inglehart may be taken for a descendant of these) expect economic progress to completely strip people of their parochial ties. More realistic theorists confine their optimism to the fact that development lessens the occurrence of violence, and some of them have worked on designing modern democratic states that may prevent ethnic conflict either by integrationist policies, which penalize politicizing along communal lines as a danger to institutional stability (Horowitz 1985), or power-sharing policies, which enable communal groups to negotiate their coexistence from quasi-equal political positions (Lijphart 1977).

12. Huntington's *Clash of Civilizations* highlights another potential consequence of globalization, the large-scale conflict among groups defined by religion and ideology, rather than by citizenship and within-country group markers. The emergence of a global Muslim identity, which often defines itself in opposition to a Christian-Western culture, is our everyday experience. Yet, on the one hand, there are strong within-Muslim (Sunni-Shiia) and within-Muslim-country (Libya, Egypt, and Yemen) cleavages and clashes, as well. On the other hand, the Muslim-Western opposition may be studied as a communal conflict in the global arena, where the intergroup inequalities are played out as inequalities among countries.

13. The KOF Index of Globalization, http://globalization.kof.ethz.ch/

14. Actually, there is proof only for the increase of the vertical (interindividual) economic inequality as a consequence of neoliberal ("orthodox") economic policies. We do not have cross-national measurements of the dynamics of intergroup (horizontal) economic inequality. As a general rule, however, in societies experiencing economic gaps between communal groups, these gaps increase when the interindividual inequality, as measured by Gini, increases.

15. Within political science, G. King is the strongest advocate of the method. Together with a team of statisticians, he produced an easy-to-handle software to impute data in lacunar datasets (Amelia II).

16. Regression models are supposed to weed out spurious causal explanations by reducing the effect of the false predictor in the presence of the real predictor. Yet, most social phenomena are overdetermined in the sense that any predictor of several that we use in a model may influence the outcome on its own, independently of the effect of others. (That is, none of them is "false," but given the association between them, they may falsify each other.) For instance, both development level and government effectiveness may reduce violence, but they are correlated, and their measurable effect in multivariate models is smaller when they are both in the same model.

17. Additional intergroup inequality indicators were developed from this basic one. First, INEQ_2 measures the distance of each minority group from the majority on the WQI (INEQ_1) scale. INEQ_3 transforms all minority-majority distances into

positive values, instead of accounting with negative values for advantaged minorities. Finally, INEQ_4 scales these distances to the country's GINI (vertical or interindividual inequality) index.

18. The correlation coefficients for the 2006 round of the FSI series inequality component are 0.269 with my standard deviation of INEQ_1 (across 142 cases), and 0.562 with the Baldwin and Huber (2010) measure (across 45 cases). St.Dev_INEQ is correlated at 0.450 with the Baldwin and Huber measure, across 46 cases. Further analyses in Chapter 7 show that the St.Dev_INEQ indicator is more narrowly focused on measuring intergroup inequality only, while the other two incorporate more vertical inequality, as well.

19. EPR also has a dummy for group regional autonomy, but lacks a measure of group concentration. Unfortunately, it does not seem to make good sense to use the autonomy indicator in models without controlling for group regional concentration.

20. Historically, this endeavor of measuring the congruence of the settlement patterns with the administrative divisions, and then accounting for the autonomy of the units, grew out from an idea of designing an *experimentum crucis* to choose between the policy proposals of Horowitz (integrationist proposal: design administrative units that crosscut the ethnic settlement patterns) and Lijphart (power-sharing proposal: design administrative units congruent with the ethnic settlement patterns, and give them maximum autonomy). Also, first, I worked on implementing it on the level of federal units. I measured the degree of federalism, and the congruence of the federal states with the communal settlement patterns; but this variable turned out to be less useful for the analyses conducted within the frames of this work, because of the relatively small proportion of federal states.

21. The reasons to override the "no grievance" rule were: a "discriminated" status of the group in EPR; borderline size coupled with obvious group disadvantages; and inconsistency within MAR (no grievance, but recorded conflicts).

22. The dummy indicates whether the group had any conflict recorded in CONIS for the respective years. The first interval variable averages the CONIS assessments for five years. Finally, the second interval variable relies on a little more complex mathematical formula, which incorporates the overall length of the conflict, and whether it is mentioned in UCDP-PRIO.

23. The suffix at the end of EPR_MAR_EXT, from "extended," refers to the fact that some variables contained in MAR and EPR have been extended to cover all communal groups included in the dataset. For instance, all EPR_MAR_EXT groups were coded on the MAR grievance variables, under the abovementioned condition that non-MAR groups were assigned the value of "no grievance." "MI" refers to the procedure of multiple imputation.

24. In May 2014 the index was renamed "Fragile States Index."

25. The other important value, which I was able to report from all models, is the significance of the coefficients, given in p-value, which specifies the possibility of the null hypothesis that the effect does not exist in the real population. This can also be taken for a more rudimentary measure of strength, a predictor with the p-value of 0.000 is certainly much stronger than a predictor with a p-value of 0.045, though the latter is still statistically significant at the most conventional alpha = 0.05 level.

26. If we take the largest group in each country for plurality, and count as minority only people who do not belong to these pluralities, their percentage is 34.9. If we count as minority everyone who belongs to communal groups smaller than 50 percent of the population, the result is 45.6 percent.

27. A number of parallel measurements could be tested against each other, to start with the very basics, the group number and group proportion estimates, and measurements of political position of the groups, as well.

Chapter 2

Why Believe in the EI-PC Nexus?

THE THEORETICAL BACKGROUND OF THE ARGUMENT

This chapter gives an account of both my readings and experiences informing the book. However, I shun framing them as an intellectual autobiography. On the contrary, I aim at presenting both the scholarly endeavors explaining intergroup hostility, on the one hand, and some recent cases of hostility outbursts, on the other, by maintaining throughout an objectifying distance. Situating these sources of inspiration and reference in a more personal "context of discovery" would suggest what I do not claim, namely, that I was the first to notice the impact of economic inequality on intergroup relations. Yet this work preponderantly inscribes in the context of demonstration, so sharply distinguished from that of discovery by Sir Karl Popper. I eagerly acknowledge all previous attempts to establish and test the impact of economic disparities on intergroup relations, and I only claim that I improved on previous trials. Again, I acknowledge that my possibility of improving was contingent on the accumulation of more conceptual clarity about types of inequality and more empirical data, primarily more disaggregated economic information.[1]

The literature on the relationships among communal groups defined by ethnic, tribal, racial, linguistic, caste, and religious group markers is scattered across several fields and subfields of social science. There is no interdisciplinary summary of these contributions, let alone a synthetic theory or central paradigm of the subject matter. There are discipline- and subdiscipline-confined summaries and, occasionally, an evolving paradigm of the subfield, such as a growing consensus of political scientists about the factors that may come into play when studying the causes of violent ethnic conflict. Unfortunately, the argument cannot be confined to the narrowly drawn political science debates. Violent conflict, the most conspicuous outcome of stressful group relationships, is a political phenomenon *par excellence*. Yet, political science is not the most versed in the study of the everyday features and trends of intergroup relations. These have traditionally been the objects of sociology and social psychology. And political science's skepticism about the impact of economic inequality on intergroup relations is likely to be fueled by the fact that the links between the two are beyond its—narrowly defined—disciplinary boundaries.[2]

The most complete, but (sub)discipline-constricted review of the claims related to the impact of economic inequality on intergroup relations is dated 1989. The author, Mark Lichbach, labeled the issue the "EI-PC nexus" (the thesis that economic inequality leads to political conflict), and concluded that this EI-PC nexus was an unsupported myth of the profession. Lichbach pointed out that the notions had been operationalized in very different ways by different authors, and he found that the "fatal flaw of statistical models of the EI-PC nexus" is the "lack of theory and explanation," more specifically, "[these] approaches are found to be deficient because they have not illuminated the assumptions and reasoning that explain how and why inequality produces conflict" (p. 434). His analysis suggests that, on the one hand, the links between the condition of inequality and political mobilization are not elaborated on, and on the other, the scholars endorsing the EI-PC nexus do not take seriously the Olson- and Hardin-type of arguments about the difficulties of collective action.

Actually, in 1989 there were already explanations of the intergroup "EI-PC nexus," just that they were formulated in the field of social psychology, not that of political science. Other reasons for advocating this nexus were promoted in the sociological literature, which resulted, for instance, in the book edited by Stewart (2008).

A main point that we have to make is that critics of the "EI-PC nexus" do not distinguish between interindividual and intergroup economic inequality.[3] The branch of sociological literature that is most interested in them uses the labels "vertical inequality" versus "horizontal inequality" to refer to the two types. The vertical type is measured with the Gini indexes and it is completely blind toward any other feature than the individuals' comparative economic position. It is quite unsuitable to compare the economic standing of groups, even if high Gini indexes are often associated with high intergroup inequality. Those who suppose EI will lead to PC expect this to happen when the economic standing of two or more groups is perceived as being unequal.

Once we focus on group inequality instead of vertical inequality, we are not left without theories explaining the linkage between the condition of inequality and conflictual outcomes. Nevertheless, a clarifying caveat may be necessary. My focus here, and the focus of those reproached by Lichbach for believing in the EI-PC nexus, has been on the relationships between communal groups. Thus, "PC" has meant intergroup struggle. I do not intend to make assumptions about "pure" class struggle in this work, which may occur as a result of increasing vertical inequality, even in communally homogenous populations. Yet, the Marxist classics have always emphasized the role of class consciousness in the workers' movement. The poor are not expected to politically mobilize only because they are poor. They are expected to mobilize following the realization that they are unjustly poor: that there is a group with ostensibly different features (such as ownership of the means of production), which gets richer as others get poorer. It is the notion of exploitation that makes Marxism "revolutionary," that is, politically mobilizing. All great religions are egalitarian and aim at the fair distribution of earthly goods, but most of them eschew support to political mobilization of the poor. Compared to Marxism, two elements are missing: defining poor and rich as two large groups with antithetical interests, and the appeal to group consciousness. On the contrary, religions tend to ontologize and exogenize the unequal distribution of wealth as given by God, and emphasize the community of all those with the same faith. They also like to picture society as gravitating toward a large middle class, an ideal shared with the liberal ideology. There is, then, in ideologies, a strong association between groupness and group consciousness, on the one hand, and political mobilization and political strife, on the other. The existence of "ranked" communal groups in a society means overlapping communal and economic cleavages, and these may be expected to be more mobilizing than the economic cleavage on its own. However, my research question concerns the other side of the issue; it asks whether the economic cleavage makes the communal cleavages deeper and harder to overcome.[4]

The quest for answers will meander through four disciplinary subfields: one in social psychology, one in sociology, and two in political science.

Social Psychology: Explaining Intergroup Behavior

Intergroup relations are an increasingly important and expanding research area within social psychology. This assessment has been reached by the psychologists themselves. Improving on previous reviews of the status of group research within the social psychological research agenda, de Moura et al. (2008) published an updated account of the field's evolution trends. The authors aimed at establishing the contribution and impact of group-related research to social psychology, and used statistical analysis of journal articles to get the numbers.

In order to determine the impact of group-related research, de Moura and her colleagues selected the ten top-cited papers from each major social psychology journal over a period of 10 years (1998–2007). They found that the proportion of group-related articles among the high-impact papers was 35.2 percent and concluded that research of group processes and intergroup relations continued to be a healthy and influential area of social psychology as a whole. The authors also identified the recurring topics and keywords of the papers. The inquiries were dominated by the themes of intergroup contact, intergroup conflict, social identity, prejudice, and stereotyping, which means that the subfield is still under the spell of the classic paradigms originated by Allport (1954; 1979) and Tajfel (1974). Concerns with stereotyping, prejudice, and contact make up the core of the Allport theory, while Tajfel's theory is most often referred to as "social identity theory" (SIT). We may wonder to which extent these paradigms rival and complement each other, seeking answers on two different levels, with Allport focusing on individuals, and Tajfel, on social environments.

There are some important commonalities between the two perspectives. First, both paradigms are set to explain behavior—even wicked, discriminative, and murderous behavior—not as unique events determined by a window of opportunity opened to evil, or by some people's bad nature, but as extreme results of everyday, normal psychological processes. At the end of this intellectual trend of "banalizing evil," there is, for instance, Moshman's 2007 paper, claiming that "genocide . . . is not so much a crime of hate as a crime of identity . . . Dichotomization enables dehumanization, which in turn enables destruction . . . To recognize that genocide is rooted in identity, then, is to recognize that the potential perpetrators of genocide include all of us, individually and in our countless collectivities."

A second commonality is their focus on operationalized and/or operationalizable features of the intergroup behavior. Intergroup conflict (tension or hostility) is operationalized with discriminative behavior and prejudices against each other, which are, in principle, measurable and vary along a continuum from mild in-group favoritism without negative prejudice toward the out-group, to dehumanizing (or infra-humanization of) the out-group, which enables their killing without moral discomfort or regret.

Yet the comprehension of intergroup conflict is quite divergent. Allport's theory aims at explaining the prejudice by classifying it as stereotyping, an unavoidable feature of human thinking. Tajfel's explanation of discrimination involves in-group favoritism, which has empirically been shown to be a universal human attitude, unavoidably present in all social situations featuring any social group delimited with any kind of group marker.

The contributors to a volume on the afterlife of Allport's prejudice theory (Dovidio et al., 2005) expressed some ambivalence about the theory, yet seemed quite confident that that the therapeutic advice derived from it may work in practice. The ambivalence of the assessments is rooted in Allport's own inconsistency about prejudice. There is some tension between his presentation of prejudice as result of "normal" stereotyping and his most often used definition of prejudice as "an antipathy based upon a faulty and inflexible generalization." The latter shifts the focus away from the universal cognitive mechanisms toward more idiosyncratic personal traits, and the circumstantial motivational impacts producing it. While the idea that prejudice is a kind of stereotype seems to enjoy widespread support, its definition as "antipathy" and as "faulty and inflexible generalization" has invited severe critiques. For instance, Eagly and Diekman (2005) point out that not all prejudices express antipathy, for example, women may be liked, but denied the qualities to be good bosses. Further, prejudices may be relatively accurate with regard to group averages, while they are inaccurate in the concrete context in which someone discriminates because of them. And prejudices may change dramatically, without changing their behavioral consequences. For instance, in the twentieth century, US Blacks became discriminated against not because of an alleged innate intellectual inferiority, but because of supposed laziness. Yet, the prejudice-is-a-kind-of-stereotype thesis may also be challenged on grounds that it is undersocialized. For instance, Fiske (2005) highlights that prejudice emerges from an interplay of cognition and social motives.[5] The social environment is highly consequential for someone's adoption of certain prejudices—actually, the impact of both overt and covert constraints may be assumed. In contrast, to a large extent, Allport's efforts were directed toward detecting the individual psychological prerequisites of prejudice. Though he admitted the role of such social constraints as parental influence, he was interested in the personality types most prone to foster prejudices. This way he remained open to the criticism of Dovidio, Glick & Rudman (2005), who state that "Allport overemphasized the role of personality in prejudice, seeing bigots as having weak personalities, as insecure, easily frustrated, and intolerant of ambiguity . . ." Nevertheless, the search for prejudice-prone personalities has been pursued by many researchers, leading to results such as Adorno's F scale for measuring authoritarianism, Rokeach's D scale for measuring dogmatism of any extreme, Altemayer's (1981) Right-Wing Authoritarianism (RWA) scale, and Sidanius & Pratto's (1999) Social Dominance Orientation (SDO) scale. All these turned out to be correlated with prejudice-proneness, but the latter two are uncorrelated with each other, and also unrelated to indices of psychopathology. As Duckitt (2005) presents the situation, there are at least two personality types with above-average inclination to foster prejudices. On the one hand, there is the right-wing authoritarian, an insecure traditionalist, who thinks about the world as a very dangerous place, in which some out-groups may be especially threatening, hence the RW authoritarian is full of hatred against them. And, on the other hand, there is a tough-minded competitor, the social dominance-oriented person, who thinks that the world is a jungle designed for the survival of the fittest, in which certain human groups have to fight each other, thus fostering negativity toward rivals and lower-status groups.

To summarize, the cognitive mechanism of stereotyping explains how the formation of prejudices is possible, but Allport's theory leaves room for a number of arguments about the causes of their formation, as well as for more research about what personality types in what social circumstances are most likely to acquire them. Fortunately, the classification of prejudice as a stereotype, despite the *lacunae* of the theory, was enough to inspire a successful social practice to combat it. This therapeutic side of the Allport theory is commonly referred to as "the contact hypothesis." Simply put, if a faulty stereotype can be surpassed by becoming more familiar with the misunderstood phenomenon, a prejudice may be defeated by personal encounters with people belonging to the out-group, who will turn out to be, guaranteed, very different from the stereotyped image that we foster about them. There is a catch, though. Not all types of contacts are suitable to allow for the stereotyped people's showing off their nonstereotypical and idiosyncratic features. Allport spoke about four criteria for making the contact work toward dismantling prejudices, called the "optimal contact conditions", which were to different degrees implemented in subsequent empirical work. Pettigrew and Tropp (2006) conducted a meta-analytic test of the contact theory. They reviewed 515 studies involving 713 samples and found that "intergroup contact typically reduced intergroup prejudice." Allport's optimal contact conditions were not always necessary for the prejudice to weaken, but where they were present, the positive impact of the contact was more convincing. Conversely, contacts without the Allport conditions may worsen the prejudice (Pettigrew & Tropp, 2005).

For the object of this book, the first Allport condition is important. Allport's four conditions for the contact leading to a positive outcome, that is, weakening the prejudice, are (i) equal group status (as perceived by both sides in the given situation); (ii) common goals; (iii) intergroup cooperation (the goals need the cooperation of the two groups); and (iv) the support of authorities, law, or custom (i.e., the contacts "enjoy the sanction of the community in which they occur"). Pettigrew & Tropp (2006) advocate the idea that "these conditions are best conceptualized as an interrelated bundle rather than as independent factors," and, indeed, it is hard to imagine, for instance, real cooperation between un-equals.[6] Yet, here I will confine to highlighting the conclusion that, in the Allport paradigm, intergroup equality is an important condition of reducing prejudice and improving the intergroup relations.

Henri Tajfel's work on intergroup relations reached maturity in the book chapter published with his student J.C. Turner in 1979,[7] but the witch-word that brands his theory was first published in 1974.[8] The Tajfel theory is known as SIT, because Tajfel spearheaded concerns related to the consequentiality of social identifications on human behavior. The behavioral pattern that his research highlighted and endeavored to explain is in-group favoritism. Social identity is the explanatory link between social categorization and the emergence of the in-group favoring behavior.

For political science, intergroup relations are a problem when they lead to intergroup violence, or, more rarely, when they lower social capital, and investment in public goods. For social psychology, the group-related issue domain is much wider, and it is propelled by the obvious fact that people have different attitudes toward their in-group than toward people classified as belonging to an out-group. Tajfel's experiments in the 1970s attempted to define the minimum conditions under which this difference of attitudes (operationalized with in-group favoritism) occurs. His team found that any arbitrary, accidental group marker introduced by the experimenters, such as the subjects' preference for the green versus the blue color, triggered biased behavior. In subsequent allocation experiments, those belonging to the blue-loving group rewarded other blue-lovers to the detriment of the green-lovers and vice versa. In-group favoritism is not necessarily coupled with negative sentiments toward the out-group, a point made emphatically by Brewer (1981), but, *de facto*, it is discrimination against the out-group, and it was shown to be associated with more favorable views about the in-group than about the out-group, and also, with a more flattering self-image of the group than outsiders have about it. Again, the positive self-image does not necessarily lead to the rejection of out-group people, but it is, for sure, a very likely source of intergroup tensions.

Since the elimination of in-group favoritism hinges on deconstructing the groups, we may wonder why and when we have groups in real life. In a plural and complex society, in which each individual is marked by several features that she shares with some and not with everyone, what makes people select one group marker above many others, as the most relevant in their environment?

Tajfel's work does not really explain the selection of certain group markers, but elaborates on the individual psychic developments leading to the adoption of social identities (social categorization, "accentuation," group identification). He also claimed that in-group favoritism is "determined by the need to preserve or achieve a 'positive group distinctiveness' which in turn serves to protect, enhance, preserve, or achieve a positive social identity for members of the group" (Tajfel 1982),[9] and believed that an increase in the salience of group membership augments in-group favoritism.

Tajfel's positions on a series of social psychology issues were prudently comprehensive. He allowed for the double demarcation of groups (by social categorization originating in ascriptive features and by internalization of group membership), for two kinds of group-related social identities (of role, such as bank clerk, and essential, such as ethnicity), and for the necessity to study phenomena on both individual and group levels—but here he was obviously biased against the individualist methodology.

According to Tajfel, human contacts (or social interaction) can be classified along a continuum from "interpersonal" to "intergroup." The latter end point is characterized by (i) the uniformity of in-group attitudes toward the out-group; and (ii) increased undifferentiation (uniformity) of the out-group, which is often described as depersonalization, social stereotyping, dehumanization, or infra-humanization. Tajfel (1982, p. 14) tells us that:

> The *antecedents* of these two kinds of uniformity seem to fall into four large classes. They are: (a) social differentials in status, power, rank, privilege, access to resources, etc., when the group boundaries are firmly drawn and/or perceived as such . . . and when the social organization on which these differentials are based loses its perceived legitimacy and/or stability . . . (b) intergroup conflict or competition, not necessarily related to previously existing status differences, as was the case in the work of Sherif and many other experimental studies to date; (c) movements for change initiated by social groups . . . . ; and (d) individually determined patterns of prejudice which have tended for a long time to occupy the centre of the stage in much of the traditional research on the subject.

The first and third factor on this list are obviously related. Typically, it is a disadvantaged group that initiates social change on its own behalf.[10] With this in mind, the "antecedents" of intergroup hostility are three: (i) inequality; (ii) Allport's prejudiced personalities (whose prejudice is expected to be reduced by contacts with the out-group in conditions of equality); and (iii) intergroup competition.

With regard to the latter, Tajfel explicitly refers to the work of Sherif in the 1940s, often branded as representing a "functional" school within the intergroup research agenda. Sherif explains in-group favoritism and out-group discrimination with the functions that group biases may serve in achieving social goals. When two groups are competing, internal cohesion, the "team spirit," enhances each group's performance. On the flip side, the group bias may disappear when the two groups pursue a common goal that needs their cooperation. These claims get firm support in experimental settings, but, unfortunately, it is very hard to apply them to real-life social conditions. In society, we have large numbers of potential group markers, both mutually reinforcing and crosscutting cleavages, and different ideologies may emerge about who should ally themselves with whom in cooperative efforts. Even the simplest economic hierarchy of a communally homogenous developed state may allow for the middle class's choice to ally itself with either the upper or the lower class. Thus, while for most real-life social situations the functional explanation cannot be put at work without preliminary assumptions about which group marker is the most salient and which can be overcome with cooperation, the existence of very sophisticated self-legitimating group ideologies, going beyond the dichotomous "we are worthy, you are nasty," has been documented. The ideologies of the dominant group have always tried to justify and legitimate their social advantages, and in the modern world, the means for this have become more sophisticated. It has been shown that in the end-of-twentieth-century United States, the primitive racism of slaveholders was replaced by a "symbolic racism" (e.g., Sears, 1993), which targets the policies that would help Blacks, and also that dominant classes may use a wider variety of legitimating discourses than simply denigrate the subordinate classes (e.g., Mary Jackman, 1996). The new upper-class arsenal contains, for instance, apparently benevolent "paternalistic" prejudices and social practices, such as "the glass-ceiling" women complain about, and promotes the ideology of individualism, while the group inequalities keep reproducing.

Further hurdles to explaining real-life intergroup behavior with intergroup competition consist in the difficulty (i) to consider three or more competitor groups, such as white, Black, and Latino candidates for city jobs; (ii) to distinguish between "pure" competition and competition involving status inequality; and (iii) to distinguish between "pure" competition and "rigged" competition (or competition perceived as rigged). When more than two groups compete for scarce resources, an alliance of two against the third is very likely to emerge. Odds are that two groups whose social status is closer to each other's will ally against the third with a more different social position. As Segura and Rodrigues (2006) put it, "cooperation and biracial coalitions are most likely to emerge between two groups of the same status and class."[11] Further, when the playground is not level, or the game is foul, the group biases grow in all involved groups, as it was convincingly shown in experimental settings as early as in the 1970s:

> [S]tudies have shown that experimentally induced illegitimacy of intergroup status differentials increases ingroup-favoring bias [in both groups, according to Turner & Brown 1978, while] Cummins & Lockwood 1979 found that in groups of boys who were equitably or inequitably advantaged or disadvantaged in rewards for the quality of their performance, the inequitably disadvantaged groups showed the most ingroup bias . . . , but the group which had inequitable advantage also showed ingroup bias. (Tajfel, 1982)[12]

I would like to emphasize that social psychology tends to equate the "hardening group boundaries" with "increasing group biases." The more salient a group, the stronger the in-group favoritism, and the more stereotypical the image of the out-group. We do not get, however, unambiguous answers about when and how a group becomes salient, and what makes certain group markers override the salience of others.

Undoubtedly, there are concerns about these issues in the social psychological literature, but this complex subject does not really lend itself to social psychology's favorite method, the experiment. The discipline reached agreement with regard to the claim that social groups come into being as results of both external and internal factors, where the "external" causes include objective features and out-group assessments, while the "internal" causes involve the members' self-identification as a group. For instance, as Ahmed et al. (2007) point out, "ethnicity is a dialectical outcome of external and internal assessments (Jenkins 1997; Nagel 1996)." But the *in-principle* interplay of the two factors does not mean that they would play out in the same way in all cases. Sometimes, the external factors, that is, ascriptive features, have a bigger role in maintaining the group boundaries, than the members' self-identification, and in other cases, it is the other way around, the group exists mainly by virtue of the members' self-identification with it. And the examples for this, provided by Ahmed et al. (2007), cut very close to our concerns about the impact of inequality on group relations.

The authors conducted a representative-sample research in four Eastern European countries, oversampling certain minorities and poor people. Roma samples were interviewed in Bulgaria, Hungary, and Romania, while in Romania and Russia, ethnic Hungarian and ethnic Ukrainian samples were also interviewed. The interviewers themselves belonged to the majority in each country (97 percent of them). Briefly, most interviewers tended to classify ethnic Hungarians and Ukrainians as belonging to the majority, despite the respondents' express claim of belonging to the minority. In the case of Roma, inversely, interviewers disregarded the respondents' self-identification as non-Roma, and classified them as Roma. The authors traced the interviewer classifications to the specifics given by the respondents about themselves in the interview. Data showed that self-identification, parents' ethnicities, and language use strongly influenced interviewer classification in all cases. Yet, in the case of Roma, the economic and demographic variables had a statistically significant effect on classification, as well. Respondents who were poor, lived in large households, and had low education were more likely to be classified as Roma. The authors conclude that Roma ethnicity has been "racialized," unlike Hungarian or Ukrainian ethnicity; but we may wonder whether "racialized," across a series of social settings, means anything else than "hierarchized," or "status-ized."

There is accumulating evidence that in developed capitalist countries, a prejudice against the poor, as such, can be detected. It was shown by experimental data,[13] and violent episodes in the real life confirmed it, as well. There have been several instances when skinhead groups battered and killed homeless people just because they were poor. Poverty is obviously an external feature, and being poor, an ascriptive group marker—no poor people internalize it as a group feature which would enhance self-esteem or reduce cognitive uncertainty. Thus, no collective action of the poor, as such, can be expected. In general, there is need of an additional group marker along which the poor people mobilize politically: either communal, as in the case of ethnoclasses, or class consciousness.

I would sum up the results of social psychology with a reference to the SIT's minimal group experiments: "when group, then bias." Bias may easily grow into overt, violent confrontation, and group inequality is the most often found cause of hardening group markers and increasing hostility. It seems that although both dominant and subordinate groups make efforts to avoid overt and disruptive collisions, sometimes inequality does breed intergroup conflict. As Hogg (2006) puts it:

> although disadvantaged or stigmatized groups have an impressive armory of protective or avoidant strategies to redirect energy from direct intergroup conflict, this is not always effective. When deprivation is very acute and a recipe for effective social change is available, disadvantaged groups will eagerly challenge the status quo by political means, or through social protest or other collective behaviors including demonstrations, riots, and uprisings. (Hogg 2006)

The role of the unfairness in aggravating group relations is often emphasized. This may be either the unfairness of the established group hierarchy or of some current procedures. Yet, since people want their groups to enhance their self-esteem, the disadvantaged groups are almost always susceptible to ideologies that portray their disadvantage as unfair—actually, the inverse situation, the resignation to disadvantage, is in need of explanation, as in the case of "simply poor."[14]

Social psychology also speaks about the ways in which group confrontation (the salience of the group markers and the group biases) can be reduced. The therapeutic advice typically aims at manipulating the group-ness. According to SIT, in-group favoritism can be altered with de-categorization and re-categorization. De-categorization, seeing another human being as an individual, and not as a specimen of a group, is possible when the group boundaries are not deeply entrenched and there are crosscutting group boundaries. De-categorization is the therapeutic advice of Allport, as well, in the form of contacts within the conditions of equality and cooperation. Cooperation is also the basis for re-categorization, meaning that a project targeting a common goal pulls the groups together into a supraordinated "we"group.

Practically, people live in social contexts interwoven with groups and group networks. We all have some nested identity complexes, such as the territorial ones (attachment to town, region, country, continent), and familial (attachment to nuclear family, extended family, clan), and several role-related identities, which change over time, such as student, professional, or retired person. Most of the time, we manage to seamlessly navigate all our multiple identities, and the coexistence with others is facilitated by the fact that most of them share at least one group with us—someone may be of other religion, but in the same town and the same party, like me. The need for a master social identity, that dominates the others, has not been demonstrated; on the contrary, arguments on behalf of the multilateral personalities, not "too" committed to any special allegiance, abound. Yet, some ideologies, such as nationalism, and religious beliefs, occasionally strive to impose themselves as master identities, and sometimes they are successful. These are the moments when people disregard all "similar" features of people belonging to a certain out-group, and persecute them because of the only group marker of salience.

Unfortunately, social psychology fails to answer the question of when and why a group marker becomes an exclusionary, that is, a master-identity-generating feature. Further, social psychology has never targeted the study of economic inequality's impact on group relations. On the contrary, researchers often have such a blind spot toward this issue, that they do not even record the comparative status of the—real-life—groups that they study (i.e., they do not control for this factor).

However, in many of its inquiries, the discipline has repeatedly stumbled across the importance of group inequality and its impact on group biases and hostile behavior has been recognized, at least in the SIT paradigm. Convergently, the Allport paradigm also takes group equality for a prerequisite of suppressing prejudices.

Political Science I: Explaining Violent Intrastate Conflict

If social psychology can be reproached for its oft-occurring amnesia regarding the role of inequality in shaping intergroup relations, the two fields of political science engaged in explaining violent conflicts—international relations (IR) and comparative politics—can be reproached for a specific blind spot toward the role of the intergroup dynamics in bringing about violent episodes.

For IR, the intrastate violent conflicts of relevance are ethnic conflicts between a minority and a plurality group (Carment & James 1997, Zhu & Blachford 2006). Religious and other communal traits are de-emphasized, as the only state-organizing principle is national (≈ ethnic) self-determination, other group markers cannot legitimate secession. IR became particularly interested in the causes of ethnic strives after 1990, when they led to dramatic changes of the post-WWII boundaries in Europe, and the international society had to take a stand, and sometimes military action, with regard to these struggles and the resulting new polities. As for the explanations of violent ethnic conflict within the IR literature, Zhu and Blachford have reported some agreement, but little accumulative knowledge on the details, and they believed that the 1997 assessments of Carment and James were still valid in 2006:

> Agreement exists that some combination of economic, political and psychological factors can explain ethnic conflicts. Consensus, however, ends at that point. The primary antecedents will vary, depending on the case(s) at issue . . . Alternative interpretations of ethnic conflict focus on class-based reinforcement of ethnic cleavages, relative equality in the size and number of groups within states, unequal resource mobilization among groups, labour market division along ethnic lines, differential activity of elites, and responses to uneven state policies. (Zhu and Blachford 2006)

Opinions can be said to range from the dominance of psychological factors to the dominance of external social factors, and even the extremes branching out in very distinctive hypotheses. We may classify as psychological both van Evera's primordialist standpoint (his creed that nationalism is the prime mover of ethnic strives, 1994) and the utilitarian take of Fearon and Laitin (2003), according to which the elites' perception of the opportunities for insurgence is the main *explanans* of internal violence. The external factors may be, as suggested by the quote above, either economic or political disparities between the groups, or a combination of the two.

Yet, while the discipline of IR is prolific in originating hypotheses about the causes of ethnic strife, the large-N empirical tests of the relevant hypotheses seem to belong to the domain of comparative politics. Both the dependent variable, violence between communal groups, and the explanatory variables, such as the groups' comparative welfare and political position, or the institutional infrastructure, are measured at the subnational or national level. In these research designs, van Evera's *explanans*, nationalism, does not really find its place, as it clearly embodies references to an interstate constellation, such as state-possessing and stateless national group-ness.[15] Further, we may avoid unnecessary confusions by reserving the term nationalism for the group consciousness of the state's plurality group, and referring to the minority group consciousness with alternate terms, as, for instance, the MAR project does. But the terms favored by the MAR theorists, group consciousness or group identity, are also missing from the literature's most known large-N studies on the occurrence of intrastate violence, and we do not always get an explanation for this omission. In some cases, it is dropped because of the authors' skepticism about its impact, while other times it is considered an intervening variable, which mediates the impact of farther external factors.

As Vorrath and Krebs (2009) put it: "Since the end of the cold war, conflict between ethnic groups has increasingly received academics' attention . . . However, the role that ethnicity plays in motivating and structuring civil wars remains an unsettled question, particularly due to the fluid nature of ethnic groups and their endogenous development during conflict" (p. 1).

In other words, scholars have different views about the degrees to which socio-territorial identities are malleable and shaped by external factors. van Evera's primordialism (or perennialism) may be taken for one endpoint of the scale, where only century-long impacts are considered to be consequential for nationalist identities. Rational choice utilitarianism is the other endpoint, which assumes the existence of a "rational" elite practically unaffected by group consciousness. These manipulative elites promote group hatred in order to benefit from the leadership position of a movement that they bring about from scratch, of a politically inert public. In between the endpoints, the Modernists, such as Bendix and Deutsch, and classics of nationalism, such as Anderson and Gellner, believed that the formation of nationalism was a corollary of historical-scale economic and social changes, namely, the evolution of capitalism. Their time horizon for a convincing change in socio-territorial identities can be said to be measurable with decades, and one or two generations. Next, we could mention the MAR theorists' position on group identity. They assume that the plurality's deliberately discriminative policies, such as economic, political, and cultural restrictions on the minority, may lead to intercommunal violence in a matter of a few years. (The minorities are believed to make credible attempts to settle the issues peacefully, before they turn to violence.)

Practically, the large-N cross-national studies, which tested a number of hypotheses about the causes of intergroup conflict, neglected the issue of nationalism and/or group consciousness. The main factors on which they focused were:

(i) the country's group structure;
(ii) the country's institutional structure;
(iii) group grievances;
(iv) the group's crave to obtain economic advantages (greed);
(v) the opportunities to conduct an armed insurrection; and
(vi) the country's development level.

The Country's Group Structure

The country's group structure involves features such as the number and size of the relevant communal groups, their territorial distribution, and histories of past conflicts. There is some arbitrariness involved in delimiting the "relevant" groups. The communal group markers may be language, religion, caste, ethnicity, tribe, and sometimes region. Language seems to be a very straightforward indicator of group-ness, and still, there is some uncertainty in language-based classifications. On the one hand, the boundary between dialect and language is blurred, and, to some extent, subject to political manipulation, such as in the case of the Serbian, Croatian, and Montenegrin languages. On the other hand, it happens that not the primary mother tongue, but the secondary *lingua franca* gets political relevance, such as in Congo DR, and in Rwanda.[16] The statistical figures adopted for analyses tend to embody the "ascriptive" perspective of state majorities and outsiders, rather than the voluntary self-identification of the concerned. With all these accounted for, we may be relatively contented with the degree of agreement achieved by researchers in delimiting communal groups in each country.

Actually, studies on the occurrence of violent conflict do not include "raw" group data in their analyses. Some special indicators have been elaborated for capturing the communal features, such as fractionalization and polarization indexes.

By definition, the fractionalization index[17] measures the probability that two randomly selected people from a population will belong to the same communal group. It is, thus, a measure of diversity, or heterogeneity, and its first uses in the 1990s and 2000s tested hypotheses on whether more heterogeneity impairs economic performance and political stability. With regard to the latter, Donald Horowitz hypothesized a nonlinear, curved pattern in the 1980s, and later empirical work tended to support his insight. For instance, Collier and Hoeffler (1998) found a nonmonotonic relationship between the level of ethnolinguistic diversity and civil war onset. States with a moderate amount of ethnic diversity were more likely to experience civil wars than states with very low and very high fractionalization. Yet, the multivariate tests of the impact of diversity did not show a convincing, consistent impact, which triggered further hypotheses about the ways in which group structure affects group behavior. The three most notable improvements to the original hypothesis were:

(i) the impact of distances along the group markers;
(ii) the impact of group polarization; and
(iii) the indirect impact of diversity.

The first improvement was introduced by Fearon (2003), who made the case for the importance of "ethnic distances" among groups in order to fine-tune the indicators of cultural diversity.[18] The second was introduced by Garcia-Montalvo and Reynal-Querol (2005a). They call polarization index a measure that captures the likelihood that the state plurality faces a large ethnic minority group. Previously, Fearon introduced the measure of "proportion of largest minority group." The "RQ" (Reynal-Querol) measure is more sophisticated, as it quantifies how far a given real distribution is from the bipolar (50:50) distribution.

Last but not least, Blimes (2006) argued that while ethnic fractionalization often fails to have a statistically significant direct impact on the onset of violence, its indirect effects are measurable. He provided a twisty proof of the impact by showing that the regression models including the significant explanatory variables most often advocated in the literature suffer from heteroskedasticity attributable to the fractionalization measures.

Institutions

The country's institutional structure matters from a number of perspectives, and for a number of hypotheses. The two most often sought for features are repressiveness and inclusiveness. A repressive state may trigger minority grievance and desperate violent moves (as claimed by Gurr and other MAR theorists), while a state unable to repress centrifugal moves may stimulate insurrection (as claimed by Fearon and Laitin 2003). Democracy may moderate violent minority mobilization against the plurality (Gurr and team), but the impact of certain types of democracy is more readily measurable than that of others. This second claim was made, for instance, by Reynal-Querol (2005), showing that democracies with proportional representation, which is her proxy for "inclusiveness," are less prone to violent ethnic strife than democracies with majority or plurality electoral rule.

Though most publications express optimistic expectations related to democracy, some counterclaims have also been formulated. Rabushka & Shepsle (1972), Horowitz (1985), and other theorists in the rational choice paradigm warn that democracy leads to the "ethnic outbidding" game of the "ethnic entrepreneur" elites. Their policy advice is, then, a type of democracy that prevents mobilization along ethnic lines, including the ban on ethnic and/or religious parties.[19]

Group Grievances

Ostensibly, group grievances are among the immediate stimulating causes of minority political action, including its violent forms. Without denying their role in exacerbating hostility, some accounts of intergroup violence treat grievances as pretexts, or manipulated perceptions, rather than serious complaints addressing real-world group disadvantages and injustices done to the group. Most famously, it is the Collier and Hoeffler (2004) paper, which makes the case for "grievance as pretext," and the Fearon and Laitin (2003) paper, which makes the case for "grievance as manipulated."

Yet, those who concur on the real mobilizing force and consequentiality of grievances still have a hard time to make a comprehensive list of them, to rank-order, and measure them. The most comprehensive approach is that of the MAR project, which records three types of grievances: economic, political, and cultural. In principle, these answer the restrictions experienced by the minority groups in each field. Unfortunately, we cannot measure the severity of grievances purely objectively, without involving some subjectivity of either the sufferers or of the observer or both. Further, in different settings and different times, different types of grievances may be of primary interest for a minority. For instance, there seems to be a historical shift from the economic grievances being more salient toward the cultural demands dominating the agenda.

Out of these three types of grievances, the impact of the political grievance is most supported thus far, although through the work of a research team, led by Cederman, which conceptualizes political disadvantages within the frames of a general "ethnopolitical configuration" of the countries.[20] From the perspective of my own classification of the causes of intergroup hostility, this "ethnopolitical configuration" includes elements of all of (a) grievances (the political exclusion), (b) group structure (history of conflicts), and (c) institutions (fragile and autocratic state). Thus, while I expect my results to be convergent with the findings of the Cederman group, my variables are slightly differently formulated.

Greed

As a metaphor in the title of a highly influent paper, "greed" sounds great, and it seems to be a convincing counterpoint *versus* "grievance." Yet, at a closer look, the theory around the role of the greed suffers from some conceptual ambiguity, as observed by Korf (2006), for instance. Further, Korf quotes criticisms against the ways in which the factors promoted by Collier and Hoeffler (2004) have been operationalized. Relying on these critical remarks, I will summarize a few issues with the Collier & Hoffler (2004) paper.

(i) The authors are right to theorize that "rebellion needs both motive and opportunity," but leave the reader in a disarray of whether greed is an opportunity for grievance-motivated movements to materialize, or a motive in its own right.[21]

(ii) The reader may also wonder whether greed typifies whole (quasi-ethnic) groups or the elites only, who then lure the masses into rebellion with an ideology of redressing grievances.[22]

(iii) The main challenge to similar projects is the normative aspects of social actions. The types of Third World minority rebellions considered by the authors can be classified as either "Al Capone-ism" or "Robin Hood-ism."

We tend to classify a group as "bandits" when they want to obtain something to which they cannot form any reasonable claim. Yet, a group forcibly and unjustly excluded from the benefits of a natural resource that their country owns may raise legitimate claims to those, and their armed fight is "Robin Hood-ism," rather than banditism. In this case, grievance and greed coincide. From a political point of view, large ethnic groups may be deemed to dissociate themselves from pure banditism, while continuing support for Robin Hoodi-sm. Further, legitimate rebellions may target redressing serious political and cultural group disadvantages by capturing economic assets in order to continue their fight—again, we hesitate to call this banditism, and would designate the grievances as causes, and the possibility to capture the assets, an opportunity only.

(iv) Last, but not least, a big issue with the Collier & Hoeffler paper is that their "proxies" are very far from validly measuring their concepts.[23]

I think that we should distinguish between banditism, which may try to operate with communal slogans, but regularly fails to get wide community support, and "Robin Hood-ism," in which greed cannot conceptually be established as a motive separate from economic grievance. Even if allowing for the possibility that misperceptions of real grievances, and expressly greedy interpretations of a group's entitlements are possible, I think that we may renounce controlling for "greed" as a separate explanatory factor of communal strife, or, more exactly, of minority mobilization against majorities.

Opportunities for Insurrection

The importance of opportunities in launching an armed insurrection has been pointed out by Fearon and Laitin (2003). This paper offers a great summary of the previous literature, it is innovative and well written, and makes a series of highly justified, welcome statements—yet, on the other hand, it makes a few challenging claims, as well. I will use the abstract to make a few comments on the most important claims:

> An influential conventional wisdom holds that civil wars proliferated rapidly with the end of the Cold War and that the root cause of many or most of these has been ethnic and religious antagonisms. We show that the current prevalence of internal war is mainly the result of a steady accumulation of protracted conflicts since the 1950s and 1960s rather than a sudden change associated with a new, post-Cold War international system. (Fearon and Laitin 2003, Abstract)

We cannot but agree: past conflicts are an important predictor of ongoing or renewing hostility, in both interstate and intrastate settings. Yet, it is hard to imagine protracted conflict without clear and persisting group boundaries, without essentializing the difference between "we" and "them." Odds are that most groups have been made entitative with reference to some communal feature.

> We argue for understanding civil war in this period in terms of insurgency or rural guerrilla warfare, a particular form of military practice that can be harnessed to diverse political agendas. The factors that explain which countries have been at risk for civil war are not their ethnic or religious characteristics but rather the conditions that favor insurgency. These include poverty — which marks financially and bureaucratically weak states and also favors rebel recruitment — political instability, rough terrain, and large populations. (Fearon and Laitin 2003, Abstract)

Incontestably, the opportunities favorable for conducting armed insurrection will stimulate the choice of this solution. I cannot but welcome the addition of the opportunity variables to the models meant to explain violent internal conflicts, and so do even the most committed supporters of the "grievance" theory. I do not concur, though, with downplaying the role of the "motive" variables, which, in this paper, is related to a social ontology that neglects the grip of "group-ness" on human minds. Fearon and Laitin (2003) take group identity as very easily manipulable by seasoned, coldly calculating elites, who, themselves, come through as completely unaffected by group consciousness, a vision that collides with that of social psychology. We will have to substantially improve our measurements of the phenomena involved so that we can accurately apportion the contribution of motives, on the one hand, and of opportunities, on the other hand, to intergroup violence. In addition, we need a more thorough account of the institutions that may offer opportunities for nonviolent political action, as well.

Development Level

The country's development level is a very likely candidate to influence intergroup relations, but we do not have 1 well-supported theory about its direction and mechanism to affect group behavior. On the one hand, the impact is mediated by multiple channels, such as political institutions (e.g., democracy), geography (e.g., ethnic concentration more likely in less developed settings), urbanism, education, and so on. On the other hand, there are historical trends to the salience of different communal features, from tribe to nation, and from religion to ethnicity and culture, which affect the formation of group identities themselves, not only the unfolding of the intergroup relations. One robust result found in cross-national empirical tests is the decline in the number of violent conflicts as societies get richer. Yet, the amount of grievances, as coded by MAR, does not always subside with increasing GDP; on the contrary, the amount of cultural grievances, for instance, goes up. Thus, the development level has become a variable for which everybody controls routinely, yet we fail to have a comprehensive theory to frame its impact.

This list of six groups of determinants covers the most important proposals, but it is not exhaustive for all suggestions coming from the international relations and comparative politics fields. For instance, as a new application of the IR logic to the subnational domain, a "domestic-level diversionary theory of war" has been promoted by Tir and Jasinski (2008). The authors claim that unpopular leaders may get their nations to rally around them by using force against a domestic minority. The logic is compelling, but the scheme involves the vilifying of the domestic minority. That is, it works through the deterioration of intergroup relations, which may have a large number of causes besides and beyond the manipulation implemented by Machiavellian leaders.

Sociological Outlook: Nationalism, Identities, and Social Justice

Social psychology and political science are not the only social disciplines that study group consciousness and group relationships. This section has been named "sociological outlook," without further specifying the subject area, because a really thorough overview of all the nationalism, collective identity, and social justice topics would have had to explore several subfields, boundary fields, and interdisciplinary fields of social research. Instead, I will confine to a relatively rhapsodic account of the ideas most pertinent to my topic.

Nation and nationalism have always been defined with reference to the state. Actually, their birth certificates are dated 1789, when the French people declared their own sovereignty over the first nation-state in a Europe of dynastic powers. This element of equality in sovereign citizenship (referred to as a "horizontal comradeship" by Anderson, 1983) has become the hallmark of nationalist thinking, explaining much of nationalisms' moral appeal, and common to both the civic and ethnic versions of it. The type of nationalism (civic or ethnic) is highly consequential to managing the state plurality's relationships with other groups in the country.

An inspired summary of the literature on nationalism and ethnic conflict, Chirot and Seligman (2001) excels in its attempts to extract information from counterexamples, such as from "major ethnopolitical warfare that stopped short of genocide," and "limited, contained, and partly resolved ethnopolitical warfare." Indeed, our streamlined explanations of violent conflicts often overlook the positive examples of coexistence such as the ethnically and religiously divided Switzerland, the forgotten tensions between the Swede and the Finns, Frisians and Dutch, or the decently handled minority issues in Uruguay, Brazil, Russia, and even China (with the exception of the Tibetans and Uighurs). The volume contains a paper by O'Leary (2001), which focuses on the most divisive theoretical issues within the nationalism/ethnicity literature. The author outlines the three dominant paradigms of primordialism, modernism, and ethno-continuism (or ethno-symbolism), and formulates two questions that widely scatter the standpoints in this field:

- Is the salience of nationalism variable across elites and masses?
- Is (or when is) nationalism strong, moderate, or weak?

The first question differentiates between those working in the rational choice paradigm—supporters of the impact of greed and opportunities—and those with a more sociological outlook, who believe in the impact of grievances. As for the second question, an answer endorsed by a plurality of social thinkers is that nationalism's strength is related to the period of transition to modernity, and will weaken thereafter. Further, nationalism may be deemed intellectually and ideologically weak, in the sense that it is "always enmeshed with other intellectual and ideological traditions because it lacks a sufficient prescriptive core to survive on its own." As a historical fact, nationalism has happened both to ally itself with, and to fiercely oppose, all of the liberal, socialist, and conservative political platforms across states.

We may wonder what happens when nationalisms weaken. Will we have cosmopolitanism, transnationalism, internationalism, or supranationalism? Or, will we have global governance, regional integrations, multinational, and plural states? As for the transformation of the nation-state, Winter (2007) answers, basically, that it depends on the minorities whether they may pressure their majorities in abandoning the old ideal of culturally monolithic state.[24]

I am a little more optimistic about the chances of postnational(ist) developments than Winter (2007). Majorities may have more reasons for endorsing minority rights and multiculturalism than just succumbing to the pressure of their minorities. As fierce assimilationist practices were observed because of the belief that a "real" nation-state is homogenous, the change of the international public opinion toward dropping this criterion from the definition of the state, and even prizing diversity, removes some important incentives of the majority to endeavor in assimilating reluctant minorities. Also, the booming industry of tourism makes colorful folk traditions such a real asset that limiting the expression of ethnic particularities is economically disadvantageous. Probably most consequentially, all of the political changes that ostensibly benefit minorities, such as proportional representation systems, decentralization, international connectedness, and regional integrations, have inherent value for pluralities.

Winter (2007) also elaborates on the distinction between civic and ethnic nationalism, another important issue of nationalism studies. Though she thinks that "both civic and ethnic dimensions are inherent in all types of nations," Winter allows for significant differences between types of nationalism. Civic nationhood is mostly affiliated with Tönnies's "Society," while ethnic nationhood is associated with "Community." Civic nations have something "artificial" in their very nature; they see themselves as contract-based, universalist, individualist, and as a 'daily plebiscite'.[25] In general, ethnic nationalisms are taken for more primitive and intolerant, but there is no convincing empirical evidence for the excellence in peacefulness of the civic type. Both basic types come in several versions. The ethnic type may emphasize either the commonality of the ancestors or of the culture, and the civic type may be either militaristic or dovish.

The sociological-anthropological approach to nationalism and ethnicity issues is preponderantly qualitative, and tends to preserve its predilection for non-quantitative methods also when it inquiries into the causes of communal conflicts. For instance, Marc Howard Ross (2011), who defined a number of causes of conflict beyond those listed in the previous section, voiced serious concerns about the nomothetic-probabilistic, crossnational, dataset-based research.

> Long-term, seemingly intractable, ethnic conflicts such as Northern Ireland, South Africa, Israel–Palestine, Sri Lanka, Kashmir, and virtually all others involve both competing interests and clashing identities (Ross, 2000). How the two are related, however, is not the same in all cases so that sometimes movement toward settlement occurs when the parties begin to bridge their interest differences, but in others—especially those characterized by high distrust, strong existential fears, and mutual denial of the legitimacy of the others' core claims—it turns out to be crucial to address the incompatible identities before any progress can be made in settling their substantive interest-based differences. (Ross 2011, p. 87)

In other words, the regression-model-based quantitative research cannot account for the structuration of causes, fails to adequately operationalize the symbolic sphere, and—a point made later in the work—resists meaningful merger with the qualitative results, thus it will not allow for the accumulation of knowledge from the two research programs.

Looked at through the prism of this skepticism toward cross-national designs in the field of nationalism and ethnicity studies, the launch of the MAR project was a morally as brave enterprise as intellectually challenging. It was initiated by Ted Gurr in 1983, and it underwent several data collection periods. The database provided empirical support for a large number of publications, most typically for Gurr et al.'s 1993 book *Minorities at Risk: A Global View of Ethnopolitical Conflicts.* The book depicts an elaborated mechanism, summed up in a flowchart (p. 125), which ties three groups of causes (collective disadvantage, group identity, and repressive control), through opportunities for political mobilization, impact of economic development, and of political institutions, with the outcomes of communal protest and communal rebellion. In addition, the dynamics and diffusion of conflict, and their feedback on group identities, are also considered. To date, this is the most comprehensive model explaining ethnic warfare.[26]

Since my theorization comes close to that of the MAR theorists, I would like to mention a difference between our views. Gurr and his colleagues tend to operationalize the "group collective disadvantage" with their variables for deliberate discrimination from the part of the majorities, rather than the measures for factual economic, political, and cultural gaps between the groups. No doubt that the two syndromes are closely related, and discrimination maintains and exacerbates inequality. Yet my insight is that horizontal economic inequality, indifferent of its causes, leads to conflict as it triggers the dominant group's prejudice and discriminative behavior on one side, and envy, a feeling of injustice and mobilization on the other.

My theoretical reasons for this belief involve the consideration that in twenty-first-century societies, economic inequality is the strongest group marker, and the more relevant the group marker, the less chance there is for peaceful co-existence. Yet, the link between inequality and group conflict may be spelled out in several ways and in the remaining part of this section I will refer to works that involve this link, outlined mainly within sociology.

First, I would like to situate the issue within the discipline of sociology. Kourvetaris (2009) reviewed the main general textbooks in sociology and reached the conclusion that the field is dominated by four main perspectives. Two were outlined by Kourvetaris by drawing on Feagin and Feagin's (2003) classification into 'order-integrative' and 'conflict-power' paradigms, but a 'gender-feminist' perspective and a 'pluralist-multiculturalist' one were also added. The order-integrative paradigm is "an extension of the structural-functionalist paradigm . . . The emphasis is on integration, stability, function and conformity. This model is close to assimilationist perspectives and their variants of Anglo-conformity, Americanization and melting-pot perspectives." In contrast, the power-conflict-stratification paradigm "frames successive generations of minority ethnics in contentious power relations." In addition, "most power-conflict-stratification theories emphasize the economic inequalities between the dominant and the subordinate groups." In Kourvetaris's account, the phenomenon called identity politics belongs to this branch of sociological thinking.

The closer an area of study is to the political field, the more dominant the power-conflict-stratification perspective becomes within it. The pluralist-multiculturalist view, celebrating diversity, flourishes in humanities that are not involved with politics and policy making. The politics-connected literature on ethnic and communal relations is premised on an insight that the existence of social groups is inherently related to a social hierarchy. Yet the basic insight is spelled out differently in a number of research traditions, of which three seem to be the most pertinent to the EI-PC nexus issue: (a) the class-struggle-inspired research on the consequences of group inequality, as exemplified by Stewart's 2008 volume; (b) versions of the civil right movements–related identity politics, and their newer mutations such as the intersectionality theory; and (c) the research on the policy consequences of diversity marked by group inequality.

The authors of the book edited by Stewart in 2008 take the stance that when social groups fight, they fight mainly because of some unequal distribution issue, though circumstances (how a political claim can be carried out in a system) and opportunities (such as external support, or surplus of unemployed young males) may shape the conflict. There is not much elaboration, indeed, on the transmission links, but a few ideas are raised. First and foremost, the biased distribution leads to complaints from the subordinate group. The grievances are more and more often expressed, until a group consciousness of unjust deprivation is formed, forming the basis for extended group support for collective action.

A main conceptual tool of the volume is the distinction between horizontal and vertical inequality. This distinction is welcome even if the labels may be opposed on logical and aesthetic grounds, and I also prefer to use "intergroup inequality" for the horizontal kind, and "individual inequality" for the vertical one, measured by the Gini index. The authors study a number of horizontal inequalities (HIs), such as the inequality of political participation and influence, economic inequality, social inequality, and inequality of the cultural status. In their shared vision, intergroup inequalities of different types may have different constellations across countries, with very different political consequences. Stewart's summary includes four configurations, which are advanced as research hypotheses to be tested in the volume[27]:

- Serious political conflict is more likely where there are significant political or economic HIs or both;
- Political mobilization is especially likely where the political and economic HIs run in the same direction (crosscutting cleavages mitigate the problem);
- Lack of cultural recognition and equity, or cultural status HIs, will be provocative, while cultural inclusion will help sustain peace;
- Political mobilization and conflict are more likely where the HIs are widening.

The theoretical counterargument challenging these hypotheses, very often expressed in rational choice approaches, is that the shared social disadvantages do not guarantee the collective action of the disadvantaged. I think that the rational-actor hurdles to collective action weaken as the group boundaries harden. In conditions of group inequality, at least one of the groups, the subordinate one, is clearly outlined by and in virtue of its deprivation, which also makes the exit from the group impossible or costly.[28] Increasing entitativity and relevance of the group involves increasing in-group bias and social groups entrapped in conflictual relations create demanding moral codes imposed on their members. Group hostilities may be exploited by political entrepreneurs and even desperate insurgents. Yet the primary constellation necessary for their success to escalate violence is a group consciousness typified by the belief that serious and/or long-term injustices have been committed against the group.

Inferences, thus far, have been confined to the simple case of two groups delimited by one or more overlapping group markers. What can we expect in the context of modern complex societies where there are several crosscutting cleavages? By disregarding the group markers' association with inequalities, we get the Modernist theory of evolution, in which crosscutting cleavages are beneficial and all parochial ties are disappearing. By assuming that the group markers become salient to the extent of their association with inequality, we follow the class-centered theorizing and classical identity movement traditions. Yet there is a third alternative, most typically represented by the intersectionality theory of Hancock (2007), and previously present in the work of the so-called third-wave feminists. The fact in focus is that some people may suffer from double or multiple social disadvantages, such as being a Black in a preponderantly white society, a Muslim in a preponderantly Christian society, and a woman in a patriarchy. Multiple disadvantages prevent the concerned from fully identifying with any movement fought by certain communal groups. They cannot fully identify with a Black movement led by Christians, a Muslim movement led by men, or with a women's movement led by white Christians. The solution suggested by Hancock (2007) is to drop the requirement of membership homogeneity in emancipatory movements and cease "to equate group unity with group uniformity."

A final brand of research that I would like to mention here, as connected to the sociological power-conflict-stratification model, is the assessment of the consequences of diversity for the society as a whole. A tradition going back to Stuart Mill takes communal heterogeneity for a risk factor that influences negatively the political life and the economy of a country even in the absence of violent conflicts between communal groups. In successive empirical tests, researchers tried to establish the impact of diversity on democracy and economic output. In cross-national literature, this work can be exemplified with Collier (2001) and Montalvo and Reynal-Querol (2005). The consequences-of-diversity topic fuses with the power-conflict-stratification model in Baldwin and Huber (2010), according to which:

(i) communal heterogeneity can be shown to have an impact on the choice of distribution policies, as it lowers social capital, the provision of common goods, and the community's investment in the public sphere; and
(ii) these negative effects can be attributed to one feature of heterogeneity, the between-group economic inequality (BGI).

In the words of the authors themselves:

> Which measure of ethnic diversity shows the strongest association with public goods provision? We do not find a robust empirical relationship between either the standard ELF measure or measures of cultural difference and public goods provision. However, the tests do reveal that between-group inequality has a large, robust negative relationship with public goods provision. Countries with higher levels of inequality between groups have lower levels of public goods, a finding that has important implications for understanding the pathways by which ethnic diversity creates governance problems. (p. 645)

These pathways can be traced from the groups' economic differences, through the diverging policy preferences of the groups, to a polarization of the political standpoints and more contentious politicizing. If, as in the United States, the wealthier group has the upper hand in politics as well, its policy preference of not sharing with others results in "minimum state" arrangements.[29]

Last, but not least, I would like to mention a few authors providing valuable case-studies pertinent to the EI-PC nexus, who do not set out from a certain theory to find empirical support for it, but rather look for the theory explaining the facts at hand. The two most relevant "empiricist" works to list is Amy Chua's 2002 book on economically advantaged minorities and Meerman's 2009 book on "stigmatized, ranked, ethnic, low-status, involuntary minorities" (SRELIM). The common observation of the two books is that intergroup economic inequality is associated with serious tension between the groups concerned.

As for the causal arrows, in the case of the advantaged minorities, it is hard to argue that intergroup hostility has induced the economic gap. The only possible causal connection is from the economic status toward the intergroup hostility—if there is any, as a skeptic would say. Generally, in the case of SRELIM, the arrows may point in both directions. However, in the case of Cuba's Blacks, the intergroup bias tracks the widening economic gap and there is no evidence at all that the widening of the economic gap was produced by intergroup hostility. This example, of the Blacks in Cuba, echoes my personal experience about the fate of Roma population in Eastern Europe after the fall of communism. The option to switch to a market economy had nothing to do with the Roma population, yet their economic decay has been associated with increasing prejudice and discrimination. Violent attacks from the part of extremists are also part of the everyday experiences of the Roma, an experience that has spared Afro-Cubans yet. The second large section of this chapter, after concluding the review of the fourth literature domain, will elaborate on these concrete examples of the interplay between economic inequality and intergroup hostility.

Political Science II: Preventing Violent Conflicts—The Policies

Most states make conscious attempts to regulate communal heterogeneity. In the domestic sphere, these include measures from complete constitutional engineering, through centralization versus decentralization, and assimilationism versus multiculturalism, to the regulation or nonregulation of hate speech. This area obviously has a strong normative dimension to it, but solutions often collide even when the goals are identical, because the policy makers' beliefs about the causal connections are widely scattered. Similarly, the political and policy standpoints for managing communal issues in the interstate system are controversial as well, and coalesce in a number of value-laden ideological platforms. Although O'Leary (2001) forwarded summaries of both sets of policy goals, I will only present his table on the domestic policies (Table 2.1). This makes a fundamental distinction between the strategic goals of ending ethnonational difference (left-side column) versus managing diversity (right-side column).

Although some policies listed in the left column have been tolerated and even advised by great powers up until the aftermath of WWII, during the second half of the twentieth century, the norms on behalf of the right-side policies have strengthened. Genocide and forceful assimilation have never happened with widespread international approval and 1945 was the last instance when ethnic expulsion (of the Germans from Czechoslovakia and Poland) happened with the support of the international community. Ever since, only a few secessions ("territorial elimination") have taken place with international consent.

Yet, the international public opinion has some preferences even within the right-side possibilities and "control" is not an option that would be encouraged. On the contrary, there is increasing consensus in the pertinent literature and practice around two principles of domestic regulation of heterogeneity. First, the legitimacy of a state involves treating its citizens impartially, with the sole exception of the positive discrimination of disadvantaged groups; and second, intergroup violent conflict should be avoided, which mandates

Table 2.1 Domestic Strategies for the Regulation of Ethnonational Differences (O'Leary 2001)

End/eliminate ethnonational difference	*Mend/manage ethnonational differences*
1. Genocide Eliminate people *Goal*: ethnic purity	1. Control Manage people *Goal*: ethnic hierarchy; organize the dominant, disorganize the dominated
2. Integration—Assimilation Eliminate relevance of ethnic differences *Goal*: eliminate differences from public life—national homogenization	2. Consociation Manage people while preserving differences *Goal*: ethnic equality and pluralism for the consociated (future integration not excluded)
3. Ethnic expulsion Eliminate people from territories *Goal*: ethnic purity	3. Arbitration Manage people impartially *Goal*: manage differences to promote accommodation or later integration
4. Territorial elimination Eliminate people and territory through downsizing or resizing *Goal*: greater ethnonational homogenization	4. Territorial management Manage people and territories *Goal*: ethnic federalism or autonomy, equality and diversity for stakeholders

peace-keeping efforts even with international armed involvement, although preventive measures are naturally preferred.

The "mending and management" of coexistence should target, then, equalizing the status of the groups and providing for the prospects of long-term peace. No policy proposal forwarded either in the scholarly literature or the UN-conform political declarations endorses values opposing these ideals. Still, the policy proposals are widely scattered, and this signals the existence of substantially diverse beliefs about the dynamics of intergroup relations.

Policy proposals may differ across states as well, in function of the specific group structures typifying them. O'Leary's "consociation" and "territorial management" in the right-side column fit different countries. Territorial management is an issue to be addressed in countries where minorities live in regional concentration. For countries with a population that is not segregated territorially, the form of consociation called "pillarization" (Lijphart) or "functional autonomy" (Kymlicka), and even everyday party politics that allow for minority parties entering the national legislature, are more suitable. And the policy proposals may differ depending on other state features, mainly development level and experience with democracy.

These latter issues have been considered in the Kymlicka and Opalski 2001 volume, tellingly entitled "Can liberal pluralism be exported?" In an introductory chapter, Kymlicka suggests the adoption of an "ethnocultural justice" principle admittedly modeled onto the five types of minority groups existing in the developed countries.[30] After 15 Eastern European ethnic relations specialists comment on the proposed model, Kymlicka rejoins by addressing four main concerns of the opponents:

(i) The role of elites in defining and manipulating minority claims. Political entrepreneurs may mobilize around inauthentic claims. Kymlicka thinks that free and fair elections weed out leaders making "inauthentic" claims.
(ii) The issue of "ethnic revenge." Groups having experienced a fate of oppressed minority in a former state-conglomerate turn intolerant majorities in their "own homeland." Again very optimistic, Kymlicka thinks that this will go away with practice in democratization.
(iii) The relative priority of democratic consolidation *vis-à-vis* minority rights. Actually, this was the way pursued by the Western countries, but they have had strong state apparatuses. Weaker states had better make peace with their minorities from the beginning.
(iv) The appropriateness of territorial autonomy. Kymlicka thinks that the Canadian-type combination of territorial and functional autonomy should be applied in accordance with the particularities of each country. He does not agree with rejection of territorial autonomy by the Organization for Security and Co-operation in Europe (OSCE) because of an Eastern European paranoia of secession.

Kymlicka's conclusions include the idea that while ethnocultural mobilization does not seem to abate in prosperous democracies, the interpersonal relations among people belonging to different communal groups have improved over the last decades. The strange pattern is likely to become more meaningful if we distinguish between types and gravity of minority demands. Dozens of peaceful demonstrations for a minority-language university, for instance, involve less intergroup hostility than the seizure of a diamond-mine by a group that was previously excluded from its benefits.

As regulation in complex systems often has side effects, some state measures may affect minorities as an unintended consequence. It is hard to imagine, indeed, any law or rule which would *not* affect intergroup relations in certain constellations. The impact of the administrative boundaries, electoral system, and language of education is intuitively clear. Yet regulations as neutral as those regarding family issues or workdays may also become communally sensitive topics in countries with Muslims and Roma, or Jews, respectively. Over the last years, more and more phenomena have been studied for their impact on communal relationships, such as the member states' integration into the European Union (Anagnostou & Triandafyllidou, 2007), the shift from one-party system to multiparty rule (Posner, 2007), and the government's involvement in the economy (Steinberg & Saideman, 2008). A latest undertaking to a synthesis of the policies affecting minorities is the volume edited by Weller & Nobbs (2010), which embodies a legal outlook to the issues and surveys the venues and guarantees of minority political participation, from the perspective of minority rights. More commonly, the disputes on the regulation of diversity are carried out from the perspective of majority legislative activity and cluster around four interrelated topics:

(i) Constitutional designs that prevent deadly ethnic conflicts;
(ii) Support for minority political mobilization and participation;
(iii) The policy goals and ideals that govern the institutions and policies pertinent to majority-minority relationship; and
(iv) Protection of the vulnerable.

Constitutional Designs That Prevent Deadly Ethnic Conflicts

The basic tension in this field is between the proposals promoted by Arend Lijphart, on the one hand, and Donald Horowitz, on the other, and may be referenced as the dispute between the "power-sharing" (consociational) model and the "integrationist" (liberal) model.

Lijphart's proposal was forwarded as an explanation for the political stability of some communally heterogeneous developed countries, such as the Netherlands and Belgium. Horowitz's 1985 book, "*Ethnic groups in conflict*," relied on cases from the developing countries, rather than the developed ones. This slight difference of perspective has persisted during the subsequent three decades of controversy. Supporters of Lijphart, such as Norris (2008) as well as Lijphart himself (2000), work on demonstrating that consociational arrangements make up for a "kinder, gentler" democracy worldwide, in heterogenous and homogenous societies alike. Supporters of Horowitz's theory work on analyzing cases in which the consociational model has broken down and they have not had a hard time to find them in the developing world.[31]

From a more general, philosophical perspective, the debate seems to be subsumed to the all-encompassing controversy between individualism (Horowitz) and communitarianism (Lijphart). This may be traced back to Locke and Montesquieu and affects all domains of social sciences and humanities. There is a large number of related ontology issues, such as whether societies consist of atomic individuals or of groups and social relations, whether people are egoistic competitors or *zoon politikon*, and whether affiliations are necessary for the psychological well-being of human beings. The controversy also involves divergent assumptions about the nature of ethnic identity and its relationships with other identity forms. In general, the individualist-liberal supporters of the integrationist model regard people's communal identities as being more superficial and more easily manipulable than the supporters of the power-sharing model do. From a Horowitzian standpoint, creating a crosscutting cleavage, such as tracing regional boundaries across ethnic lines, will lead to a new regional identity in competition with the old ethnic identity and will allow for interethnic cooperation in both regions. From a Lijphartian standpoint, if the same ethnicity is the underdog in both regions, they will not stop fighting either for a region of their own or for guaranteed political powers in both, that is, either for territorial autonomy or for consociationism. It seems that the idea of communal justice and its impact on human behavior is a main divider between the two conceptions. Individualists, such as O'Flynn (2005), argue that people should be treated as "inherently valuable individuals," rather than members of a group, but most individuals expect others to recognize them in the totality of their communal-cultural particularities, that is, they demand respect as French Canadians or Japanese Peruvians, not as abstract human beings. Furthermore, we cannot easily tolerate injustices happening to a group to which we belong.

The Lijphartian and Horowitzian proposals are discussed in the context of "constitutional engineering," because the pursuit of any of these ideals needs deep-rooted institutional regulation, of the kind that is generally included in the basic laws of a country. The examples *par excellence* are the definition of the state as national or multiethnic, determining the official languages and providing for state secularism. Federalism and types of pillarization are also constitutionally encoded. Determination of subnational divisions, degrees of decentralization, and some features of the electoral system may or may not be elaborated on in the constitution, but they are very important corollaries of the principles adopted in it, as are the cultural and educational policies as well. Norris (2008) makes the important point that the institutional solutions develop and improve over time—there are more choices to implement either the Lijphartian or the Horowitzian project than there were four decades ago.

Support for Minority Political Mobilization and Participation

While full-scale constitutional engineering is typically carried out with UN sponsorship in war-torn areas, a number of more common and less dramatic policy choices, which, nonetheless, may deeply affect minorities, are essentially made by the country's plurality ethnic (or religious) group. Beyond the issue of territorial autonomy, which is regularly debated within the Lijphart-versus-Horowitz framework, the main questions are whether the majority (i) should allow for the formation of ethnic or religious parties, and (ii) should coopt representatives of communal-feature-based organizations in the branches of government.[32]

Not all identity-based political mobilization is confined to minorities. Religious parties may include a part of the majority ethnic group and may represent the majority's religion, as the Muslim Brothers in Egypt. There are also ethnic parties of the majority ethnic group, the nationalist parties, such as that of Le Pen's in France. Other identity-based movements may split both majorities and minorities, such as the women's movement. Thus the controversy over identity movements goes beyond the international community's minority-protecting concerns. The larger written liberal-individualist tradition is, in general, uncomfortable with the idea of mobilization around social identities and strives to depict society as basically homogenous, revolving around a large middle class. Identity movements challenge the universalist claims of the nation-state cultures and highlight the segmentation of the society. The debate has been going on for decades and an agreement is still far.

In the domain of ethnicity, a salient issue is whether ethnic mobilization, mainly the creation of ethnic parties, exacerbates intergroup cleavages or helps solve social malfunctions. As already referred to, Rabushka and Shepsle (1972) argued that ethnic politicizing leads to conflict (because of a mechanism of "ethnic outbidding"), while Lijphart promoted power-sharing schemes to smooth out animosities. Ishiyama (2009) presents the evolution of the debate up to the twenty-first-century contributions of Chandra (2004), Stroschein (2001), Birnir (2007), and Posner (2004, 2006). Ishiyama himself engages in an empirical analysis of the pertinent data and does not find support for the claim that ethnic parties cause or exacerbate ethnic conflicts. This finding received further support from Basedau & Moroff (2011) who studied 12 Sub-Saharan countries in order to answer the question whether the ban on ethnic parties may or may not promote peace. Their conclusion is, simply, that "empirically speaking, hardly any general patterns in the effects of bans can be detected."

Thus, while there is no evidence that either the ethnic parties or their prohibition affect the probability of intergroup violence, there is evidence that advanced democratic environments depress intergroup violence. Since advanced consensus democracies generally do not ban identity-based movements and parties,[33] we have to conclude that allowing for minority political mobilization is beneficial for the intergroup relations. Or conversely, that political exclusion of the minorities increases the risk of violence, as Cederman and his coauthors have established.

Policy Goals and Ideals That Govern the Institutions and Policies Pertinent to Majority-Minority Relationship

The institutions and policies pertinent to the majority-minority relationship can be said to pursue one of three ideals—though mixed solutions are also possible. The basic policy ideals to choose from are assimilation (as practiced by France), civic patriotism (as practiced by the United States), and multiculturalism (as practiced by Canada). Good summaries of the pertinent views and debates can be found in Brown (2000) and Joppke (2004). The issue has taken center stage in the debates around the emergence of a European identity, as the "thickness" of the common group consciousness is widely believed to be connected to the legitimacy of a polity (Garcia, 1993; Jansen, 1999). Multiculturalism may be inimical to legitimacy, while civic patriotism (or constitutional patriotism in Habermas's rendition) has to be defended against both false universalist pretensions and anemia in fostering "real" patriotism.[34]

In the previously quoted Kymlicka & Opalski (2001) volume, the emphasis was on practical solutions, on whether an arrangement working in a developed Western country may work in less developed environments. More generally, this debate is about values and principles to choose from. We badly miss attempts to compare the three policy systems (assimilation, civic-ness, and multiculturalism) from the point of view of their impact on intergroup relations. With regrets, I have to abandon the temptation to elaborate on this comparison within the frames of this book. Although I will be testing the impact of a number of institutional arrangements, I won't systematically subsume them under the served policy ideals.

Protecting the Vulnerable against Discrimination and Abuse

According to generally accepted norms, a legitimate state cannot discriminate against any group, in any of its functions and services. What is more, there is consensus around the fact that a legitimate state should fully protect every citizen against physical, economic, and psychological harm caused by others. But there is no consensus on whether the vulnerable groups should be protected against hate speech as well. Effective antihate speech legislation is often opposed in the name of free speech and even where such laws are in place, the prosecution of hate crime may be lax and dependent on the demographics of the microsociety.[35]

Further, it is less consensual whether the state ought to intervene to protect the victims against discrimination by other groups. Advanced welfare states tend to implement laws targeting equal hiring practices and they may intervene to prevent housing segregation. Part of these measures, branded as "affirmative action" in the United States, are also fiercely opposed by the US conservatives and individualist-liberals.

More radical solutions aim at redressing the negative conditions attached to the definition of certain groups in order to crush the prejudice that leads to discrimination.[36] A recent endeavor in this sense is the initiative for

Roma integration called "Decade of Roma inclusion 2005–2015," launched by 10 Eastern European countries, now including 11 Eastern countries and Spain. As their website states, "the Decade focuses on the priority areas of education, employment, health, and housing, and commits governments to take into account the other core issues of poverty, discrimination, and gender mainstreaming." The initiative is institutionally innovative, as well. Except for the indigenous peoples, there have not been international joint ventures to address the plight of an ethnic group. And further, it relies on a public-private cooperation in minority affairs, which has also been a rarity thus far.

The need for this initiative will be documented in the next section. As for a concluding word at the end of our inquiry in the scholarly literature, I would highlight that of the fields overviewed, political science is the most skeptical about the EI-PC nexus. In contrast, there is serious theoretical support for the impact of economic inequality on intergroup relations in the social psychology literature and there is both theoretical and empirical support for this impact in sociology and development economics.

THREE CASES SUPPORTING THE IMPACT OF ECONOMIC INEQUALITY

Roma in Eastern Europe

Most Eastern European countries have significant percentages of Roma population, up to an estimated 7–10 percent in Romania, Hungary, Bulgaria, and Slovakia.[37] Official population figures regularly promote much smaller numbers of Roma than scholars estimate. On the one hand, Roma are hard to find during censuses, many of them lacking stable and visible accommodations within the official residential areas and, on the other hand, large proportions of Roma declare themselves as belonging to other groups than Roma. Their reasons to do so are probably mixed. Fear of extremists can be expected to play a large role, but real identity crises may be another. During communism, Roma were expected to assimilate and the assimilation policies offered, uncontestably, real chances for getting ahead in the society.

We can and should distinguish between integration and assimilation, as policies toward minority communal groups. Integration is the ideal of a multicultural society which does not want to erase the cultural differences among the constituent groups, but aims at assuring their economic and political equality. Assimilationist states impose cultural homogeneity and political equality in these countries is defined in individualist terms, not as the equality of groups. Most assimilationisms, such as in France, are blind toward the group economic inequality issue. This was not the case with the communist assimilationism. To their credit, they promised not only political, but economic equality also to those who played by the rules of the regime.

The Roma started from very disadvantaged positions at the end of the WWII: they were devastated by the Nazi genocide, in addition to their historically marginalized status. For centuries, they had been denied personal freedom in the countries where they had immigrated during the Middle Ages and in the Romanian principalities, for instance, they were legally set free only after 1854. In Central and West Europe, they often suffered from bloody pogroms and forcible sedentarization; in the Balkan areas under direct Ottoman rule, they fell in a second-class category of "infidels." Without any property in real estate, either land to cultivate or house to dwell in, they lived on seasonal agricultural work, migrant artisanship, and occasional musical performance. With the turmoil of wars behind and the rigid communist administration strengthening, the Roma lost both the opportunity to freely move and camp in unsupervised countryside and their sources of revenue, except for music. What the communist state could offer to them, in exchange, was free education, cheap housing, and a stable workplace in developing industries. Since education and work needed the use of the official language and housing meant sedentarization, all these came as a strong assimilationist package. On the positive side, they helped large masses out of poverty and, obviously, there were no restrictions on the use of the Roma languages in private life, while Roma music was widely accepted by the population and promoted by the states' official cultural policies.

Before the fall of communism, Roma presence at any level of the social hierarchy was nothing unusual. There were large numbers of educated Roma in higher-level intellectual positions, at universities, state and party apparatus, and in the arts. Significant amount of intermarriage also happened, contributing to a vanishing Gypsy group consciousness. As an Eastern European specificity, Roma sometimes tended to assimilate to another minority group, not to the state majority. For instance, in Romania, Hungarian school classes usually had a few Roma students as well, whose family spoke Hungarian at home, rather than Romanian or Romany.

Yet, the social integration of the Roma was far from complete in 1989. Though most of them had regular paid jobs (in Hungary, for instance, an estimated 70 percent), they were overrepresented in the lowest qualified jobs and their educational attainment, as well as health records, were much lower than those of other groups.

In the economic domain, the fall of communism meant the collapse of the previous economic structures and a decade-long recession, the economies getting back to their pretransition output levels in the new century only. The first to be shut down were the communist-era industrial giants, which employed the most unskilled labor. Urban unemployment soared, forcing out many people from the cheap communal housing and pushing them toward the countryside where plots of land became available from the disbanding of the communist-era cooperatives. Yet, the Roma were not among those who could prove any entitlement to plots of land. Most of them had a choice between the life of urban paupers and rural ghetto dwellers.

Unfortunately, the "most of them" is not exaggerated. We have both national and international data on the life of Roma, which support this claim.

In the 2000s, the UNDP conducted two waves of research on Eastern European Roma, the results of which are publicly available at http://vulnerability.undp.sk/. The situation typical for most of the countries taking part in the survey (including former Yugoslavia and Albania) is reflected in Table 2.2 on Bulgaria and Romania.

The UNDP results on Hungary are, unfortunately, underestimating the poverty of the Roma.

In the countries featured in Table 2.3, the rates below the national poverty line were not recorded and, in Hungary, the lower international threshold of

Table 2.2 Economic Situation of Roma in Bulgaria and Romania

Roma population	*Bulgaria*	*Romania*
Below $4.30 (PPP) per day poverty line		
Income-based poverty rate	49	67
Expenditure-based poverty rate	46	66
Below national poverty lines		
Income-based poverty rate	70	63
Expenditure-based poverty rate	69	62
Share of population not having access to		
essential drugs	75	77
secure housing	33	29
improved sanitation	81	88
improved water source	10	68

Table 2.3 Economic Situation of Roma in the Czech Republic and Hungary

Roma population	*Czech Republic*	*Hungary*
Below $11 (PPP) per day poverty line		
Income-based poverty rate	25	
Expenditure-based poverty rate	45	
Below $4.30 (PPP) per day poverty line		
Income-based poverty rate		8
Expenditure-based poverty rate		9
Share of population not having access to		
essential drugs	27	74
secure housing	14	36
improved sanitation	10	46
improved water source	8	34

$4.30 was applied instead of the $11 threshold applied in the Czech Republic. For sure, the material standing of Roma is better in the Czech Republic than in Hungary. In Hungary, the below-$4.3 per day is the deep poverty level, not the "total poverty" category.

It seems that the "access to improved sanitation" indicator comes closest to the experienced poverty. Two Hungarian researchers conducted a three-country survey based on random samples of Roma and non-Roma in 2000, following a previous round of similar surveys carried out by them in 1988.[38] In all three countries, the poverty level increased during these years for non-Roma also, but much more for the Roma. Table 2.4 summarizes their findings from the two rounds. In Hungary, the best-off country of the three, 16 percent of the Roma classified themselves as poor or very poor in 1988, and 49.5 percent classified themselves as poor and very poor in 2000.

Though the Eastern European economies came out of the prolonged recession and reached the pretransition GDPs in the early 2000s, the poverty rates have not really subsided, and they definitely have not in the case of Roma. In general, accession to the European Union and sporadic periods of leftist governing mitigated both the poverty of and the expression of hostility toward the Roma, but the latter spiraled out from any state control. The everyday experience of the Roma became one of discrimination and persecution. In 2008, the Human Rights First advocacy group dedicated a special edition to hate crimes against Roma,[39] speaking about widespread popular hostility and governmental inactivity toward or complicity with prejudiced attacks on the Roma:

> Roma, like members of other visible minorities, routinely suffer assaults in city streets and other public places as they travel to and from homes, workplaces, and markets. . . . These widespread patterns of violence are sometimes directed both

Table 2.4 Economic Situation of Roma Compared to that of Non-Roma

Country	*Year*	*Sample*	*Very poor (%)*	*Poor (%)*	*Not poor (%)*	*Total (#)*
Bulgaria	1988	Non-Roma	1.3	6.6	92.1	808
		Roma	15.0	23.6	61.4	435
	2000	Non-Roma	13.4	38.4	48.2	901
		Roma	66.7	27.3	6.0	557
Hungary	1988	Non-Roma	2.3	3.3	94.4	871
		Roma	7.4	8.6	84.0	428
	2000	Non-Roma	6.1	11.3	82.6	902
		Roma	21.4	28.1	50.5	459
Romania	1988	Non-Roma	4.8	12.7	82.5	825
		Roma	16.7	17.1	66.2	294
	2000	Non-Roma	15.5	27.5	57.0	997
		Roma	51.7	23.0	23.3	397

> at causing immediate harm to Roma—without distinction between adults, the elderly, and small children—and physically eradicating the presence of Roma in towns and cities in several European countries. . . . The principal reports of harassment against Roma concern abusive treatment by agents of governments, [such as] police ill-treatment . . . . The language of public discourse on Roma in Europe regularly refers to the *expulsion* of Roma, to *evictions,* to the *dismantling* of settlements, to the *destruction* of Roma homes and communities, to wholesale *incarceration*, or the *deportation* of Roma as a national objective. . . . Popular language concerning Roma is also rife with terms reflecting stereotypes portraying Roma as *untrustworthy*, *dishonest*, *dirty*, *lazy*, *violent*, and often as *criminals*, *thieves*, or *kidnappers* (Human Rights First).

If express violence is occasionally (but, unfortunately, more and more often) claiming the lives of some Roma, discrimination is the silent killer that prevents Roma from breaking the vicious circle of poverty. Out of two equally poor and similarly educated people, the Roma are always less likely to find housing outside the ghettos and long-term employment than the non-Roma.

Yet the Roma's educational attainment is clearly inferior to the non-Roma averages. The UNDP survey reported between 26 percent (Hungary) and 71 percent (Montenegro) Roma people without education beyond the primary four grades.[40] This "no education beyond 4 years primary" category includes cases of no schooling at all and, as an increasing problem, years completed in special schools for the mentally handicapped. This is probably the most pervasive form of school segregation in Eastern Europe, though other forms, such as private schools and schools in wealthy neighborhoods far from Roma settlements, have also developed. In 2007, in a high-profile court case against the Czech Republic, the Open Society Institute, supporting the 18 applicants before the European Court of Human Rights,[41] highlighted the reality of ethnicity based school segregation backed by convincing statistics. According to these, in 1999, in the Czech city of Ostrava:

- Over half of Roma children were placed in "special schools";
- Over half of the students in "special schools" were Roma; and
- Any randomly chosen Roma child was more than 27 times more likely to be placed in a "special school" than a non-Roma child.

Even where Roma children managed to avoid the trap of placement in "special schools", they were most often enrolled in substandard and predominantly Roma urban ghetto ones.

Though the decision of the European Court of Human Rights was favorable to the Roma, the school segregation is not over in Eastern Europe and the problem might still be worsening in certain countries. The fully integrated education would need much more than the tolerant predisposition of the majority. Most Roma children start school from a disadvantaged position, for instance, with little proficiency in the language of the majority. Their regular attendance is jeopardized by lack of clothes and means of transportation as well as by health issues. As they repeat classes and become older than their classmates, their hostility toward school and teachers may take violent expressions. Moreover, the girls often quit their studies to give birth in their early teens.[42]

We fail to really quantify the amount of hostility against Roma in order to draw a historical trajectory of it. For sure, indiscriminate hate attacks on Roma families have not happened under the communist rule. School segregation was minimal, as there were no private schools, and the communist state did not like to invest in "special schools"—it preferred to include everybody in the regular ones, which was a cheaper solution. Intergroup relations were smoother also because the "lazy" and "criminal" stereotypes could not take hold of minds. The Roma lifestyle was much closer to that of the majority: they held jobs and had legal incomes.

The authorities in the Eastern European countries are often accused of fostering prejudice and acting prejudicially against Roma. What is less known is that they are often accused by their own majority for not protecting the interests of those for whom the coexistence with Roma has become very difficult. Yet the success of extremist movements and parties is often rooted in this type of discontent. It is very hard to distinguish between rejecting someone for their skin color and rejecting someone for their irritating behavior. Living on welfare is certainly something irritating for all taxpayers, mainly those who make little money themselves. Sadly, the deeply marginalized population further attracts public ire with petty, but constantly recurring thefts and by sending their children sick and dirty to school.[43]

Officials in Eastern Europe seem to be caught between the legitimate ideals of antidiscrimination and the fact that a large number of majority complaints against Roma cannot be dismissed as false and racist. To their credit, they have realized that the way out is closing the economic gap between majorities and the Roma, while simultaneously maintaining the antidiscrimination standards. It is in this context that we have to praise the participants and contributors of the Decade of Roma Inclusion initiative. Nonetheless, the way to economic emancipation of the Roma will be long and hard; 2015 does not seem to be its end, by any means, but, at most, a promising beginning. As of 2011, two of every three Hungarians thought that there was a "big tension" between Hungarians and Roma—more exactly, 68 percent of the respondents, as compared to 52 percent believing that there is a big tension between the poor and the rich.[44]

Blacks in Cuba

This story was brought to the light of scholarly investigation by Jacob Meerman in a book published in 2009.[45] The book elaborates on the concept of *stigmatized, ranked, ethnic, low-status, involuntary minorities (SRELIM)*. They are involuntary minorities because, on the one hand, they did not want to come into contact with what is now their majority: their ancestors were either conquered or enslaved against their will. On the other hand, today they would like to become integrated in the larger society, but this is very hard.

In the sixth chapter, entitled "The Afro-Cuban story: a brief success," the author claims that during 1959–1989 the Afro-Cubans achieved complete parity with whites with regard to education, job status, and income, the only differentiating aspect remaining their higher deviance levels.[46] Meerman's explanation of how the racial gap was so smoothly closing within a few decades involves a historical account. Blacks in Catholic countries were not "dehumanized" so much as in the United States: actually, they were in ascension before Castro came into power. They supported the revolution and the fast communist-style economic growth helped them achieve parity with the lighter-skinned Cubans. The state promoted color-blindness ("ni clase, ni raza"), and the state's ways changed the folkways, informal private discrimination became almost imperceptible by 1990.

Yet, since 1991, when Cuba embarked on a liberalizing course, the gap has been opening up again.[47] The reason lies in the existence of some hidden social advantages of the whites, which passed unnoticed before liberalization, but have become highly consequential later. For instance, white citizens were allocated community housing in more desirable neighborhoods than their Black counterparts. When it came about opening a shop or renting out extra living space, the better placed real estate brought much more revenue for whites than for Blacks. Whites also tend to have more overseas connections, relatives, and friends, who could help them in several ways, with remittances and capital to establish and run a business. With the opening gap, the almost-completely absent stigmatization of Afro-Cubans as lazy and prone to addiction made a comeback. There is, also, new evidence for discriminating against the Afro-Cubans in employment and education.

Their workplace disadvantages come from the sectoral particularities of the Cuban economy. In the traditional industrial sectors, developed under communist rule, Blacks achieved parity. Yet in the newly emerging service sectors, in tourism and foreign trade, whites have obtained the higher echelons and more profitable jobs: "blacks and mestizos are overrepresented among professionals and technicians in the traditional sector and underrepresented in the emergent sector and among managers, which suggests that their low presence in these sectors is not due to lack of skills" (Espina Prieto et al., 2010). Also, "in tourism, blacks and mestizos are concentrated in internal support jobs that do not bring them into direct contact with tourists," that is, they do not get tips, which in services are a very substantial part of the realized revenue. Here the workings of either prejudice or in-group favoritism can clearly be seen. The decision makers favoring whites for direct-contact jobs are either convinced that tourists prefer being attended by white people or simply reward their own nieces and the friends' nieces with the most coveted jobs such as tourist guide and stewardess, for instance.

Discrimination in education is harder to support with hard statistical data, since the pure school enrollment figures may be misleading. Beyond enrollment, it is the quality of the education and the market value of the diplomas that make the difference. Nonetheless, the overall tertiary enrollment reveals some group disparities. It has been shown that in 2004 whites were clearly overrepresented in the day-time higher education. The admission rate of the white test takers was 70 percent as compared to 51 percent of the Black test takers, and 57 percent of the Mestizo test takers.[48] In turn, the gap in the admission test performance may be explained with the quality of the high schools attended previously and the family support.

Chinese Diaspora in South-East Asia

Amy Chua's 2002 book has been a statement against the creed informing the policies promoted by the United States since the 1970s, "the assumption that markets and democracy go hand in hand." Uniquely, in this book, this assumption is challenged on purely empirical grounds, not in the name of a rival social theory, such as Marxism, Third Worldism, or Keynesianism, which have not ceased criticizing it for decades. Chua pulls together hundreds of empirical facts with the intent to show the failure of the free-marketeer doctrine in ethnically heterogeneous countries—and the rough reality is that all of the developing world is ethnically heterogeneous. Of the communal heterogeneity cases, Chua is interested in those in which an advantaged minority is economically definitely better placed than the country's majority or plurality population, which may control the politics in fully democratic conditions. She marshals examples for this combination from all continents (except West Europe and North America), but her personal experience lies with the case of Chinese diaspora in South-East Asia. Below there are two excerpts summing up Chua's main thesis:

> The point, rather, is this. In the numerous countries around the world that have pervasive poverty and a market-dominant minority, democracy and markets— at

> least in the form in which they are currently being promoted—can proceed only in deep tension with each other . . .
>
> When free market democracy is pursued in the presence of a market-dominant minority, the almost invariable result is backlash. This backlash typically takes one of three forms. The first is a backlash against markets, targeting the market-dominant minority's wealth. The second is a backlash against democracy by forces favorable to the market-dominant minority. The third is violence, sometimes genocidal, directed against the market-dominant minority itself.

I think Chua is right that market liberalization in the presence of a highly market-advantaged minority may have only the three outcomes portrayed above. Yet, I do not completely agree with the way she conceptualizes democracy. Here, as in most parts of her book, democracy is equal with "free market democracy," that is, only democracy that promotes economic free-marketeer orthodoxy (à la Reagan and Thatcher) is considered democracy. Yet Chua's argument includes the claim that West Europe and North America followed other development paths than those that they want to impose on the Third World now. This past definitely includes egalitarian and equalizing economic policies (land reform, Marxism, social democracy, Keynesianism). Should we claim that the Unite States during the New Deal or Sweden in the second half of the twentieth century were not democratic?

Applying a more general notion of democracy and also assuming that in a democratic state the economic policies will serve the majority, the three outcomes described by Chua can be formulated as:

(i) Democracy triumphs, the country's ethnic plurality or majority implements equalizing economic policies and ends the minority's market-dominance;
(ii) Democracy fails, the country's market-dominant minority imposes a plutocratic rule;
(iii) The state fails, state authorities cannot stop violence against the market-dominant minority.

There are, obviously, some overlapping and intermediate cases, as all the above processes take time to unfold. When democracy is established but is slow in transferring market positions from the advantaged minority toward the majority, pogroms and crime against the former may still occur. One possible happy ending is when the dominant minority blends in the majority, as it has happened, for instance, in Thailand. Policies aiming at equalizing the groups' material standing may greatly precipitate this.[49]

Yet the existence of a market-advantaged or simply rich minority invites communal hostility in all parts of the world, not only in poor developing countries. We do not see this today in West Europe, but it was only 80 years ago that the most murderous genocide of all times took off with the—democratic!—election of Hitler into power.

We still fail to realize how deep the poverty of the majority and how wide the wealth gap between the groups have to be in order to trigger intergroup violence. Peter Glick, in his "Choice of Scapegoats,"[50] seems confident enough that the scholarship's findings about the mechanism of scapegoating explain pogroms and genocide against "successful" minorities, but notices that lethal hostility may outlast the conditions that originally induced them. The preparation of the Holocaust and its actualization stretched on for 12 years, much after Hitler put, first, margarine, and later (after conquering a few West European countries) butter, on the table of the Germans. And the genocidal strategy continued after the victory over the French, as well.

Glick's account of aggression against "successful" minorities (such as Armenians and Tutsies, besides the Jews) emphasizes that scapegoating occurs (i) when the aggressor group suffers a frustration or trauma as a group; (ii) when the aggressor group experiences severe life conditions and relative deprivation; and (iii) when the scapegoated group is perceived as powerful and malevolent, that is, some power to harm the aggressor group can be believably attributed to them, besides their intention to do so. These conditions seem to go further than the "simple" economic gap emphasized in Chua's account. Actually, Chua also warns the reader that it is not poverty alone that turns the poor majorities against wealthy minorities. "Poverty by itself does not make people kill. To poverty must be added indignity, hopelessness, and grievance" (Chua, 2002, Introduction).

Unfortunately, poverty in unequal societies invites and generates indignity and hopelessness by itself. Being poor among the wealthy is a lifelong experience of inferiority, if not outright humiliation, for everybody except the monks and nuns who choose poverty on purpose. Belonging to the middle class and being inferior to the upper class are tolerable only because there are others inferior to the middle class. As for hopelessness, people in the developing countries are much less optimistic about the power of the market to generate well-being and to make the wealth trickle down, than the US Republicans are, for instance. The developing countries have a long record of opposing the Washington Consensus packages, because they do not trust "free" markets to help them catch up with the wealthier. Typically, they place their hopes on political action, domestic and international, rather than on the Invisible Hand, to improve their lot, even if the scope of political action is limited in the presence of hegemonic powers. As for the developed world, there were series of rebellions, revolutions, civil wars, and centuries of labor movement enforcing those equalizing measures that make them "welfare states" today.

The Commonalities

In all three cases above, interethnic tensions are associated with economic inequality between the groups. The distance between them may be either on behalf of the majority or to their detriment; the tension invariably occurs nonetheless.

From the point of view of a causal claim, the case of the advantaged minority is the simplest. We either admit that inequality causes the intergroup hostility or deny the existence of the latter; in no way can hostility cause intergroup inequality. Disadvantaged minorities, however, may become poorer due to the hostility of the majority, as actualized in discriminative policies and behavior. Here, the causal arrows may run both ways, in addition to the third possibility of denying the existence of intergroup hostility. This latter happens when political science (i) does not pay attention to low-intensity hostility at all; (ii) takes "grievances" for either greed or manipulated group consciousness (Collier & Hoeffler, 2004; Fearon & Laitin, 2003); and (iii) expects group grievances to disappear with the creation of cross-cutting identities (Horowitz, 1985). Within the limits of the reasonably feasible, my research design aims at addressing these concerns by (i) formulating dependent variables that measure lower intensity hostility, as well; (ii) controlling for the "manipulated group consciousness" hypothesis; and (iii) comparing the impact of the power-sharing and Horowitzian institutions. I do not deny the possibility that majority hostile behavior worsens the condition of the minority, but my emphasis is on highlighting the strength of the other sense impact, from economic inequality to intergroup hostility.[51]

The last alternate causal model to consider would include an omitted factor that causes both inequality and hostility. We were very happy to have an overarching explanation of what causes economic inequality between groups. Unfortunately, such a unique explanation does not exist and cannot exist.[52]

Beyond the association of economic inequality and intergroup hostility, the three case examples may reveal some further details of this relationship and guide the selection of the control variables as well.

The comparison of Roma and Afro-Cubans may suggest that the magnitude of intergroup hostility covaries with the economic distance between the groups, that is, the larger the economic gap, the more the hostility. The cases of Roma and of the Chinese show that the occurrence of murderous impulses against other groups does not necessarily need such a historical-scale national trauma, as those suffered by Turks and Germans at the conclusion of the First World War. Nor do they need an economic depression as deep as the one experienced by Germany in 1929–1933. Actually, intergroup hostility may develop even in conditions when the economy, generally speaking, is not in a downward spiral or serious trouble, but inequality is experienced as increasing. However unfortunate this may be for the real-world developments, methodologically it is good news, as it absolves us from controlling for "national traumas." The various circumstances in which the intergroup tension occurs include a number of continents, countries with very different historical trajectories, and groups with different status on the indigenous-immigrant scale.[53]

The kind and degree of the distance between groups in these three cases, however, do not cover the whole possible spectrum. On the one hand, there is racial, but no linguistic, or cultural difference between Afro-Cubans and Cubans. On the other hand, there is both racial, and cultural difference between Chinese and the Filipinos and Malays. Roma are situated in-between, they are racially different, but culturally half-assimilated to their majorities. Other possible combinations are, for instance, cultural difference without racial difference, and even discrimination and hatred without definite racial, linguistic, or religious group markers, such as in the case of Japan's Burakumin and Rwanda's Tutsis. Yet the variation that exists on these communal measures in the three cases does not indicate any strong impact of the "group structure" indicators, which, hopefully, may simplify the analyses.

Ultimately, both the scholarly literature and the case examples at hand encourage the creed that horizontal economic inequality is a significant determinant of intergroup hostility, whose impact may come across in regression models beyond and despite the idiosyncratic causal complexes governing each minority's relationship with its plurality group.

NOTES

1. I have often wondered whether there is as much room for "real" discoveries in social science as in natural science. To the extent to which our societies resemble the Greek *polis*, for instance, they do not leave room for large-scale revolutionary observations that completely escaped the eyes of Plato, Aristotle, Zeno, and so on. I would say that, at least since the early twentieth century, social science advances through gradual small steps in which the context of demonstration has to be emphatic because of the paradigmatic controversies. In the context of demonstration, having several antecedents of the thesis advocated is an asset rather than a liability.

2. There seems to be a subdisciplinary fragmentation issue, as well, at the root of this neglect. Political psychology asks questions about the evolution of intergroup relations, and the US minority research has relied on, and contributed to, this literature. Yet, psychological explanations going beyond the plain rational choice (RCT) assumptions are very rare in the cross-national political science literature (comparative politics and international relations).

3. Fearon & Laitin (2003) included inequality among the predictors of violent conflict, namely, they included a Gini index, the measure of vertical inequality, as

a control variable. This failed to turn up as significant, thus justifying the authors' express skepticism toward it.

4. I also allow for the perverse effect that a communal group marker hardened by economic distance becomes more consequential for group behavior than the economic distance in itself. This involves the idea that communal differences hinder the collective action of the poor. Yet this work is confined to arguing for the impact of economic inequality on communal group behavior.

5. "Social sharing among ingroup members—gossip, rumor, opinions, stories, media—contribute to consensus in stereotyped beliefs . . . Usually, one is less motivated to be accurate about outgroup members and more motivated to share the ingroup's understanding of them" (Fiske, 2005).

6. The game-theoretic definition of cooperation implies symmetrically situated players, while in psychology, Piaget, for instance, included in the definition of cooperative relationships the equality of the participants.

7. Tajfel, H. & Turner, J. C. (1979). "An Integrative Theory of Intergroup Conflict."

8. Tajfel, H. (1974). "Social Identity and Intergroup Behaviour."

9. Tajfel's insight in this regard has been confirmed by later research. For instance, a 2007 paper by Hunter et al. tested two related hypotheses. "The first was that *intergroup* discrimination leads to increased self-esteem. The second was that threatened self-esteem (i.e., operationalized here as the extent to which people believe that the in-group is negatively evaluated by an out-group) would lead to increased *intergroup* discrimination. Support was found for both hypotheses." A rival theory of the motivation for belonging to a group, called "cognitive uncertainty avoidance" (Greenberg et al. 1997), claims that the need of validation of world-perceptions, and terror management are also important. "People are more likely to identify with groups when they are faced by self-conceptual uncertainty. When such uncertainty is very high they will seek out totalist groups that are highly orthodox, have simple and consensual prototypes, high entitativity, and strong charismatic leaders, and that engage in extreme forms of intergroup behavior" (Hogg 2006). The attraction that human minds feel for simple, streamlined ideologies is well supported. Yet the facts do justice to Tajfel in the sense that the extremist groups' ideologies always flatter their self-image (Übermensch, Messianism etc).

10. Some social movements such as environment protection, or disarmament, may also militate for social change, indeed, but participants of these movements are not classified as "out-group" by others.

11. They refer to results obtained by Giles & Evans 1985. And continue with added details, such as "if the two groups are unbalanced in size or relative political power, the racial or ethnic group with the most representation in city and county government is likely to fare better than the others in terms of public service jobs and other government benefits. Thus, the better-positioned group might reasonably be less than eager to form a coalition (Deutsch 1985; see also Browning et al. 1984, Butler & Murray 1991, Meier & Stewart 1991, Sonenshein 1986, Warren et al. 1986). In fact, they may attempt coalition with whites, and may themselves be attractive to whites as a coalition partner. Such an environment will produce far more interminority competition than cooperation."

12. A version of the competition theory was promoted by Lawrence Bobo, who believes that intergroup competition is represented in the minds of the concerned people as out-group threat, and they react with hostility, prejudice, and discrimination, to this threat. Beyond Bobo's contribution, numerous literature on threat hypothesis has been unfolding in the recent decades, and the findings were summed up in a meta-analysis written by Riek et al. in 2006. They found that, across 95 studies, the types of intergroup threat tended to have a positive relationship with negative out-group attitudes. Yet, when they briefly surveyed other factors, as well, the impact of group inequality also emerged. "Status differences between groups also relate to higher levels of threat, such that as the difference in status increases the degree of perceived threat increases (W.G. Stephan et al., 2002). Moreover, out-group status differentially influences reactions to threat. Cadinu and Reggiori (2002) found that group threat led to stronger devaluation of low status relative to high status out-groups." Yet, the threat-testing studies rarely paid attention to the impact of the status inequality; on the contrary, they often did not record the comparative status of the groups at all.

13. Yzerbyt & Corneille (2005) refer to a previous experiment of Yzerbyt et al. (1994). After an ambiguous film about a girl performing scholastic tests, those who were told that she comes from a wealthy family were much more likely to say that she performed well, than those who were told that she comes from a poor family.

14. For instance, research by Wright, Taylor, and Moghaddam (1990) shows that when members of a disadvantaged group believe that entry to an advantaged group is open, even only slightly open (only a token percentage of people can pass), they shun collective action and instead individually try to gain entry to the advantaged group. Subsequently, the chances of collective action grow when entry to the advantaged group is closed, or it is not sought for, as in the case of communal groups who do not want to assimilate to the advantaged majority.

15. The relationships with kindred abroad also exceed the country boundaries; these may be taken into account by measuring them at group level. The logic of the Fearon & Laitin (2003) paper, emphasizing the role of the opportunity in bringing about violent conflict, clearly parallels IR realism's explanation of war, but the empirical test of it follows a comparative politics design.

16. With religion, we have to be aware that the distance between two religious groups is not necessarily proportional with the difference of their beliefs: Sunni Muslims in Pakistan are more hostile against Ahmadi Muslims, than Hindus, for instance. Yet, the group marker the most difficult to establish for classification purposes is ethnicity, when it is unassociated or only probabilistically associated with language or other clearer group markers. This is the case with the difference between Hutus and Tutsis, for instance, or with heavily Russified Belarus groups. Latino and Asian groups within the United States tend to foster national identities, such as Mexican, Cuban, and Japanese, rather than pan-Hispanic and pan-Asian group identities, and the same happens with the Roma in Europe, as they often identify with Roma subgroups, such as Lovari, Beash, and Sinti, rather than with Roma in general.

17. The first fractionalization index, the ethnolinguistic fractionalization index (ELF), was calculated by Soviet geographers in the 1960s, and it was updated by the

American Philip G. Roeder in 1985. In the early 2000s, three new batteries of fractionalization indexes were published by American researchers, motivated by the goals of focusing on one type of cleavage only (for instance, Annett, 2001 and Alesina 2002 worked out separate ethnic, linguistic, and religious fractionalization indexes), and by the necessity to answer the changed political landscape, that is, changes in state boundaries, and in population figures (Fearon, 2003).

18. Fearon measured these distances in terms of a tree diagram of the language families.

19. The policy proposals will be reviewed later in section 4 of the "Theoretical Background of the Argument" part.

20. In the beginning, this group of researchers relied on the EPR dataset originated by Cederman & Girardin, and they repeatedly demonstrated the impact of political grievances on ethnic mobilization and occurrence of violence. Later the dataset was upgraded into a geocoded information base. In this research program, the idea of political grievance is captured as "political exclusion," and the conclusion reached by Wimmer, Cederman, and Min (2009), as well as by Cederman, Wimmer, and Min (2010), is that "armed rebellions are more likely to challenge states that exclude large portions of the population on the basis of ethnic background." The list of variables making up the ethnopolitical configuration includes, besides political exclusion, past conflicts, segmented elites, and regime changes.

21. Their reasoning seems to parallel that of Skocpol, whose list of causes of social revolution disregarded the grievances of the peasants. Skocpol argued that "peasants always have reasons to rebel," thus she looked for the opportunities of the revolution, and portrayed these as causes.

22. This paper of Collier & Hoeffler suggested to me that they meant whole groups. Yet, in their later work they got much closer to the standpoint familiar from Fearon & Laitin 2003, which emphasizes the distinction between elites and followers.

23. "We consider four objective measures of grievance: ethnic or religious hatred, political repression, political exclusion, and economic inequality" say the authors, and this sounds great. Yet, ethnic or religious hatred is measured with the fractionalization and polarization indexes, political repression of the groups with general autocracy levels (versus democracy), political exclusion of the groups with the proportion of the state's plurality group, and group economic inequality, with the individual inequality measure of Gini index. Further questions may be raised about the use of the "ratio of primary commodity exports to GDP" as a proxy for natural resources, a component of "greed." Primary commodity exports seem to be a good proxy for the country development level, as well, about which we know for sure that is correlated with the probability of violence.

24. She asks the question of "how does the nation become pluralist?" following the recognition that "Nations—whether civic or ethnic—usually overemphasize homogeneity . . . There are, however, nations that thrive upon 'diversity'. In recent years, Canada, for example, has made a name for itself by emphasizing the cultural and linguistic heterogeneity of its population. Canada was also the first country in which normative pluralism as an essential dimension of Canadian nationhood became officially implemented through policy (1971) and law (1988)."

25. They are individualists in two respects: because individuals are perceived as the primary unit (which precedes the nation chronologically and ontologically), and because the collectivity's goal is often defined in terms of protecting and maximizing individual liberty. Ethnic nations are, on the other hand, organicists, particularists, and collectivists.

26. The dataset itself contains hundreds of variables, a result of careful planning for multidimensional tests. Criticisms are generally leveled against the case selection, rather than against the variables. Briefly, it can be said to be a "selection on the dependent variable": only minorities "at risk" are included, which have an above-average chance to get into conflict with their majorities. As the MAR homepage formulates it: "MAR tracks 283 politically-active ethnic groups throughout the world from 1945 to the present—identifying where they are, what they do, and what happens to them. MAR focuses specifically on ethnopolitical groups, nonstate communal groups that have "political significance" in the contemporary world because of their status and political actions. Political significance is determined by the following two criteria: the group collectively suffers, or benefits from, systematic discriminatory treatment vis-à-vis other groups in a society, [and] the group is the basis for political mobilization and collective action in defense or promotion of its self-defined interests." Thus, though 283 is an imposing number, if we want to get information about how a minority-majority relationship gets so tense that the majority discriminates, and the minority mobilizes, and not only about how the already tense relation results in violence, we have to include in our dataset the minority groups omitted by MAR, as well.

27. The authors allow for the impact of several other factors, such as centralized vs. decentralized state, institutional accommodation of peaceful striving for group goals, "cultural demography" (size, proportion, cohesion, distance of the groups), economy (in backward societies violence is more likely), and dispute over natural resources.

28. In the terminology of the US group research, a sense of "linked fate" is forming, in which the emancipation of the whole group is seen as a more realistic perspective than the social emancipation of a single member of the group.

29. I would mention that previously Alesina and La Ferrara (2000) found the impact of racial heterogeneity and economic inequality as paralleling each other, each of them having, separately, the same magnitude negative impact on public good provision. That is, high vertical inequality in communally homogenous communities may also reduce social capital and public good provision, but the impact of horizontal inequality can be expected, and was shown to be, by Baldwin & Huber (2010), much more substantial.

30. All contributors to the volume emphasize that there are types of minorities in Eastern Europe, which are completely missing in the West: the Roma (ethnoclass, whose ancestors immigrated voluntarily), the Baltic Russians (involuntary immigrants), the Crimean Tatars (returning population), also the Russians in some Commonwealth of Independent States (CIS) countries, where the Russian language has higher prestige than the "titular" language, and so on.

31. René Lemarchand, who does not seem convinced by either party in this controversy, brings powerful arguments against the epistemological value of case studies in this domain. In a paper published in 2007, he reflects on Rwanda, Burundi, and the

Democratic Republic of the Congo, chosen to illustrate a clear failure (Rwanda), a success (Burundi), and a half-failure-half-success (DR Congo) of the power-sharing model. He points out how deep-rooted social processes shape the opportunities for the success of certain institutions and that any constitutional engineering may work only where there is a state that can enforce any rule. In other words, a failed state cannot be taken for a refutation of either the power-sharing or the integrationist model, whichever was introduced there in the wake of the collapse.

32. If the answer is yes to the latter, then questions about proportions may follow. In law enforcement, for instance, the population-proportional employment of minorities is the most advocated solution.

33. Yet, some institutional features, such as single-member electoral districts in countries where minorities do not live in concentration, may render minority political mobilization ineffective, even when it is not prohibited.

34. A cluster of working papers produced by the ARENA Centre for European Studies gives a good overview of the complex and ramifying dispute (Føllesdal, 2000; Fossum, 2003a and 2003b; Olsen, 2005) which obviously extended onto a much larger segment of the European literature (Delanty, 2002; Habermas & Derrida, 2003; Bellamy & Castiglione, 2004; Herrmann, Risse & Brewer, 2004; Harmsen & Spiering, 2005; Risse, 2005). Yet, one of the most influential thinkers of the domain is the Canadian Will Kymlicka (1995, 2007).

35. For instance, King (2008) showed that hate crime prosecutions are fewer in US districts where political conservatism, Christian fundamentalism, and Black population size are higher.

36. In the US sociopsychological literature, this idea was first endorsed by Krech and Crutchfield (1948), who stated that it is not the black skin that leads to prejudice, but the "correlated cues" of poverty, lack of education and low social status. Thus the task is to eliminate these "correlated cues." The origins of the idea can be traced back through Gunnar Myrdal's 1944 work to a social-democratic theoretical tradition, sensitive to the socioeconomic differences between groups, which likens the relations between communal groups to relations between classes.

37. An extensive book has been published in English by Barany, Zoltan D. (2002), which includes a plethora of statistical and historical information on this issue. I use the term Roma for both the singular and the plural form of the demonym, as in the Romani language Roma is plural. However, I have come across the "Romas" version, as well.

38. Ladányi János & Szelényi Iván, 2002: "Romas and the poor in Hungary, Romania, and Bulgaria," *Szociológiai Szemle* [Sociological Review] 2002/4., 72–94.

39. Violence against Roma and Sinti: 2008 Hate Crime Survey, http://www.humanrightsfirst.org/wp-content/uploads/pdf/fd-080924-roma-web.pdf

40. Compared to 12 percent (Hungary) and 8 percent (Montenegro) of the plurality population.

41. http://www.soros.org/initiatives/justice/litigation/czechrepublic, D.H. and Others v. Czech Republic

42. There is an ongoing dispute around the fact of whether the early-age marriages are a cultural feature of the ethnic group to be preserved or a feature of the "culture of poverty," both as result of loose social control and as means of obtaining more welfare

money. For sure, the age for marriage and childbirth is strongly correlated with the overall well-being of the human groups. With rising welfare, the number of births per woman decreases, while her age at first pregnancy increases by itself, without any constraint added.

43. Violent crime was neither typical nor typically attributed to Roma until the last 10–15 years, but lately the number of victims of alcohol-fueled quarrels, robberies, and burglaries turning violent has been on rise.

44. TARKI Omnibusz 2011.

45. "Socio-Economic Mobility and Low-Status Minorities: Slow Roads to Progress." The groups studied are, besides the Black Cubans, India's Dalits, the US Blacks, Japan's Burakumin, and Bolivia's Indigenous peoples (Aymara and Quechua).

46. We may take for granted that the education levels were high indeed, as the 1997 standardized tests conducted by pan-American and UNESCO organs showed Cuban students being much better at both mathematical and linguistic skills than their peers from twelve other Latin American countries. Willms & Somers (2001) state that "one of the most prominent findings of the First Report was the remarkable success of Cuba: its average test scores were about two standard deviations above the Regional mean in both reading and mathematics" (p. 411). The cross-national test was applied in Argentina, Bolivia, Brazil, Colombia, Costa Rica, Cuba, Chile, Honduras, Mexico, Paraguay, Peru, the Dominican Republic, and Venezuela, and entailed testing over 50,000 pupils, in the third and fourth grade. This test is sometimes referred to as PEIC-UNESCO (Primer Estudio Internacional Comparativo) and other times as the LLECE (Labouratorio Latinoamericano de Evaluacion de la Calidad de la Educacion) test.

47. Scholars have relatively quickly reacted to these developments. As of 2012, there has already been a well-sized sociological literature on the changing racial relations in Cuba, in both English and Spanish. I have relied here on English-language sources, such as the Meerman book, a couple of English publications by Cuban scholars, and an electronically available synopsis of Esteban Morales Domínguez, written to his 2008 book (Challenges of the Racial Problem in Cuba, published by the Casa de la Fundación Don Fernando Ortiz; the Introduction is posted at http://etnocuba.ucr.edu/?p=143.), which highlights the lack of publications on race in Cuba for the last 45 years, but also draws attention to the increasing scholarly and popular interest in it over the last few years.

48. Rodrigo Espina Prieto: "The racial perspective in equity studies in Cuba," Seminar paper, UNDP/IPC, Brasilia, January 2007. Not meant for circulation, but the data is credited to González, Niuva (2006). *Familia, racialidad y educación.* Trabajo de Diploma, Departamento de Sociología, Universidad de La Habana (Inédito)—and it is convergent with survey results from Espina Prieto et al. (2010), whose subjects claimed that admission to university is harder for Blacks.

49. Unfortunately, a collusion of the assimilated market-dominant minority with the majority elite may as well lead to plutocratic rule as the machinations of an unassimilated market-dominant minority on its own. In the first case, however, the issue can be conceptualized in simple class-struggle ideologies, no communal overtones are necessarily emerging.

50. Cf. Dovidio et al., 2005.

51. There are no serious reasons to conduct a full-fledged comparison of the two directions of impact, such as with a technique of simultaneous equations. A number of historical and theoretical reasons buttress the absolute dominance of the "from inequality toward hostility" direction above the opposite. Empirically, MAR's ECDIS variable codes 31 groups out of the 762 in the MAR_EPR_MI dataset as suffering from economically oppressive policies, and most cases can be shown to exacerbate preexisting economic gaps, rather than to create them.

52. For diverse groups around the world, there are different factors contributing to their relative poverty. There is, for instance, the lack of industrial development in most of the world in the sixteenth century, when Europe started its expansion. Colonialism aggravated the inherited economic disparity of whole continents, while conquest, slavery, and colonial politics brought about deep differences of wealth and status of the communal groups in most countries. On a smaller scale, regions within the same country might have experienced different development velocities and paths, as result of natural endowments and catastrophes, exposure to foreign conquests, or presence of social capital, as suggested by Putnam. Finally, on the basis of preexisting smaller differences in resources, unleashed market conditions may induce polarization of wealth.

53. Blacks in Cuba are at parity with whites on this scale, while the Roma are many-century-old-immigrants, and the Chinese relatively new immigrants.

Chapter 3

Explanatory Model and Hypotheses

May the Odds Be in My Favor?

Chapter 2 showed a scarcely flattering image of the scholarly undertakings in the field of intergroup relations. It suggested that there are deep-rooted structural causes to the fact that the impact of economic inequality on intergroup hostility has not firmly been asserted and has not convincingly been demonstrated thus far. The logic of the situation is that, if we believe in the causal potency of inequality, then we have to blame science for failing it thus far. More exactly and less dramatically, we get to believe that science failed to give the EI-PC nexus a fair shot to force the threshold between hypothesis and thesis. And some issues with science, which challenged its dealings with this nexus, are undeniably, ostensibly real.

The first issue is the disciplinary fragmentation of social research, which breaks down my subsequent critiques as well. Inadequate conceptualization of economic inequality, such as failure to distinguish between intergroup (horizontal) and interindividual (vertical) type, has incontestably contributed to marginalizing economic inequality as a causal factor, but the failure is typical to the political science field, not to sociology and development economics. Another discipline-specific conceptualization is political science's focus on violent conflicts resulting in battle deaths, and its neglect of lower intensity manifestations of intergroup hostility, such as discrimination, oppression, and pogroms. Indeed, political science tends to collapse the category of violent communal conflict with that of violent noncommunal social conflict (such as violent forms of class struggle) and to study civil wars in general, rather than take violent communal conflict for the endpoint of a scale ranging from weaker forms of communal hostility toward stronger ones. And finally, it is much more typical to political science than to other social fields to focus on minority-majority relations, not on communal relations in general.

The lack of satisfactory empirical data on horizontal inequality—and on a number of features pertinent to communal groups and group relations—affects all social disciplines, but those relying on quantitative methods are more touched than the experiment-based social psychology and small-N oriented anthropological research.

All these issues with social research contributed to the pattern found, that social psychology and sociology are more supportive of the EI-PC nexus than political science. The formers' specific disciplinary focus and conceptual tools allow for a very different framing of this relationship. Concern with intergroup disparity, as a group marker, refocuses the old allegation that economic inequality makes the poor rebel onto the conjecture that economic inequality causes group enmity and group rivalry. The consequences of this difference in framing are not trivial,[1] and they also call for different methodologies. "Simple" rebellions, as well as civil wars, have often been explained from individualist utilitarian stances, while the explanation of group interactions tends to involve holistic or communitarian perspectives.[2]

Yet without believing in some favorable auspices foreshadowing the chance of success, it would have been premature to attempt a new research focused on the EI-PC nexus. The first favorable circumstance to mention is the academia's relative normative consensus around rejecting communal intolerance. State secularism, pluralism, diversity, and tolerance get support, while attempts to suppress heterogeneity either through expulsion or through forced assimilation, are repudiated. The legitimacy of the state hinges on its treating all citizens fairly, and domestic violence may be put down by international intervention. The relative normative consensus, however, does not mean agreement with regard to the policies to follow in heterogeneous countries, nor common vote with regard to the application of the responsibility to protect, nor concurring views with regard to the positive discrimination of disadvantaged groups.

A further encouraging circumstance is the emergence of cumulative knowledge in the field. It is primarily the cross-national large-N research of political scientists that allows for pooling results from several studies and leads to delimiting a number of determinants—or groups of determinants—that have been shown to have an impact on the occurrence of intergroup hostility. In multivariate regression models, these determinants keep being tested against each other and have reinforced the belief that the explanation of domestic violence is multicausal. Whichever we think is the main explanatory variable, we have to allow for the impact of the country's economic development level; its political institutions; the opportunities of the groups to mobilize; and the special features of the communal group structure, such as group size, regional concentration, cultural distances, and overlapping versus crosscutting cleavages. In addition, beyond all externalized and objectified features of the social world, some ideational factors, ideologies, and group consciousnesses or identities, may have their impact. Yet in multicausal settings, concerns with aggregation (or "structuration") of the influences are unavoidable. Can we model the impact of all these determinants in simple additive ways, or we are bound to account for their intricate and idiosyncratic interrelatedness? Neither alternative is universally shared. By succumbing to the prudence involved in the choice of the latter, we would lose the grip on certain phenomena whose impact on intergroup hostility comes through in regression models even if their effect is modified by other features of the respective cases. To do justice to defenders of the idiographic approach, odds are that some determinants are interchangeable. When we measure the causal impact of both political inequality and economic inequality on a large number of cases, we cannot exclude the possibility that in some cases it was political inequality without economic gap, and in other cases it was economic inequality without political gap, leading to intergroup hostility. There are also cases of more complicated interplay between causes such as crosscutting economic and political inequality, which is supposed (for instance in Stewart 2008) to mitigate the impact of both. Yet setting up a list of probable causes, even if we do not claim that all of them are always necessary to produce the undesired outcome, has an undeniable practical value analogous to that of the list of carcinogenic substances in modern medicine.

Finally, the third reason for optimism is the availability of better data than those on which previous research had to rely. Chapter 4 will give details about the origins of my data. Here I mention only the large-sample surveys carried out by the UNICEF and USAID, so necessary for measuring intergroup inequality in a large number of countries, and which were not available a few years ago.

This chapter presents an explanatory model of intergroup hostility that draws on the *acquis communautaire* knowledge base brought about by research in the field, primarily the quantitative type.[3] That is, it embraces all major explanatory variables promoted by political scientists, but also tries to address concerns related to the structuration of the causes and the temporal unfolding of intergroup relations.

THE EXPLANATORY MODEL

Though scholars of intergroup conflict diverge in their choice of the main explanatory variable, they greatly concur about the sphere of determinants that should be taken into consideration. We may find the same basic concerns in the work of the MAR theorists, of the utilitarian approach of Fearon and

Laitin, and of the sociologist and economist contributors of the volume edited by Stewart (2008). With the sole exception of economic inequality, whose impact is admitted by some and denied by others, researchers agree that the country's developmental level and institutions, the group structure and history, as well as the international circumstances, all have an impact on the intergroup relations.

These concerns come together in the flowchart model represented in Figure 3.1.

The chart highlights an important choice I have had to make in order to make the hypotheses testable. Social psychology and sociology tend to speak about communal groups without reference to their position as majority or minority in a nation-state. Political science speaks, almost exclusively, about minority-majority relationships. And data for cross-national empirical tests exists only for minority-majority relationships.

When we substitute the minority-majority relations for intergroup relations, we restrict the sphere of potential group-dyads, but automatically control for an important variable, the political inequality. (At least at the simplest

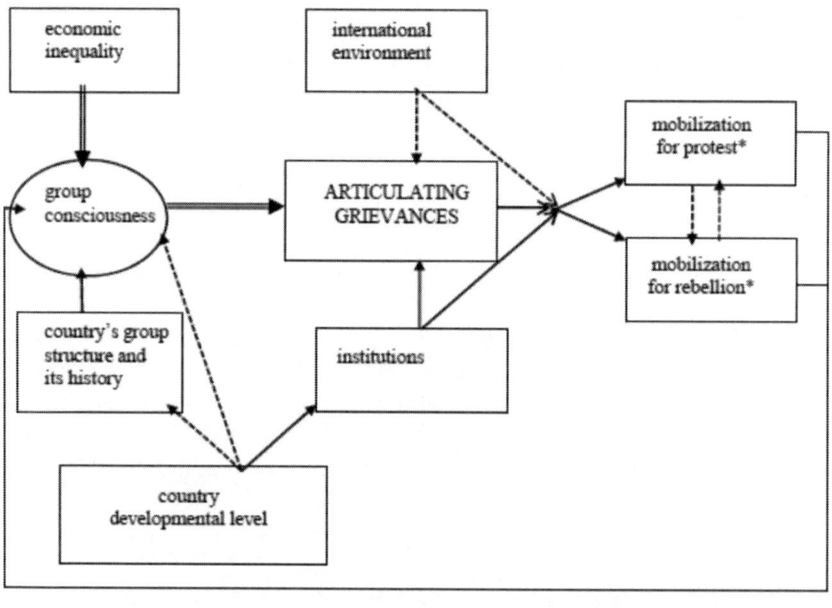

*"Protest" and "rebellion" are used approximately in the sense in which they occur in the MAR database, as well. "Protest" includes all non-violent forms of political action, from peaceful demonstrations through ethnic party politics to, say, road blockages. "Rebellion" means violent means, during which physical clashes with other groups occur.

Figure 3.1 Factors Explaining Minority Attitudes and Behavior I.

dichotomic level—this distance can be further refined by introducing either institutional variables of democracy, inclusiveness, and power-sharing, or the comparative power rank of the groups, as in the EPR data.) Further, when our dependent variable is violent conflict, the minority-minority horizontal relationships are not really relevant. Practically, violence between two small minorities can be expected to be put down by state authority, while in case of sizeable minorities at fight, the alliance of the plurality with one of them is very likely to occur, which transforms the problem into the basic minority-majority issue.

Thus, although my basic insight about the impact of economic inequality comes from theories with a more general outlook, Figure 3.1 is focused on minority-majority relationships. This is obvious from the causal link "articulation of grievances," a term meaningful only in the context when one group uses the state authority against the other. (In case of power-wise symmetrical groups, the link would be called "articulation of reasons for group hostility.") And the two basic options of acting upon the grievances, "protest" and "rebellion," are terms borrowed from the MAR vocabulary.

Yet, I would like to point out my divergence from the previous scholarship in this regard. A large part of the literature seems to assume that the tactics of peaceful "protest" are doomed to grow into violent "rebellions."[4] My contention is that in the more developed parts of the world, most minority political participation is meant to stay within the frames of democratic political strife and does not carry larger chance of reverting to violence than political strife along class and other issues, such as environmentalism. And I hope that a move in the opposite direction is also possible: that the warriors may be brought back to negotiating their coexistence. This may become feasible, indeed, when the international community intervenes and mediates between the parties. The bifurcating, double arrow from the bloc of institutions to the formulation of grievances and beyond, intends to visualize the complexity of the institutional impacts. Some features of the institutional structure, for instance, lost autonomy, and political discrimination, are determinants of grievances, as such. Other features, for instance, inclusive democracy, which allows for the effectual political participation of the minorities, will have an impact on the tactics that a minority chooses when it seeks redress to their grievances. The larger written institutional structure includes features such as government effectiveness, economic and social policies, and cultural organizations—a sizeable number of factors that can be taken for influencing either the grievances, or the choice of the tactics, or both. The same can be said about the impact of the international environment. Social globalization, for instance, which fosters a cosmopolitan outlook of the population, is likely to reduce intergroup hostility, that is, to affect the grievance levels.

Yet, the availability of foreign military aid to rebel groups will increase the temptation of choosing violent solutions to redress their plight.

Since this chart shows the dynamics of intergroup relations from the point of view of the minority only, it does not capture my belief that economic inequality has an impact through modifying the attitudes of both parties to the relationship toward each other. Actually, my contention about and my explanation for the mechanism of impact of economic inequality is to trace it both ways. Minorities react to the fact of inequality with the feeling that an injustice is happening. In majorities, inequality triggers a vicious circle of finding legitimating myths for their privileges, blaming the subordinate group, developing prejudices, and discriminating, which worsens the situation of the minority, who become even poorer with all the negative corollaries of this situation, including substance abuse and crime.

Also, the model is better at explaining the typical case when the minority is poorer. In case of the much rarer situation of advantaged minorities, it is the majority feeling frustrated and acting upon this frustration. When majorities have a safe grip on political power, they use state authority to level the economic conditions, through nationalization, land reform, positive discrimination on behalf of the poorer majority, and so on. When their own political ideology does not allow for market-contrary measures, or their foreign allies or relations with international lenders do not allow for them, the popular frustration often leads to pogroms, widespread discrimination, unpunished and "undetected" crimes against the wealthy minority, as experienced by whites in Zimbabwe and the Chinese in diaspora. In these cases it is not the economic inequality *per se*, but the persecutions suffered at the hand of the frustrated majority that will become the object of minority grievances.

Lastly, group consciousness is a very important intervening variable, but I cannot rely on it in the empirical work. It is impossible to get data on the hostility levels of each group. Thus, my actual regression models have to skip the link of group consciousness, with the result that the factors impacting group consciousness will become direct explanatory variables. By dropping group consciousness from the model, the feedback from mobilization back to articulating grievances can be traced through the history of group relations, as in Figure 3.2.

Models are, obviously, simplifying. They simplify both the real-world processes and the scholarly claims about them. In the case of this model, for instance, despite the full agreement that development levels have an impact on intergroup conflict, there are controversies about the ways and direction of this impact. I will proceed below to explicate and sharpen my assumptions related to these impacts and operationalize them in testable hypotheses.

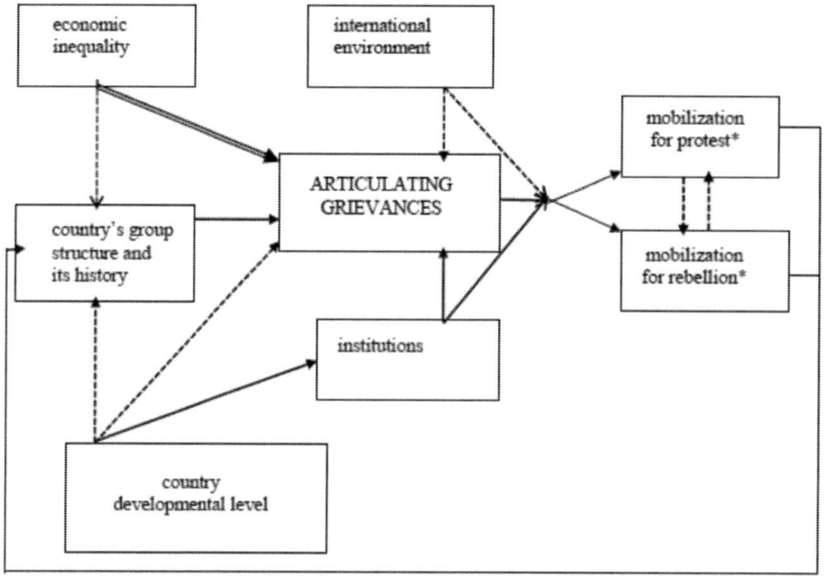

* "Protest" and "rebellion" are used approximately in the sense in which they occur in the MAR database, as well. "Protest" includes all non-violent forms of political action, from peaceful demonstrations through ethnic party politics to, say, road blockages. "Rebellion" means violent means, during which physical clashes with other groups occur.

Figure 3.2 Factors Explaining Minority Attitudes and Behavior II.

THE EXPLANATORY VARIABLES AND HYPOTHESES

Economic Inequality

My basic conjecture stipulates the impact of economic inequality on intergroup relations and intergroup conflict. The direction of the impact is unambiguous: the larger the welfare gap between the groups, the more hostile and conflictual their relationship.

There are, however, impediments to sharpening this conjecture into a testable hypothesis. We cannot measure hostility levels, as such, in large-N samples. Most of the pertinent cross-national literature works with violent intergroup conflict, as their dependent variable, though violent conflicts are neither necessary nor proportionate expressions of intergroup hostility. On the positive side, we may hope that certain intergroup issues are solved in relatively peaceful ways, that is, the accumulating tension and hostility can be diverted from discharging into violence. On the negative side, severe oppression may impede or delay the rebellion of the minority. Certain idiosyncratic conditions may have the same effect, such as the geographical dispersion of the minority, their fresh immigrant status, crosscutting cleavages, and internal discord.

I assume that economic inequality always leads to tension and hostility between groups, but will lead to express violence only probabilistically, within certain particular circumstances. The application of the "*ceteris paribus*" clause is nothing unusual in research; this is why we use a large number of control variables. But besides relying on control variables, I would also experiment with a dependent variable that is closer to "tension and hostility," than to violent conflict.

Operationalized for tests, the hypothesis doubles itself so that it allows for the use of two types of dependent variables:

- H1a Economic inequality between groups increases the likelihood and intensity of violent conflict between them.
- H1b Intergroup economic inequality increases the number and severity of the grievances forwarded by minorities.

I would sum up the reasons for believing in this "EI-PC" nexus starting from social psychology's Tajfel paradigm, which claims that the continuing salience of group-ness is a source of tension in itself. In our modern world, economic inequality is a very powerful group marker, and the more unequal the groups are, the more closed, "barricaded," impermeable they are toward each other. In the language of the political science methodology, this is a constructivist claim, which endogenizes the sheer existence of the groups and their relationships. Intergroup violence is likely when we have well outlined groups without common grounds and without cooperative tasks—but when do we have well outlined groups without common grounds and without cooperative tasks within the same state? What makes a group stick out in a society? Why is the group membership salient for its members, and why is it salient for the out-group?

I suggest that a main reason for the groups being salient is that they are parts of a social hierarchy, in the sense in which gender is considered to be a hierarchy. When we speak of majorities and minorities, the underlying political power hierarchy is obvious. Yet, economic inequality may be at least as consequential as political inequality. Unequal status of any kind hardens the group boundaries and prevents interaction, cooperation, and blending together. The walls are erected from both sides: the better-placed group originates legitimizing mythologies and prejudices, while the disadvantaged group fosters grievances and imposes a moral code of hostility on their members.

Beyond political inequality, studied, for instance, by Cederman et al, and the economic inequality of which impact I intend to prove here, there are several other forms of intergroup inequality for which I won't be able to control within the frames of this project. The two most significant seem to be social inequality, which mars the life of India's Dalits and Mauritania's

Haratins, and cultural inequalities, which affect almost all minority groups to some extent.[5]

A number of thought-provoking sources supporting the EI-PC nexus have already been referred to, such as (i) Stewart (2008), which makes a very clear distinction between horizontal and vertical economic inequality; (ii) work of the MAR group, which highlights the importance of group comparative disadvantages; and (iii) case studies by Chua (2002) and Meerman (2009), which show the strong association between intergroup economic gaps and intergroup hostility.

Development Level and Modernization

In cross-national studies we cannot imagine empirical tests without controlling for the countries' relative wealth and well-being. Yet, in the case of intergroup hostility and violence, we do not have clear expectations related to the impact of the development indicators. The absence of a well-coalesced dominant paradigm of the field allows for a number of hypotheses free-floating around the issue, and even for some antithetical predictions. As an empirical generalization, we may claim that in the most developed countries, intergroup violence is much rarer than in the developing world. Yet, the most developed countries are also the most homogenous, and the most democratic, features that are much more likely to reduce violence levels than higher GDP on its own. Plus, industrialization reduces the geographical concentration of the minority groups, hindering their military mobilization.

The roots of the disarray in this domain may be traced back to the debate between perennialist (or primordialist) theorists claiming that ethnicities are unchanging attributes stamped on us for good, and the modernist (constructivist) theorists claiming that the scope and importance of national entities are social artifacts, particularly of the capitalist modernization,[6] and all socioterritorial identities are historically changing. While the nineteenth century was typified by the nationalist mobilization of majorities, since WWII we may speak about the strengthening of the postnational[7] loyalties in an increasingly globalized world.

Policy choices are deeply affected by beliefs about the changeability of the socioterritorial consciousness. We may define a continuum of these beliefs, ranging from most transient to least ephemeral. On the transient end of the scale, there are, for instance, Dahl and Inglehart, who think that economic progress will automatically strip people of their parochial ties. Lijphart is on the least ephemeral end. He does not think that intercommunal disputes will get solved from themselves and suggests power-sharing schemes, which enable communal groups to negotiate their coexistence from quasi-equal political positions. In between the extremes, but closer to the Dahl/Inglehart position, there is Horowitz, who intends to facilitate the communal groups' melting together with political arrangements that reward interethnic cooperation and punish politicizing along communal lines.

It seems that a majority of theorists expects development to reduce the salience of communal ties and levels of intergroup hostility, but there have been a number of opposing claims forwarded, as well, which refer to certain particular social and historical circumstances within which modernization fails to improve the intergroup relations. Such conditions were highlighted by Huntington (1968: too rapid modernization), Scott (1976: collapse of rural social structures without being replaced by new forms of social control and solidarity), Gurr (1971: certain groups remain excluded from the benefits of modernization), and Chua (2002: imposition of individualist free-marketeer policies in developing countries with unsolved group inequality problems).

As of today, there is no overarching theory linking development and intergroup relations, and we may wonder whether it is possible at all. Modernization processes may be deemed to affect group relations in diverse, often antithetical ways, such as:

(i) Geographical concentration versus urban rivalries. In preindustrial societies, communal groups tend to cluster together geographically and have most of their interaction among themselves, rarely interfering with other groups. This reduces chances of both syncretizing and conflicts. Urbanization involves "melting together," but also some rivalry for jobs, housing, and education.

(ii) Tolerance versus rivalry in education. Education leads to more tolerant attitudes, but longer schooling involves issues about who pays for it and who controls the language and content of public education.

(iii) Nation-building versus globalization. As a matter of fact, most of the globalization affects the already developed countries only, which went through their nation-building era by the twentieth century. The countries that have become independent after WWII still have to work a lot on approaching the nation-state ideal promoted by the developed, and generally approved of by the developing, countries. The latter, then, may be assumed to be exposed to nation-building and globalization simultaneously, a mixture of whose impact on ethnic relations is incalculable.

(iv) Pacifying democracy versus Westernist democratization. Democratic institutions allow certain conflicts to be played out in peaceful ways. But some developing countries resist West-imposed democratization because this comes with the imposition of individualist free-marketeer capitalism. This latter may be opposed either on mercantilist grounds (such as in the Asian tigers), or on Marxist or Keynesian grounds, which also involve the idea that unleashed markets prevent the application of equalizing policies that would assure long-term ethnic peace.

I think that our solution to the problem of accounting for the impact of such an elusive determinant is to take apart as many of its component factors as possible. I included measures of group concentration, urbanism, globalization, and democracy in my models. In order to control for development level, I used the simplest country wealth (GDP/cap, GNI/cap) and population well-being indicators (HDI, life expectancy). With regard to the impact of these, my predictions for the two dependent variables are different.

- H2.a More well-being in a country reduces the likelihood of violent conflict. This converges with our empirical observations, though those may be an artifact of the confounding factors, mainly of democracy. On utilitarian grounds, however, we may expect people to venture into violence when they have little to lose and the goods absolutely necessary to their survival are in very short supply.
- H2.b More well-being in a country does not reduce the amount of grievances voiced by minorities. This is not a direct impact of the well-being, but an outcome of all corollaries of economic development, such as the isolated evolution of the groups coming to an end, and a general increase of the mass political activity levels. In the fortunate conditions of a healthy democracy, oft-voiced grievances may count on some redress without serious costs or side effects, what lends a utilitarian support to the hypothesis. And, obviously, a growing pie generally does not impede disputes about the size of the slices.

Group Structure and Group History

By a country's group structure I mean the number and relative size of the relevant groups, and also their distances on the group markers such as race, ethnicity, language, and religion. We often refer to it as "diversity" or "heterogeneity," but the usage of these terms varies greatly, and they carry some emotional connotation, as well. The literature tries to capture the features typifying diversity with the concepts of fractionalization, polarization, and group distance.

Fractionalization indexes were the first to be introduced, their history starting in 1961 with the Soviet ethnolinguistic fractionalization index (ELF). Today we have a very large number of similar measures, because researchers kept multiplying them in function of the communal group markers of interest to them. The original ELF relied on ethnolinguistic groups; others distinguished between ethnic groups and linguistic groups (e.g. Annett, and Alesina), and religious fractionalization has also been added. As of today, Alesina's triplet (ethnic, linguistic, and religious) covers the most countries and it relies on statistical data contemporaneous with that of Fearon's indexes.

It seems that the relationship between the proportion of minorities, on the one hand, and group relationships, on the other, is not monotonic. When controlling for other factors, highly homogenous and highly fragmented societies seem to experience less communal conflict than those in which a clear majority (i.e., one above half of the overall population) faces one or more sizable minorities. The thesis of nonmonotonic relationship was first suggested by Horowitz (1985), and later researchers tried to work out indicators that allow for measuring the structure of fragmentation, not its size only. Fearon (2003) introduced measures for the proportion of plurality and of the largest minority, while Garcia-Montalvo and Reynal-Querol (2005) showed that their index of polarization was a significant predictor of intercommunal conflict.

Based on these results, it is obvious that we have to control for fractionalization,[8] but it makes sense to make predictions only about polarization.

- H3.1a The likelihood of violent conflict increases with the relative size of the minority.

This claim incorporates some concerns making up the "opportunity for insurrection" hypothesis advocated by Fearon & Laitin 2003, addressed in section 3.6. Yet, the behavior of the plurality seems to contribute to the larger minorities' increased feeling of oppression. Pluralities do not feel comfortable in the presence of large minorities and overstress their efforts to homogenize the population. Thus, I expect larger minorities to voice more grievances than smaller minorities:

- H3.1b Larger minorities have more grievances.

Other exogenously given factors that may affect the minority-majority relationship are the group markers. Is it the language, the customs, the religion, or the race most effectively separating the groups? Again, there is a consensus that the nature of the difference and the distance of the groups on the feature that separates them (e.g., distance on language) may have an impact on group relations, but there is no unique and overarching theory of what to expect, and little if any empirical support for any salient pattern. Modernization theory, for instance, expects the effacement of all communal differences, but primarily that of religion; thus, it expects religious collisions in backward countries only. Some accounts (such as work by Jonathan Fox 2002, 2004) claim that religious clashes are more violent than clashes between ethnic groups.

I do not have a theory to explain why any exogenous group marker should be more important than others in bringing about hostility and violence,[9] and we do not have good comprehensive (worldwide) data to control for the impact of any of them. It is only the MAR dataset containing information about the group markers, for its 282 groups out of more than 700 which would make the full list of minorities to study. Given the lack of any salient theoretical expectation to test, and the difficulty to find the appropriate measurements, I have given up to control for the group markers and the distance on them.

There are, however, two other group features that are unavoidable in models explaining intergroup relations: group concentration and group history.

The geographical concentration of the groups may count for both the chances and nature of group mobilization. Geographically compact groups have better opportunities to organize for collective action, and their political activity is likely to target territorial autonomy. Geographically dispersed groups have traditionally faced more difficulty to organize themselves, a condition that is increasingly mitigated by the modern gadgets for networking. Yet, their political goals are less predictable. These may range from support for a number of minority cultural institutions through establishing a minority party to full-fledged power-sharing along communal lines, such as in the Dutch pillarization.

Geographical concentration does not mean more conflictual relationships on its own, since isolated groups have less contact and therefore less chance to clash. Geographical concentration, however, is more frequent in the less fortunate parts of the world, where all disputes are more likely to turn violent, and it means an additional vulnerability of the minority, which cannot ever forgive a majority that breaches on their territorial autonomy. The importance of this issue is highlighted by MAR's effort of elaborating an indicator called "lost autonomy." That is, the main difference is made not by the geographical concentration *per se*, but by the majority's tolerance toward the autonomy of such areas and its willingness to evenhandedly help their development. This is partly a group history issue, and partly an institutional one. Practically, my models:

(a) control for the group concentration as part of the "opportunity for insurrection" hypothesis;
(b) control for past conflicts; and
(c) include a predictor measuring to what extent the country's administrative boundaries are drawn with respect to minority concentrations, and its interaction term with a decentralization measure.[10]

The reason for (b) are my hypotheses that:

- H3.2a A history of violent conflicts makes further conflicts more likely.
- H3.2b A history of violent conflicts makes minority grievances more likely.

The following section articulates the argument for including the variables mentioned in (c).

The Country's Institutional System

The three most important features of the institutional system, relevant for the intergroup relations, seem to be efficiency, repressiveness, and inclusiveness. The concerns with these features come from a number of theoretical traditions. State efficiency has mainly been focused on by the proponents of the opportunity for insurrection hypothesis. Repressiveness is a concern of the MAR theorists and of those working within social conflict perspectives. Inclusiveness became an issue of the ethnic policy debates between the Horowitzian and Lijphartian approaches, and got its cross-national empirical support from Reynal-Querol in 2005.

Since the beginning of the scholarly preoccupation with minorities, the repressiveness of the state operated by the majority has seriously been considered as an important factor shaping intergroup relations. We may distinguish, however, between formal and informal majority attitudes toward a minority, and the two may be desynchronized. It often happens that the state credibly strives to treat all its citizens impartially, but the majority practices discrimination against a minority in education, jobs, and housing, or violent hostility against an either disadvantaged or advantaged minority.[11]

On the flip side, individual majority attitudes toward a minority may be quite tolerant, while the state applies policies that restrict the political, economic, and cultural rights of a minority as a group. This was the experience, for instance, of a number of ethnic minorities in Eastern Europe during communism. The policies of the socialist state were geared toward homogenizing and assimilation, and prevention of civil associations of any kind, but the individual career of persons belonging to minorities was not hindered, and actually often promoted with a quota system applied in the ruling party's and state's leadership positions. I introduced the term "de-synchronized" for these discrepancies because it seems that time is an important factor here, and ultimately the state's ways and the folkways tend to get more concerted, either on behalf or to the detriment of the minority.

Moving upward, for instance, were the Blacks in the United States from the 1970s through the new century (a state-led upward spiral) and Hungarians in Romania since the fall of communism (a popular mood-led spiral), while moving downward are the Roma in Hungary, on their way to lose state support at the hands of a rightist government pandering to a strong extreme right movement.

Thus my take on the impact of the phenomenon labeled "repressive control" by the MAR theorists, which is one of their three main groups of causes explaining the occurrence of intergroup violence (out of the triad of collective disadvantage, group identity, and repressive control), is that indeed, higher repression leads to more grievance and more violence. Just that, unfortunately, it may not explain the whole variation in intergroup hostility and may lack real proportionality with it. Since there are practical impediments to testing the assumption, as well, I do not forward express hypothesis in this regard, but I control for two forms of state repressiveness. First, in all datasets, I have included a democracy measure, most often a political terror scale. And second, where possible, that is, in the chapter 6, I explore the impact of MAR's specific measures of political and economic discrimination and of the cultural (religious and language) restrictions—these are the best measures that we have on group-specific repressiveness.

Finally, state inclusiveness is a complex and controversial issue. While there is agreement that an inclusive state allows for the well-being of the minorities, there is no consensus about what helps minorities flourish in a state which is not their "own." The most often mentioned policy goals are integration and assimilation, while the most relevant policy tools are districting, decentralization, and support for political mobilization along communal lines.

As a policy ideal, integration denotes a majority-minority coexistence in which minorities are not constrained to radically change their ways of life and identity in order to be a prosperous part of the country's population. In contrast, assimilationism offers the prospect of individual prosperity while imposing the majority culture upon minorities. The so-called civic nationalism, which is regularly branded as leaving cultures alone, and requiring the homogenization of the political attitudes only, is very often experienced as assimilationism by the subjected minorities. It seems that the truth comes somewhere in the middle. The US civic nationalism, for instance, has done a decent job in securing secularism as the religious neutrality of the state, and allows for the pursuit of a large number of cultural traditions as leisure-time activities. However, this civic nationalism has a hard time accommodating the programmatically nonindustrial way of life of the Native Americans and Amish, for instance, as well as to duplicate the state language in areas with Hispanic majority.

The constitutional blueprints forwarded by Horowitz, on the one hand, and Lijphart, on the other, target different things, both legitimate and meaningful. Horowitz would like the residents of a country to come together in a color-blind and language-deaf citizenry, the real "horizontal comradeship" of Benedict Anderson, under the aegis of civic nationalism. Lijphart aims at minority-friendly designs, which enable the groups to accommodate to existing state boundaries by devaluing state-ness and empowering subnational authorities. It is his policies that can be termed "integrative," "inclusive," or maybe "accommodating," though Horowitz also conceives of his own proposals as helping the citizenry integrating into one nation. Yet, the essence of the Horowitzian advice is to prevent minority politicizing along ethnic lines, in order to curb the desire of some ethnic entrepreneurs to exacerbate intergroup hostility. Unfortunately, this advice seems to involve the idea that a grievance that is not loudly voiced does not exist, and also the elitist conception that the "entrepreneurs" are affected by group plights in other ways than the rank-and-file, and have full command of the beliefs of the latter.

For long, researchers have been working on devising tests that would help us choose between the two policy proposals. A number of case studies evidence the superiority of either one or the other, regularly by pointing out flaws in the workings of one prescription in a certain country. Lijphart's "accommodating" policy goals can be operationalized for large-N empirical tests in a number of ways. Reynal-Querol (2005) measured inclusiveness with proportional representation versus plurality electoral system, and she found that "democracy is not enough to deter social conflicts. The level of inclusiveness of the political system is important in explaining the probability of civil wars."

I think that there are at least two aspects of inclusiveness. For geographically concentrated minorities, territorial autonomy is the most important political achievement. For geographically dispersed minorities, the way of having a say in politics goes through political parties, whose success measures their incorporation into the country's political life.[12] Thus, I would formulate a hypothesis that takes into account both types of inclusiveness:

- H4.2a Political arrangements that allow for more autonomy of the minority and/or more success of the minority parties lead to less intergroup violence.

And, since lack of autonomy and electoral systems that exclude minority parties are grievances on their own, I would add the corresponding hypothesis involving the other dependent variable:

- H4.2b Political arrangements that allow for more autonomy of the minority and/or more success of the minority parties mitigate the severity of minority grievances.

This pair of hypotheses may best justify the need for the double arrow illustrating the impact of the institutions in the flowchart-models (Figures 3.1 and 3.2). A minority excluded from the country's political life, which experiences a large political inequality gap, has good reasons to harbor discontentment and hostility, and forward grievances against the state-operating plurality. Yet, political grievances, as any grievance, of any type, such as of economic and cultural, may lead to peaceful settlement of the issues only in the conditions of a democracy that allows for the articulation of the minority demands within the system. Hence, the inclusiveness of the political system is also an opportunity for avoiding violence, in the same sense in which large rural areas and large proportions of unemployed young males increase the probability of a militarized outcome.

The International Environment

There are countless ways in which the international environment may affect intergroup relations in a country, but no outstandingly strong impact or generalizable pattern has been detected thus far.

An oft-formulated conjecture is that support from kindred increases the likelihood of violence. Yet, there are cases in which the kindred support is directed toward impeding or mitigating violence (such as Ireland's in the North-Ireland conflict), and there are cases in which unrelated countries and groups support the fight of a minority against their majority, either on humanitarian grounds or as part of a selfish political strategy.

Though I do not deny the possibility that types of external support increase the likelihood of the hostility turning violent, I could not control for all these idiosyncratic influences for all countries and all groups in my sample. I have tested the impact of external support on the MAR_EPR_MI dataset only, since MAR is the only source for this rare indicator.

Yet, I am interested in some other influences of the international environment, for which we have dependable data. The single most important phenomenon shaping the interstate system nowadays is globalization. This is, however, a complex phenomenon with diverse facets and aspects, affecting the states in various, uneven, and possibly antithetical ways. The KOF globalization indicators[13] cover three areas: economic, social, and political interconnectedness. Of these, economic globalization cannot be expected to make the states more minority-friendly; on the contrary, Amy Chua's claim can be operationalized as:

"$H_{(Chua)}$: The more a developing country is economically integrated within the global economy, the more hostility we may find there toward their advantaged minorities."

This claim should be tested on a restricted sample containing advantaged minorities only. The small number of such cases hardly allows for including 11–14 control variables, as the full-sample regression models do, and as a further complication, economic globalization is very closely associated with the development indicators. This means that in full-sample modeling economic globalization would follow the impact pattern of the GDP/capita and life expectancy variables, leading to less violence, but more grievance.

If we found the same pattern in the case of the advantaged minorities, this would not refute the Chua claim, but the full support for it would be more grievance and more violence—in conditions of reasonably full control for a large number of concurrent influences. Subsequently, since the accurate test of this claim would need a digressing from the general research design, I refrain from advancing $H_{(Chua)}$ as a research goal within the frames of this book. Yet, with a lingering suspicion toward the impact of economic globalization, I also refrain from advancing a hypothesis that would attribute positive impact to economic globalization, as I do in the case of social and political globalization.

I think that we may hope that social interdependence and dovish foreign policy contacts have a positive impact on states' behavior toward their minority groups. Social and cultural ties with people in other countries reduce nationalist attitudes and spread a more cosmopolitan—or more internationalist—outlook. The real endorsement of integrative policies by a state is signaled by their ratifying the main treaties of minority rights protection. Yet, this is a sign of, not a cause of their minority-friendliness! If we want to single out the impact of the international environment on majority behavior, the general political globalization is probably the best indicator that we have. The general deference to international norms shows to what extent they internalized the values informing the United Nations system. Thus, I forward the hypotheses that:

- H5.1 Higher social globalization of a country reduces intergroup hostility.
- H5.2 Higher political globalization of a country reduces intergroup hostility.

In addition, the KOF economic globalization measure has also been included in some models.

The Opportunity for Insurrection Hypothesis

Fearon and Laitin (2003) emphasize the role of opportunities in bringing about intrastate violence. Their claim is that ethnic wars do not occur where grievances are the hardest—they occur where there are better opportunities for armed insurgency, such as geographic conditions, large rural areas, state failure, group concentration, lots of unemployed young males, and support from kindred.

I think that these factors are more likely to direct the choice between "protest" and "rebellion," after the grievances have emerged under the impact of other determinants. The divergence between the two standpoints may be tested by comparing the weight of grievances, on the one hand, and the opportunity for insurrection variables, on the other, in bringing about violent conflict.[14] In order to address this issue, I pursue two tracks of hypothesis testing, labeled one-step resolution and two-step (or two-stage) resolution. Practically, in all three parts of the data analysis, I build both all-inclusive "omnibus" regression models, in which all explanatory variables exogenous to hostility are included to explain violent conflict, and two types of partial models, which substantiate my intuition that a number of exogenous factors influence group grievances, while the occurrence and severity of violence hinges on both the grievance levels, and on a series of opportunities. Opportunities may either facilitate the nonviolent settlement of the differentials, or push the participants toward violent solutions. The basic "opportunity for insurrection" hypothesis is that:

- H6 A group's opportunities to launch an insurrection with reasonable chances of success increase the likelihood and intensity of intergroup violence.

Yet we may imagine lots of factors having an impact on the chances of a rebellion, thus this claim needs a number of measurements to operationalize. Though they are specific to the measurement of "opportunity," most of them may be conceptualized as belonging to one of the explanatory clusters displayed in the flowchart-models, and actually, some of them double themselves and affect intergroup relations in multiple ways, not only through increasing the probability of violence.

We can substantiate H6 with a long list of circumstances, but many of them have serious issues that hinder their inclusion in models as "pure" measures of the opportunity for insurrection hypothesis. Table 3.1 sums up a number of concerns.

In addition, the Fearon and Laitin paper (2003) contained a measurement of the "mountainous terrain," which I cannot reproduce in my datasets. Yet, since the reason for accounting for the adverse geography is its role in hindering or delaying state repression against dispersed groups of rebels, I think that a substantial part of it is captured by the "state effectiveness" indicator.

In a final analysis, the opportunity for insurrection hypothesis is tested in my models with two group-structure variables (group proportion and group concentration), an international-environment indicator (external support, in the MAR_EPR_MI dataset), one specifically institutional (government effectiveness), and two that may be labeled as institutional in the larger sense (proportion of unemployed young male, and of the rural population).

Table 3.1 Issues with the Operationalization of the Opportunity for Insurrection Hypothesis

Operational claim	*Drawback*
Communal groups that have a larger proportion within the population are more likely to rebel	The test of this claim confounds with testing for the polarized group structure, as suggested by Garcia-Montalvo & Reynal-Querol 2005.
Communal groups that live in regional concentrations are more likely to rebel	Regional concentration facilitates mobilization, but also brings about specific minority demands for territorial autonomy (i.e., increases grievances, as well).
Large rural areas facilitate insurrection	I have reliable measurements for the proportion of rural population, not for areas. And urbanism is a par-excellence development indicator, highly correlated with measures such as GDP/cap and life expectancy.
External support to rebels, such as from kindred, facilitates insurrection	Measurable with the MAR_EPR_MI data only.
State effectiveness inhibits proneness to insurrection	There is a dependable measurement of state effectiveness, as part of the Worldwide Governance indicators, but it is highly correlated with development indicators.
Large supply of unemployed young males makes insurrection more likely	In principle, this can be measured, but practically, comparable indicators exist only for a reduced number of countries. And a further concern may be the impact of unemployment benefits, where they exist.

RESEARCH DESIGN

The project was set up as a large-N cross-national study that provides empirical support to hypotheses in virtue of the predictors' strength in multivariate regression models. Yet since the beginning there has been some tension between my explanatory model, stipulating a stepwise approach to the explanation of violent conflict, and a truly streamlined modeling, with only one dependent variable. During work, more problems emerged that increased the complexity of the analysis. As briefly referred to in the introductory chapter, the main issues leading to the multiplication of the regression models have been:

1. Lack of a unitary dataset containing all variables of interest, for comparable number of cases, and time spans. This problem was addressed by involving two different, though partially overlapping, group-level datasets, EPR_MAR_EXT and MAR_EPR_MI.
2. A level of analysis issue. Intergroup relations, and specifically violent intrastate conflict, may be studied at both the group and country level. This led to the addition of one more dataset, a purely country-level one.

3. My conjecture about the occurrence of violent conflict involves a process in stages. Thus, I defined two types of regression models: (i) causes of intergroup hostility explaining grievances and (ii) grievances explaining violent conflict. Both types of models have involved, obviously, a large number of controls taken from the predictor categories outlined in the previous section of this chapter. Yet, my findings may be compared to previous scholarly results only if I build comparable regression models, thus I could not spare the (iii) classic "omnibus" models, which connect the causes of hostility with the violent outcome. In addition, as a quick test of the power of my main explanatory variable, I ran (iv) generalized linear models with the intergroup economic inequality measures and the country factor, which is the equivalent of all pertinent country dummies.
4. I have had to use multiple dependent variables, such as grievances on the one hand, and violent conflict, on the other. The group level and the country-level analyses needed different indicators, and I also had to face the fact that MAR's grievance measures are taken along three different dimensions: economic, political, and cultural, without the possibility to combine them in a common scale.
5. Missing data made me resort to a technique of multiple imputations twice, in Chapters 6 and 7. In Chapter 6, I attempted to extend several MAR variables from the 282 MAR groups onto 727 minority groups included in my larger group-level sample. In Chapter 7, the data missingness was less pervasive, but the multiple imputation provided much needed values of the unemployed young males variable and of the measures that—uniquely in the literature—distinguish between conflicts of communal nature and other social conflicts.

Further challenges also tended to lead to an overproduction of regression models. I experimented with multilevel (nested) models to address the shortcomings of concatenating group-level and country-level measurements in the same models. Because of high association among predictors and danger of collinearity, I ran trials with several versions of parallel measurements. Sometimes, the multiplication of analyses answered the complexities around the definition of minority group.

I tried to bring order to the chaos induced by all these complications by structuring the three analytical chapters in very similar ways, and the conclusions include a more technical part that synthetizes information from Chapters 5 through 7. Actually, I have had to renounce a number of enticing alternate paths of research in order to keep the analyses and their presentation relatively simple and streamlined. For instance, I minimized the number of tests with special subsamples and dropped group consciousness from among the explanatory factors.[15]

By the nature of the enterprise, however, I cannot spare the reader a detailed presentation of the datasets with which the regression models have been built. Chapter 4 introduces the largest dataset of the three, named EPR_MAR_EXT.

NOTES

1. For instance, when speaking about the fight of the poor against the rich, we expect all poor people, without regard to their communal features, to join in—as the "workers of the world, unite" call has it. Yet, if unequal economic status is fused with easily noticeable communal group markers, poor people may fight other poor people who are perceived to belong to a communal group with a different *average* wealth. The pure utilitarian logic is diverted by a group stereotyping logic. In the light of what we know about the spell of group loyalties on our minds, and our predilection for acting upon "satisficing" pieces of information, not complete knowledge, this is not an anomaly, but rather the norm for the *zoon politikon*. Herbert Simon's bounded rationality, and the prospect theory of Kahneman & Tversky seem to reinforce this opinion.

2. One well-known counterexample is Fearon & Laitin's 1996 work on the effects of intragroup policing on intergroup relations, which inscribes in the individualist rational choice theory (RCT) paradigm.

3. Most factors of influence advocated in qualitative or small-N research make their way into quantitative research. In this case, for instance, I referred to small-N studies of the EI-PC nexus (Chua, Meerman), but did not trace causes already integrated in quantitative research to their previous occurrences in the small-N literature. Yet the plus point of the good small-N research is its study of the structuration of predictors, which cannot be rendered fully lucrative in the quantitative environment.

4. This is, for instance, the basic argument for banning ethnic and religious parties. Other consequences of this belief are certain variables constructed in the way that "protest" becomes a lower stage of "rebellion."

5. Legal inequality, such as slavery, is almost completely missing from today's world, except for expressly illegal forms, result of human trafficking and other criminal activities.

6. As in Hobsbawm 1992, and A. Marx 1996, 1998.

7. There are diverse hypotheses about how the socioterritorial identities may develop after the era of nationalism. One scenario is cosmopolitanism, but the possibility of a supra-national identity layer, thus the formation of multi-level territorial allegiances, has also been contemplated (e.g., Medrano and Gutiérrez 2001). Further, regional allegiances may completely overwrite national loyalties as part of the "federalization of Europe" scenario, in the Spinnelli tradition. The typical cosmopolitanization-believers are the developmentalists, such as Inglehart & Welzel 2005, 2009, and Norris & Inglehart 2009. One form or venue of forming cosmopolitan identities is transnationalism, the condition when people are existentially tied to two

or more countries. This phenomenon has also developed a burgeoning literature of its own, see for example, Howard 2011.

8. Chapter 2 has already mentioned that the fractionalization index performs poor in multivariate models.

9. In several countries, race seems to be the group marker the most associated with intergroup hostility, but in those countries the racial cleavage is indistinguishably confounded with the economic gap. Asians, who are not typically separated by persisting economic cleavages from the host population, have not had problem with successfully integrating in either the North American or Latin American, or Australian societies, while the indigenous populations and the Africans have had. Among the Asian immigrants to the United Kingdom, religion seems to be the group marker with the most predictive power with regard to the chances of integration: Indians and Pakistanis of non-Muslim religions (such as Hindus and Sikhs) seem to blend in seamlessly, while Indians and Pakistanis of Muslim religion still happen to show anti-British hostility. (The most tragic manifestation of this latter was the terrorist attack in London on July 7, 2005).

10. This is a country-level measure of group autonomy formulated to be used with the country-level dataset, but I have also had to use it with the EPR_MAR_EXT data, because of the lack of more appropriate measurement. With the MAR_EPR_MI dataset, I have been able to use MAR's own autonomy measures.

11. In any of the three cases quoted in the previous chapter, hostile actions against the Roma, Afro-Cubans, and wealthy Chinese (to the extent of the atrocities narrated by Chua), have not been initiated or openly sponsored by the state.

12. The Dutch pillarization goes beyond this solution for dispersed minorities, but it is so unique that in a cross-national dataset it's no point in controlling for that solution. Less elaborate forms of functional autonomy may be more widespread, but we do not have good cross-national data on it.

13. Original source of the data was Dreher, Axel (2006): "Does Globalization Affect Growth? Evidence from a new Index of Globalization," *Applied Economics* 38, 10: 1091–1110. Yet, it has repeatedly been updated, and the http://globalization.kof.ethz.ch/ site has several series for later years as well.

14. Originally, I was planning on a more sophisticated test of the Fearon & Laitin (2003) claim, in the sense to check on whether the opportunity for insurrection variables have an impact on grievances. This test would have addressed the part of the claim that attributes important consciousness-forming powers to some political entrepreneurs. (The political entrepreneurs, whose choices are, actually, made on grounds of opportunity calculation, are said to be capable of turning the minority group consciousness against their majorities when they want to.) Yet, for a more streamlined research design, and also because of data availability, I had to drop this project. For instance, there is no decent measure of the proportion of unemployed young males.

15. Since for many theorists thinking in a communitarian/holist paradigm, the absence of this explanatory factor won't go unnoticed, the Appendix 1 will briefly address the issue of whether group consciousness should and could have been included in these cross-national analyses.

Chapter 4

Presentation of the EPR_MAR_EXT Dataset

THE BASIC DESIGN

It is not really common in political science that the presentation of data to analyze takes a full chapter. Quantitative work in this field typically relies on a few widely known datasets, brought about as the collective venture of a few like-minded scholars, such as the Correlates of War, Polity, Worldwide Governance Indicators, Comparative Manifesto Project, and Freedom House ratings. In the field of the relationship among communal groups, however, there is a serious shortage of quantified, systematized, and generally accepted cross-national data.

First of all, there are some special issues with delimiting the groups of relevance within countries. There are a number of communal features which may either crosscut, or overlap with each other, thus the definition of groups involves some arbitrariness rooted in our rank-ordering of the group markers. Importantly, both the populations concerned and the scholars who study them, may develop selective sensitivity toward certain communal traits. For instance, it is widely known that in Switzerland the religious divisions were more important in the beginning, and the salience of ethnicity increased only in the nineteenth century. An inverse path of evolution, from more salience of ethnicity first, and more salience of religion later, may be attributed to Eritrea.[1] Political science tends to pay most attention to the ethnic group marker, which is the only one taken for legitimizing requests for secession. This bias persists even in face of evidence that religion is more likely to cause violent conflicts (Fox 2004), and that the inclusion of racial minorities is harder to achieve than that of ethnic minorities. The two most comprehensive datasets on communal groups worldwide, the MAR[2] and the EPR[3], both applied a practical criterion to define the groups that make their list. MAR was more restrictive, selecting the groups (i) which are minorities, and (ii) whose relationship with the majority-dominated government has already turned problematic. EPR included groups with political representation, that is, groups that were claimed to be represented by certain political organizations (in or outside the government), but confined its concerns to the citizen population. In contrast, the Minority Rights Group International (MRG)'s World Directory of Minorities looks at (i) residents, rather than citizens; (ii) lists all minority groups, not only those with political representation; and (iii) is equally interested in ethnic, linguistic, religious, regional, and, sometimes, caste or tribal group markers.[4] Yet, on the flip side, the MRG data is predominantly qualitative, hard to be accurately sorted into the cells of a spreadsheet.

As for my intentions, I wanted to avoid the pitfalls of focusing on the politically relevant groups only, and endorsed MRG's sociologically more sensitive way to account for the whole 100 percent of the population, including groups that do not have distinct voices in politics. Yet, I relied on EPR's scaffolding of—predominantly—ethnic group composition of each country, and I completed it with—predominantly—ethnic groups mentioned by MRG, which typically have little, or no political representation of their own.

Another conceptual issue to address is the level of analysis. While intuitively we think that group relationships are best measured at group level, a number of group-related phenomena have convincingly been measured at country level, as well. Possibly the best-known examples are the group composition measures, the fractionalization, and polarization indexes.[5] Approximately a third of the EPR variables are country-level measures. For instance, after determining which communal groups had been excluded from power, the authors were able to calculate the proportion of population excluded from power in each country, the ratio of included versus excluded, and so on. MAR provides data on groups involved in violent conflicts; other datasets, such as the GPI (of the Vision for Humanity), and FSI (of the Fund for Peace) classify countries on the basis of their domestic peacefulness or bellicosity. I think that the existence of an association between two variables, and the nonspuriousness of the impact of one on the other, that is, the persistence of the impact in the presence of controls, can be tested on both the group level and country level.[6] The mechanism of the causal impact, however, is likely to be demonstrable on the lower level only. The dataset to be presented here and analyzed in the next chapter, is basically group level, in the sense that most variables pertinent to the intergroup relationships are measured on the level of communal groups. It contains, however, country-level variables derived from group level measurements (analogous to EPR's measure for the politically excluded population), and some developmental and institutional variables, which have originally been measured on country level.

A last theoretical issue to be mentioned right in the beginning has to do with the term, "minority." Actually, it seems that within the scholarly community there is more consensus about who are the minorities, than among the concerned people themselves. Not as if scholars would always agree, but they more often do than not. In the case of countries with clear majorities, such as Sweden or Italy, the delimitation of the groups is largely converging in sources such as Fearon (2003) and the World Directory of Minorities. Differences may emerge, however, with regard to countries composed of several smaller groups, without a clear majority, and where either alliances or certain groups' closeness on the group markers may result in capricious shifts between plurality and minority status. For instance, in Ivory Coast, EPR's "Northerners (Mande and Voltaic/Gur)" group is the plurality, with 27 percent, while the Baule have 14 percent, and "Other Akans" (e.g., Agni, and Ebrie) carry 18 percent. Yet, the Baule, an Akan group, and other Akans, are no more different from each other than ethnic groups making up the "Northerners." If we collapsed the "Baule" and "Other Akan" categories, we would get a group of 32 percent, trumping the Northerners' bid for the plurality position.

Closeness on the group marker, however, may bring some uncertainty of the classification on its own, even in conditions of clear majority in the state. There are, for instance, some regional identities which occasionally may become politically very emphatic, but their salience may also vanish fast, such as the Lombardian identity in Italy, and Moravian in the Czech Republic. The strengthening of subnational identities in Europe over the past couple of decades was an unexpected phenomenon, diametrically opposed to what has happened in the most fortunate parts of Africa, such as Zambia and Botswana,[7] where reasonably cohesive national populations have come about out of tribal segmentation.

The point that I need to make here is that lay people may hold a very different notion of "minority" than scholars. In political science, in everyday politics, and in mass media, too, the term minority designates a group of people who, as measured along a communal group marker, differ from the largest group in a country. There is also a consensus that ethnicity and language are such communal group markers. Yet, according to scientific opinion surveys, such as the European Social Surveys, most Catalans in Spain, and Frisians in the Netherlands, do not classify themselves as "minority." That is, when asked whether they belong to a "minority group in this country," they give a negative answer, but when asked about their language at home, they do not hesitate to admit that they speak something other than the majority language. They have an identity as, say, Catalans, but do not classify Catalans as a minority of Spain. It seems that in Spain, it is the immigrant Africans, and possibly the Gypsies, taken for "minority" by the population concerned, and this pattern of "racializing" minorities is quite widespread in West Europe.

The same does not happen in East Europe. The ethnic and ethnolinguistic minorities to the east of Hungary have well-developed and politically consequential minority consciousness, with the sole exception of Vlahs in Greece, who have officially stated that they do not seek recognition as a minority.

I think that the concerned people's self-definition as a group (i.e., their group consciousness) has to maximally be taken into consideration, but their self-classification as a minority or nonminority can be overridden by the plain, universally applicable principle that differences on a communal group marker create groups of various sizes. The largest group is labeled "plurality," and the smaller ones are labeled "minority." (I prefer to use the term "majority" for groups larger than 50 percent of the population—clearly, not all pluralities are majorities in this sense.) The objective criteria for delimiting groups along the communal group markers are (i) language use at home or native/first language; (ii) self-declared ethnic, tribal, and religious affiliation; (iii) self-declared regional consciousness, or self-declared relevance of the regional identity (such as in the case of Lombards and Moravians); and (iv) racial and caste belonging. Unfortunately, in the case of these last markers we cannot say that it is the self-declared identity that only counts. In some societies, skin color may be consequential for someone's social position even in the absence of a racial self-identification, which, otherwise, almost always occurs, with the exception of people of mixed heritage, who may experience some identity crisis, mainly in racially more permissive societies. In the United States, for instance, where the "one-drop" rule was the law of the land, people of mixed descent were expected to develop nonwhite identity, and I am not sure whether we may speak of this in past tense.

Practically, the diversity data circulated by the most authoritative sources, UN Statistics, and CIA World Factbook, primarily come from censuses, in which communal features are recorded on the basis of the subjects' self-declaration. The same is true for most scientific surveys, from the USAID's Demographic and Health Surveys to Inglehart's WVS, they all rely on self-identifications. Yet, in France and some former French colonies, there is a ban on asking about ethnicity,[8] and in these countries ethnic diversity is estimated from language and/or religious diversity. Other censuses may neglect either the language question, or the religious question,[9] which creates a need for independent expert estimates. The linguistic diversity of the world is continuously monitored by Ethnologue, while religious movements, such as the missionary group around the Joshua Project, piece together very detailed information about the faiths pursued in each country. Obviously, all these sources have their specific issues to be aware of, and try to correct for. We may never be sure that we really capture the accurate group composition figures. The typical error of the censuses is the "omitted variable," failure to ask about a socially salient fact, but under- and over-estimations may also occur.

For instance, the size of the Roma population is typically underestimated in censuses, while the size of the majority is often boosted by not allowing for choices that would outline some minority, for example, India's census on religion does not allow for the "nonbeliever, atheist" option.

Since the comprehensive and accurate datasets on communal groups that I dream about have not existed, I embarked on seriously modifying the existing datasets for my purposes. MAR has an unequalled wealth of variables, but a restricted number of cases, which are not randomly drawn from the sampling universe. It includes only the groups whose relationship with their majority has already gone sour, thus offers a biased sample of minority groups worldwide. The EPR dataset has a much larger coverage of minority (and majority) groups, but has fewer variables that I could use in my models. The idea of combining them emerged immediately and naturally, but the implementation of the project turned out to be far from unproblematic, and the addition of a number of new groups emerged as imperative in order to approximate the standard of completeness that we may find in the MRG database.

After obtaining the final list of groups, I worked on adding my main explanatory variable, the intergroup (horizontal) inequality, by collecting disaggregated economic data from a large number of sources. My group-level dataset received its final form after I assigned values on a number of EPR and MAR variables to the newly added groups, and imported data on communal conflict from the CONIS[10] and UCDP/PRIO datasets. In the last step, I added country-level variables, such as aggregated economic, developmental, and institutional measures, and calculated a few derived measures, such as the group inequality measure scaled according to the country's Gini index.

This chapter aims at detailing the sources of my data, and explaining the choices that I had to make. It is complete with the dataset itself, and with the codebook serving it.

Physically, I put together a group-level dataset that tries to illustrate the sources of every data point—this is what I call the "data collection dataset." Its plain version, with the elimination of comments and parallelisms, is the "operational dataset," to be fed into the statistical software for analysis.

The presentation of the dataset will follow the chronology of work, and will focus on issues that are doomed to remain disputable. The topics of the following sections will be:

1. The merger of the parent datasets and addition of new groups;
2. Inclusion of my intergroup inequality measure (INEQ);
3. Assigning values to the new groups on certain EPR and MAR variables;
4. Adding CONIS and UCDP/PRIO data; and
5. Appending country-level data and computing a few indexes.

STEP I: MERGING EPR AND MAR, EXPANDING THE LIST OF GROUPS

EPR is a historical-longitudinal dataset covering the years 1946 through 2005, while the MAR newest release is confined to the years 2004–2006. I set up my data collection datasheet for the period 1999–2006. Though my sympathies lie with a time-series design, I could not reasonably count on acquiring inequality data for more than one point in time in the twenty-first century, for various years in various countries. I opted for the 8-year span for being able to accurately document the provenience of every datum which is included in the dataset to be analyzed. The target year has been 2005. I think that most variables involved in the project, such as group numbers, proportions, grievances, and inequality, have a warranty of at least five years in normal conditions.[11] The simplest solution for data analysis is to take into consideration one year only, either 2004 or 2005, with a preference for the later.

Another choice I had to make was about the size of the countries and groups to be taken into consideration. In this regard I follow MAR, and my data is limited to countries with at least 500,000 people in 2005, and groups of at least 100,000 people or at least 1 percent of the population of their country. This means that a few small groups—about 50—included in EPR have been dropped, but new countries and new groups had to be added.

Technically, in a first step I cut back EPR to the interval 1999–2005, and this short version was copied together in an Excel file with the MAR 2004–2006 data, resulting in a datasheet with eight years for each communal group and more than 200 variables wide. Two types of problem were encountered here: conflicting information about the number and proportion of the groups; and different group names, or different constitution of the communal groups within a certain country.[12]

Different Group-Size Estimates

Since smaller differences of 1–5 percent between the EPR and MAR estimates were the rule rather than the exception, I dropped the first plausible idea to halve the difference between them for my EPR_MAR. Instead, I ventured in inviting a third authoritative opinion, the Minority Rights Group International's (MRG) accounts. Occasionally, this helped me to choose on the basis of its concrete references to census data or credible survey estimates. But it often happened that MRG did not give a concrete number, and allowed for a range of values, which again, left me with the duty to pick up the most likely estimate. Work with the MRG data also resulted in adding a number of groups to the EPR list, and leaving me with the task to assign values on some EPR variables to them.[13]

Neither MAR nor EPR aimed at listing all groups in a country, but I pursued completeness, thus the proportions not adding up to 100 percent have seriously challenged me. The EPR numbers for Australia, for instance, were 2 percent Aboriginal and 84 percent White. What to do with the 14 percent difference up to 100? It is believed that there are some 7 percent of Asian origin, and a few percent of mixed origin, as well. But should I create a new group for Asians, for instance, when the Asian group seems smoothly and unproblematically blending into the Australian mainstream, and it is only the indigenous people who are economically, socially, and politically distinct? Yet, if I do not create new groups for Asians and for those of mixed heritage, I have to rebaptize the category into "nonindigenous" and increase their proportion to 97 percent, which may not be well covered by the EPR variables conceived for 84 percent Whites. And this example is from a country where we have a reasonably good overview of the population! Unfortunately, in the case of many, mainly African and Asian countries, I have been unable to bridge the difference between the numbers given to known groups and the total of 100 percent. For instance, in Benin, EPR lists four ethnic group(cluster)s to a total of 81.5 percent. From MRG data and two surveys that I consulted for this country (DHS and Afrobarometer) I got convincing evidence for the existence of approximately 4 percent of Peulh (Fulani). This group was included in my datasheet, but I am still wondering who are the missing 14.5 percent?

Different Group Names, or Different Constitutions of the Communal Groups within a Certain Country

Different names *per se* mean only some additional work for the compiler to identify the synonyms. Yet, sometimes the different names refer to diverging construction of the group. Most typically, there have been differences between my sources in regards of tracing the boundaries between races. "Black" is sometimes "African and Mulatto and African/Amerindian," other times more strictly African only. Similar problems occurred at the boundaries between whites, Mestizos, and Indigenous Amerindians.

Unfortunately, it often happens that EPR and MAR demarcate the groups differently.

For instance, in Bolivia, EPR speaks about 23 percent Aymara, 37 percent Quechua, and 3.2 percent "Guarani and other Eastern indigenous groups." MAR speaks about 50 percent Indigenous Highland Peoples, and 5 percent Indigenous Lowland Peoples. As for the SOWIP,[14] it gives its estimates about the comparative disadvantages of the indigenous people for all three groups taken together. I think that in cases of "simple" disaggregation, when one dataset uses a common term for what is a group cluster in the other, the solution is to keep the smaller units and allocate the same aggregate-level values to all from the other dataset. There are, though, more complicated cases, as well.

In Argentina, the MAR estimate of the indigenous population is 6 percent (2.3 million), while EPR speaks about 1 percent (400,000) Quechua only. MRG also speaks about 400,000 Quechua, but this is the minimum number for the Quechua foreigners entering from Bolivia in search of work. Argentina's own indigenous population, composed of some 16–20 groups, among which the Mapuche are the most numerous, is estimated to 1 percent altogether. Yet, on the one hand, there are another 0.5 percent declaring their indigenous roots, but not living with indigenous communities. And on the other hand, there are 8 percent Mestizos in the country, who are not added either to the category "Argentinian" or to that of "Quechua" by EPR, but may contribute to the high percentage given by MAR to indigenous people. In my "data collection" datasheet, I included separate categories for "Quechua guestworkers" (2 percent) and "Argentinian other: Mestizos, Asians, Arabs" (12 percent). Yet, in the operational dataset, I keep only the "Quechua guestworkers" as a separate entry, while the "Argentinian other" comes to be collapsed into the preexisting "Argentinian" category. The data collection sheet intends to document all choices that I had to make, and I tried to facilitate its navigation with a color coding. The original EPR and MAR data are on black fonts; my additions are on red font. Groups that are included in MAR, but not in EPR, are marked with blue color. I have also used a double heading. The lower header is the variable name, while the upper header refers to the source of the variables.

In this first phase I have expanded the dataset in four ways:

(i) I added cases, mainly additional groups in already included states, but also 30 countries. There are 62 independent states that did not make the EPR country list, of which 32 do not satisfy the criteria to be included in my dataset, either. Most of them are too small, and some do not have any well-outlined minority group comprising more than 1 percent of the population. The rest of 30 countries acquired entries in my dataset, and 12 of them have minority groups that occur in MAR, as well. The new countries are Bahrain, Bhutan, Burkina Faso, Cyprus, Denmark, Djibouti, Equatorial Guinea, Fiji, Germany, Guyana, Iceland, Ireland, Italy, Korea Republic, Libya, Mauritius, Montenegro, Norway, Oman, Papua New Guinea, Portugal, Quatar, Singapore, Somalia, Suriname, Swaziland, Sweden, Tanzania, United Arab Emirates, and Uruguay.[15] Basic information about the newly added groups, such as size and proportion, was taken from the MRG knowledge base, and this latter also helped me to allocate values on two main EPR variables, expressing the power status of the groups, and their past conflicts with each other.

(ii) I imported a variable of country population size from the US Census Bureau website (US_CPOP), which helped me calculate the EPR group sizes on the basis of their proportion estimate.
(iii) I established three columns (variables) for capturing the MRG size and proportion estimates, as well as other important information about the groups. These columns are not meant to be variables, and they are not copied into the operative datasheet.
(iv) I introduced three variables of my own, labeled "My_proportion" (for group proportion), "Minority," and "Minority_type." *My_proportion* refers to the size of the group that—after consulting a number of sources—I deem to be the most accurate. *Minority* distinguishes between minority and plurality groups, while allowing for a multiple plurality third option. The decision rule was to take the largest citizen group for plurality, and all others for minority. Multiple plurality cases emerged when two or three communal groups occurred aggregated in one of my sources and disaggregated in the other. Yet, another way to distinguish between minorities and pluralities is to take for minority all groups in a country that are below the 50 percent threshold. I think that both decision rules are legitimate and defensible.[16] *Minority_type* replicates the plurality (p) and multiple plurality (m_p) values, but the minority groups are further classified as historical, new immigrant (after WWII), noncitizen, and secessionist groups. Secessionist minorities are those who live in *de facto* separated regions but without the plurality's consent for separation (e.g., Turkish Cypriots, and Transnistrians), or (ii) without the terms of separation being settled between minority and plurality (e.g., Palestinians in West Bank and Gaza).

I think that these distinctions are important, and that there are real conceptual and methodological challenges to lumping together noncitizens and new citizens, or migrant workers and immigrants, as minorities. On the one hand, the interest protection activity of newcomers is strictly circumscribed as compared to that of old, citizen minorities, even in democracies. For instance, the fact that both Germany and France are democracies does not mean that Turks in Germany can act in the same ways as citizen Arabs in France—let alone the choices available to Bretons or Occitans in France. On the other hand, economic inequality affects guestworkers and immigrants in other ways than the in-born population. The former typically come from poorer countries, and compare their condition not only with that of the host country nationals, but also with what they left behind. Subsequently, it is only the second and third generation of immigrants who develop the feeling that their group's disadvantage is a social injustice.

In the next step, I worked on collecting and recording information on intergroup economic inequality.

STEP II: ADDING THE GROUP INEQUALITY VARIABLE

This has been the lion's share and the heart of the data preparation work. I believe that previous trials to empirically support the claim that economic inequality breeds political conflict (i.e., the EI-PC nexus) have only failed because of poor data.

Unfortunately, using first-rate inequality data is not an act of good intentions and diligence from the part of the researcher. Despite an expanding demand for them, we still do not have indicators of "vertical inequality" (either Gini or the share of certain wealth categories) for all countries, obtained with the same dependable methodology. Gini indexes, however, are much more readily available than measures comparing the welfare of communal groups. The only dataset that had a group-level measure of "economic difference" (ECDIFF) was a previous edition of MAR, while the newest has only a measure of "economic discrimination" (ECDIS). In addition, over the last few years, two country-level horizontal inequality measures were made public, one belonging to the FSI (of the Fund for Peace) series, and the other covering 46 states (Baldwin and Huber 2010).

The reasons for not having measures of horizontal inequality are various, and "simple" neglect is only one of many. Some countries oppose collecting data on the race, ethnicity, or religion of the population on ideological grounds, claiming that the importance of an overarching national identity should override these accidental traits. Often, the lack of data is related to trials of manipulating the statistical figures. In a world under the spell of nation-state ideologies, ruling elites have a visceral attraction toward denying the existence of salient minorities, downsizing their official figures, and creating as much illusion of homogeneity as possible. (Still more humane than *de facto* getting rid of minorities, through genocide, expulsion, forced assimilation, and so on!)

Also, it often happens that the information is diligently collected in censuses, microcensuses and official surveys, but the national statistical office does not pay attention to preparing the crosstabulations which make the material standing of the communal groups visible. As far as I know, the strongest push thus far to change this practice and make public the disaggregated economic measures, has come from the International Work Group for Indigenous Affairs (IWGIA) and was endorsed by the UN Permanent Forum of Indigenous Peoples, on behalf of the indigenous communities. My case with China may show a new dimension of the issue. On the official website of the Statistics Bureau, I could not access any economic or educational data disaggregated along minority group lines. Yet, an institution hosted by the University of Michigan, called "Chinadataonline," has had some minority*education cross-tabs, based on the 2005 Chinese official 1 percent microcensus—just that they charge a fee for accessing their treasures.

The case for most countries is that there is no officially collected statistical data available for comparing the economic standing of the communal groups, not even with proxies such as educational attainment, health condition, and life expectancy. My project would have been doomed without the possibility of relying on surveys.

Surveys come in many types and flavors, such as:

(i) Official surveys, carried out by the national statistical offices, on large representative samples. For instance, many countries have periodic, institutionalized household income and expenditure surveys. (In my accounts of sources of information, these surveys are classified with other official statistical—national or international—data.)

(ii) Large-sample living conditions surveys. The first of these were initiated in Third World countries by USAID in the 1980s. The surveys were meant to support charity work, to help channel aid where it was most needed. The flagship survey series is called Demographic and Health Surveys (DHS), but the same institution carries out malaria and HIV surveys too. DHSs are focused on health and reproductive health issues, record the educational level of the respondents, and take measurements of the household possessions (living arrangements, animal stock, land), on the basis of which the households are classified in to five wealth quintiles. A very similar survey series is UNICEF's Multiple Indicator Cluster Survey (MICS), also recording educational attainment and wealth quintiles, with less emphasis on health conditions. Yet, none of these series has really targeted comparing ethnic groups within countries. Most surveys resulted in published reports, but only accidentally do these mention any intergroup difference, and these accidental comparisons may not include all groups of interest. For my purpose, the reports have not been useful at all—I needed the complete datasets to mine out the information of interest to me.[17] Fortunately, in 2006 UNESCO had the bright idea to put together a compilation of educational data from previous DHSs and MICSs. This dataset was a kind of backbone of my enterprise, though UNESCO also often neglected to give disaggregation along ethnic or language lines, and I had to go to the original sources to get them.

(iii) Group-centered regional surveys of living conditions carried out under the aegis of international organizations. I have used two of these, for the Roma, and for the indigenous peoples. In the 2000s, UNDP conducted a two-wave survey series on the conditions of Roma in 11 Central-East European countries. The reports, and part of the data are freely available on a website hosted in Slovakia. In 2009, the International Labour Organization (ILO) published the conclusions of a research project carried out together with the African Commission on Human and Peoples' Rights

(ACHPR).[18] The project aimed at detecting and pointing out the legal practices that further the indigenous peoples' disadvantages, rather than measuring these disadvantages in themselves. Yet, a few statements, for instance, the claim that the health condition of the indigenous peoples is inferior to that of the nonindigenous peoples in all 24 countries studied, can be used as rules of thumb in comparing the groups. Some individual country reports are also available, I have used the one on Eritrea. There is a similar publication by the UN Department of Economic and Social Affairs, more exactly by the Permanent Forum on Indigenous Issues, "State of the World's Indigenous Peoples" (SOWIP), which I list with a next category of data-source because technically it is a compilation rather than a survey (in the sense of relying on fieldwork specially carried out for this publication). There is, on the other hand, a survey that concerns only one country, but seems to fit this category. In 2009, the ACHPR and IWGIA published a "Report of the African Commission's Working Group on Indigenous Populations/Communities," making public the results of a research and information visit to Libya in August 2005, where they studied the conditions of the Amazigh (Tuareg, Berber) population. With some hesitation, I would mention here the reports and other publications of the UN High Commissioners on Refugees and on Human Rights. Though dependable and authoritative sources, and providing a plethora of background information on the life conditions of certain groups, they are not really suitable sources for quantitative comparisons.

(iv) Opinion surveys. For this project, I used them in a very unusual way. I dealt with the demographics of the respondents only, such as race, ethnicity, religion, and language, and cross-tabulated these with income and/or education levels. Opinion surveys use much smaller samples than the above mentioned DHS and MICS, but specialists are pretty confident that when they are properly done, they are really representative of the whole population. Unfortunately, with smaller minority groups, it often happens that no representative gets in the sample; and it is really a great leap of faith to believe that, say, one Sorb picked up in a Germany-wide sample, is the average Sorb in all regards: education, income, ideology—I wonder what his/her gender should be? I admit that very small minority samples are not the really dependable data. In general, I would not rely on information conveyed by samples below 20, with the exception of cases when two or more independent surveys concurred on the basic trends. (I took two separate waves of the same survey series as satisfying this criterion.) The opinion surveys that I used were the World Value Surveys, the International Survey Series Programme's 2003 round on National Identities, and a number of regional Barometers. I was able to use the surveys that asked about one or more of the race, ethnicity, language, and religion of the respondents. I have not ventured in

> trying the Eurobarometers, for instance, because I know from previous experience that they neglect these questions. So do the Arab Barometer surveys, with the sole exception of the Lebanese survey. On the positive side, I was very lucky with the Afrobarometer, which systematically recorded all four of the above traits in most cases. Besides the four regional Barometer series (African Barometer, Arab Barometer, Asian Barometer, and Latinobarometro), I was fortunate enough to be able to consult opinion survey data on Afghanistan collected by a research team commissioned by the Asia Foundation.

Further, a few compilations of data have helped me greatly. These are sources maintained by either international organizations or NGOs with global reach, and offer information collected by country or area specialists.

I have already mentioned the Minority Rights Group International, which has a hard copy publication called "World Directory of Minorities," and also maintains a website where we can search for either countries or groups. Another NGO, IWGIA, publishes widely on "The Indigenous World," and also maintains a website for easy access to their knowledge base. I think that the UN/DESA publication SOWIP can be best labeled as a "compilation," too. And I do not think that there is anything pejorative in this term when applied to a publication that pulls together statistical and survey information from dozens of countries to give an accurate picture of the disadvantages suffered by aboriginal peoples. Last, but not least, I also used the US Library of Congress Country Studies series (http://www.loc.gov/rr/frd/), and, occasionally, the websites of certain minority groups (such as of the Buraku in Japan, Dom/Roma in Iran). More idiosyncratic sources were Amy Chua's 2002 book on advantaged minorities (such as the Chinese diaspora in Asia and the Pacific) and, for instance, the website of the Bougainville Copper Inc. mining firm on clarifying the situation in Papua New Guinea.[19]

The sources used for each country are summed up, in Word format, in Appendix 3, and are included in the Excel-format codebook accompanying the EPR_MAR_EXT dataset. All sources are mentioned, with the sole exception of MRG, because it has some information about all countries and all minority groups—that is, I have used it for each country and each group.

Out of these sources, I managed to mine out several indicators of intergroup inequality. I recorded 16 educational, and 13 economic indicators, plus 2 that involve health conditions as well (life expectancy and HDI). The list is given in Table 4.1 in a tabulated form.

The next task was to make these indicators comparable by converting them into a unique inequality scale. First, I considered working out a replica of the older MAR versions' ECDIFF indicator. Yet, the existence of the Wealth Quintile Index (WQI) in DHS and MICS suggested a different method that led to a slightly different result.

Table 4.1 Indicators of Intergroup Economic Inequality

Educational indicators	
mo_literacy_A	Women's literacy rate (from the Unesco DME file)
eduyears_17_22_A	Average number of years of schooling in population aged 17–22 years
eduyears_23_27_A	Average number of years of schooling in population aged 23–27 years
illiteracy%	Rate of illiterate people
primary_compl%	Rate of those who completed primary education
high_sch_compl%	Rate of those who completed secondary education
<=4 sch_yrs	Rate of those with less than primary education
>12 sch_yrs	Rate of those with more than secondary education
edu_yrs_17+	Average number of years of schooling in population above 17 years
sch_yrs 15+	Average number of years of schooling in population above 15 years
ED3a	Average educational attainment on a 6-point scale used by MICS
educ.att_1–10	Average educational attainment on a scale used by Afrobarometer
educ.att_ 0–6	Average educational attainment on scales used by other surveys
Economic indicators	
Wealth_Quintile_Index	Average on the Wealth Quintile Index value of households
wealth	Household wealth (assets) assessments (e.g., in the United Kingdom)
Pisa_ESCS	Average on the Pisa tests economic and social classification of the students
poverty%	Rate of the poor (below a certain poverty line)
income_gap	Difference between the average (or median) incomes of the groups
consumption_gap	Difference between the average (or median) expenditures or consumption
unemployment%	Rate of unemployed people
WVS_income	Average on the 10-point income scale used by the WVS series
ISSP_income	Average of the family incomes recorded by ISSP polls
ISSP_self-placement	Average of self-placements on a 10-point material well-being scale
niveaux_vie	Disposable income in euros
GDP_subnational	GDP/cap (mostly in PPP) of certain subnational regions
development_small_area	Regional development index based on several economic indicators
Health and composite indicators	
life_expectancy	Life expectancy at birth
HDI_subnational	HDI calculated for certain subnational regions

Note: A series of mo_literacy_B, eduyears_17_22_B and eduyears_23_27_B have been used along the series ending in "A." They measure the same things as the "A" series, but "B"-s refer to a different definition of the group. If "A" was calculated according to ethnicity, then "B" was calculated according to language or region.

1	1.25	1.5	1.75	2	2.25	2.5	2.75	3	3.25	3.5	3.75	4	4.25	4.5	4.75	5

Figure 4.1 Wealth Quintile Index Scale Values.

Since I had the "real" WQI in a number of countries, I decided to include an inequality measure that simply spells out the position of the groups on this WQI scale. I only made a slight modification of the original values: I brought them to the closest value divisible with 0.25. Instead of a fully continuous scale between 1 and 5, I set up a 17-point scale, visualized in Figure 4.1.

This measure I labeled "INEQ_1."[20] Next, I included a second inequality measure (INEQ_2), which is closer to being a replica of the ECDIFF indicator. As a conceptual difference from INEQ_1, this involves determining, in each country, who is the majority group, and who are the minorities. This may be controversial in certain cases, because of various reasons.

First, several countries do not have a clear majority, but are composed of a large number of communal groups, of which the largest may not exceed 20 percent of the overall population. INEQ_2 accounts for the distance between the group with the largest percentage, termed plurality, and each of the other groups, defined as minorities.[21] There are three issues with this approach:

(i) Groups in the developing countries, and mainly in Africa, are often fluid coalitions of tribal groups. One group that today is the plurality, may split by tomorrow, while other two or more groups may come together in a unitary cluster. Providentially, my analysis is narrowed on such a short time span that the groups can be taken for reasonably stable.

(ii) The most numerous group may not be the politically most significant, and the one that traditionally controls the state. Mainly in Africa, political power has long been possessed by small elite groups such as whites, American Liberians, and Tutsis. Yet, our political ideals and sense of social justice say that these are anomalies. The norm is or should be that the most numerous groups have the most voice in politics. And there is, undeniably, a historical trend toward this condition. As of my target year of 2005, Africa had only one ruling minority, the Tutsi in Rwanda. The current salient examples of ruling minorities are in the Arab world, rather than in Africa. A typical example is Bahrain, where a Shi'a majority has been ruled for centuries by a Sunni dynasty.

(iii) Yet, in the Gulf Arab countries, the "ruling elite" problem has a special dimension to it: citizenship. The largest communal group happens to be that of nonnationals. There are 58 percent Palestinians in Jordan versus 40 percent Jordanian Arabs; there are 75 percent noncitizen guestworkers in Qatar versus 25 percent citizens; there are 80 percent foreigners in

> the United Arab Emirates versus 18 percent national Sunnis; and there are 35 percent Palestinian Arabs in Israel versus 24 percent Ashkenazim Jews, if we take, as it is *de facto*, the Israel-occupied Palestinian territories for part of Israel. In these circumstances, I opted to take for plurality the largest citizen group, and non-citizen groups, however large, are coded "minority."[22]

Once the INEQ_1 variable was achieved and the plurality/minority classification decided, the INEQ_2 coding has become easy. But achieving the INEQ_1 values raised issues of converting educational and health data into WQI estimates. This part of the work was greatly helped by a number of countries in which I had the WQI measurements in parallel with other indicators. Table 4.2 shows a sample of equivalences, which served as guides for my conversion activity—I would call this my "Rosetta Stone." Unfortunately, these Rosetta Stone cases allow for probabilistic conversion rules only. They have not led to absolutely rigorous equivalences. The value of an education year, as expressed in WQI values, ranges from 0.25 to 1. There are a number of idiosyncratic factors that influence the relationships among

Table 4.2 Sample List of Measurement Equivalences

Poverty rates (UNDP, UN_ESA):
- In Macedonia: 33 vs 7% is 2 units on the WQI scale
- In Montenegro: 27 vs 1% is 1.75 units on the WQI scale

One education year in the adult population:
- In Bangladesh: approx. 0.25 on the WQI scale
- In Bosnia-Herzegovina: approx 0.5 on the WQI scale
- In Cameroon: approx 1.00 on the WQI scale
- In Cote d'Ivoire: approx. 0.25 on the WQI scale
- In Macedonia: approx. 0.75 on the WQI scale
- *In Montenegro: approx 0.75 on the WQI scale
- In Sierra Leone: approx 0.50 on the WQI scale
- In Vietnam: approx 0.50 on the WQI scale
- In Laos: approx 1.00 on the WQI scale
- In Uzbekistan: approx 1.00 on the WQI scale

Illiteracy rate (IWGIA):
- In Vietnam: 3% literacy vs 90% is 2.5 on the WQI scale

% below primary (or <4yrs of school):
- In Macedonia: 43 vs 15% is 2 on the WQI scale
- In Montenegro: 71 vs 8% is 1.75 on the WQI scale

% above secondary (>12yrs of school):
- In Macedonia: 0 vs 16% is 2 on the WQI scale
- In Montenegro: 0 vs 26% is 1.75 on the WQI scale

*This is based on the relation between Montenegrins and Serbs. When Muslim populations are involved, the education gap for the same WQI scale distance may be larger, because Muslims invest less in the education of women. In Montenegro, women's literacy for the preponderantly Muslim Albanians and Bosniaks is 75 and 73%, respectively, while among Christians and atheists it is 89%.

the features of interest. For instance, in the case of Muslims, lower education values may be associated with a certain WQI score, than in the case of non-Muslims. In countries with national health service, better life expectancy and general health indicators may be associated with a certain WQI score, than in countries with fully market-based health care systems. All these impacts are uncharted territory, and I was left with the responsibility to pick up a unique value within the interval determined by the stochastic conversion rules. My choices can be scrutinized in the data collection sheet, which contains both the original datapoint and my value allocation based on it.

Some further randomness of the conversions comes from the fact that I had to work, as the DHS and MICS did, with quintiles—as opposed to using more fine-ground intervals, such as deciles or percentages. In the case of quintiles, the upper category may be very heterogeneous, consisting of 19 percent of the population who are only imperceptibly slightly richer than the rest of 80 percent, and of 1 percent who are *extremely* rich. Thus, I also took into account the country-specific distribution of the indicators (e.g., average schooling, minimum, maximum education) besides applying the average value inferable from the above examples. I hope that most of my coding is reasonably adequate; but there are cases where I hesitated a lot before making my choices.

On the one hand, it happened that my data contained slight inconsistencies which allowed for different coding. With an example personally affecting me as a Hungarian, the condition of Hungarians in Romania and in Slovakia allowed for coding either equality or slight difference (0.25 on the WQI scale).[23] I chose, finally, the values less favorable for Hungarians on the basis of the general rule that it is always harder for minorities to maintain their living standards than it is for the majorities. Whatever is their condition, it takes them more effort to maintain it, as they incur extra costs.

On the other hand, I was seriously disturbed by cases when the "traditional" economic patterns were disrupted for the period studied and I am afraid that these cases may weaken the support for my main hypothesis. For instance, for the period 2003–2006, I had to code Bougainvilleans in Papua New Guinea as equal with the rest of the population, as the copper mine in Bougainvillea, the cause of a long secession war, was closed down. It is also the case of the Russians "in the near abroad" and of whites in Zimbabwe, that their relative wealth, which, according to my hypothesis, motivated animosity against them, mostly dissipated after more than a decade of adverse policies (in the CIS), or land expropriations (in Zimbabwe).

The INEQ_2 indicator is the best replica of MAR's ECDIFF that I could achieve, and I hope that it may become a useful tool for mapping the relative wealth status of minorities worldwide. Yet, my basic hypothesis about the impact of economic inequality is basically symmetrical: I think that the wealth gap induces animosity in both cases, be the minorities either richer or poorer than the majority. This means that my main explanatory variable is, in fact, INEQ_3, a measure in which the distances of the advantaged minorities occur not with a minus, but with a plus sign.

A last issue that I had to address with the creation of a new INEQ variable is the fact that the economic distances between the lowest and the highest quintile are not the same in each country. I used the Gini indexes, which express the distance between the poorest and the wealthiest individuals or households in a country, to synthesize information from the intergroup and the vertical inequality measurements. Technically, Gini was multiplied by my variable measuring the economic distance of each minority group from the country's plurality, in absolute values, and the resulting variable, substantially INEQ_3 scaled to Gini, was labeled INEQ_4.[24]

Yet, before implementing this step, which involved adding country-level measurements to EPR_MAR_EXT, I worked on adding more group-level data.

STEP III: ASSIGNING VALUES TO THE NEW GROUPS ON CERTAIN EPR AND MAR VARIABLES

The basic version of EPR is the first, which can be obtained from the Harvard dataverse, labeled "EPR_groupyear_v.1.1". The authors of the dataset have not ceased making improvements to it, but the new developments go beyond a simple group-year-political status spreadsheet. The Swiss ETHZ has established a data portal called "GROWup" (http://www.icr.ethz.ch/data), which, as of February 2012, offered:

(i) a geographically referenced version of EPR (GeoEPR-ETH Version 2.0);
(ii) a short completion to EPR v1, called EPR v2; and
(iii) a dataset called ACD2EPR Docking Version 1.2, which is said to link the conflicts recorded in ACD v.4-2010 to the groups listed in EPR v.2.0. The codebook attached to this, called "GROW^{up} Research Front-End Documentation, RFE Release 1.0," compiled by Philipp Hunziker in November 2011, highlights the existence of a new variable, computed from the simple nominal [power-]status variable that occurs in EPR v.1. The nominal scale is transformed into an ordinal, and is being labeled "pwrrank." Its description states that "higher values correspond to more powerful groups, i.e. variable ranges from 1 (Discriminated) to 7 (Monopoly), whereas Regional Autonomy and Separatist Autonomy are both assigned the value 3." Since this transformation is very useful for analyses, I decided to compute the analogous ordinal measure for my groups, as well.

Yet, previously I had to assign values on some basic EPR variables. I estimated that the three EPR variables the most useful for my purposes are the [*power-*]*status* (string), *warhist* (War_history), and *gpeaceyrs* (Group_peace_years). From *status*, a number of other variables, such as *Stat* (numeric), *Egip* (ethnic group in power), and *Excluded* (ethnic group excluded from power) can immediately be computed, besides the *Pwrrank* (Power_rank).

A total of 324 new groups were added to the 733 original EPR groups. Of the 324, 71 have been groups contained by MAR 2004–2006, while others were included in EPR_MAR_EXT based on MRG data.

As already mentioned, EPR neglected the noncitizen groups, and small, weak groups without significant political representation also tended to remain below its radar. Yet, a number of groups, mainly the MAR groups, had to be added because of the different definition of certain groups in the two sources. For instance, in Canada, EPR has one common entry for "French speakers," while MAR distinguishes between "Quebecois" and "French Canadians." This means two groups added, but, in the final version of my dataset, I have dropped the collapsed category of "French speakers," thus the real lengthening of the group list is one, only.

In the case of these partly overlapping groups, the values on the *status, warhist*, and *gpeaceyrs* measures were simply copied from the corresponding EPR v1.1 measures. In a number of other cases, such as Bahrain, Butan, Fiji, and Guyana, I could rely on EPR v.2. For all other cases, I mainly relied on MRG summaries, but obviously, the MAR accounts have also been of great help, where they existed. The sources used for assigning values are referred to in the codebook (its sheet labeled "EPR completing"). There is a separate column to mark whether the group is included in the MAR database or not. Some value allocations based on trivia, such as "discriminated" for Roma, and "no war" for noncitizen groups, are marked "general."

In the first step, I have just tried to emulate the EPR's value assignment on *status, warhist*, and *gpeaceyrs* measures. In the second step, I transformed the [*power-*]*status* variable in an ordinal scale, following the suggestions found in GROWup. The scale values are as follows: 1 = discriminated; 2 = powerless and non-citizen; 3 = regional autonomy, separatist autonomy, and irrelevant; 4 = junior partner; 5 = senior partner; 6 = dominant; and 7 = monopoly.

The *war_history* and *group_peace_years* measures have not perfectly been suitable for my purposes. I wanted to include a variable summarizing the history of the groups (whether they experienced high animosity, violence against each other in the past, or not). The problem with the EPR measures is their very accuracy. EPR counts the conflict episodes since 1946, but for newer states, such as for Latvia, from 1992 only, and for new immigrant groups, such as Israel's Russians, since the 1980s. Thus, some post-1946 conflicts, which happened within the frames of another state formation, do not show up in the accounts, and the number of violent episodes is not comparable across groups, since they do not refer to the same time interval. The years of peace are incomparable, as well, because of the same concerns. I think that the best available solution is to take the ratio of the two measures: *war_history* divided by *group_peace_years* (and multiplied by 100, to spare decimals) should give a comparable measure of conflictual past (Past_violence), though the problem of the newly created states which experienced violence between groups before breaking free, still persists. Most typically, this is the problem of the former colonies. The small groups of whites living in Swaziland or Zimbabwe are obviously coded with "0" violent episodes; yet, the populations concerned have not forgotten the ordeals of colonialism and liberation war. Any correction to Past_violence in this sense could be done only manually, on a case-by-case basis, bringing about Past_violence2, with the corrections documented in the codebook.

The completions made to the MAR data were simpler. I needed the MAR grievance indicators as my dependent variables for measuring intergroup animosity below the violent conflict level. MAR included three types of grievance measures: political, economic, and cultural grievances, all three conceived as ordinal scales. For my purposes, a unique measure of grievance would have been more advantageous, but the three types cannot be combined in a unique ordinal scale because of too low correlation values among them (maximum 0.59). Thus, I created a simple dummy for marking the presence of a grievance of any type and any strength during the three years included in the newest MAR dataset, named "any_grievance_in_MAR," and proceeded to allocate values on all four grievance indicators (any_grievance, political, economic, and cultural grievance,) to all groups. For the groups included in MAR, I used the original values unchanged. For the groups not included in MAR, which otherwise would have satisfied the MAR size criteria (above 100,000 members, or above 1 percent of the population of a country with a population of more than 500,000), the default value is 0, that is, no grievance, on all three variables. I diverged from this rule in five cases:

(i) Groups classified by EPR as "discriminated" received "1" on the political grievance measure;
(ii) Groups classified by EPR as "separatist autonomy" received "4" on the political grievance measure;
(iii) In countries whose population is not convincingly above 500,000,[25] or in the case of groups not convincingly above 100,000 members (or above 1 percent of population), thus in cases in which MAR could have refrained from including the group because of the size threshold, I assigned the values which seemed the most plausible based on other sources,

primarily MRG. Ultimately, there was only one such case added: the Inuits (Greenlanders) of Denmark.

(iv) Two (clan) groups in Somalia, torn by internal conflict, were not assigned values on grievance indicators.

(v) Since no human enterprise and no dataset is fully immune to error, I devised a method to check on the comprehensiveness of the MAR grievance indicators by testing both the internal cohesiveness of the MAR data, and their compatibility with another conflict dataset. This resulted in corrections made to 30 cases.[26]

The idea was to test whether MAR recorded "grievance" in all cases when MAR itself indicated high political mobilization or other expressions of inter-communal tension; and when the CONIS dataset marked the presence of a conflict. Technically, I relied on three dummies:

(i) One dummy ("any grievance in MAR") showing "1" when any grievance of any strength existed[27];
(ii) One dummy ("any conflict in MAR") showing "1" when MAR detected any of six expressions of conflict[28];
(iii) One dummy ("any conflict in CONIS") showing "1" when the CONIS data marked conflict.

The theoretical expectation was that:

any_grievance_in_MAR ≥ any_conflict_in_MAR ≥ any_conflict_in_CONIS

Out of 876 cases, only 68 showed a different pattern (including the two groups with internal issues in Somalia).

I checked on these 68 cases one by one, and in 30 cases I decided to change the grievance values from 0 to 1. The reasons are documented in the codebook. Some corrections seem to have the support of the MAR qualitative summaries. For instance, the quantitative MAR dataset codes the Russians in Turkmenistan without grievance, while the qualitative comments admit that they have experienced very tough times since the early 1990s, and suffered various discrimination policies. Yet, they cannot voice their grievances directly, and their main interest protection mechanism is to ask for the support of the Russian government. And further, since their main defense against oppression is emigration, they are near to dropping out of the monitored-size minority lists completely.

As a final outcome, the "any grievance in MAR" indicator was doubled with a second version, in which 30 cases were changed in order to achieve more consistency with other information available. This measure, labeled "any_gr_MAR2," was used in analyses in Chapter 5, as a general grievance measure, along the domain-specific economic, political, and cultural grievance indicators.

Yet, beyond the grievance indicators, I needed measures of communal conflict for my models. EPR's war history is about the past; I was looking for data documenting communal violence in a period succeeding the time span for which I had measurements of the explanatory variables.

STEP IV: ADDING HIIK'S CONIS AND UCDP/PRIO ARMED CONFLICT DATA

The most comprehensive dataset on violent conflicts worldwide is Uppsala University's and PRIO's common venture, officially called UCDP/PRIO Armed Conflict Dataset, of which the 4th version (Version 4-2010) was the one that I downloaded and used. The UCDP/PRIO defines conflict as: "a contested incompatibility that concerns government and/or territory where the use of armed force between two parties, of which at least one is the government of a state, results in at least 25 battle-related deaths." It is to be added that the 25 battle-related deaths have to occur per year, in order that a certain year be recorded in UCDP/PRIO. Thus it is only relatively very bloody and militarized conflicts making their way into this dataset. UCDP reacted to this limitation by bringing about a dataset on "low-intensity conflicts," but currently this is available only up to the year 2004, which does not help in searching for conflicts after 2005.

Fortunately there is an alternative. The Heidelberg Institute for International Conflict Research (HIIK) in the Department of Political Science, University of Heidelberg, has been publishing annual "Conflict Barometers" since 1992, grounded in a database called CONIS. The violence threshold for inclusion in CONIS is lower than that for inclusion in UCDP/PRIO. They classify conflicts in five categories, on an ordinal scale of intensity levels: 5 = war; 4 = severe crisis; 3 = crisis; 2 = manifest conflict; 1 = latent conflict. The yearly reports, that is, the Conflict Barometers, are publicly and freely downloadable, thus I could use the Conflict Barometers for the years 2006 through 2010.

The CONIS data provide the country, the parties to a conflict, the conflict items, the start date of the conflict, and its intensity on their 5-point scale. I worked on singling out the conflicts pertinent to my intergroup relations-focused project. I selected the conflicts that

(i) involved at least one domestic group (i.e., intrastate conflicts);

(ii) were intercommunal as compared with my existing list of groups (i.e., intracommunal affairs were neglected); and
(iii) can be defined as minority versus power-holding group (i.e., fought by a minority excluded from power against a group coded as junior partner, senior partner, dominant, and monopoly; or fought by a junior partner against a senior partner).[29]

Applying these criteria to the UCDP/PRIO dataset, too, we get a sample of UCDP/PRIO cases that are CONIS cases, as well. Or otherwise, the UCDP/PRIO cases are the bloodiest CONIS cases. I worked on assigning one summative CONIS intensity measure to all cases imported in my dataset, and then on a more synthetic intensity measure, which takes into account the UCDP/PRIO data, as well. The first is the 5-year average of the CONIS intensity levels (Conis_intensity), while the second is a more complicated formula, taking into account the length of the conflict, and, with increased weight, the years during which the conflict was so intense that it was recorded in the UCDP/PRIO Armed Conflicts Dataset (Intensity_index).[30]

STEP V: ADDING COUNTRY-LEVEL DATA AND CALCULATING A FEW INDEXES

A last important step was merging the group-level dataset with a dataset that contains country-level measurements. This latter was prepared for covering a longer timespan than the group-level data, because of reasons unrelated to the analysis to be done in Chapter 5.[31] That is, my country-level dataset covers the years 1999 through 2010, though most variables are available for a part of these years, only.

The full list of variables included in the country-level dataset, with their sources, is shown in Appendix 4 in Word format; a more elaborated form of this codebook occurs in the Excel file (codebook and notes). I collected data on ethnic, linguistic, and religious fractionalization, on economic development level (such as GDP/capita, Human Development Index (HDI), life expectancy), on democracy (such as the Freedom House ratings, FH_iPolity2, and political terror scales[32]), on electoral family, on economic, social and political globalization (known as the KOF measures), on good governance (such as the Worldwide Governance Indicators) and state repressiveness, on the unemployment of young males, as well as on vertical inequality. Most of these measures are meant to serve as control variables in the regression models, but the Gini index has also been used for scaling my group-level communal inequality index (that is, for calculating INEQ_4 from INEQ_3).

A number of variables, such as the country-level violence indicators (GPI, FSI), will be dealt with only in Chapter 7.

There are two institutional variables that need some explanation, labeled "Communal_division" and "Communal_sub_division." They are related to my attempt to compare the impacts of the Lijphartian (power sharing) and Horowitzian (integrative) institutional designs. An institutional feature that could distinguish between the two proposals is decentralization along communal lines versus decentralization crosscutting the communal lines, which addresses the difference between Lijphart's advocacy of communal power sharing, and Horowitz's advocacy of communally mixed regions that create new loyalties. I experimented with two new variables meant to capture the ways in which subnational administration is done. Communal_division measures the degree to which the federal boundaries are traced with respect to the settlement patterns of the communal, mainly ethnic, groups, while the other ("Communal_sub_division") measures the congruence of the administrative subdivisions with these settlement patterns. I worked out a 5-point ordinal scale, on which 1 means "no concern for ethnic settlement patterns" (the Horowitzian ideal), and 5 is the full respect for them, such as in the Belgian federalism. This latter can be said to be the Lijphartian ideal, but only when it is paired with high decentralization values, the measurement of which involves separate Federalism_index and Decentralization_index measures. My federalism measure has been compiled from six federalism measures (four contained in the Quality of Government dataset, two contained in Pippa Norris's Democracy dataset), while the decentralization index has been compiled from five decentralization measures contained in the Database of Political Institutions (DPI) 2011. While my main purpose in the data analytic step is to demonstrate the impact of the INEQ variables on intergroup hostility, testing the impact of the institutions is a theoretically and morally challenging task, without which our picture about the impact of other explanatory variables would not be complete. Unfortunately, some exploratory tests indicated serious collinearity issues with the federalism variables, and my reported models include only the variables pertinent to administrative subdivisions.

The last steps of the data preparation involved merging a cleaned and simplified version of the group-level dataset with the country-level dataset, and some extrapolation of the existing datapoints. A number of variables, which in the data collection versions were displayed for the target year 2005 only, such as the group proportion, group size, minority-plurality and minority type classifications, as well as the INEQ measures, have been extended onto neighboring years, from 2003 to 2007. And two technically necessary variables have been created, the numeric versions of Minority (Minority2) and Minority_type (Minority_type2).

With this, the dataset became ready to be fed into SPSS, and I could embark on the analytical work.

Yet finally, in order to check on the validity of my INEQ values by comparing them to similar measurements elaborated for countries, I have constructed a country-level intergroup inequality measure out of my group-level horizontal inequality measures. For each country, I calculated the standard deviation of the groups' WQI values, as captured by INEQ_1. The resulting country-level variable, "standard deviation of INEQ_1," was tested for correlation with the two measurements of horizontal inequality that we possess. One measure, due to Baldwin & Huber (2010), exists for 46 countries only, and my "St_dev_of_INEQ" is correlated with it at 0.450 across these cases. The other measure has been brought about by the Fund for Peace as a part-indicator of their FSI, and it covered 142 countries in 2006. Across these 142 cases, my "St_dev_of_INEQ" is correlated with it at 0.269, while the Baldwin and Huber measure achieved a correlation of 0.562 (across 45 cases). While these associations may not seem to be high, they are certainly highly significant, and Chapter 7 will provide support for the claim that they affect the dependent variables in very similar ways.

On group level, it is only the MAR economic discrimination measure that can be compared with my INEQ measures, and the correlation coefficient between the MAR measure and my INEQ_1 is −0.452 across 282 common cases. Again, the affinity between the measures is tested through their behavior in regressions. Chapter 6 features a number of models in which MAR's ECDIS and my INEQ perform very similarly, they both increase the intergroup hostility levels, and their effects have comparable magnitudes.

NOTES

1. During the fight for independence from Ethiopia, the ethnic identities (more exactly the anti-Amhara sentiment, unifying all of the Tigrinya, Tigre, Saho, Afar, Bilen, Kunama, and Nara groups) seem to have been more decisive, while later the religious identities have developed so much salience that Eritrea's human rights records are heavily stained with religious persecution.

2. http://www.cidcm.umd.edu/mar/

3. Lars-Erik Cederman; Brian Min; Andreas Wimmer, 2009-05-01, "Ethnic Power Relations dataset," http://hdl.handle.net/1902.1/11796UNF:5:k4xxXC2ASI204QZ4jqvUrQ==V1 [Version].

4. MRG does not attempt to hierarchize these, but some may emerge as particularly salient based on the historical narrative and the presentation of "current issues." These later focus—analogously to the MAR selection criteria—on communal conflicts that bring about human suffering: violence, discrimination, internal or external displacement, and social injustice.

5. And these also reveal the difficulty of choosing among communal group-markers, since we have a number of ethnic, linguistic, religious, and ethnolinguistic fractionalization indexes.

6. This "can" is of the kind that originates an "ought:" if possible, then it is necessary to endeavor to test the hypothesized relationships on both levels.

7. Not very long time ago, Mali could be listed with this group. And even after the bloody domestic conflict there in 2012, it is not erroneous to say that the Black (Sub-Saharan) tribes in Mali have come together in a reasonably cohesive citizenry; and it is only the "Whites" (mainly Tuaregs) who contest the legitimacy of the central power.

8. Versions of this ban may occur in several other countries, without French influence, as well. In Austria, for instance, the ethnic roots of the newly naturalized citizens are not registered anymore, which makes difficult the estimation of the fresh immigrant population (e.g., the number of naturalized Turks).

9. This is most typical for some Arab countries, where the religion of the respondents is not asked, or, not asked in detail, which makes Sunni, Shi'a, and followers of other branches of Islam undistinguishable. Yet, a question on religious denomination may be missing in countries in which it does not really have relevance anymore, such as the United States.

10. CONIS is the abbreviation of Conflict Information System, a database that previously was known as Cosimo or Kosimo, maintained by the HIIK in the Department of Political Science, University of Heidelberg. They have been publishing annual "Conflict Barometers" since 1992.

11. Nonnormal conditions are cases of genocide, pressuring communal groups into exile, large-scale land reform, nationalizations, and so on. These are events that make the headlines, and the chances to overlook them are minimal.

12. It also happened that EPR conflicted with itself, that is, it had two versions of the group configuration in Eritrea, one religious (Christians and Muslims), and one ethnic (groups like Afar, Bedawi, and Bilen).

13. It is mainly the very disadvantaged groups missing from EPR, such as the Roma, and new immigrant groups. EPR did not include noncitizens.

14. State of the World's Indigenous Peoples, a United Nations Department of Economic and Social Affairs (UN DESA) publication.

15. There is a smaller dataset labeled "EPR version 2," which, as of February 2012, contained data on Bahrain, Bhutan, Cyprus, Djibouti, Fiji, and Guyana, but practically on only one variable, the power status. I used this source for the additional cases, as documented in the codebook and the data collection sheet.

16. My INEQ_2, INEQ_3, and INEQ_4 variables are calculated with reference to a clear plurality (or multiple plurality) in a state.

17. The datasets are available with permission only. MICS is more generous, with one request I got access to the whole third round of surveys. USAID expects separate requests of permission for each geographic country-group, and has a higher proportion of restricted data, which are not accessible at all.

18. Overview report of the research project by the International Labour Organization and the African Commission on Human and Peoples' Rights on the constitutional

and legislative protection of the rights of indigenous peoples in 24 African countries. International Labour Office.—Geneva, ILO, 2009.

19. The mine was the single main cause of the Bougainvillean separatist movement, and its closure and then reopening have tightly been interwoven with the evolution of the majority-minority relationships in the country.

20. "INEQ" is obviously the abbreviation of "inequality." I hesitated between its use in the all-caps version *versus* the simple "Ineq" form. I think "INEQ" is more unambiguous when used in the text (it makes immediately clear that it refers to a variable), but in the tables and figures I often resorted to "Ineq" because of reasons of space.

21. Technically, I coded the poorer-than-the-plurality groups with positive values, and the wealthier-than-the-plurality groups with negative values. One unit of INEQ_2 scale difference is equal with a 0.5 WQI distance, thus the maximum distance between two groups may be 8 units. (In the data collection sheet the negative values are preceded by an "x" placeholder, to avert Excel's adverse reactions to cells whose content starts with minus sign.)

22. In Israel, since Palestinians living in the West Bank and Gaza are not really citizens of Israel, the Ashkenazim Jews were coded as plurality.

23. In Romania, the life expectancy values suggested equality, the education data slight disadvantage. In Slovakia, regional data suggested slight advantage, ISSP survey results suggested equality.

24. Since the plurality groups are coded 0 in INEQ_3, the INEQ_4 variable does not carry information about the vertical inequality typifying the majority group, and in this sense INEQ_4 is not a full-fledged interaction term of vertical and horizontal inequalities. Thus I have also computed the INEQ_3*Gini interaction term by adding 1 to all INEQ_3 values and multiplying with Gini afterwards. I expected this latter variable, INEQ_5, to save me the separate use of Gini in certain models. However, later analyses have evidenced that horizontal and vertical inequality have different impact patterns, horizontal inequality affecting communal conflicts, while vertical inequality affecting noncommunal social conflicts, and their interaction term is torn between opposite tendencies.

25. Suriname's 2004 census found 492,829 people there. The UN estimate is that in 2005 Suriname crossed the 500,000 threshold, but the CIA World Factbook lists it with a below-500,000 population. I included Suriname in my dataset, but left out Solomon Islands, which is in a very similar situation, around 500,000 in 2005.

26. The details are included in the codebook's "MAR completing" sheet.

27. As previously specified, this means a value of 1 of the dummy when any of the 9 entries to the three grievances in three years (2004–06) is different from zero.

28. The following MAR codes were taken for expression of conflict: live separatism (SEPX > 0); group mobilization beyond parties (GOJPA > 2); intercommunal conflict (INTERCON > 0); larger protest activity (PROT > 2); and rebellion (REB > 0).

29. Since conditions (ii) and (iii) are difficult to conclude on, in the data collection sheet there are more conflicts included than in the operational. It took me some time to reach decisions with regard to some of them. The final choices are on black fonts. Also, where a communal group appeared to be involved in more conflicts (supporting

two or more militant groups), the intensity indicators of the most violent conflict were included in the operational dataset.

30. The formula is the sum of Conis_intensity (=HIIK average intensity), HIIK years out of 2006–2010/10, HIIK historical years/100, and UCDP years out of 2005–2009.

31. They are related to the possibility of an independent, country-level test of the EI-PC nexus, based on some newer country-level measurements available for the years after 2006 only. This analysis is presented in Chapter 7.

32. These two scales, by Amnesty International and the US State Department, measure the terror exerted by the regime toward its citizens.

Chapter 5

Analyzing the EPR_MAR_EXT Dataset

THE GROUPS

This chapter aims at exploring the group-level dataset, the creation of which was detailed in the previous sections. My main analytic goal has been to build regression models with maximum explanatory power, and reveal how inter-group economic inequality contributes to this explanatory power, yet I think that it is important to evidence all important features of the context within which these regression models function. Thus, the chapter unfolds through two exploratory data analysis sections before introducing the regressions and the subsequent concluding thoughts.

The dataset contains 876 groups, out of which 16 cannot be included into analyses. These are minority groups in China, all below 1 million people, for which I failed to get data on their economic standing, and subsequently I did not allocate values to them on a number of variables.[1] Of the 860 groups for which I have achieved most essential indicators, 153 are plurality groups, and 4 are multiple pluralities. This also means that there are 155 countries in the sample.

The number of minority groups is 703. As Table 5.1 shows, most of them are old, historical minorities, but approximately 10 percent are newer. Thirty-three groups that migrated into their country of residence after 1945 are considered to mostly be citizens there, while 35 groups are not.[2] The nine secessionist minorities are all historical dwellers of their land. (They are the Turks in Cyprus, Abkhazians and Ossetians in Georgia, Palestinians in Israel, Transnistrians in Moldova, Saharawis in Morocco, Issaq and Dir in Somalia, and the Southerners in Sudan).

Beyond the numbers associated with the groups, there are the individual people, and we may be both surprised by and impressed with the figures evidenced by the data. In 2005, not less than 34.86 percent of the population

Table 5.1 Cross-Tabulation of the "Minority" and "Minority_type" Variables

	Minority or plurality			
	Plurality	*Multiple plurality*	*Minority*	*Total*
Plurality	153	0	0	153
Multiple plurality	0	4	0	4
Historical minority*	0	0	626	626
New minority (after WWII)	0	0	33	33
Secessionist minority	0	0	9	9
Noncitizen	0	0	35	35
Total	153	4	703	860

*In most analyses, an extended-sense *historical minority* has been used, which includes the nine secessionist minorities and the four multiple pluralities, as well, for a total of 639 groups.

Table 5.2 Population as of 2005

	Number of groups	*Total people belonging to groups*	*Percent population*
All countries (155)		6,364,692,050	100.00
Plurality	153	4,129,725,941	64.88
Multiple plurality	4	16,896,789	0.27
Minority	703	2,218,069,319	34.85

belonged to minorities, versus 64.88 percent belonging to pluralities. I have to admit, however, that I am providing these data for the 155 countries included in my sample, not for the whole world. In exact figures, my sample covers 97.5 percent of the world's population (more than 6.34 billion people), not the whole 100 percent, which was estimated at 6.5 billion in 2005.

The surprise may be augmented by counting as "real" plurality only those who belong to groups which include more than 50 percent of the population. As a matter of fact, there are only 104 groups out of the 153 marked as plurality that satisfy this criterion. The number of people making up these 104 groups is 3,464,219,598 versus the 2,900,472,452 people belonging to groups equal or smaller than 50 percent.[3] This is 54.4 percent versus 45.6 percent: my dataset shows the humanity as being almost evenly shared between people who may think in terms of "*our* nation-state" and people for whom this notion is problematic.[4]

The numbers are important because minorities are thought to be discontented groups almost by default. Indeed, 42 percent of the historical minorities score 1 on the "Any grievance in MAR" indicator. It happens, however, that there are not only minorities logging grievances, but 17 percent of the plurality groups as well, and 6.7 percent of the large, "real" pluralities comprising more than 50 percent of their country's population, also do. Table 5.3 names the seven large pluralities scoring 1 on the "Any grievance in MAR" indicator, as they are telling examples for the power of the accidental and contingent in history.

Table 5.3 Plurality Groups above 50 percent of the Population with Grievances

	Plurality groups larger than 50% of the population	*Any_grievance in MAR* *None*	*Yes*	*Total*	*Concrete case*
EPR power rank ordinal scale	Powerless or noncitizen	2	1	3	Rwanda Hutus (pol.gr)
	Regional autonomy, separatist autonomy, or irrelevant	1	1	2	Bolivia Indigenous Highland Peoples (pol,econ,cult.gr)
	Junior partner	2	0	2	
	Senior partner	24	4	28	Belgium Flemings (cult.gr); Burundi Hutus (pol.gr); Iraq Shi'is (pol.gr); Taiwan Taiwanese (cult.gr)
	Dominant	42	1	43	Fiji Fijians (econ.gr)
	Monopoly	26	0	26	
Total		97	8	104	

Note: The Hutus of Burundi and the Shi'a of Iraq reached their power position only recently, and they still harbor complaints and fight for assurances of their new condition.

The main question we may ask with regard to types of groups is whether any group feature makes the communal groups more likely to have and express grievances. Data suggest that variations of the plurality/minority condition definitely count. Yet, the feature which is most often hypothesized to count toward the existence of hostility and conflict, is the size of the groups. In my sample, neither the size nor the proportion of the minority groups emerges as a serious predictor of grievances in bivariate relationships. Smaller pluralities, on the other hand, are significantly more likely to be grieved than larger pluralities. And one more meaningful pattern emerges from a correlation matrix of the Alesina fractionalization indicators with the grievance indicators. For minority groups, increasing fractionalization is negatively correlated with the amount and severity of grievances, while for pluralities, the pattern is opposite. Pluralities are likely to have more grievances (and conflicts) when the country's fractionalization is higher.

Yet, before any bi- or multivariate analysis of the variables, I would like to give some further details about my cases, the groups. One important issue we have to bear in mind is that numerical majorities are not always the ones that have controlled the state, the power relations are a little more complicated, as Table 5.4 reveals.

Of the weirdest cases, the discriminated plurality and one of the historical minorities in monopoly position are in Bahrain, while the other monopolist minority is Bhutan's Drupka (Ngalong) Buddhist elite. Despite the exceptions, the table makes it clear that pluralities have a significant edge on the power rank, and their advantages may be highlighted by comparing the group means, as well. Table 5.5 summarizes the groups' position on three measures that may greatly influence their objective and subjective well-being: on the political and economic ladders, as well as on the likelihood that they foster memories of recent violent episodes.

Table 5.4 Group Type and Power Rank Cross-Tabulation

		Minority type					
	Plurality	*Multiple plurality*	*Historical minority*	*New minority*	*Secessionist minority*	*Non citizen*	*Total*
EPR power rank ordinal scale: Discriminated	1	0	63	9	0	3	76
Powerless, noncitizen	13	0	187	16	0	32	248
Regional autonomy, Separatist autonomy, irrelevant	7	0	180	3	9	0	199
Junior partner	11	3	142	5	0	0	161
Senior partner	45	1	34	0	0	0	80
Dominant	47	0	18	0	0	0	65
Monopoly	29	0	2	0	0	0	31
Total	153	4	626	33	9	35	860

Table 5.5 Differences among Types of Group with Regard to Power and Wealth

	EPR Power Rank ordinal scale		*Group's Wealth Quintile Index value*		*Past violence index*	
	N	*Mean*	*N*	*Mean*	*N*	*Mean*
Plurality	153	5.24	153	3.14	152	4.80
Multiple plurality	4	4.25	4	3.25	4	0.00
Historical minority	626	2.93	624	2.79	624	7.97
New minority (after WWII)	33	2.12	32	2.55	33	3.84
Secessionist minority	9	3.00	9	2.67	9	80.07
Noncitizen	35	1.91	31	2.04	35	0.29
Total/average	860	3.28	853	2.81	857	7.66

Typically, minorities are poorer than pluralities, and new minorities and non-citizens are poorer than the historical minorities. These trends are mitigated by the existence of a few advantaged minorities, as well as some wealthy expat communities, such as the European Union retirees in Spain.

Table 5.6 aims at visualizing the relationship between wealth and political power positions. In order to produce this table, I have created a dummy separating groups that are above 3, the middle value on the WQI, (also my INEQ_1 measure), and others that are below 3 or are exactly 3.[5] Table 5.6 shows that while pluralities are reasonably likely to hold power be they either poor or rich, poor minorities are significantly less likely to be included in government than wealthier minorities. Unfortunately, both inclusion rates are low, but the 45.7 percent inclusion rate for relatively well-off minorities is much better than the 26.1 percent inclusion rate for poor historical minorities.

Most theorists expect beneficial effects from crosscutting cleavages. This is a belief shared by Donald Horowitz, for instance, and the sociologists contributing to the Stewart 2008 volume. I also expect political empowerment to mitigate the frustration caused by economic disadvantages. In general, the

Table 5.6 Group Type and Power Position Cross-Tabulation

Groups above 3 on the Wealth Quintile Index	*Ethnic group in power*		
	Excluded (%)	*In power (%)*	*Total (%)*
Plurality	4 (6.2)	61 (93.8)	65 (100)
Multiple plurality	0 (0)	4 (100)	4 (100)
Historical minority	100 (54.35)	84 (45.7)	184 (100)
New minority (after WWII)	8 (88.9)	1 (11.1)	9 (100)
Secessionist minority	4 (100)	0 (0)	4 (100)
Non citizen	1 (100)	0 (0)	1 (100)
Total	117 (43.8)	150 (56.2)	267 (100)
Groups <= 3 on the Wealth Quintile Index	*Excluded (%)*	*In power (%)*	*Total (%)*
Plurality	13 (14.8)	75 (85.2)	88 (100)
Historical minority	325 (73.9)	115 (26.1)	440 (100)
New minority (after WWII)	19 (82.6)	4 (17.4)	23 (100)
Secessionist minority	5 (100)	0 (0)	5 (100)
Non citizen	30 (100)	0 (0)	30 (100)
Total	392 (66.9)	194 (33.1)	586 (100)

groups' position on the political power rank can be shown (as it has been shown previously by Cederman and coauthors) to be highly consequential for their animosity levels expressed in grievances and occurrence of intercommunal conflicts. Yet, my aim is to go a step farther: I would like to have a look at the institutions that may empower minorities. There is, unfortunately, a serious technical hurdle to this task, an artifact that I would call the "modernization paradox effect." In simple bivariate relationships, minorities seem to be politically better off in less developed countries. The EPR-based "power rank" ordinal variable and the "ethnic group in power" (egip) indicator are negatively correlated with indicators such as GDP and life expectancy. Further, the "modernization paradox effect" overspills onto a number of phenomena usually associated with development, such as democracy, proportional representation, and decentralization. Their measures are also negatively correlated with the power status measures, though these negative associations sink into insignificance in partial correlations or multivariate regression models in the presence of a modernization or development indicator. The emergence of this "modernization paradox effect" seems to be explained by two facts. On the one hand, there are larger pluralities in more developed countries, which never fail to be the politically strongest, and on the other hand, developed countries host a larger proportion of noncitizen and new immigrant groups, which are, almost by definition, powerless.

On the economic side, the "modernization paradox effect" means that minorities tend to get relatively poorer, while pluralities, relatively richer, as the country's GDP increases. The Pearson correlation value between

Table 5.7 Historical Trends of Horizontal and Vertical Inequalities

	INEQ_2	*INEQ_3*	*INEQ_4*	*INEQ_5*	*GINI*
	WQI distance from plurality (+, –)	*WQI distance from plurality (+ only)*	*Group WQI distances scaled to Gini (Ineq3 *Gini)*	*Interaction term ((Ineq3+1)*Gini)*	*Gini index*
GDP per capita, PPP	0.176				–0.353
Life expectancy at birth, female	0.221	0.091			–0.460
Overall globalization index (KOF)	0.083		–0.085	–0.126	–0.318
Economic globalization index	0.109			–0.101	–0.298
Social globalization index	0.128			–0.117	–0.349

Note: All Pearson correlation coefficients reported are significant above the alpha = 0.05 level.

minority WQI and GDP/capita is minus 0.143 across 696 cases in 2005, while the same WQI of the pluralities was correlated with GDP/capita at plus 0.3 (across 153 cases). Economic globalization of the country has the same negative association with the WQI position of minorities ($r = -0.1$), and both the economic development and globalization measures are positively associated with larger intergroup inequalities. There is an antithetical trend of intergroup and interindividual inequalities emerging here. The Gini index is known to be curvilinearly associated with the development indicators: it increases at the beginning of the modernization process, and starts to shrink with the establishment of welfare states in the most developed societies, resulting in an overall negative linear pattern. As for my dataset, these antithetical trends are clearly marked by the correlation values between the various inequality measures and a number of development and globalization indicators (Table 5.7).

Modernization also affects the articulation of grievances. While the rate of expression of economic and political grievances is almost even across developmental levels, people in developed countries are significantly more likely to log cultural grievances than their counterparts in less-developed countries. Yet, details about the grievance variables are the subject of the next section.

THE VARIABLES—DESCRIPTIVES AND BIVARIATE RELATIONSHIPS

From a purely statistical point of view, violent episodes between communal groups are not really common events. From 2006 through 2009, there were only 52 communal conflicts that made the threshold to be included in the

UCDP/PRIO dataset. There were, however, more conflicts of lower intensity included in CONIS, and the frequency of minority grievances recorded by MAR has been even greater.[6]

My effort to use several dependent variables is rooted in the belief that not all lower-level expressions of hostility are doomed to evolve into violent episodes. Since violent conflicts are rarer in developed countries, the question of whether there is less lower-level hostility in developed countries than in the less developed, is not trivial. My dataset contains 144 CONIS conflicts, out of which 36 concerned the 282 groups living in the most developed countries (for a rate of 12.8 percent), while 108 conflicts happened to the 594 groups in less developed countries (for a rate of 18.18 percent).[7] Yet, the distribution of grievances is biased to the detriment of the advanced. In developed countries, 33 percent of communal groups expressed cultural grievances, as compared to 13 percent of groups in less developed countries. The rate of political grievances is practically the same in the two groups (33 versus 31 percent), while the rate of economic discontentment is 28 percent in the developed world versus 19 percent in the less developed countries. Subsequently, the overall pattern is more grievance in developed countries, but less violent conflict; and this means that the developed countries are much more successful in diverting the intergroup tensions from discharging in violence, than the less developed ones.

The next tables, Table 5.8 and 5.9, review the bivariate relationships of some potential explanatory variables with seven dependent variables.[8] These latter include the three MAR ordinal grievance scales (political, economic, and cultural), and a binary indicator showing the presence or absence of any grievance during the years 2004–2006. A second dummy shows the presence or absence of any conflict included in the CONIS dataset for the years 2006–2010. Two further variables aim at quantifying the severity of the CONIS conflict, one intensity measure being based on CONIS information only, while the other taking into account the UCDP/PRIO rankings of those events, as well. The tables distinguish between minorities and pluralities, and have separate entries for both pluralities above >50 percent of the population, and historical minorities in extended sense (i.e., including the nine secessionist and the four multiple plurality groups). Only the tables pertinent to two explanatory variable groups, economic inequality (Table 5.8) and political institutions (Table 5.9) are presented here.[9]

The first section of Table 5.8 tells us that poor groups, be they either minorities or pluralities, are more likely to have grievances and get into conflict with other groups, than rich groups are. The correlation coefficients are the strongest with the economic grievances, yet the other two types of grievances are also affected. In the second through fourth sections, INEQ_2, INEQ_3, and INEQ_4 are zero by default for all plurality groups. The coefficients

Table 5.8 Bivariate Relationships of the Dependent Variables with Inequality Measures

	Political grievance	Economic grievance	Cultural grievance	Any grievance	Any conflict	Conis intensity	Intensity index
INEQ_1: Group average Wealth Quintile value							
Historical minority (639)	-.144	-.225	-.159	-.173	-.101	-.125	-.151
Minority (703)	-.111	-.207	-.132	-.141		-.083	-.111
Groups <50% (756)	-.123	-.197	-.142	-.145		-.087	-.117
All groups (860)	-.149	-.219	-.159	-.175	-.084	-.105	-.133
Plurality (153)							
Group >50% (104)	-.229	-.261		-.252			
Development trend: Correlations with grievances grow (max. -0.323), those with conflict fade away							
INEQ_2: Group WQI distance from plurality (+, --)							
Historical minority (639)	.117	.216	.129	.167	.095	.128	.155
Minority (703)	.085	.193	.102	.131		.086	.115
Groups <50% (756)	.094	.187	.111	.133		.086	.117
All groups (860)	.119	.208	.128	.162	.075	.104	.132
Development trend: Correlations with grievances grow (max. 0.302), those with conflict fade away							
INEQ_3: Group WQI distance from plurality (+ only)							
Historical minority (639)	.168	.214	.164	.195	.105	.118	.149
Minority (703)	.126	.189	.124	.149		.083	.113
Groups <50% (756)	.143	.180	.143	.154	.072	.086	.118
All groups (860)	.194	.224	.177	.217	.109	.123	.149
Development trend: Correlations with grievances grow (max. 0.304), those with conflict fade away							
INEQ_4: Group WQI distances scaled to Gini (Ineq_3*Gini)							
Historical minority (639)	.155	.221	.171	.187	.086	.101	.127
Minority (703)	.124	.203	.135	.153		.077	.104
Groups <50% (756)	.141	.194	.152	.157		.081	.109
All groups (860)	.190	.235	.185	.217	.102	.117	.140
Development trend: Correlations with grievances grow (max. 0.353), those with conflict fade awayr							

Note: The numbers in parentheses refer to the frequency of the respective category in EPR_MAR_EXT, and indicate the upper bound for calculating the correlation coefficients. As pluralities have been coded with WQI=0, their INEQ_2, 3, and 4 values do not produce meaningful correlation coefficient with the hostility measures.

typifying the "Historical minority" group are higher than those of the politically more inert new and noncitizen groups.[10]

Overall, the correlation coefficients do not promise that the intergroup inequality measures will explain a high percentage of variation, but they point toward a consistently present relationship with meaningful variation across types of groups and developmental levels.[11] It is also important that the correlation coefficients measure the linear component of some relationships which are obviously not perfectly linear. For instance, the relationship between the ordinal-scale inequality measures and the two binary dependent variables (Any_grievance, Any_conflict), are best expressed by a logit or probit curve, while the two intensity measures are very far from the normal distribution, both peaked and skewed.

Table 5.9 Bivariate Relationships of the Dependent Variables with Institutional Features

	Political grievance	Economic grievance	Cultural grievance	Any grievance	Any conflict	Conis intensity	Intensity index
EPR power rank ordinal scale							
Minority (703)		-.137	-.076	-.188			
Groups <50% (756)	-.080	-.133	-.089	-.188			
All groups (860)	-.179	-.206	-.151	-.285	-.098	-.093	-.098
Plurality (153)	-.302	-.291		-.343	-.224	-.222	-.221
Groups >50% (104)	-.316	-.216	-.228	-.332	-.234	-.271	-.284
Development trend: In less developed group, negative with conflict, in developed, no correlation							
Freedom House ranking with imputed Polity							
Minority (703)	.076	.130	.127				
Groups <50% (756)	.078	.129	.133				
All groups (860)		.112	.122				
Development trend: No clear trends							
Political terror scale (from the US State Department)							
Minority (703)	.090		-.083		.179	.218	.226
Groups <50% (756)	.093		-.086	.074	.178	.216	.223
All groups (860)	.116			.099	.174	.210	.216
Plurality (153)	.258			.211		.163	
Groups >50% (104)	.227						
Development trend: Same tendencies (+) in both developmental groups.							
Decentralization index of administrative subdivisions							
Minority (703)	.076		.082				
Groups <50% (756)	.096		.098				
All groups (860)			.077				
Development trend: No clear trends							
Administrative subdivisions fall along communal lines ("Communal_sub_divisions")							
Minority (703)	.085				.137	.161	.179
Groups <50% (756)	.097				.142	.164	.187
All groups (860)	.097				.138	.155	.174
Plurality (153)	.168		.198		.185	.161	.196
Development trend: Same tendencies (+) in both developmental groups.							
Interaction term of Decentralization index and "Communal_sub_divisions," my autonomy measure							
Minority (703)						.076	
Groups <50% (756)	.090				.072	.088	.088
All groups (860)	.070					.075	.074
Plurality (153)			.199		.193		.213
Development trend: No significant values in any of the developmental groups							

Note: All correlation coefficients displayed are significant above Alpha=0.05. The empty rows (with no significant correlation) have been deleted.

Though theoretically all groups of explanatory variables are equally important, for political and policy practice the institutional features are of special importance. Table 5.9 has a first section that is not about the institutions themselves, but about the effective power position of the groups, as measured by the EPR data.[12] This is followed by variables that tap into the institutional settings that make it possible for minorities to climb the power ladder: democracy (as measured by the Freedom House/imputed Polity variable and the political terror scale); proportional electoral system (of which influence was so weak, that it was left out from the table); and opportunities of territorial autonomy.

This latter feature was measured as the interaction term of two indexes. On the one hand, I measured the country's decentralization with a variable calculated as average of four measurements promoted by the Database of Political Institutions. The association between decentralization and grievances emerged as weakly positive, since decentralization is development-related: the more advanced countries have more decentralized institutions. On the other hand, I worked out a measure called "administrative subdivisions fall along communal lines" (or "communal_sub_divisions"), which intends to be a proxy for group concentration,[13] and this produces a series of positive correlation coefficients with the hostility measures.

With both the decentralization index and the concentration proxy being positively associated with the dependent variables, we may expect their interaction term (i.e., their product) to show an even stronger positive correlation with the dependent variables, but this does not happen. In the two minority samples, the positive association with grievances is lower in the case of the interaction term than in any of the component factors, and the association with conflict is substantially lower than in the case of the concentration proxy Communal_sub_divison. This suggests that allowing for the territorial autonomy of territorially concentrated minorities reduces the chances of intergroup conflict, an effect doing justice to Lijphart in his dispute with Horowitz.

Unfortunately, all of our analyses are doomed to be hurt by what I dub the "Modernization paradox effect." The development level is associated with a number of group structure and institutional features, and this collusion produces unexpected results, such as making decentralization liable for increasing intergroup hostility. Development's association with those features may lack any sound causal relationship. We cannot reasonably claim that higher GDP *causes* some countries to have larger plurality groups and less ethnic or religious fractionalization, nor that GDP *causes* minorities to be relatively less wealthy and less powerful in the developed states than in the less developed. The impact of a specific Western evolution path, which has been associated with the creation of homogenous populations, is an account to be considered, but there is no evidence either for the claim that communal homogeneity is a prerequisite of development or for the claim that homogeneity is necessarily produced by development. The issue resembles the complexities around the relationship between development and democracy. Though strongly associated, and impacting each other at the level of each individual country, there is no overarching causal pattern to describe their relationship beyond the empirical generalization that democracies are more likely to survive at higher levels of GDP. Maybe the most palpable developmental impact on communal relations is the dispersion of communal groups as result of industrialization and urbanization.

I reviewed the other groups of explanatory factors, as well, and most of the time the bivariate relationships confirmed the theoretical expectations. Yet there were some surprising details emerging, such as:

- The group proportion variable showed significant negative correlations with the grievance and conflict indicators, suggesting that as the proportion of the group increases, they tend to become more contented and more peaceful, which is the exact opposite of what is theoretically expected. Yet the separation of plurality and minority groups saves the theory. It is the plurality groups that get more contented and peaceful as they grow in size—minorities do not. Odds are that previous work has often failed to find a positive relationship between group proportion and conflict because in many countries it is very hard to distinguish between plurality and minority groups. Their logics of behavior, however, are understandably contrasting.[14]
- Though in general the emergence of grievances and conflict is importantly affected by past violent episodes, cultural grievances are fairly inert to their impact.
- The KOF globalization indicators replicate the pattern of the development indicators, such as GDP, HDI, and life expectancy. (i.e., the likelihood of violent conflict goes down, the incidence of minority grievances increases, and pluralities grow more contented and peaceful with globalization.)
- Of the measurements actualizing the hypothesis that opportunities for insurrection increase the chances of violent conflict, government effectiveness reveals an ability to reduce the likelihood of violent conflict, as expected, but produces an anomalous positive correlation coefficient with the measure of cultural grievances. Unfortunately, the "unemployed young males" variable belonging to this group is very lacunar, and this has seriously impaired its performance in the correlation matrices. The predictor has values for 553 cases out of 860, and the developed countries are heavily overrepresented in the sample of 553. The next two chapters do justice to the hypothesis of opportunity for insurrection by applying a multiple imputation method, which assigns values to all cases on the "unemployed young males" variable. The difficulty with the measure of rural population, namely, that it is correlated with the development indicators above $r = 0.65$, will be addressed in Chapter 6 by using a measure of urbanism specific to the MAR dataset.

This chapter proceeds to build models that explain the most variation of the dependent variables, and will also try to clarify the specific conditions, mainly institutional conditions, within which the grievances lead to violent conflict.

REGRESSION MODELS

The substantively most important element to explain about intergroup relations is the occurrence of violence, here operationalized with the variables that express the presence of violent conflict and its intensity (Any_conflict, Conis_intensity, Intensity_index). My contention, however, has been that the factors that make the groups hostile toward each other lead to the articulation of group grievances first, and the group strategy to achieve redress for the plights is later formulated in function of a series of institutional possibilities, including the opportunity for—or, maybe more correctly, the cost-benefit analysis of—insurrection. This suggests a two-step analysis of the causal mechanisms: in a first step, I would like to explain the occurrence and severity of grievances, and in a second, the transition from grievance to violent conflict.

Yet the whole data analytic work will articulate four types of explanations:

(i) Explanations of intergroup hostility, while controlling for countries. I intend to show that the impact of intergroup economic inequality may be detected behind the idiosyncratic effects of various country contexts. Thus in a number of models I have included my INEQ measures along the functional equivalent of all country dummies. Afterward, the next three steps of the regression analysis implement the Przeworski & Teune (1971) epistemological project of substituting individual names with variable names. That is, the country factor is being replaced with a number of variables impersonating the country context with a few salient features of these, such as the developmental level, fractionalization, and inclusive democracy.

(ii) Explanations of grievances with group-level and country-level variables, such as those expressing intergroup inequality, and the country's group structure.

(iii) Explanations of violent conflict with grievances and a selection of controls, meant to tap on the institutional circumstances and the opportunity for insurrection.

(iv) "Omnibus" explanations of violent conflict. These models include the causes of grievance together with the circumstantial and opportunity for insurrection variables, by bypassing the grievances themselves.

Unfortunately, all steps involve a mixture of group-level and country-level measurements, whose concatenation in models is not absolutely unproblematic. And a further difficulty to struggle with in these complex regressions is collinearity.

The regression analyses are confined to the subset of historical minorities. The political action of new and noncitizen minorities is much more limited by institutional and opportunity issues, but we may hypothesize that within a few decades they will adopt the behavioral patterns of the older minorities.[15]

Explaining Intergroup Hostility (both Grievances and Conflict) with Group-level Variables, while Controlling for Countries

I worked with the SPSS statistical software, and for this task I was mainly relying on the procedure called "Generalized Linear Models" (GENLIN or GLM). Within this procedure, all three model types pertinent to my dependent variables (binary, ordinal, interval) are available, and all take string variables as factors. Given that introducing the country dummies uses up 154 degrees of freedom, and this triples in the case of the interaction terms, in this step I did not restrict the cases to a single year. This increased the maximally available case number to 639*2 = 1278 for models with the political grievance measure; and to 639*3 = 1917 for the two conflict intensity variables.[16]

Originally, I intended to run seven regression models with only two independent variables: the intergroup economic inequality measure and the country factor. The country factor is a variable which, in the GENLIN procedure, replaces the totality of country indicators, or otherwise, it is the functional equivalent of 154 country dummies. Yet in practice, the GENLIN procedure objected to the use of binary and ordinal outcome variables, and it gave good results, without technical issues, only for models with interval dependent variables. These are called by SPSS "linear models." Out of my seven dependent variables, there are two that were originally conceived as interval variables, and the 5-point ordinal political grievance variable may also be used in linear models.

Table 5.10 shows the results from three GENLIN models with the economic inequality variable and the country factor. Here and in all subsequent regression models reported, I use a graphic coding for highlighting the

Table 5.10 The Economic Inequality Measure in Additive Models with Country Effects

	Political grievance	Conis intensity	Intensity index
Model fit information from Generalized Linear Models (linear option)			
Log likelihood	-2899.0	-1748.7	-2458.6
Likelihood Ratio Chi-2	836.8	1293.6	1346.3
Parameter coefficient information from GLM: the significance value (p) of the predictors			
Inter-group economic inequality (Ineq_3_ln)	.002	.063	.001
Country factor (Statename)	.000	.000	.000

Trellis pattern shows significance above alpha = 0.05; vertical lines show significance between alpha = 0.05 and 0.1.

significance of the regression coefficients. These are given, in all cases, in *p*-values, and p-values below 0.05 are highlighted with trellis patterned cells.[17] Further, I use light vertical lines for significances between alpha = 0.05 and alpha = 0.1, and dots for coefficients that turn up as significant with the theoretically unexpected sign. The *p*-values show the country factor maximally significant. The intergroup economic inequality measure turns up with convincingly low *p*-value twice, and only in the case of the CONIS intensity measure does it score a second-class significance with a *p*-value of 0.063. Unfortunately, the GENLIN output does not contain any easily interpretable measure of model strength, and this is unfortunate also for testing my intuition that multilevel models are better than additive models. I think that the fact that the communal groups are nested in their countries should be modeled with multilevel regressions, and I expect these to have more explanatory power than the "additive" models, which do not account for the nested relationship.

I have also experimented with increasing the model strength by including three more highly relevant group-level variables besides the intergroup economic inequality. The other three predictors are political inequality, past violence, and group size. Tables 5.11 and 5.12 show the results, in two versions: in additive models and in nested models.

In Table 5.11, group proportion turns up as a significant predictor of conflict, but the single strongest group-level *explanans* of intergroup hostility is past violence. Unfortunately, it is correlated with both economic and political inequality, which resulted in a weakening of the measured impact of my economic inequality variable and contributed to preventing the EPR political inequality measure from reaching significance. In addition, political inequality is associated with economic inequality, as well. Table 5.12 presents three nested models, in which the three main group-level predictors are included as interaction terms with the country factor. Visibly, the Log Likelihood values are smaller, and the Likelihood Ratio Chi-squared values are higher in the

Table 5.11 Four Group-Level Variables in Additive Models with Country Effects

	Political grievance	Conis intensity	Intensity index
Model fit information from Generalized Linear Models (linear option)			
Log likelihood	-1799.8	-899.4	-1273.2
Likelihood Ratio Chi-2	803.0	1045.2	1175.6
Parameter coefficient information from GLM: the significance (p-) value of the predictors			
Inter-group economic inequality (Ineq_3)	.016	.133	.011
Power status ordinal variable	.558	.414	.748
Past violence	.000	.000	.000
Group proportion	.000	.052	.048
Country factor (Statename)	.000	.000	.000

Trellis pattern shows significance above alpha = 0.05; vertical lines show significance between alpha = 0.05 and 0.1.

Table 5.12 Four Group-Level Variables in Nested Models with Country Effects

	Political grievance	Conis intensity	Intensity index
Model fit information from Generalized Linear Models (linear option)			
Log likelihood	-1468.4	-390.4	-756.7
Likelihood Ratio Chi2	1465.8	2063.3	2208.7
Parameter coefficient information from GLM; the significance (p-) value of the predictors			
Country factor * Economic inequality (Ineq_3_ln)	.000	.000	.000
Country factor * EPR Power status (Powr_rank)	.000	.000	.000
Country factor * Past violence	.000	.000	.000
Group proportion	.000	.012	.017

Trellis pattern shows significance above alpha = 0.05; vertical lines show significance between alpha = 0.05 and 0.1.

case of the nested model than in the case of the additive model, which supports the superiority of the nested modeling.

I have not included regression coefficients in these tables, as the GENLIN procedure does not give summative coefficient estimate for the interaction terms. There are partial coefficients given for each country, such as "[Statename=Belgium]*ineq_3_ln," which is –6.383. Where summative coefficients are given, and they are significant, they all point in the theoretically expected direction.

Explaining Grievances with Group-level and Country-level Variables

This section endeavors to explain the emergence of hostility as measured with the severity of grievances expressed by the minority population. Since the impact of political institutions on the articulation of grievances is mediated by the actual political inequality experienced by minorities, in this step I will use the EPR measures of political inequality, rather than the institutional indicators themselves. The explanatory variables to be considered here are partly group-level, and partly country-level measurements, as summed up in Table 5.13 (Checklist 1).

The variables belonging to each group are arranged in two columns. The pairs displayed next to each other measure very closely related phenomena, and are very highly correlated between themselves, thus I refrained from using them in the same model. By alternating the closely related explanatory variables, as well as the dependent variables, and experimenting with two time spans (2005 only and 2003–2005), ultimately, I ran 40 models plus two stepwise modeling tests.

The first observation to highlight is the consistency of the findings. Models with 12 predictors often behave capriciously in slightly altered conditions. My models were consequent in indicating that:

Table 5.13 Checklist 1. Independent Variables Considered in Models Explaining Minority Grievances

	Group-level variables	
Intergroup economic inequality	Ineq_3_ln	Ineq_4_ln
Intergroup political inequality	Power status (Pwr_rank)	Ethnic group in power (EGIP)
Group proportion	Group proportion	
Group history	Past violence	
	Country-level variables	
Country's group structure	Ethnic fractionalization	Linguistic fractionalization
	Religious fractionalization	
	Proportion of plurality	Largest minority
	Group concentration proxy	
Country development level	GDP/capita (PPP)	Life expectancy (female)
Country international embedness		Globalization index
	Economic globalization	
	Political globalization	
	Social globalization	

- When a predictor turned up as significant, it had the same sign in all models. This suggests that minority grievances of all kinds have a similar set of causes, though certain causes may be more relevant for one type and less relevant for other types. For instance, the religious fractionalization indicator emerges as a significant predictor of cultural grievances, but not of political grievances. The political inequality indicator inversely, is significant in the ordinal regression model explaining political grievances, and insignificant in the model explaining cultural grievances.
- The predictors that turn up as significant in a model confined to 2005, are always significant in the many-year versions, as well, but these latter may allow for more explanatory variables to cross the significance threshold.
- The sign of most indicators is in the theoretically expected direction. While intergroup economic inequality increases the level of grievances, higher position on the power ladder reduces it. Past violence, which is the strongest predictor in these models, acts toward boosting grievances. Larger groups are more likely to express grievances, and further, the larger the plurality group in the country, the more likely that the minorities express grievances. These results have to be interpreted against the background condition that there are larger pluralities in the developed countries. The impact of the development measure is positive, that is, there are more grievances in developed countries. Five other predictors, of globalization and fractionalization, have turned up as significant in a limited number of models only. Religious fractionalization contributes to the reduction of cultural, and occasionally, of economic grievances, while

ethnic fractionalization increases these, but the results are sensitive to the kind of development indicator used. (In other words, the association between fractionalization and development level shapes the impact of diversity on grievances).

- The explanatory strength of the models varies around 20 percent, with the cultural grievances being the less elucidated, followed by the economic grievances, and models explaining political grievance are the strongest.

Tables 5.14 and 5.15 report the strongest model in each category, from the series confined to year 2005 (in which less predictors turn up as significant than in the multi-year resolutions). Yet, before the overview of the results, I would like to make two remarks.

First, my intergroup economic inequality variable turned up as significant 36 times out of 40, always with the expected sign, and there were only two models explaining political grievance (those confined to 2005), in which the measure scaled to Gini (Ineq_4) failed to reach significance, while the original measure (Ineq_3) did.

Table 5.14 Explaining Grievance with Inter-Group Inequality and Control Variables: The Ordinal Models

Dependent variable	Economic grievance		Cultural grievance		Political grievance	
Case number	624		622		623	
-2 Log likelihood	830.6		667.5		1225.2	
Cox & Snell Pseudo-R2	.152		.136		.242	
Nagelkerke Preudo-R2	.196		.192		.271	
McFadden Preudo-R2	.110		.119		.123	
Likelihood Ratio Chi-2	102.9		90.7		173.0	
Warnings	Empty cells (66.5%), Pearson Chi-2 <0.05 (but Deviance is 1)		Empty cells (66.6%)		Empty cells (79.9%), Pearson Chi-2 <0.05 (but Deviance is 1)	
	Estimate	Sig.	Estimate	Sig.	Estimate	Sig.
H. economic inequality (Ineq_3)	.741	.000	.636	.005	.409	.024
EPR power status rank	-.272	.005	-.118	.266	-.221	.009
Group proportion	3.192	.010	4.643	.000	3.677	.001
Ethnic fractionalization	1.189	.103	1.716	.032	.142	.825
Religious fractionalization	-.169	.736	-.591	.280	-.245	.586
Proportion of plurality	1.120	.129	1.687	.040	1.592	.015
Past violence	.012	.000	.007	.014	.034	.000
Group concentration proxy	-.526	.260	-.433	.386	-.186	.661
Economic globalization	.002	.942	-.011	.666	-.034	.086
Political globalization	.028	.000	.018	.011	.005	.370
Social globalization	-.013	.464	-.004	.853	.016	.339
Life expectancy (female)	.042	.014	.077	.000	.037	.011

Trellis pattern shows significance above alpha = 0.05; vertical lines show significance between alpha = 0.05 and 0.1.

Table 5.15 Explaining Grievance with Inter-Group Inequality and Control Variables—A Binary and an OLS Model

	Binary model		OLS model			
Dependent variable	Any grievance		Political grievance			
Number of cases	624		623			
-2 Log likelihood	708.1		Adjusted R-squared = 0.215			
Cox & Snell R2	.203					
Nagelkerke R2	.273					
Predicted %	72.1					
Likelihood Ratio Chi-2	141.5					
					collinearity statistics	
	Coeff.	Sig.	St.Coeff.	Sig.	Toler.ce	VIF
H. economic inequality (Ineq_3)	.563	.003	.091	.014	.919	1.088
EPR power status rank	-.386	.000	-.032	.426	.762	1.312
Group proportion	4.351	.001	.111	.005	.802	1.247
Ethnic fractionalization	-.138	.840	.093	.163	.285	3.504
Religious fractionalization	-.104	.826	-.009	.831	.719	1.390
Proportion of plurality	.816	.229	.226	.000	.306	3.271
Past violence	.045	.000	.393	.000	.938	1.066
Group concentration proxy	-.837	.069	.019	.640	.799	1.251
Economic globalization	-.044	.030	-.158	.211	.079	12.680
Political globalization	.007	.221	.046	.278	.705	1.418
Social globalization	.028	.105	.089	.536	.061	16.271
Life expectancy (female)	.029	.058	.153	.025	.273	3.666

Trellis pattern shows significance above alpha = 0.05; vertical lines show significance between alpha = 0.05 and 0.1.

Second, I tested the best two models for redundancy. I asked for a stepwise elimination of the predictors from the binary model explaining Any_grievance, on the one hand, and the OLS model explaining political grievance, on the other. In neither case led the elimination to a superior model. This shows that all explanatory variables contribute to the models, and the explanation of intergroup hostility is truly multicausal.

Table 5.14 contains information on the three ordinal models. Though the results seem meaningful and congruent with results from other models, the regression models themselves have some technical issues. The ordinal regression environment is not really hospitable for interval variables, here called "covariates."[18]

Table 5.15 contains a clean, technically healthy binary logistic model, and a technically healthy ordinary least squares model, which, however, suffers from dangerously high levels of collinearity. (Two predictors, social globalization and economic globalization, barely exceed the 0.05 threshold for VIF tolerance).

The results from the ordinal model and the OLS model to explain political grievance are very similar, with only one difference to be mentioned. The political inequality measure does not turn up as significant in the linear model, though it is significant in the ordinal one. But in Tables 5.14 and 5.15, I have included the stricter 2005-confined models only. When we increase the case number, the predictors get better chances to turn up as significant or to show more impact on the dependent variable.[19]

Explaining Conflict with Grievances and a Selection of Circumstantial and Opportunity Variables

In this section, I would like to find the predictors of violence while controlling for the grievance level. The research question is that once the group grievances have been articulated, in which conditions do they lead to violent episodes and when is there a chance to achieve a peaceful solution? Not unimportantly, the models also test whether grievances are significant causes of domestic violence. In the strongest forms of the opportunity for insurrection hypothesis, grievances have no autonomous impact, as they are artifacts of the political entrepreneurs guided by greed.

Table 5.16 (Checklist 2) summarizes the predictors that may typify the road between grievance and violence. There are, on the one hand, circumstances that push the grievance-harboring groups toward insurrection, and there are, on the other hand, circumstances that make the peaceful political action more attractive. A number of factors have to be taken into consideration either because they facilitate minority political action of any kind (such as larger minority group, and smaller plurality group), or because they are significant determinants of, causing or shaping, actions of any kind (such as country development level). Sadly, the set of concrete variables available falls a little short from what we may deem to be really adequate and complete representation of the theoretical categories.[20]

I ran regression models with all three conflict measures available, ordinary least squares models with the "Conis_intensity" and "Intensity_index" measures, and binary logistic models with the "Any_conflict" variable. All models contained the same 13 predictors, while the 14th, the grievance measure, was alternated: I included the four grievance indicators successively in the explanations. I also tested the time factor. I ran the models for year 2005 only and for all available years, which were again, either 2003–2005 or 2004–2005. This means 24 models (3*4*2) to report on, but actually I ran 21 additional models, as well.

Twenty of the additional models included the measure for unemployed young males, as the 15th predictor, and its presence kept slashing the number of cases to less than half. I compared each model containing this unemployment measure with the corresponding model lacking it, and the presence of the measure meant little if any change in the impact of the other variables, and it definitely not affected the four strongest predictors. The unemployed young male variable itself has never emerged as significant.

Table 5.16 Checklist 2. Independent Variables Explaining Inter-Group Violence

Theoretical concept	*Operationalized concept*	*Instrumentalized concept*
Grievance level	Communal grievances	Economic, cultural, and political grievance
		Any_grievance
Opportunity for insurrection (rebellion)	Government effectiveness	WGI government effectiveness
	Rural settlements	Proportion of rural population
	Supply of unemployed young males	Proportion of unemployed young males
	Foreign military aid to group	
Opportunity for peaceful political action	Democracy	Freedom House/iPolity2
		Political terror scale (US State Dept.)
	Inclusive democracy	Electoral family (based on Norris)
		Proportional system dummy (from DPI)
	Minority territorial autonomy	Decentralization index* regional concentration proxy (Commnl_s_divisions)
	*Minority functional autonomy	
Country-level controls	Development level	GDP/capita (PPP)
		Life expectancy (female)
	Country international embeddedness	KOF globalization index
		Economic globalization (KOF)
		Social globalization (KOF)
		Political globalization (KOF)
	Plurality proportion and/or minority proportion	Proportion of plurality group
	Fractionalization	Ethnic fractionalization (Alesina)
		Linguistic fractionalization (Alesina)
		Religious fractionalization (Alesina)
Group-level controls	Group proportion	Group proportion (My_prop)
	Group concentration	Regional concentration proxy (Communal_sub_divisions)
	Foreign aid to group	
	*Group organization potential**	

*These entries (marked with asterisk on the left) cannot be addressed with the currently existing measurements
**Groups' organization potential hinges on a number of country and group features that have already been included, such as democracy and group concentration, but may involve idiosyncratic issues that go beyond what can be addressed here, such as cross-cutting divisions (e.g., Sunni and Alevi Kurds), high in-group economic inequality, urbanism and occupational features, choice of exit over voice, and so on.

The 21st model was actually the very first that I ran in this series. It included the measure for social globalization, and the SPSS output showed very high collinearity (two VIF values above 10, and the corresponding tolerance levels very close to zero). Subsequently, I dropped social globalization from the models studied, and this relieved the collinearity problem.

Table 5.17 reports on the explanatory strength of the models, while Table 5.18 reviews the impact of the predictors. Again, I would like to

Table 5.17 Strength of the Models Explaining Conflict

Dependent Variable	*Included grievance predictor*	*Adjusted R^2*	*Cox & Snell R^2*	*Nagel-kerke R^2*	*Predicted %*	*Number of cases*
2005 only						
Any conflict	Any grievance		0.296	0.468	84.4	620
	Economic gr.		0.185	0.292	83.4	620
	Cultural gr.		0.131	0.207	82.4	618
	Political gr.		0.282	0.445	86.3	619
CONIS intensity	Any grievance	0.278				620
	Economic gr.	0.200				620
	Cultural gr.	0.123				618
	Political gr.	0.336				619
Intensity index	Any grievance	0.292				620
	Economic gr.	0.213				620
	Cultural gr.	0.135				618
	Political gr.	0.358				619
All years available						
Any conflict	Any grievance		0.296	0.468	83.5	3105
	Economic gr.		0.181	0.287	83.4	1860
	Cultural gr.		0.128	0.202	82.1	1856
	Political gr.		0.287	0.453	86.3	1856
CONIS intensity	Any grievance	0.281				3105
	Economic gr.	0.212				1860
	Cultural gr.	0.133				1856
	Political gr.	0.353				1856
Intensity index	Any grievance	0.303				3105
	Economic gr.	0.224				1860
	Cultural gr.	0.144				1856
	Political gr.	0.374				1856

emphasize the relative stability—or robustness—of the findings. The variations of the model strength are the same in the two halves of the table, and they make good sense. Political grievance, for instance, is a stronger predictor of conflict, than cultural grievance. The sign of the significant coefficients is also stable across the board.

The explanatory power of the OLS models, as expressed by the adjusted R^2-s, varies from 12.3 percent to 37.4 percent of variation explained. The very generous Nagelkerke Pseudo-R-squared measure indicates even higher explanatory power of the binary model (up to 46.8 percent), but if we take the average of the two Pseudo-R-squared measures, the explanatory potential of the binary model is at parity with that of the OLS models. Table 5.18 details the contribution of the individual predictors to this performance. Yet, Table 5.17 has already revealed the power of some grievance indicators. Models with the political grievance indicator may be 20 points stronger than models with the cultural grievance indicator, which tells us

Table 5.18 Significance and Sign of the Predictors in the 24 (Plus 20) Models Studied

Theoretical concept	*Instrumentalized concept*	*% significant (2005)*	*% significant (all years)*	*Sign*	*Reading of the sign*
Grievance level	Any grievance (6 models)	100.00	100.00	Positive	more grievance, more conflict
	Economic grievance (6)	100.00	100.00	Positive	more grievance, more conflict
	Cultural grievance (6)	100.00	100.00	Positive	more grievance, more conflict
	Political grievance (6)	100.00	100.00	Positive	more grievance, more conflict
Opportunity for insurrection (rebellion)	WGI Government effectiveness	8.30	66.70	Positive	anomalous
	Rural population	100.00	100.00	Positive	less urbanized, more conflict
	Unemployed young males (20 models)	0.00	0.00		
Opportunity for peaceful political action	Political terror scale	100.00	100.00	Positive	less democracy, more conflict
	Electoral family	0.00	0.00		
	Minority autonomy proxy (decentr*commnl_s_div)	58.30	100.00	Negative	more autonomy, less conflict
Country-level controls	Life expectancy (female)	0.00	100.00	Positive	anomalous
	Economic globalization	0.00	16.67	Positive	economic globalization increases conflict
	Political globalization	0.00	8.30	Negative	political globalization reduces conflict
	Proportion of plurality	16.67	66.70	Negative	larger plurality, less conflict
	Ethnic fractionalization	0.00	66.70	Negative	more fractionalization, less conflict
	Religious fractionalization	0.00	91.67	Negative	more fractionalization, less conflict
Group-level controls	Group proportion	0.00	0.00		
	Reg. concentration proxy (communal_sub_divisions)	100.00	100.00	Positive	more concentration, more conflict

Note: The table gives the percentage of coefficients that turned up as significant above $\alpha = 0.05$ level. The number of models run with each predictor, when not marked otherwise (in parentheses), is 24.

that political grievance, on its own, explains more than 20 percent of the variation of conflict measures. Other three predictors, which never failed to turn up as significant in these models, were the percentage of rural population, the group's regional concentration, and democracy. Table 5.18 shows convincing support for the belief in the political institutions' power to avert violent conflicts. Two of the three institutional variables considered have performed as theoretically expected.[21] The terror scale measure did not falter at all, while the measure for minority regional autonomy was a little better than the table suggests. This latter is listed in the table with a 58.3 percent performance for the 2005 set of models, but actually there were, besides the seven models in which it scored p-values below 0.05, four other models in which its p-value was between 0.05 and 0.1. Further, it manages to emerge with negative sign despite the ubiquitous significant and strong positive impact of the group concentration measure, with the help of which it was constructed.

There is relatively less support for the impact of the opportunity for insurrection variables in these models. The only strong predictor is the proportion of rural population. The measure for the proportion of unemployed young males has failed to emerge as significant in the separate models I ran with it, which may be due to the poor quality of the data. Most disturbingly, though, the government effectiveness indicator reaches significance, when it reaches, with the wrong sign. Since in bivariate relations both the government effectiveness and the life expectancy indicators are negatively correlated with violent conflict, it may be the case that there are the strong rural population and terror-scale measures pushing the government effectiveness and life expectancy variables to turn up with the opposite sign. Though the model diagnostics do not show dangerous collinearity effects, the four development-related variables are strongly associated among them. Their correlation matrix contains values between 0.343 and 0.625, as measured across more than 3100 cases.

The controls, with the sole exception of the development indicator life expectancy, show up as theoretically expected, when they do. The curvilinear relationship between fractionalization and conflict is captured by the fact that both a larger plurality and more fractionalization may mitigate the likelihood of violent conflict.

Yet, we may not be perfectly happy with the overall performance of the country-level variables used in these models. The models in the first section of this analysis suggested that the countries, when they are introduced as a single factor (replacing 154 dummies), may explain some 40 percent of the variation in intergroup hostility levels. Grievances may add another 25 percent to this, which means that these models with R-squared values below 0.4 fail to capture most of the cross-country variation.

"Omnibus" Explanations of Conflict

In this final section of the regression analysis, I build models that explain violent communal conflict while bypassing the grievance indicators, that is, I connect the violent outcome directly with the factors that affect intergroup behavior. Regarded from the point of view of the models in section 3, this means to replace grievances with their causes, such as economic and political inequality, and past violent episodes. There have been, unfortunately, a few issues with this project.

First, the control variables selected for accounting for the specific country effects, such as development level, and fractionalization, do not seem to do a good job, they capture very little of the variation explainable with the country context. Other relevant country features may be needed to increase the explanatory potential, such as the vertical economic inequality, exposure to immigration, membership in regional integrations, and so on. The price of inclusion of any new variable is, however, increased risk of collinearity and odd behavior of the weakly significant predictors.

Second, there are some conceptually distinct factors that we cannot measure with empirically distinct indicators. Intergroup political equality means that minorities are fairly and proportionally represented in the political institutions of the country, this is what EPR's power status ordinal variable (Power_rank) intends to measure. Yet, on country level, we measure intergroup political equality with the institutional *opportunities* for minorities to reach fair representation, and these institutions are identical with those that may divert communal groups from violent ways of action, and make them to pursue peaceful ways of politicizing. Democracy, proportional representation electoral system, as well as various power-sharing arrangements, are both determinants of political grievance and frameworks that shape communal action once the grievances have been formulated. I hoped that it would not be redundant to include in the models both the power rank indicator and the institutional variables, but actually, they ostensibly reduced each other's measurable impact.

Third, we have already known that models that conceptualize the groups as nested in their countries outperform simple additive models in explanatory power. On the flipside, the inclusion of a large number of interaction terms to model the relationship between group-level and country-level variables, leads to technically less perfect models, increases the risks of nonnormal residuals, collinearity, and heteroskedasticity. There is an unavoidable trade-off between loss of explanatory power and loss of technical validity. And occasionally the difference between group-level and country-level analysis may cut deeper. In my datasets, the vertical inequality measure Gini index, a country-level indicator, is positively correlated with country-level measurements of violent conflict. Yet, when it is correlated with the group-level violence indicators, across the 639 historical minorities, it leads to a significant negative coefficient of about –0.1, as if higher Gini reduced conflict proneness. If we select only one group from each country (such as the plurality group), all association between the Gini and the group-level conflict indicators is gone, the coefficients are insignificant. That is, the relationship between a country-level indicator and the group-level indicators is sensitive to the distribution of groups across countries, which is not completely random from the perspective of a number of important variables, such as development levels. There are more and larger historical minority groups in less developed, less democratic, less well governed countries. Vertical inequality is believed to be curvilinearly associated with development: increases at the beginning of modernization, and decreases at the highest levels of postindustrial and democratic development. Communal violence occurs mainly in the least developed settings, where the number of groups is also high. That is, additive models involve the assumption of isomorphism between levels of analysis, such as the creed that the correlation between $X_{\text{group-level}}$ & $Y_{\text{group-level}}$ is the same as between $X_{\text{country-level}}$ & $Y_{\text{country-level}}$—and this is not always the case.

Taking into consideration the possibility of using alternative measurements for a number of predictors, as well, the model fitting in this step is doomed to be a trial and error procedure. I might rely, however, on a few lessons from the previous sections, for instance, to avoid using all three globalization indicators in the same model. Models containing the measurement of unemployed young males have also had to be run separately. And I left some of the trial-and-error work on the software. The variables considered to be included in the models are summarized in Table 5.19 (Checklist 3).

I ran two additive models with each of the three conflict variables, the Any_conflict, Conis_intensity, and Intensity_index measures, as dependent variables. The basic models contained 16 predictors, while the second model in each category included the unemployed young male measure as the 17th predictor. Models with 16 predictors had 1848 cases (for the interval 2003–2005), while the models with 17 predictors had 383 cases only.

Table 5.20 reports the explanatory power of the three basic omnibus models, with 16 predictors.

As in the case of a model with 16 predictors, we may wonder whether they are all needed for good results, I asked the SPSS software to perform a backward elimination of the redundant explanatory variables. In the OLS models, the increase of the adjusted R-squared values was only 1–2 points even after the elimination of five predictors, while the nonadjusted R-squared kept decreasing. In the binary model, the 2 Log Likelihood value started to increase right after the first elimination. These outcomes suggest that there

Table 5.19 Checklist 3. Independent Variables Explaining Inter-Group Violence

Theoretical concept	*Operationalized concept*	*Instrumentalized concept*	
Grievance level's determinants	Violent past	Past violence	
	Intergroup economic inequality	Ineq_3	Ineq_4
	Intergroup political inequality	EPR Power status rank	Ethnic group in power
	Assimilationism, cultural restrictions		
	Informal discrimination & hate crime		
Opportunity for insurrection (rebellion)	Government effectiveness	WGI Govt Effectiveness	
	Rural settlements	Rural population	
	Unemployed young males	Unemployed young males	
	Foreign military aid to group		
Opportunity for peaceful political action	Democracy	Political terror scale	Freedom House/iPolity
	Inclusive democracy	Electoral family	Proportional system
	Minority territorial autonomy	Decentralization idx* Cmmnal_s_divisions	
	Minority functional autonomy		
Group-level controls	Group proportion	Group proportion	
	Group concentration	Cmmunal_s_divisions	
	Foreign aid to group		
	Group organization potential		
Country-level controls	Development level	Life expectancy (female)	GDP/capita (PPP)
	Country international embeddedness		Globalization index
		Economic globalization	Social globalization
		Political globalization	
	Plurality proportion and/or minority proportion	Proportion of plurality	
	Communal fractionalization	Ethnic fractionalization	Linguistic fractionaliz.n
		Religious fractionaliz.n	

Table 5.20 The Explanatory Power of the Main "Omnibus" Models

Dependent variable	*Model type*	*Adjusted R-squared*
Intensity_index (with logarithmic transformation)	OLS	0.245
Conis_intensity (with logarithmic transformation)	OLS	0.198
Any_conflict	Binary	About 0.200
Cox and Snell Pseudo R-squared = 0.160		
Nagelkerke Pseudo R-squared = 0.255		

are no strong reasons for eliminating any of the predictors that were included in the models on theoretical grounds, even if some of them fail to turn up as statistically significant in these models. The intergroup economic inequality variable Ineq_3_ln was kept in both OLS models all along the elimination procedure, up to the eighth step, where the software stopped because of the sharply declining model parameters. In the binary logistic model, Ineq_3_ln was eliminated in the second step. Its absence increased the –2 Log Likelihood by one point, and reduced the Nagelkerke Pseudo-R-squared by one point, thus we cannot claim that its elimination improved the model.

A further modeling issue to address is the additive versus nested combination of the predictors. Since in these models the country effects are represented by the 8 country-level variables, in a nested model the impact of the group-level variables can be mimicked with 32 (8*4 group-level variables) interaction terms. Practically, though, unfortunately, a regression model with 40 closely related predictors does not allow for an accurate and fair test of the contribution of the variables.[22]

Tables 5.21 and 5.22 contain three models each. The first is a simple OLS regression, with the advantage of revealing the explanatory power as adjusted R-squared statistics, and we also have some standardized coefficients (Beta-s) to compare the impact of the predictors. The second model is the same regression performed in the GENLIN procedure, which uses maximum likelihood estimation, and gives Wald statistics instead of t-statistics, but calculates the significance of the predictors within two thousandth difference for the 2*16 predictors. We do not get, unfortunately, Pseudo-R^2-s from this procedure, the model is described with the Log Likelihood and Likelihood Ratio Chi-2 statistics.

The third model reported in the tables is a nested model with interaction terms. Yet, instead of interacting the group level variables with the country-level variables, I interacted them with the countries themselves, at least the three group level variables of main interest. These interaction terms are at the bottom of Tables 5.21 and 5.22.

This change has dramatically improved the model strength statistics. The Log Likelihood values shrank to less than half, while the Likelihood Ratio Chi-squared statistics more than tripled. The nested model has obviously

Table 5.21 Explaining Violent Conflict, as Measured by the Intensity Index Variable

DV: Intensity index (w/ logarithmic transformation)	**OLS additive model**		**GENLIN additive model**		**GENLIN nested model**	
Number of cases	1848		1848		1848	
Adjusted R-squared	0.245					
Log Likelihood			-1551.4		-723.5	
Likelihood Ratio Chi-squared			535.4		2191.2	
	St. coeff.	Sig	Wald Chi^2	Sig.	Wald Chi^2	Sig.
Horizontal economic inequality (Ineq_3_ln)	.052	.015	6.0	.014		
EPR power status (Power_rank)	.015	.512	0.4	.510		
Past violence	.381	.000	330.2	.000		
Group proportion	.034	.139	2.2	.137	7.4	.006
Ethnic fractionalization	-.015	.709	0.1	.708	0.8	.365
Religious fractionalization	-.046	.058	3.6	.056	4.3	.038
Proportion of plurality	.014	.727	0.1	.726	7.4	.006
Regional concentration proxy	.230	.000	32.3	.000	4.8	.029
Life expectancy (female)	.231	.000	34.9	.000	1.9	.172
Economic globalization	.078	.136	2.2	.134	1.3	.250
Political globalization	.078	.005	7.9	.005	4.2	.040
Political terror scale	.181	.000	39.1	.000	0.0	.974
Electoral family	-.007	.773	0.1	.772	0.3	.584
Minority autonomy proxy	-.270	.000	35.7	.000	4.2	.040
WGI government effectiveness	.038	.392	0.7	.390	1.2	.281
Rural population	.156	.000	24.1	.000	7.0	.008
Ineq_3_ln*Country factor					517.1	.000
Power_rank*Country factor					587.5	.000
Past_violence* Country factor					1095.5	.000

Trellis pattern shows significance above alpha = 0.05; vertical lines show significance between alpha = 0.05 and 0.1.

much higher explanatory power than the additive model, but, unfortunately, we lack the algorithms to express its strength in simple terms such as percentage of variance explained.[23] Undeniably, most of the improvement comes from the incorporation of the country variation itself in the models; but the results also strengthen the belief that the three group-level variables included in the interaction terms (horizontal economic and political inequality, and past violence), are significant predictors of violent conflict.

For the binary ordinal model explaining Any_conflict, no nested GENLIN version could be executed. It was also the model that allowed for the smallest number of predictors to turn up as significant. What was significant in this model, has been significant in the above OLS models, as well, with only one exception. The proportion of plurality scored a significant p-value (0.022) in this model, which did not happen in the OLS models, as it was only in the nested models that the proportion of plurality reached significance again.

Table 5.22 Explaining Violent Conflict, as Measured by the CONIS Intensity Variable

DV: Intensity index (w/ logarithmic transformation)	OLS additive model		GENLIN additive model		GENLIN nested model	
Number of cases	1848		1848		1848	
Adjusted R-squared	0.198					
Log Likelihood			-1179.1		-364.9	
Likelihood Ratio Chi-squared			424.9		2053.2	
	St. coeff.	Sig	Wald Chi^2	Sig.	Wald Chi^2	Sig.
Horizontal economic inequality (Ineq_3_ln)	.041	.061	3.6	.059		
EPR power status (Power_rank)	.019	.445	0.6	.443		
Past violence	.330	.000	233.0	.000		
Group proportion	.043	.067	3.4	.066	8.1	.004
Ethnic fractionalization	-.031	.449	0.6	.447	0.9	.332
Religious fractionalization	-.050	.047	4.0	.046	4.1	.042
Proportion of plurality	.000	.995	0.0	.995	10.2	.001
Regional concentration proxy	.197	.000	22.3	.000	3.1	.077
Life expectancy (female)	.219	.000	29.7	.000	1.3	.263
Economic globalization	.109	.041	4.2	.040	1.9	.172
Political globalization	.082	.004	8.3	.004	4.9	.026
Political terror scale	.189	.000	40.1	.000	0.0	.917
Electoral family	-.010	.690	0.2	.689	0.2	.634
Minority autonomy proxy	-.237	.000	25.9	.000	2.4	.124
WGI goverment effectiveness	.007	.875	0.0	.875	1.4	.243
Rural population	.158	.000	23.4	.000	5.7	.017
Ineq_3_ln*Country factor					566.2	.000
Power_rank*Country factor					695.8	.000
Past_violence* Country factor					833.0	.000

Note: The country variable in itself cannot be included in models (as a "main effect"), because in its presence the software refuses to calculate values for a number of country-level variables.

Trellis pattern shows significance above alpha = 0.05; vertical lines show significance between alpha = 0.05 and 0.1.

Finally, I would like to report on the results from the models in which the measurement of the proportion of unemployed young males has also been included. For all five dependent variables, the case number shrank to 391 with the addition of this variable. It tended to be significant, and to persist during the backward elimination procedures.

DISCUSSION AND CONCLUSIONS

The size and proportion of the minority populations worldwide sanction extraordinary interest in the intergroup relations. While the main phenomena to learn about and to avert are violent conflicts, we are little likely to get a good grip on these without a deeper understanding of the dynamics of intergroup hostility, a process subject to a number of influences and their idiosyncratic structuration. Data here have extensively supported that the explanation of intergroup hostility is multicausal and complex, one salient aspect of the complexity being the interplay between the group level and the country level.

With a possible bias toward the importance of my subject, I would complain about the profession's neglecting to elaborate a series of measurements that could profitably be used for the explanation of conflict in cross-national analysis. It is not only the intergroup economic inequality measure which has been missing from our toolkit. We need measurements of functional autonomy, and better, all-inclusive and detailed measurements of the minority territorial autonomy, of the regional concentration of communal groups, and some other features that have been addressed by MAR, but effectively measured for only 282 groups.

These two circumstances are the main excuses for the first statement that I have to make with regard to the results obtained in this chapter. The explanatory power of the regression models is not too high. It seems that the country factor (state name) explains some 40 percent of the overall variation of the grievance and conflict measures. The theory-driven selection of a set of group-level and country-level predictors led to models that explain about 20 percent of the variation of grievance—less of the cultural grievance, and more of the political grievance. The occurrence and intensity of violent conflict can be explained with the selected group-level and country-level predictors in the range of 12.3–37.4 percent, depending on which grievance indicator is used. Political grievance, on its own, explains more than 25 percent of the variation of violent conflict. By tracing direct links from the causes of grievance to the occurrence of violence, as in the "omnibus" models, we can explain 25 percent of the variation of conflict intensity, when we rely on additive models. Nested models increase the amount of variation explained, but we do not have the tools to plausibly estimate the magnitude of the improvement.

The second observation refers to the consistency of the results. All types of regression models in all four sections of the regression analysis were tested with several versions, and either there were not significant differences, or they made good sense, such as the relative weakness of the models containing cultural grievance as a predictor as compared to models containing political grievance. Further, there were relatively few predictors that reached significance with the theoretically unexpected sign, and this has always been related to the modernization cluster.[24] In models with large numbers of associated predictors, which explain multicausal phenomena subject to several weak influences, it is not uncommon that weaker predictors turn up with the wrong sign as a result of their correlation with a stronger predictor, which manages to keep its expected sign. All together, the models managed to tell a convincing story about the process-like unfolding of intergroup hostility through grievances to violence, in which most predictors promoted in the literature found their place.

Third, I would like to comment on the performance of the individual predictors in these models, starting with my main explanatory variable. This predictor, the intergroup economic inequality measure showed a consistent and persistent, even if not very strong impact on the dependent variables. The basic version of the variable, Ineq_3 has never failed to turn up as significant above alpha = 0.05 level in the explanation of the four grievance variables in the models without the country factor. In the presence of the country factor, the economic inequality measure has been significant above alpha = 0.05 in models explaining political grievance, and also in models explaining conflict as measured with the Intensity index variable.

In the omnibus models, faced with the strong competition from 15–16 rival predictors, horizontal inequality emerged as significant above alpha = 0.05 level in the explanation of the most complex conflict intensity indicator. It scored a little less-convincing p-value of 0.06 in the explanation of the other conflict intensity measure, Conis_intensity. The only additive conflict model in which the economic inequality measure failed to reach a conventional level of significance, was the binary logistic model explaining Any_conflict—but even this model can be shown to be a little stronger when the Ineq_3 variable is included among the predictors. Since the performance of the economic inequality variable varies across the models with the three conflict measures, we may wonder which of the three conflict measures is the most adequate measurement of high level intergroup animosity. As a matter of fact, the correlation matrix of these three variables with the MAR conflict measures shows that the Intensity index is the strongest associated with the MAR rebellion indicator, at a correlation coefficient of 0.599, a reason to give primacy to the results suggested by this.[25] What I hoped to measure with the EPR_MAR_EXT violent conflict measures, was the type of conflict classified by MAR as rebellion.

Of the group structure/group relations cluster of variables, the measure for past violence has had the strongest impact, both in the explanation of grievances and in the explanation of violence. It virtually never failed to turn up as significant, always with positive sign. Next, the group proportion variable has proven its significance in most models, also keeping its positive sign. The hypothesis of a curvilinear relationship between fractionalization and intergroup conflict has received support through a combination of weak negative impact of the fractionalization indicators and some positive impact of the measure expressing the proportion of the plurality group in the country. My proxy variable for the regional concentration of the groups has also emerged as significant in a number of models, always with a positive sign.

Of the institutional variables affecting the choice between peaceful and violent ways, on the one hand, but presumably the grievance levels themselves, as well, the democracy indicator political terror scale, coded toward increasing terror levels, has shown significant positive impact in each additive model. The measure of minority territorial autonomy has had almost the same stable and good performance. It was only the variable for the proportional representation electoral system that kept failing to reach significance. Yet the institutional variables in my models had to cope with two kinds of competitor predictors. In the omnibus models I have used the Power_rank measure borrowed from the EPR dataset in parallel with the above three institutional measures (democracy, autonomy, PR system). While the institutions create the opportunity for minorities to climb the power ladder, Power_rank measures the extent to which this has been realized. Other serious competitors of the institutional measures have been those related to the developmental-modernization complex, such as female life expectancy, rural population, government effectiveness, and the globalization indicators. Because of different reasons, partly, to control for the opportunity-for-insurrection hypothesis, and partly, to control for the impact of the international environment, I included all these highly correlated variables in my models, and this resulted in some predictors reaching significance with a confusing sign. I think that the problem can be addressed by creating subsets along the development variable, but this group-level focused dataset is not the most suitable for clarifying the relationships among institutional and developmental variables measured on country level. Chapter 7, which explores a country-level dataset, elaborates more on the impact of the development level and its correlates.

Of the predictors belonging to the opportunity-for-insurrection complex, the measure for the rural population has always emerged as significant, always with the right sign. Actually, its strength may be the cause of the failure of the other opportunity measure. The proportion of rural population, conceptualized as a topic-specific modernization indicator, has substantially contributed to the trouble experienced with this cluster of variables. Unfortunately, the government effectiveness indicator also belongs to this cluster—and subsequently, it has very often become insignificant in my models, and also happened to turn up with the wrong sign. The special smaller-N models including the unemployed young male measure showed the little paradox picture that this measure has never emerged as significant when a grievance indicator was in the model, but tended to be significant in the omnibus models without grievance measures. Since there are no significant correlation coefficients between the unemployed young male measure and the grievance indicators, except for a unique, low but significant $r = 0.092$ with the Any_grievance, the answer seems to involve a more complicated relationship of the unemployment measure with the modernization and institutional complex.

Finally, I would like to highlight the ontological implication of some findings. In some regressions presented here, a number of variables defined at group level showed that their impact may be measured even in the presence of the country factor, and/or in the presence of potent country-level indicators. That is, communal groups exist, and they are causally consequential for their sub-, supra-, and national environments. Yet, the group features whose impact has been considered here and found to persist beyond the country variation, are relational attributes, such as the group proportion, economic and political inequality, and past intergroup hostility.

In this chapter, I have tried to capture the interplay between the group-level and country-level phenomena, but I have often run into technical hurdles. In the next chapters, I will try to correct for two main issues with the above-presented analysis. I have not had good measures for the group concentration, for foreign aid to the group, neither for the organization potential of the groups. In Chapter 6, relying on the MAR dataset, I will try to address the impact of these. And on the other hand, as already mentioned, I will try to sort out the issues around the modernization cluster with the help of a country-level dataset. Checking on this, however, is not the only reason for involving new datasets and new analyses. My motivation to proceed with a country-level analysis is mainly rooted in the recognition that group-level and country-level results may be divergent, as they are in the case of the correlation between the Gini index and conflict. And we may not be sure that we have really captured the big picture without comparing the results and explaining the discrepancies, where they are.

NOTES

1. Their names are Daur, Dongxiang, Gelo, Kirgiz, Lahu, Lisu, Maonan, Mulao, Naxi, Quiang, Salar, Sha, Shui, Tu, Wa, and Xibe. They are part of the EPR data, typically have regional autonomy, and none of them is included in MAR.

2. At an even closer look, some of the noncitizen groups struggle to obtain the citizenship of their new country, such as the Turks in Germany, while others aim at getting certain citizenship rights extended onto lawful residents, such as the European Union expatriates in Spain, for instance.

3. Actually this group includes three numeric pluralities, as well, out of which, though, two are noncitizen groups (foreigners in Qatar and UAE), and one is a new minority (Palestinians in Jordan).

4. The countries of the European Union and the Commonwealth of Independent States (CIS) are accounted here one by one, without reference to the European Union or CIS. The possibility of supranationalism, however, adds one more dimension to the argument that nation-states are obsolete (or obsolescent).

5. Most really big pluralities take the value 3, this is how the WQ index and my INEQ_1 indicator were defined.

6. The low frequency of violent episodes had to be addressed with transforming the variables before use in regression models, and I produced the logarithmic transformations of two conflict variables (Conis_intensity, Intensity_index). Some economic inequality measures needed similar transformation.

7. The developmental groups for these tests were defined with reference to the female life expectancy variable, the threshold being at 75 years.

8. I have used simple Pearson correlation coefficients, rather than bivariate regression coefficients. Their sign and significance are the same, yet the correlations are much easier to handle.

9. The correlation matrices were limited to year 2005, and all Pearson correlation coefficients reported are above the alpha = 0.05 significance level. Because of the importance of the developmental level, the tables contain references to how certain relationships show up in the file split along the developmental dummy "Female life expectancy above 75 years."

10. The development trend is the same for "simple" poverty (as measured by INEQ_1) and horizontal inequality (as measured by INEQ_2, 3, and 4). In developed countries, the association between group poverty and grievances, mainly economic grievances, gets stronger, while the association between group poverty and violent conflict disappears, suggesting that in the developed world violence is not a means to address or redress group economic disadvantages. Similarly, the association between the inequality measures with the grievance indicators is stronger in the developed countries, while their association with conflict weakens and disappears in the developed group.

11. The highest correlation coefficient in these series is $r = 0.367$, between INEQ_5 and economic grievance, in the developed country group (containing 282 cases). In terms of explanatory power, this means an R^2 of 0.135, that is, 13.5 percent of the variation explained.

12. As repeatedly shown by Cederman and coauthors, groups included in power are more likely to be contented and peaceful. Table 5.9 displays EPR's power rank indicator only, but the correlations with the "ethnic group in power" (EGIP) variable are very similar. Unfortunately, both are strongly correlated with my economic inequality indicators, with coefficients exceeding 0.3, mainly in the case of minorities.

13. More exactly, since it is formulated at country level, it approximates an aggregative measure expressing the average or typical concentration of all groups in a country, which otherwise might be measured as a weighted mean. The regional concentration of communal groups has always been considered a factor that increases the opportunity of minorities to organize politically, but at the same time, it is very likely to breed requests for territorial autonomy, thus political grievances, as well.

14. The opposite logic of behavior is attested by other correlation coefficients between the country's group structure and the hostility variables. When significant, these statistics carry different signs for minorities and pluralities. In the case of all three types of fractionalization, growing values are associated with less grievance and less conflict from the part of the minorities, and with more grievance and more conflict from the part of the pluralities.

15. For instance, the first generation of Hispanics tends to come to the United States with relatively random political preferences, quasi-evenly shared between rightist and leftist views. It is in the second and third immigrant generations that the better known 66:33 asymmetrical political support pattern emerges, which nears the US Blacks' 90:10 distribution on behalf of the Left.

16. For the first, I have had overlapping values for two years (2004, 2005), while for the latter two, values are available for 2003, 2004, and 2005.

17. The *p*-values measure the probability of the null hypothesis that the featured impact does not exist in the real population. Thus a *p*-value below 0.05 means a regression coefficient significant above the alpha = 0.05 level, which is the most often reported significance level.

18. There is a known problem with calculating the goodness-of-fit indicators when the model contains covariates, rather than factors. SPSS gives two goodness-of-fit indicators, the Pearson Chi-squared, which is very low in all my ordinal models, and occasionally sinks below the acceptable threshold of 0.05, and the Deviance, which is reassuringly high in all models, more often reaching the maximum value of 1 than not. (In the case of my reported models, it is 1).

19. I think this is an honest pursuit, as here we face issues of overdetermination, rather than spurious relationships. For instance, development level and the size of the plurality group are not in causal relationship with each other, but they ostensibly co-vary, and both seem to have an impact on grievance levels, seemingly independently from each other. Yet, the truth of "both have an impact" comes through in regression models only after both variables pay some toll for their covariance.

20. There are a few operationalized concepts for which we do not have good cross-national measurements at all. This is the case of the minority functional autonomy (also called "pillarization"), and the foreign aid to communal groups. Further, the variable for the proportion of unemployed young males does not cover all cases, and the quality of these data is also challengeable.

21. Even a third, the electoral family variable happened to turn up as significant in some of the reduced-case-number models containing the young male unemployed indicator.

22. The covariance of the explanatory variables may push some predictors below significance level even if the impact of these latter is real in the sense that their presence is enough to objectively affect the dependent variables. As already mentioned, in the case of development level and proportion of plurality group there is clear overdetermination.

23. We may speculate that if the Log Likelihood value of –1551.4 is equal with an Adjusted R-squared of 0.245, then a Log Likelihood value of –723.5 approximates an Adjusted R-squared of 0.525, but I have no knowledge of any statistical theory addressing the issue of such inferences.

24. In my models I had several measurements of development, as I could not spare including in the models indicators for development itself, rural population, globalization, and government effectiveness; all of which are further related to the democracy and other variables, as well.

25. The correlations of MAR's rebellion with the other two measures are lower, as reported in Chapter 6 in detail. This gives a very serious edge to Intensity index above the other two measures. Yet, the other two are also plausible indicators, and even if they seem to be less affected by my INEQ variable, we may be more confident about a finding when it is supported by parallel measurements.

Chapter 6

Analyses Based on MAR_EPR_MI Data*

SIMILAR AND YET SO DIFFERENT: THE NEED FOR MAR_EPR_MI

The EPR_MAR_EXT dataset, presented in Chapter 4 and analyzed in Chapter 5, includes the full Minorities at Risk (MAR) dataset, or more exactly, its last version pertinent to years 2004–2006. However, the MAR variables could not fully be included in the analyses run in Chapter 5, because of the authors' particular sampling method. MAR does not cover all minority groups of the world, and has not targeted to select a random, representative sample of it. The criteria for inclusion in MAR have been, on the one hand, size-related, and on the other, related to the status of the minorities in their country. It is this second feature that has been reproached as MAR's "selection bias." By neglecting minority groups that either get on well with their majorities, or are too weak to formulate complaints, MAR prevents inquiries into constellations and factors within which minorities can successfully be integrated in their countries. MAR contains an impressive number of 282 communal groups, but the number of minority groups worldwide, even applying the size limits imposed by MAR,[1] is much higher. EPR_MAR_EXT identified 860 groups, out of which 153 are pluralities. I use the term *plurality* for the largest communal group in each country, and *majority* (or *real majority*) for groups larger than 50 percent of their country's population. Smaller plurality groups are less likely to have a safe grip on state power, as a coalition of two other groups may easily render them a minority population.

*A previous version of this chapter has been published in *The International Journal of Diversity in Organizations, Communities and Nations*. Annual Review, Vol. 13, pp. 1–21.

MAR covers roughly 40 percent of all minority groups. Yet, if we distinguish between types of minorities, such as noncitizen versus citizen, historical versus new immigrant, and secessionist versus nonseceded, the number of MAR groups in these subsets may not be enough for conclusive tests.

Chapter 5 made use of MAR data by exploiting its selection bias. The groups not included in MAR were coded, by default, with a small number of exceptions, as NOT having grievances. This chapter would like to benefit from the information contained in MAR about two features which have not adequately been addressed in Chapter 5, and for the study of which we lack country-level variables, as well. Both are pertinent to the ability of communal groups to successfully organize and carry out collective action. One is the geographical concentration of the groups, which facilitates their organization, and the other is the external support to them, from kindred groups and state or nonstate foreign actors, which may alter their cost-benefit calculations when they make strategic decisions. Technically, Chapter 6 aims at explaining the same dependent variables as Chapter 5, by introducing a few new explanatory variables which supplant or complement less adequate measurements of group features and international impacts. With slightly changed measurements, the findings related to the impact of my main explanatory variable, the intergroup horizontal inequality, have an opportunity to show their robustness.[2] In addition, MAR has two variables that can be used as complementary dependent variables, with the great advantage that they distinguish between peaceful (*Protest*) and violent (*Rebellion*) political activism.

In order to bridge the difference between 282 MAR groups and approximately 700 minority groups worldwide, the dataset has had to be submitted to a multiple imputation procedure, carried out with the software Amelia II.[3] I strived to increase the adequacy of imputation by feeding into the software the maximally possible number of related variables, such as data about the group power status taken from the Ethnic Power Relations (EPR) dataset, conflict data from CONIS, and Alesina's fractionalization indexes. I have also included a large number of country-level indicators in order to make up for Amelia's blindness toward the fact that the groups are nested in their countries.

The multiple imputation method set some limits on what I could reasonably use of the wealth of variables in MAR. I dropped the idea to test the impact of various group markers, such as ethnicity, race, and language. The variation of these has no relationship with any known variable, thus any value assigned by Amelia could not be considered but as a random number. Fortunately, these group features have never been found to be significant predictors of intergroup relations. It would be helpful to control for them, but we may be confident enough that they do not covary with either hostility or violence.

Similarly, predictions about group cohesion, as a determinant of the group's strength of organization for collective action, could not receive really adequate testing here. Older versions of MAR had a variable to directly measure group cohesion. The 2004–2006 version is restricted to a variable indicating the presence of violent intracommunal conflict, which is a relatively rare phenomenon, occurring in 14 percent of the cases (i.e., in 40 cases out of 282). Since this feature is quite unpredictable from the variables that we have, I gave up considering it in my analyses.

This chapter continues with the presentation of the dataset MAR_EPR_MI, followed by a section of bivariate analysis. Afterward, the basic explanatory models will be run on both the original dataset and the datasets obtained with multiple imputation.

PREPARING EPR_MAR_EXT FOR ANALYSES FOCUSED ON MAR

The large EPR_MAR_EXT dataset had to be reduced and concentrated in order to be successfully submitted to multiple imputation. Actually, I applied truncating in three dimensions: (i) reduced the number of variables, (ii) shrank the number of cases, and (iii) cut back on the number of years. The final version of the dataset for the analyses in the chapter has been named MAR_EPR_MI, where MI refers to the method of multiple imputation.

(i) As for the variable reduction process, MAR itself was cut back to 13 variables, out of which four synthetized information from several original MAR variables, and two were obtained by recoding a complex variable. External support from all three sources listed by MAR separately (kindred groups, states, and nonstate actors), were added as "External_support," and their military support as "External_military_support." Three dummies referring to whether the group is represented in the executive and the legislative of the country have been collapsed in one measure of group representation, and two types of cultural restrictions (on religion and on language) have been collapsed into a "Cultural Restrictions" variable. MAR's original "Group organization for political action" (GOJPA) measure either cannot be used as an ordinal variable, or it suggests that peaceful umbrella and party organizations are doomed to grow into military organization. I created two ordinal measures out of it, one capturing the group's organization toward peaceful political action, and the other capturing its organization toward violent political action, as summarized in Table 6.1.

Further, although collapsing information from several variables is my preferred method to reduce the number of variables, I refrained from applying this in case of two seemingly closely related measures, "Group concentration" and "Proportion of group members in regional base," which showed some inconsistency in 37 instances, in the sense that highly concentrated groups were coded as not having a regional base. Thus these two indicators are to be tested separately in models.[4]

Table 6.1 Recoding MAR's Group Organization for Political Action (GOJPA) Variable

MAR codebook's description of values	*GOJPA*	*GO_Party*	*GO_Milit*
No political movements or organizations represent group interests	0	0	0
Group interests promoted by umbrella organizations	1	1	0
Group interests promoted by conventional political parties or movements	2	2	0
Group interests promoted mainly by conventional movements or parties, but also by militant organizations with limited support	3	0	1
Group interests promoted mainly by militant organizations, but also by some conventional organizations	4	0	2
Group interests promoted only by militant organizations	5	0	3

Besides the MAR variables, all seven group-level conflict variables used in Chapter 5 have been integrated into MAR_EPR_MI, along with the group political inequality measure from EPR (Power_rank), and four group economic inequality measures. Several country-level conflict variables were added, and selected measures of country economic development, democracy, decentralization, good governance, and vertical economic inequality. The final number of variables included in MAR_EPR_MI was 61.

(ii) Analyses in this chapter are confined to the study of minority groups, and pluralities have been excluded from the dataset. Yet, not all pluralities. I adopted the rule of eliminating only "real" majorities, that is, plurality groups above 50 percent of the population. I also think that a plurality is "real" plurality when this fact is reflected in its political position, that is, it has been included in power at least since the first year of my EPR_MAR_EXT dataset, 1999. (Nonincorporated groups relate to state as minorities, not as majorities.) This interpretation of the notion of plurality led to leaving in the sample six above-50 percent plurality groups, as specified in Table 6.2.[5]

I have also deleted 16 minority groups from China, all between 100,000 and 1,000,000 people. China has 55 minority ethnic groups, of which 34 have more than 100,000 members. EPR_MAR_EXT included all 34, plus the majority Hans. All minority groups are well documented in several aspects, but for the smallest ones is impossible to find data about their comparative economic standing. Politically, groups below 1 million don't have any significant presence in the national government, but are eligible for some regional autonomy. MAR_EPR_MI includes 18 minority groups from China, and I think that this number is sufficient to give adequate weight to the specificities of similar minorities (very small in comparison with their majorities, and suffering from historical neglect, rather than deliberate discrimination).[6]

(iii) Finally, of the 12 years between 1999 and 2010, featured in EPR_MAR_EXT, the shorter dataset preserved only eight. I deleted the years

Table 6.2 Plurality Groups above 50 percent of the Population Left in the MAR_EPR_MI Dataset

Country	*Group*	*Group proportion*	*EPR EGIP code**	*Group included in MAR*
Bolivia	Indigenous Highland Peoples	0.60	0	Yes
Burundi	Hutus	0.85	0/1 since 2002	Yes
Iraq	Shi'a Arabs	0.60	0/1 since 2003	Yes
Niger	Hausa	0.56	0/1 since 2000	No
Rwanda	Hutus	0.84	0	Yes
Syria	Sunni Arabs	0.54	0	No

*EGIP stands for "Ethnic group in power," a variable introduced by EPR, available for years up until 2005 (inclusively).

1999–2002, in order to spare effort to Amelia; and for the same reason, I have extended a few slowly changing variables onto 2008, 2009, and 2010. In the case of these, the best guess is constancy. The affected variables are the minority type, group proportion, intergroup economic inequality, and a few variables defined as referring to a certain time span.[7]

Since Amelia is recommended for cases when the missingness is random, it is very important to have an image of the extent and direction of biases inherent in MAR. We know that the authors selected, on purpose, minorities whose coexistence with their majorities has become problematic, thus from the perspective of my project, which aims to explain the rise of hostility and occurrence of violence between groups, this is a selection on the dependent variable. We know little if any, however, about to extent to which the explanatory variables are affected by the selection bias. Benefiting from the possibility of comparing the set of MAR groups with a reasonably complete set of all minority groups, I have run a few tests to get a hint about the characteristics of the selection bias. Technically, most tests were done by creating a "Group included in MAR" indicator variable, and checking on its correlations with a number of variables of interest.[8]

First of all, I checked on the extent to which different types of minorities are represented in MAR. As Table 6.3 shows, there are the noncitizens who are relatively neglected. Multiple pluralities are so rare—only four in EPR_MAR_EXT—that their number does not allow for any conclusion with regard to the representativity of MAR.

Above the threshold of 100,000 or 1 percent, inclusion in MAR is completely independent of the size of the group, and groups that represent a larger proportion of the population are only very slightly more likely to be included than small-proportion groups ($r = 0.092$). On the other hand, the groups tend to come from countries with larger pluralities. The association between the inclusion in MAR indicator and the proportion of the plurality group ($r = 0.151$) is paralleled by the positive association of the former with the development measure female life expectancy ($r = 0.105$), and weakly significant negative associations with ethnic and linguistic fractionalization. There is, thus, a slight tendency in MAR to select groups from more developed countries, but this cannot be substantiated with all development indicators. The association with GDP/cap, and with the percentage of rural population, for instance, is insignificant.

Further, I inquired about whether selection by MAR has seriously been associated with the political and economic inequality of the groups. Table 6.4 shows the findings. On the right side, the coefficients between my economic inequality variables and the "Selected in MAR" dummy indicate the presence of a weak association. The correlation coefficient between the EPR's power rank variable and presence in MAR is –0.066, with a p-value of 0.070 only. Thus, I included in Table 6.4 the whole crosstabulation of the power status

Table 6.3 Cross-Tabulation of Groups in MAR_EPR_MI and in MAR (2005)

	Groups in MAR_EPR_MI	*All groups*	*Groups included in MAR* Number	*Groups included in MAR* Percentage
Minority type	plurality below 50% of the population	55	21	38.2
	multiple plurality	4	1	25.0
	historical minority (incl. secessionist)	635	241	38.0
	new immigrant group	33	14	42.4
	noncitizen	35	5	14.3
Total		762	282	37.0

Table 6.4 Inclusion in MAR's Association with Political and Economic Inequality

Cross-tabulation of "Inclusion in MAR" and the group's power rank

	All groups	MAR groups #	MAR groups %
1. Discriminated	76	47	61.8
2. Powerless	247	75	30.4
3. Regional autonomy/ Irrelevant	198	73	36.9
4. Junior Partner	160	59	36.9
5. Senior Partner	54	21	38.9
6. Dominant	22	7	31.8
7. Monopoly	5	0	0.0
Total	762	282	37.0

Correlations between "Inclusion in MAR" and inter-group economic inequality

	Corr.coeff.	Signif.
Ineq_1	-.095	.009
Ineq_2	.066	.068
Ineq_3	.116	.001
Ineq_4	.119	.001

Number of cases for correlations: 755

Note: Calculi have been restricted to year 2005.

ordinal scale and inclusion in MAR. This shows that only the scale ends, the discriminated and the monopoly groups are disproportionately represented. (And, actually, the overall number of monopoly groups, five, is too small to allow for conclusions.)

MAR's known bias is, however, toward including groups involved in conflict, and this bias can be measured only with conflict measures independent of MAR. The dataset contains a number of such variables, and Table 6.5 shows the pertinent parts of the correlation matrix. The lower half of the table may be surprising: selection into MAR is not associated with any country-level measure of conflict. It is only associated with the groups' involvement in conflicts to which they are parties. The correlation coefficients around 0.35, across 762 cases, show moderate-to-strong association with the group-level conflict indicators derived from the CONIS and UCDP/PRIO datasets.

The associations between inclusion in MAR and the institutional variables such as democracy, proportional representation, and decentralization are just as elusively weak nothing as the association of inclusion in MAR with the development level. Based on all these relationships, I would conclude that the multiple imputations based on MAR may inflate the strength of the factors that have an impact on the occurrence of conflict in contrast with the inconsequential

Table 6.5 Association between Inclusion in MAR and Diverse Conflict Measures

	Correlation coefficient	Significance	Number of cases
Group-level conflict measures			
Any conflict in CONIS (of any intensity)	.369	.000	760
Average intensity of conflict in 5 years (2006-2010)	.349	.000	762
Conflict intensity based on both CONIS & UCDP_PRIO	.342	.000	762
Country-level conflict measures			
Refugee population as per 1000 of country of origin	-.023	.531	762
Internally displaced persons as % of population	.039	.281	762
Battle-related deaths	.021	.570	762
Banks Weighted Conflict Index	.058	.109	759
Global Peace Index (highest the worst)			0
Failed State Index (1--120, highest the worst)	-.043	.361	451
FS Group Grievance (1-10, highest the worst)	-.017	.716	451
WGI Political Stability and Lack of Violence	-.064	.077	757

Note: In Table_6.5, and throughout the chapter, I continue using the same pattern coding as in the previous chapter. The cell of coefficients significant above the alpha=0.05 threshold are marked with (green) trellis. Completely insignificant coefficients are not marked, but those with p-values between 0.05 and 0.1, which may be taken for significant above alpha=0.1, are highlighted with (yellow) vertical lines. (Pink) dots are reserved for coefficients that turn up as significant with the theoretically unexpected sign. I use this visualization technique for both correlation and regression coefficients, except for the tables in which I do not include insignificant coefficients at all.

variables, but we have no reason to think that any of the explanatory variables will get unfair advantage to the detriment of others. Fortunately, my main goal with rerunning the explanatory models with MAR data is the inclusion of new explanatory variables, not really to establish a rank order of the determinants.

I am interested, however, in whether the MAR sample is biased toward violent conflict versus conflict carried out with peaceful, democratic political means. The overall count of groups involved in peaceful actions classified as "Protest" is 138, versus 58, the overall count of groups involved in violent actions classified as "Rebellion." As Table 6.6 shows, some groups were not involved in either protest or rebellion (124), and some groups were involved in both (40), which leaves us with 98 groups which protested only and 18 that rioted only in 2005. There is no factual data on whether this proportion of more than 5:1 typifies minority behavior worldwide. Yet, we know that the proportion of democracies to autocracies was 6:4 in 1994 (Gleditsch & Ward 1997), and still much below 5:1 in 2005. Since minorities have no real chances to peacefully promote their interests in autocracies, a proportion of Protest-to-Rebellion above the proportion of democracy-to-autocracy refutes the assumption of a selection bias on behalf of Rebellion.

It seems that further crosstabulations may reinforce the belief that minorities prefer peaceful political action over riots, and in fortunate circumstances they do not contemplate violent means at all.

Table 6.6 Cross-Tabulation of Two Forms of Political Activism: Protest and Rebellion

	PROTEST						
REBELLION	None 0	Verbal opposition 1	Symbolic resistance 2	Small demonstrations 3	Medium demonstrations 4	Large demonstrations 5	Total
0 None	124	26	8	57	6	1	222
1 Political banditry, sporadic terrorism	10	1	0	16	4	0	31
2 Campaigns of terrorism	0	0	0	2	0	0	2
3 Local rebellions	0	0	0	0	0	0	0
4 Small-scale guerilla acitivity	3	0	0	3	1	0	7
5 Intermediate guerilla activity	5	0	1	2	3	0	11
6 Large-scale guerilla activity	0	1	0	5	1	0	7
7 Civil wars	0	0	0	0	0	0	0
Total	142	28	9	85	15	1	280

Note: Calculi have been restricted to year 2005.

Table 6.7 Cross-Tabulation of the "Group Organization for Political Action" (GOJPA) Variable with "Protest" and "Rebellion" (2005)

	Group organization for political action						
	None	Umbrella organizations	Parties	Mainly conventional, also militant	Mainly militant, also conventional	Militant organizations	Total
Protest							
0 None	6	27	70	27	5	7	142
1 Verbal opposition	0	4	15	7	2	0	28
2 Symbolic resistance	0	0	4	4	1	0	9
3 Small demonstrations	0	8	34	26	17	0	85
4 Medium demonstrations	0	0	8	3	4	0	15
5 Large demonstrations	0	0	1	0	0	0	1
Total	6	39	132	67	29	7	280
Rebellion							
0 None	6	39	127	41	6	4	223
1 Political banditry, sporadic terrorism	0	0	6	16	8	2	32
2 Campaigns of terrorism	0	0	0	1	1	0	2
3 Local rebellions	0	0	0	0	0	0	0
4 Small-scale guerilla acitivity	0	0	0	4	3	0	7
5 Intermediate guerilla activity	0	0	0	4	6	1	11
6 Large-scale guerilla activity	0	0	0	2	5	0	7
Total	6	39	133	68	29	7	282

Table 6.7 shows that out of the 282 groups with grievances, only 104 had some military organization promoting their cause, and 68 of these military organizations were dominated or counterbalanced by "conventional" (i.e., nonviolent) political organizations. On the extreme, umbrella organizations do not engage in riots, and military organizations do not engage in peaceful protests. The 133 minority parties organized 62 protest events of all intensities in 2005, while they were involved in only 6 actions qualifying as Rebellion, all of them of the lowest intensity recorded in MAR.

BIVARIATE RELATIONSHIPS

Bivariate analyses are seldom reported, but here they may deserve a brief section because of the possibility to compare measures from MAR with measures from other datasets, and even with country-level data.

Measurements of social phenomena are always disputable, including even the hardest economic indicators, such as GDP. There is, for instance, GDP measured at current US dollars, on a fixed US dollar parity, and either on purchase power, or unadjusted to this latter. These versions of the GDP measure covary to different extents, and they certainly may lead to different results in regression models. The maximum for which we may hope in this regard is a convergence of the results.

The variables which describe group features and country features related to the group structure are much less standardized and precise than the economic indicators. They are replicable, but only by replicating the whole method of calculating them—different methods are likely to lead to different measures, which may not be, unfortunately, very closely associated among themselves. Tables 6.8 and 6.9 present the MAR variables' association with other measurements with which they can reasonably be expected to show significant correlations. The tables contain larger sections of the overall correlation matrix, but I highlighted with thick box frames (and yellow shading) the areas in which associations are theoretically expected. Only the correlation coefficients are displayed, without case numbers (which come in the range of 270–282) and significance values (which are above alpha = 0.05 for all coefficients included). Table 6.8 shows that the group power status variables imported from EPR are reasonably well correlated with MAR's measurement

Table 6.8 Correlation of MAR Measures with Other Group-level Measurements

Other measures \ MAR measures	Group representation in government	Group autonomy	Political discrimination	Economic Discrimination	Religious restrictions	Language restrictions	Separatism Index	Protest	Rebellion
Past violence			.139	.129	.128		.212	.162	.621
EPR Power rank	.374		-.469	-.446		-.194			
EPR EGIP	.477		-.356	-.381		-.140			
INEQ_1	.146		-.366	-.453	-.122			-.152	
INEQ_2	-.149		.366	.440	.122				
St. dev. of INEQ_1			.165	.223					
Political grievance		.339				.133	.782	.382	.313
Economic grievance			.282	.367			.214	.300	
Cultural grievance			.146	.214	.189	.280	.203	.225	
Any grievance (MAR)			.225	.244	.148	.137	.278	.246	.131
Any conflict (Conis)		.183			.210		.389	.200	.285
Conis intensity index		.152			.221		.395	.200	.425
Intensity index		.160	.147	.135	.237		.391	.177	**.599**

Table 6.9 Correlation of MAR Measures with Selected Country-Level Measurements (2005)

MAR measures / Other measures	Group concentration	Proportion in regional base	Group autonomy	External support to group	Military support to group	Representation in government	Political discrimination	Economic Discrimination	Religious restrictions	Language restrictions
Decentralization Index		-.162	.318				-.163			
Communal_sub_divisions	.230	.275	.240						.183	
Decentraliz*Commnl_s_div			.377							-.153
Economic globalization	-.265	-.281		-.121			-.121			
Political globalization				-.160					-.126	-.224
Social globalization	-.258	-.297	.120	-.196						
Freedom H./imputed Polity	-.125	-.190	.121				-.166		-.287	-.204
Political Terror scale (US)	.221	.270		.204	.145					
Electoral family	-.122	-.169							-.237	-.121
House electoral rule (PR)		.140								

of group political representation and political discrimination, but fail to capture the group's autonomy status. MAR's variable for economic discrimination is also reasonably well correlated with my economic inequality measures Ineq_1 and Ineq_2. At this point, I included the country-level measure derived from Ineq_1, as well, in order to observe the difference between the two levels of analysis. The associations between the MAR conflict indicators (Separatism Index, Protest, and Rebellion), and the conflict measures based on CONIS and UCDP-PRIO reveal that it is the most complex Intensity index measure which best captures the violence coded by the MAR team.

Table 6.9, which includes correlations between group-level and country-level measurements, features much lower correlation values than Table 6.8. In the context of Table 6.9, the two above-0.2 coefficients between the MAR group concentration variables and my measure of congruence between settlement patterns and administrative subdivisions, seem to be acceptably high. Most importantly, the association between MAR's group autonomy indicator and mine (Decentralization * Communal_sub_division) is a comforting 0.377.

On the negative side, a country's globalization is not associated with the possibility that a group receives external help (either from kin, or foreign states, or nonstate actors); on the contrary, the two phenomena tend to be negatively correlated. Finally, there is evidence that democracy, as measured by the Freedom House/imputed Polity scale, may safeguard minorities from experiencing political discrimination, and restrictions on their religion and language—it is only economic discrimination that is not affected by higher democracy levels. Also, proportional representation is significantly associated with less restriction on religion and language.

The next tables summarize the bivariate relationships between dependent variables and predictors, with a special focus on the two types of *explanans* specific to MAR: group concentration, and external assistance to minority groups. Noncitizen groups were taken out of the sample, both because MAR does not represent them proportionally, and because their political action is constrained. They have to be politically much less active than other groups, which leads to an unnecessary watering down of the impact of all variables of interest. Without noncitizens, the number of groups in the sample is 727, and that of the MAR groups is 277.

The next tables, presenting correlation results, include only coefficients significant above alpha = 0.05. Special background pattern (and color) helps identifying the explanatory variables borrowed from MAR, but the predictors are listed along the main clusters typified by the nature of impact, independent from the origin of the variables. Table 6.10 comprises the economic inequality measures, and those expressing either the reality or the possibility of political inequality. I also included a set of variables from MAR, which expresses the degree of discrimination of and restriction on minorities, in four domains: political, economic, religious, and linguistic. Though the formulation of these variables assumes the deliberate oppressive action of the state-operating groups, they do, *de facto*, express the distance between majorities and minorities in the respective areas. A look at Table 6.10 shows that all inequality/oppression variables affect at least one of the conflict measures. The impact of the MAR oppression and my INEQ variables is the strongest and most consistent across several outcome variables, while the country-level institutional measures perform a little weaker. Yet, my country-level autonomy measure (Decentralization * Communal_sub-_divisions) parallels MAR's group-level autonomy measure (AUTON2), and they both seem to increase intergroup hostility. This is hard to understand without the data included in Table 6.11, referring to the groups' regional concentration.

Table 6.11 relates some group features and group-structure features to the conflict measures. Group proportion and the size of the largest minority do not affect conflict, and group size is not a weighty predictor of it, either. Past violent episodes do considerably increase the probability of conflict, and as expectable, of rebellion, rather than of protest. And last, but not least, we have the geographical concentration measures in this group of *explanans*. Their impact on conflict is not very strong, but considerable, and definitely higher than the impact of the corresponding autonomy measures. That is, regional concentration of the minorities increases the chance of conflict, including

Table 6.10 Significant Correlation Coefficients between Dependent Variables and Three Groups of Determinants (2005, Citizen Groups Only)

	Political grievance	Economic grievance	Cultural grievance	Any grievance	Any conflict	CONIS intensity	Intensity index	Protest	Rebellion
Political discrimination (MAR)		.289	.173	.223			.163		
Economic discrimination (MAR)		.369	.235	.242		.130	.150		.123
Religious restrictions (MAR)			.172	.149	.214	.225	.241		
Language restrictions (MAR)	.135		.285	.139					
Cultural restrictions (MAR)*	.126		.290	.182	.129	.146	.174		
INEQ_1	-.147	-.217	-.165	-.174	-.089	-.110	-.140	-.158	
INEQ_2	.116	.210	.134	.162	.080	.110	.140	.121	
INEQ_3	.168	.204	.170	.185	.098	.111	.143		
INEQ_4	.160	.214	.176	.183	.083	.098	.127		
EPR Power rank	-.092	-.148	-.107	-.203					
EPR Ethnic group in power (EGIP)	-.115	-.090		-.133					
Gr. representation in govt (MAR)								.128	
Group autonomy (MAR)	.338				.179	.147	.156	.146	
Decentraliz*Communl_sub_div	.097				.073	.089	.091		.140
Freedom House/iPolity	.083	.141	.142	.076				.190	
Political terror scale (US)	.081		-.102		.162	.203	.212		.328
WGI Regulatory Quality		.099	.144				-.073	.157	-.154
Electoral family (Norris-based)			.109		-.076		-.075		
Decentralization Index	.107	.080	.102					.179	

*This "Cultural restrictions" variable is the simple sum of the Religious restrictions and Language restriction values, created with the intent to simplify the regression models. Though MAR was right to distinguish between religious and language discrimination, here I do not need to address the cultural components in so detailed manners.

separatist movements and rebellion, but where there are autonomy arrangements in place, the likelihood of violence is smaller.[9]

Further, Table 6.11 replicates the general pattern noticed in Chapter 5. On higher development levels, we may have more grievances (expressed, promoted), but there is less violent conflict. MAR's Protest versus Rebellion dichotomy allows for an illustration of the fact that development goes with more protest movements, but fewer riots. External support to groups, either military or of mixed nature, is associated with higher conflict levels. The surprising information with regard to this group of variables is that the presence of intracommunal conflict is positively associated with measures of intercommunal conflict. This goes against all theoretical expectations,

Table 6.11 Significant Correlation Coefficients between Dependent Variables and Four Groups of Determinants (2005, Citizen Groups Only)

	Political grievance	*Economic grievance*	*Cultural grievance*	*Any grievance*	*Any conflict*	*CONIS intensity*	*Intensity index*	*Protest*	*Rebellion*
Group proportion									
Group size								.168	.132
Past violence	.392	.200		.268	.376	.426	.552	.159	.620
Ethnic fractionalization (Alesina)	–.099		–.118	–.117					
Proportion of plurality	.141	.092	.181	.149					–.122
Proportion of largest minority									
Difference plurality—Largest minority	.124		.142	.124					
*Group concentration (MAR)	.292				.128	.163	.169		.130
*Proportion in regional base (MAR)	.290		–.163		.200	.197	.214		.221
Communal sub divisions	.094				.133	.157	.183		.228
GDP/capita (PPP)			.109				–.075	.171	–.138
Life expectancy (female)	.123	.127	.249	.135					
*External support to group (MAR)	.242	.169		.159		.173	.223		.384
*Military support to group (MAR)	.193				.195	.257	.270	.130	.414
*Intragroup conflict (MAR)	.270				.200	.248	.254	.168	.394
*Group urbanism (MAR)	–.148	–.227			–.129	–.164	–.210		–.158
Proportion of rural population			–.166		.074	.089	.109	–.214	.122
WGI government effectiveness		.096	.166					.157	–.139
Unemployed young males (%)			.100	.134					
*Group organization (GOJPA, MAR)	.452			.186	.446	.517	.529	.244	.491
*GO_Party (organization for protest)	–.294		.156		–.333	–.431	–.433	–.120	–.432
*GO_Military (organiz. for rebellion)	.397		–.154		.463	.558	.583	.188	.535

Note: The MAR variables are marked with an asterisk.

both psychological, claiming that intergroup animosity is associated with intragroup cohesion (Tajfel 1982), and political, claiming, for instance, that wars are the midwives of nations (Raymond Aron, 1962: Peace and war), or that rallying around the flag creates the national cohesion necessary for a bad leader to maintain in power (Ostrom& Job 1986: A diversionary theory of war). Yet, MAR codes as intracommunal conflict only incidents involving violence, even if low-intensity violence, such as with knives, between communal antagonists. And violent disputes over pastures, fisheries, or mines, for instance, may occur even if a minority group is very monolithic in its demands toward the majority population. That is, the high correlation between intracommunal violence and intercommunal violence gets an explanation from the fact that both occur in less developed settings.

The last three variables in Table 6.11 show the impact of group organization on the dependent variables. The coefficients are impressive, the largest of all explanatory groups reviewed. The conceptual issue here is whether they are indeed explanatory variables. It is hard if not impossible to distinguish between these levels of political organization and the political action itself. Party is, for instance, defined as an entity that vies for power; and minority military organizations negate the majority's bid to the legitimate monopoly of power by their very existence. Subsequently, I do not intend to use these variables as explanation of hostility or violence; I am more interested in the causes that push a group toward either party-type or military-type organization.

The next sections aim at building efficient explanatory models with these groups of variables. Preference has been given to group-level measurements, where possible, and to MAR's own variables.

REGRESSION MODELS WITH THE ORIGINAL DATASET

The logic of model building follows the two-step impact mechanism that I explored in Chapter 5. In the beginning, I built a number of models explaining grievance. The next steps involved the explanation of conflict, in two ways: first, by including grievance variables in the model, and second, by tracing grievances back to their causes. These latter regressions are the typical omnibus models of conflict.

Analyses were restricted to the 762 citizen groups. All models could be run either by restricting the sample to one year, or by including several years, but my original dataset has had a built-in limit in this regard. The MAR variables are available for years 2004–2006, while a variable that I included in all models as an important control and was imported from EPR, the measure of past violence, is available for until 2005 only, as its last year. Thus the choice of years was limited to either 2005 only, or to 2004 and 2005. As for the second version, we may be concerned about the presence of serial correlation in the data. I experimented with both versions, and as a general pattern, the model explanatory strength turned out to be almost identical for the two. The estimates of the coefficients showed very little difference, as well. What differed, was the significance value calculated for the predictors, and the models with more cases are more generous in this regard, as they allow for more coefficients to turn up as significant. Since the significance of the predictors in my models is severely diminished by multiple correlations among them, I thought that it was fair to give them more chance by keeping more cases in the model. Yet, in order to address the issue of serial correlation, the models involving two years were run with robust errors, in SPSS's Generalized Linear Models procedure. The ordinal models in Table 6.12 are presented in the one-year resolution.

Table 6.12 reports three ordinal logit models explaining the three types of grievance recorded in MAR. They include a large set of control variables, selected from the group—group structure, developmental and institutional predictor groups. The main predictors of interest are the first three, expressing special types of inequality and oppression. All three of these have significant impact on their respective grievance indicators, in the order displayed, economic discrimination having the strongest impact, and political discrimination having the weakest. Yet, the strength of the models is different, and

Table 6.12 Types of Grievance Explained with MAR's Oppression and Inequality Variables

Dependent Variable	Economic grievance		Cultural grievance		Political grievance	
Number of cases	273		272		273	
Cox and Snell Pseudo-R2	.199		.180		.281	
Nagelkerke Pseudo-R2	.224		.210		.295	
McFadden Pseudo-R2	.101		.102		.108	
	Estim.	Sig.	Estim.	Sig.	Estim.	Sig.
Economic discrimination	.625	.000				
Cultural restrictions			.464	.000		
Political discrimination					.157	.070
Group proportion	-3.942	.001	-.591	.624	-1.299	.208
Past violent episodes	.001	.678	-.002	.434	.018	.000
Linguistic fractionalization	-.007	.991	.450	.487	-.031	.958
Religious fractionalization	.013	.982	-1.422	.024	-.662	.250
Diff. plurality-largest minority	-.503	.384	.186	.764	.764	.168
Proportion in regional base	.228	.025	-.145	.159	.331	.001
GDP per capita, PPP	.000	.208	.000	.054	.000	.219
Political Terror Scale (US)	-.080	.565	-.349	.016	.020	.881
Group political representation	1.351	.001	.376	.362	.313	.419
Group autonomy	-.247	.479	.331	.362	1.539	.000

Trellis pattern shows significance above alpha = 0.05; vertical lines show significance between alpha = 0.05 and 0.1.

the one explaining political grievance seems to be the strongest, though all three models can be classified as explaining around 20 percent of variation.[10] Remarkably, some control variables tend to affect the three types of grievances in different ways.

Of the variables belonging to the group- and group-structure cluster, linguistic fractionalization fails to become significant in any model, while religious fractionalization affects cultural grievances only. Past violent episodes increase the likelihood of political grievance, but do not have significant impact on the other two dependent variables. Three predictors happen to turn up with unexpected sign, that is, their impact is the opposite of what was theoretically expected, and two of these are probably related to the "Modernization paradox effect." The counterintuitive findings are that economic grievances intensify when the group proportion is smaller, and groups with more political representation have more grievances.

It seems that grievances are more often formulated and expressed in modernizing settings, due to social transformations facilitating group awareness. In developed countries, minorities are smaller, and democratic conditions allow for more group representation. The third variable emerging with an unexpected sign is the group autonomy measure. This, too, may also be related to the "modernization paradox," as autonomy is positively correlated with development indicators such as life expectancy and social globalization, but group concentration issues may also have a part. In the group- and group-structure cluster there is a variable that could be retrieved from MAR only, here called "Proportion in regional base." If we look at it across types of grievances, it tells an interesting story. Political and economic grievances increase in the presence of more regional concentration, while cultural grievances do not. It may well be the case that geographically dispersed minority groups tend to militate for cultural, rather than for political or economic rights. Within the model explaining political grievances, autonomy seems to increase the demands, and it is obviously in competition with the impact of political discrimination, also having some positive impact on grievance.[11] Yet the impact of the autonomy indicator should be examined with reference to that of the group concentration measure. This latter never fails to turn up as significant—and substantively strong—in the explanation of economic and political grievances, and of conflict intensity. Territorial autonomy is the problem of groups with regional concentration; geographically dispersed groups aim at functional autonomies.

As for the political institutional structure of the country, the models show that more political representation helps in articulating more economic grievances. Increasing terror silences cultural demands, but fails to do the same to economic and political demands as well.

Table 6.13 presents variations of the model explaining political grievance, with cases from 2004 and 2005.[12] Its important message is that *economic* discrimination is a powerful predictor of *political* grievance. And it is not because of, or mainly because of, the perceived wrong intention of the discriminating plurality. The last two models in this table show that MAR's economic discrimination variable may be replaced with my economic inequality measure with very little loss of explanatory power.

The next step of this analysis is to explain violent conflict with grievance, in the presence of the opportunity for insurrection variables and the necessary controls.

Table 6.14 contains four robust linear models which all have the same dependent variable, a measure of the intensity of conflicts included in Conis and UCDP/PRIO.[13] There are four predictors that are consistently significant above alpha = 0.05 across all models. Past violent episodes increase the likelihood and intensity of violence. Development reduces the likelihood of violence, while political terror breeds more violence, and military support from kindred, foreign states, or nonstate actors also boosts it. (External assistance to minority groups in other forms also increases conflict intensity significantly,

Table 6.13 Robust Linear Models Explaining Political Grievance

Dependent Variable	Political grievance		Political grievance		Political grievance		Political grievance	
Number of cases	543		543		541		541	
Log Likelihood	-923.888		-920.697		-917.617		-917.132	
[Adj.R^2 of corresponding OLS]	[0.237]				[0.246]		[0.243]	
	Est.	Sig.	Est.	Sig.	Est.	Sig.	Est.	Sig.
Political discrimination	.071	.096						
Cultural restrictions			.143	.001				
Economic discrimination					.135	.002		
Ineq_3_ln							.334	.003
Group proportion	-.876	.048	-.874	.045	-.789	.081	-.432	.340
Past violent episodes	.007	.000	.007	.000	.007	.000	.007	.000
Linguistic fractionalization	.140	.551	.033	.887	.215	.362	.224	.349
Religious fractionalization	-.580	.031	-.510	.052	-.530	.045	-.634	.016
Diff. plurality-largest minority	.695	.001	.525	.016	.743	.001	.810	.000
Proportion in regional base	.266	.000	.244	.000	.271	.000	.277	.000
GDP per capita, PPP	.017	.019	.017	.018	.017	.017	.016	.025
Political Terror Scale (US)	.082	.213	.088	.175	.094	.154	.093	.152
Group political representation	.269	.151	.228	.208	.318	.085	.226	.200
Group autonomy	.933	.000	.962	.000	.971	.000	.858	.000

Trellis pattern shows significance above alpha = 0.05; vertical lines show significance between alpha = 0.05 and 0.1.

Table 6.14 Explaining Conflict Intensity with Grievance, Opportunity, and Control Variables

Dependent Variable	Intensity index		Intensity index		Intensity index		Intensity index	
Number of cases	493		491		493		490	
Log Likelihood	-507.81		-489.811		-513.226		-511.159	
[Corresponding OLS's Adj.R^2]	[0.288]		[0.333]		[0.272]		[0.271]	
	Est.	Sig.	Est.	Sig.	Est.	Sig.	Est.	Sig.
Any grievance in MAR	.355	.000						
Political grievance			.154	.000				
Economic grievance					.031	.436		
Cultural grievance							-.021	.627
Group proportion	-.441	.148	-.292	.321	-.399	.191	-.428	.164
Past violent episodes	.006	.000	.005	.000	.006	.000	.006	.000
Linguistic fractionalization	.245	.103	.235	.097	.211	.151	.196	.172
Religious fractionalization	-.265	.074	-.177	.221	-.282	.057	-.315	.038
Diff. plurality-largest minority	.227	.106	.135	.322	.256	.068	.249	.078
Proportion in regional base	.065	.022	.012	.666	.065	.025	.061	.036
GDP per capita, PPP	-.014	.018	-.015	.017	-.013	.034	-.013	.026
Political Terror Scale (US)	.096	.024	.102	.012	.104	.016	.101	.018
Urban/rural distribution	-.034	.162	-.038	.118	-.039	.127	-.046	.058
WGI governmnt effectiveness	.273	.000	.261	.000	.280	.000	.294	.000
External military support	.712	.038	.573	.064	.820	.020	.801	.022

Trellis pattern shows significance above alpha = 0.05; vertical lines show significance between alpha = 0.05 and 0.1.

but not as substantially as military support.) Group concentration is related to more conflict. The challenging finding is the overall significance of the government effectiveness variable—with the theoretically unexpected sign.

As a first circumstance to consider, there is a correlation of 0.798 between GDP/cap and government effectiveness, which may explain at least part of this anomaly. Yet, there may be more to it. "Real" government weakness leads to a war of everyone against everyone, the country breaking down in indiscriminate warring factions. Conflicts included in my dataset are between government and a minority group. And the state apparatus that can uphold armed violence against a group, has to have some power, that is, some "government effectiveness." The rational choice explanation of intergroup conflict claims that would-be insurrection leaders embark on a violent course when the state is weak (for instance, in Fearon and Laitin 2003). Yet, the grievance explanation of conflict (such as Gurr) claims that when the oppression is intolerable, minorities rebel even against strong states able to exert political terror. This claim gets confirmation by the models above, in which political terror occurs with significant positive coefficients. Finally, it cannot be excluded that the conflict intensity measure, drawing on CONIS, not only on UCDP-PRIO, contains a portion of nonviolent conflict, which would be classified by MAR as "Protest", rather than "Rebellion." If we look at separate models explaining these two different types of conflict, government effectiveness has a positive impact on Protest (as expected), and no significant impact on Rebellion.

But before considering models with Protest and Rebellion, I would like to highlight the differences among the impact of different types of grievance. In these models, it is only the political grievance that preserves its significance in the presence of controls. (In bivariate relationships, economic and cultural grievances are also significantly related to conflict intensity.) The differences may be further analyzed by distinguishing between Protest and Rebellion. Models run on these two forms of activism as distinct dependent variables make clear that Protest is predicted by all three types of grievance (political, economic, and cultural), to comparable extent. In contrast, Rebellion is substantially predicted by political grievances only, and some weakly significant impact of the economic grievances may show up in models. Cultural grievances do not seem to result in Rebellion at all.

The last types of models reported here aim at supplanting grievances with their causes, that is, tracing direct links between some causal variables and the conflictual outcome. Previously I tried to explain grievances with MAR's three variables of political discrimination, economic discrimination, and cultural restrictions; thus, these are the main candidates for replacing grievances in the regressions. In addition, I explore the power of my intergroup economic inequality variable. The obstacle to packing all these measures in the same model is the association among them, for instance, political and economic discrimination are correlated at $r = 0.764$. Yet, the association with the cultural restrictions measure is lower, which precludes, on the other hand, their combination into an index. Thus, Table 6.15 presents a series of models in which these inequality and oppression variables are included one by one.

The models show the convincing impact of past violence, political terror, regional concentration, and external military support, all in the hypothesized direction. The development indicator GDP/cap is significant with a negative sign, thus violence is rarer in developed countries. It is only the government effectiveness variable that turns up consistently with the unexpected sign. The inequality and oppression variables are all significant when added to the model one by one, but thwart each other's measurable impact when added to the model at the same time.

We may wonder how it happens that cultural restrictions and economic inequality outperform political discrimination in the explanation of conflict intensity, when political grievance has been shown to have much important impact on both conflict intensity and rebellion, than economic and cultural grievances? There are two answers to this question, and any combination of the two is plausible, as well. One explanation is what I would call the

Table 6.15 Explaining Conflict Intensity with Different Types of Inequality and Oppression

Dependent variable	**Intensity index**		**Intensity index**		**Intensity index**		**Intensity index**	
Number of cases	492		493		491		491	
Log Likelihood	-511.418		-507.608		-509.641		-507.810	
[Adj.R^2 of corresponding OLS]	[0.277]		[0.289]		[0.279]		[0.277]	
	Est.	**Sig.**	**Est.**	**Sig.**	**Est.**	**Sig.**	**Est.**	**Sig.**
Polit. discrimination	.046	.048						
Cultural restrictions			.091	.001				
Econ. discrimination					.051	.041		
Ineq_4_ln							.045	.014
Group proportion	-.385	.202	-.405	.181	-.392	.202	-.177	.573
Past violent episodes	.005	.000	.005	.000	.005	.000	.006	.000
Linguistic fractionalization	.232	.117	.149	.294	.254	.092	.257	.078
Religious fractionalization	-.219	.149	-.195	.181	-.224	.138	-.258	.088
Diff. plurality-largest minority	.277	.050	.159	.260	.287	.044	.322	.022
Proportion in regional base	.077	.009	.065	.022	.080	.007	.072	.013
GDP per capita, PPP	-.014	.023	-.016	.007	-.014	.021	-.013	.036
Political Terror Scale (US)	.101	.020	.109	.010	.100	.021	.101	.018
Urban/rural distribution	-.038	.115	-.047	.055	-.034	.170	-.041	.091
WGI government effectiveness	.299	.000	.329	.000	.294	.000	.276	.000
External military support	.836	.017	.899	.014	.826	.016	.823	.014

Trellis pattern shows significance above alpha = 0.05; vertical lines show significance between alpha = 0.05 and 0.1.

"crossed impacts," and it is related to the relationships between types of grievances and types of discrimination. Factually, it can be described as a correlation of 0.593 between political grievances and economic grievances, and a correlation of 0.764 between political discrimination and economic discrimination (and continued with some correlations above 0.4 with the cultural aspects). The associations among the three aspects of both discrimination and grievance are so high because (i) some phenomena cannot be neatly classified in one category only, they are multifaceted; and (ii) the problem and the solution may fall in different categories. For instance, demands for the decentralized administration of a minority concentration area may strike us as a political issue; but if the main goal of it is to use the minority language in the local government and run the local school in the minority language, then the community's goal is as much cultural as political. Or, if an economically disadvantaged group fights for getting a larger share from state budget by increasing their representation in the national government, then an economic discrimination issue leads to political grievances.

The other answer is not really an explanation, but reference to a slightly diverging constellation of facts. The imputed models differ to some extent from the models built on the original dataset—and the most notable divergence is that they show a serious impact of the economic and cultural grievances on both conflict intensity and rebellion.

REGRESSION MODELS ON THE IMPUTED DATASETS

The creators of the multiple imputation Amelia software are very confident about the possibilities of this tool to fill in missing data. They suggest that in case of divergence between the results from the original and the imputed datasets, we should trust the imputed data.

I am a little more skeptical about the powers of Amelia to make up for missingness, and I tend to take for well-supported result only the observations confirmed by both the original and the imputed data. Fortunately, a series of basic findings are the same or very similar in the two types of regression models. Issues on which the original and the imputed data do not concur perfectly, I would refer to further analysis.

Actually, my skepticism is not directed against Amelia as such, but I think that the MAR_EPR_MI dataset is a particularly difficult case to be subjected to multiple imputation. The main special issues with it are:

(i) We have original data for only 37 percent of the cases considered;
(ii) Groups are nested in countries, which practically cannot be modeled in Amelia;
(iii) The association of the MAR variables with out-the-system variables such as country features is relatively low;
(iv) We have original data for 3 years only out of 8 in the MAR_EPR_MI.

I have tried to address these issues by:

(i) Asking for six replications, rather than five, to allow for more randomness;
(ii) Packing the file to be replicated with country-level variables;
(iii) Packing the file to be replicated with all available parallel measurements of group political and economic inequality, and institutional and conflict variables;
(iv) Running the final models on year 2005 only, for which we have the original measurements for almost all cases included in MAR.

The final number of variables introduced in Amelia for multiple imputation was 61, with three identifiers (year, country-, and group-name).[14] Besides the MAR variables themselves, the procedure produced much needed imputed values for the variable "unemployed young males," which I could not use with the original dataset because of its dramatically (and selectively) reducing the number of variables. Here it is added to all models involving the "opportunity for insurrection" hypothesis, and in a few trial models that I ran in parallel with and without this variable, its presence did not affect the behavior of other variables.

The logic of model-building followed the same steps as those presented in the previous section; first I explained grievances, then conflict. This latter, in its turn, is explained first with grievances and opportunities, and later with omnibus models bypassing the grievance stage.

With regard to the models explaining grievances, I ran into an unexpected problem which slightly limits the comparability of the models run on the original and the imputed data. My dependent variables of economic, political, and cultural grievances, the same set of variables that I used in Chapter 5, as well, and which has been reasonably complete for all (not only the MAR) groups, still contained some 16 missing values for year 2005. Amelia filled in these with not-integer intermediate values, transforming the ordinal scale into interval scale, which made me use ordinary least square (OLS), rather than ordinal logit models to explain grievance.[15]

Because of space limits, the tables reporting on the imputed data include the pooled models only. (Appendix 5 shows some of them one by one.) From the pooled models procedure we do not get R-squared values and standardized coefficients. Tables 6.17 through 6.20 include, instead, an average of the R-squared values reported for the six imputed models, and simple OLS coefficient estimates. In addition, a column shows the p-values, that is, the significance of the coefficients.

The first table in this series, Table 6.16, includes models explaining economic grievance. For easy comparison of the imputed models with the original, I copied this latter in the grid, as well. It makes visible that there are two uncontested predictors of economic grievance: regional concentration and economic inequality or oppression. My own economic inequality predictor is weaker than MAR's ECDIS, but still powerful, and second only to the impact of the past violence in the six imputed models in which it was included. The "modernization paradox" effect, that more political representation means more grievance, is mitigated in the imputed models, and we have, instead, a negative impact of autonomy on grievances. Previously, Chapter 5 reported models that showed the regional concentration of communal groups increasing the risk of hostility, and autonomy reducing it. Those results were obtained with my own variables of "administrative subdivisions fall along communal lines" and its interaction with a decentralization indicator. The same effect is here obtained with a set of different measurements, and hopefully this convergence of the results establishes the validity of the finding.

The other important difference between the original and the imputed models is the emergence of past violence as highly significant in the latter. Since past violence has emerged as significant predictor in other models here and in Chapter 5, as well, the imputed models may be closer to the reality than the original model with regard to this variable's impact on economic grievances.

Table 6.16 Explaining Economic Grievance

	Original data (ologit)		POOLED Model (OLS)		POOLED Model (OLS)	
Dependent variable	Economic grievance		Economic grievance		Economic grievance	
Number of cases	273		727*6		727*6	
Approximate Adjusted R^2	0.199 (Cox&Snell)		0.144 (average)		0.097 (average)	
	Est.	Sig.	Coeff.	Sig.	Coeff.	Sig.
Economic discrimination	0.625	0.000	0.196	0.000		
INEQ_3 (ln)					0.251	0.000
Group proportion	-3.942	0.001	-0.221	0.389	0.077	0.770
Past violence		0.678	0.004	0.000	0.004	0.000
Linguistic fractionalization		0.991	-0.014	0.914	-0.082	0.534
Religious fractionalization		0.982	-0.014	0.913	-0.086	0.473
Diff. plurality-largest minority		0.384	0.203	0.083	0.178	0.140
Proportion in regional base	0.228	0.025	0.092	0.004	0.078	0.017
GDP/ capita (PPP)		0.208	0.000	0.118	0.000	0.188
Political terror scale		0.565	0.004	0.885	0.014	0.637
Group representation in govt.	1.351	0.001	0.296	0.007	0.123	0.245
Group autonomy		0.479	-0.340	0.000	-0.439	0.000

Trellis pattern shows significance above alpha = 0.05; vertical lines show significance between alpha = 0.05 and 0.1; dots highlight coefficients that turn up as significant with the theoretically unexpected sign

Table 6.17 includes the same predictors as Table 6.16, but the dependent variable is political grievance. Happily, the variance of this can be explained to larger extent with my explanatory variables, the adjusted R^2-s reach 0.250. This time my economic inequality variable performs better than MAR's economic discrimination measure, but the strongest predictor of political grievance is history, as measured by the past violence variable. The impact of the regional concentration keeps high, but the unexpected-sign impact of the autonomy arrangements is weaker in the imputed models than in the original.

The models from the imputed dataset are decently healthy, those with the dependent variable economic grievance have 0–2 outliers, and those with political grievance, 2–4 outliers, all within the 3 to 4 standard deviation band. As for the next models to be presented, the residuals from models with Intensity index as their dependent variable are a little peaked, and have some 6 to 9 instances above 3 standard deviations. These smaller deviations from the normal are unlikely to influence the results in any systematic way. Table 6.18 presents results from models explaining conflict intensity, in which the grievance indicators compete against 12 controls. As a difference from the original model, the imputed models include a measure of the proportion of unemployed young males, which seems to have only marginally affected the results.[16] The single most important difference between the original and the imputed models is the convincingly strong impact of all types of grievances (not only of political grievance) on conflict intensity.

Table 6.17 Explaining Political Grievance

	Original data (Robust linear)		POOLED Model (OLS)		POOLED Model (OLS)	
Dependent variable	Political grievance		Political grievance		Political grievance	
Number of cases	541		727*6		727*6	
Adjusted R-squared			0.225 (average)		0.237 (average)	
	Est.	Sig.	Coeff.	Sig.	Coeff.	Sig.
Economic discrimination	.135	.002	.113	.018		
INEQ_3_ln					.384	.000
Group proportion	-.789	.081	.236	.599	.670	.143
Past violence	.007	.000	.015	.000	.014	.000
Linguistic fractionalization	.215	.362	-.237	.304	-.220	.334
Religious fractionalization	-.530	.045	-.269	.203	-.302	.145
Diff. plurality-largest minority	.743	.001	.691	.001	.694	.001
Proportion in regional base	.271	.000	.276	.000	.281	.000
GDP/ capita (PPP)	.017	.017	.000	.464	.000	.477
Political terror scale (US)	.094	.154	.050	.336	.050	.324
Group representation in governm.	.318	.085	.102	.593	.009	.959
Group autonomy	.971	.000	.165	.419	.118	.557

Trellis pattern shows significance above alpha = 0.05; vertical lines show significance between alpha = 0.05 and 0.1; dots highlight coefficients that turn up as significant with the theoretically unexpected sign

Besides grievances, two further variables are consistently strong predictors of violent conflict: past violence and political terror. This latter may leave room for divergent theorizations. On the one hand, it is an institutional circumstance of carrying out political action: lack of democracy constrains groups interested in change to choose violent, rather than peaceful-parliamentary means. On the other hand, it is a political grievance in itself, sign of, or means of political discrimination, and definitely a reason for turning against the regime in place. Yet, despite some significant association between the terror and grievance measures, here they both manage to turn up significant. Government effectiveness keeps having an impact in the theoretically unexpected direction, but it is substantially weakened as compared to the original model. The last variable that always shows up with significant, even if weakly significant, coefficient values, above the lower threshold of alpha = 0.1, is religious fractionalization. The negative sign on it suggests that more religious fractionalization means less violence, and this is good news for an increasingly plural world, even if we are aware that these fractionalization indexes are not linearly associated with most variables in the models.

In a final balance, there have been two predictors in the original models whose impact on the conflict intensity variable have not been confirmed by

Table 6.18 Explaining Conflict Intensity with Grievance and Controls

	Original model (Robust)		POOLED model (OLS)		POOLED model (OLS)		POOLED model (OLS)	
Dependent Variable	Intensity index		Intensity index		Intensity index		Intensity index	
Number of cases	493		727*6		727*6		727*6	
Adjusted R-squared			0.375 (average)		0.306 (average)		0.286 (average)	
	Est.	Sig.	Coeff.	Sig.	Coeff.	Sig.	Coeff.	Sig.
Any grievance	.355	.000						
Political grievance			0.190	0.000				
Economic grievance					0.220	0.000		
Cultural grievance							0.220	0.000
Group proportion	-.441	.148	-0.055	0.755	-0.018	0.922	-0.100	0.594
Past violent episodes	.006	.000	0.005	0.000	0.007	0.000	0.008	0.000
Linguistic fractionalization	.245	.103	0.166	0.089	0.145	0.158	0.092	0.374
Religious fractionalization	-.265	.074	-0.162	0.066	-0.211	0.023	-0.189	0.046
Diff. plurality-lg.minority	.227	.106	0.040	0.663	0.168	0.077	0.105	0.278
Proportion in regional base	.065	.022	0.012	0.593	0.056	0.010	0.062	0.005
GDP per capita, PPP	-.014	.018	0.000	0.289	0.000	0.631	0.000	0.635
Political Terror Scale (US)	.096	.024	0.088	0.000	0.093	0.000	0.104	0.000
Urban /rural distribution	-.034	.162	-0.029	0.133	-0.013	0.544	-0.040	0.082
WGI gov. effectiveness	.273	.000	0.120	0.002	0.081	0.051	0.098	0.021
External military support	.712	.038	0.058	0.778	0.083	0.715	-0.124	0.578
Young male unemployed			0.000	0.824	0.002	0.365	0.002	0.312

Trellis pattern shows significance above alpha = 0.05; vertical lines show significance between alpha = 0.05 and 0.1; dots highlight coefficients that turn up as significant with the theoretically unexpected sign

the imputed model series: the development indicator (GDP/capita), and the external military support. The bivariate analysis, and a number of previous observations, have shown the GDP/capita negatively correlated with conflict intensity, which lends some support to the original model. In the original model, the effect of the GDP/capita measure comes through despite its significant association with a number of other variables that amassed more strength in the imputed models, primarily the cultural grievance indicator, insignificant in the original model and highly significant in all imputed models. External military support is also correlated with conflict intensity in bivariate relationships (at 0.237), but it has a higher correlation value with the past violence indicator (at 0.391), which keeps significant in the imputed models, seemingly to the detriment of the external military support measure.

Table 6.19 reports the most complex models in which inequality and oppression variables supplant the grievance indicators. The models' explanatory power is lower this way, and the inequality and oppression variables perform weaker than the grievance variables, but the contribution of the controls

Table 6.19 Explaining Conflict Intensity with Economic Inequality and Controls

	Original model (Robust)		POOLED model (OLS)		POOLED model (OLS)	
Dependent Variable	Intensity index		Intensity index		Intensity index	
Number of cases	491		727*6		727*6	
Adjusted R-squared			0.262 (average)		0.259 (average)	
	Est.	Sig.	Coeff.	Sig.	Coeff.	Sig.
Economic discrimination	.051	.041	.047	.038		
Ineq_3_ln					.080	.059
Group proportion	-.392	.202	-.010	.958	.054	.786
Past violent episodes	.005	.000	.008	.000	.008	.000
Linguistic fractionalization	.254	.092	.124	.244	.115	.277
Religious fractionalization	-.224	.138	-.210	.029	-.233	.015
Diff. plurality-largest minority	.287	.044	.151	.126	.152	.125
Proportion in regional base	.080	.007	.069	.004	.064	.006
GDP per capita, PPP	-.014	.021	.000	.550	.000	.607
Political Terror Scale (US)	.100	.021	.103	.000	.102	.000
Group urbanism	-.034	.170	-.036	.133	-.038	.104
WGI government effectiveness	.294	.000	.122	.004	.113	.009
External military support	.826	.016	-.331	.137	-.336	.133
Unemployed young males			.004	.130	.004	.137

Trellis pattern shows significance above alpha = 0.05; vertical lines show significance between alpha = 0.05 and 0.1; dots highlight coefficients that turn up as significant with the theoretically unexpected sign

to the models is basically the same as in the models presented in Table 6.18. I have run models on the imputed datasets with all inequality/oppression variables. Economic discrimination turned up as the strongest predictor of the four, followed by cultural restrictions and my economic inequality variable, while political discrimination remained the weakest, scoring only two p-values between 0.05 and 0.1, on two imputed datasets. Since my main concerns lie with the impact of economic inequality, there are the models with MAR's economic discrimination (ECDIS) and my intergroup economic inequality (INEQ_3_ln) included in the table. Compared to the results obtained with the original dataset, it is again the impact of the development indicator GDP/capita and of the external military support that are differently assessed in the model run on the original dataset and the model series run on the imputed datasets. The impact of past violence, political terror, group concentration, and religious fractionalization gets strong support. On the other hand, government effectiveness keeps significant with the unexpected sign.

While the positive sign on the government effectiveness measure can be explained with a combination of collinearity and factual causes, there is no good explanation of why the impact of the external military support became insignificant in the imputed models. As the most important change of these models as compared to the original models has been the addition of the unemployment variable, the phenomenon is probably related to the relationship between the two. In the original dataset, there is no association between the proportion of unemployed young males and the external military aid, but after large-scale imputation to both variables, this has occurred. In the imputed dataset number five, for instance, the correlation between external military aid and proportion of unemployed young males, as measured for year 2005 and citizen groups only, is 0.105, significant at the 0.01 level.

DISCUSSION AND CONCLUSIONS

The single most important hurdle to the cross-national study of group behavior is data availability. Most of the time we have to realize some limitation of the empirical toolkit to be used.

The MAR data has been not only widely used, but also widely criticized; its previous versions as well as this latest edition. It is mainly its case selection criteria that has been targeted, but other features, such as the construction of variables, and even concrete value assignments, can and have also been challenged.[17] Though my task has been to make the most constructive use of the given knowledge base, I had to face the weaknesses of MAR in order to extend some of its variables onto a more complete sample of minority groups worldwide. I think that my EPR_MAR_EXT dataset offered a unique opportunity to review the direction and depth of the MAR selection bias, and also to compare some of its variables with other measurements of analogous phenomena. In addition, the variables imported from EPR_MAR_EXT were also useful for the multiple imputation procedure.

Despite similarities, and common variables, I would like to emphasize that the datasets explored in Chapters 5 and 6 are quite different. There is a difference, on the one hand, with regard to observations, and on the other, with regard to variables. Chapter 5 studied historical minorities, while Chapter 6 includes new minorities and relatively smaller pluralities, as well. In Chapter 5, the main explanatory variable was my intergroup economic inequality measure, in Chapter 6, the main explanatory variable is MAR's "economic discrimination" variable, though most of the time I paralleled the models with ECDIS with models featuring my own INEQ measures, as well. The models run in this chapter included MAR's measures for group concentration, and its values for external support to minorities, as main controls of interest, and occasionally, variables of political inequality and institutional features (representation, autonomy, urbanism) have also been imported from the MAR inventory.

These differences are important because the logic of analysis and fortunately the results, as well, are similar in the analyses presented in the two chapters. The research objective has been to obtain support for three related claims:

(i) that economic inequality leads to intergroup hostility expressed in grievances;
(ii) that grievances increase the probability and intensity of violent conflict; and
(iii) that economic inequality has an impact on violent conflict, which, despite its mediation by grievances, may be directly measured.

These tasks involved the construction of three types of explanatory models, all of which have been packed with the controls most advocated in the literature. They included measures addressing group features and the country's group structure, the development level, variables pertinent to the group's political status in the country and the institutions that shape the minorities' chances of political success, a measure of the foreign aid to groups, and indicators of the opportunity for insurrection. Most of the resulting models have had their explanatory power in the range of 20–25 percent, which is not very high, but still shows some real knowledge about the phenomena. The explanatory variable "economic discrimination" has been significant in most (i) and (iii) type models with which I experimented, and in all of those reported, and its impact has regularly been paralleled by a weaker impact of my own horizontal inequality (INEQ) measure. The only crack in the logical sequence was marked by the failure of the economic grievance variable to be a significant predictor of violent conflict intensity, but only in the model run on the original dataset. In the imputed datasets, economic grievance is a significant predictor of violence, and anyway, economic inequality predicts not only economic grievance, but political grievance, as well. (This latter, in its turn, has been a significant predictor of conflict intensity in the models run on both the original and the imputed dataset.)

Though economic discrimination (and my inequality measure) is a significant predictor of both grievance and conflict, it is not the strongest of them all. Through all models, original and imputed, the most powerful predictor of intergroup hostility is past violence. This may seem to be a slightly tautological finding; but actually, it does justice to a group-consciousness-based theorizing as opposed to individualist approaches, represented mainly by the rational choice paradigm. The same can be said about the also consistently strong impact of the group concentration measure, though here conceptualization in the terms of the opportunity-for-insurrection framework is also possible. The impact of a third control, the political terror scale, may also allow for divergent conceptualizations, as cause of grievance and as lack of opportunity for peaceful strategies, but it does not support the opportunity-for-insurrection hypothesis.

The group- and group-structure measures have been as elusive here as they tended to be in previous scholarly work, as well. Yet, there is a relatively consistent finding emerging from most models: religious fractionalization lowers conflict levels.

The variable for the proportion of unemployed young males does not seem to have been successfully imputed by Amelia. There is too much variance of its performance from one imputation to the other. As a final balance, it can be classified as a potential, but not confirmed, predictor of violence.

Last, but not least, there are a few variables that happened to emerge as significant with the theoretically unexpected sign. Most cases of this type can be attributed to idiosyncratic cross-effects of some highly associated variables, but at least one, the measure of government effectiveness, seems to have been misconceptualized. In the utilitarian tradition, I expected a strong state to deter rebellion. However, my dependent variable of conflict intensity involves the existence of a strong state. The isolation of the deterrent and the inherent effects of government effectiveness cannot be solved through work with either the EPR_MAR_EXT or the MAR_EPR_MI datasets. It becomes possible, however, by relying on a country-level dataset, in which the group-level conflict intensity variable is supplanted with country-level measurements.

The next chapter, Chapter 7, presents and analyzes a country-level dataset. There are serious reasons to believe that our knowledge about social phenomena is not complete without studying them from different perspectives and on different levels of analysis.

NOTES

1. MAR considers only countries above 500,000 people, and groups above either 100,000 members, or 1 percent of the population. These numeric thresholds have been applied to the EPR_MAR_EXT dataset, as well.

2. Scientific testing requires the findings to be replicable. Yet, in the case of multivariate regression models, simple rerunning of the regression, with the same measurements, does not satisfy all expectations related to replication, which involve obtaining the same results with different cases. Rerunning the regressions tests the computational algorithm, but robustness tests (with slightly altered measurements), and validity tests (such as on split samples, and comparing similar measurements), come closer to the methodological ideal of replication.

3. Please see description and availability at http://gking.harvard.edu/amelia/.

4. Another inconsistency discovered during the task of cutting back on variables was that the MAR coders left blank a number of values of the AUTPRO variable. This measures the proportion of a communal group living in their autonomous region, and is by default 0 for groups not benefiting of an autonomous area. In 21 cases, when AUTON2, a dummy indicating the existence of autonomous region, was coded 0, the

by-default zero on AUTPRO was missing. I filled in these, but did not interfere with the really missing values, that is, with cases when AUTON2 was coded with 1.

5. There are further 3 numeric pluralities in the sample, but these have not been coded as pluralities at all, since they are not citizens—it is the foreigners in Jordan (54 percent), Quatar (75 percent), and the United Arab Emirates (80 percent).

6. Though the plight of the Tibetans seriously mars China's human rights records, there are only 3 out of the country's 34 above-100,000 minority groups that are included in MAR, for a percentage of below-10. This is below the world average of inclusion in MAR, which comes to 37 percent. (The Chinese groups in MAR are the Tibetans, the Hui, and the Turkmen/Uyghurs; all three are strongly defined by their religion.)

7. "Any grievance in 2004–2006," "Any conflict in CONIS 2006–2010," and the Intensity indexes calculated for these years.

8. This indicator variable is not part of the dataset subjected to multiple imputation.

9. Since the same does not necessarily apply to the expression and promotion of grievances, we may wonder what causes further minority complaints, once their condition is classifiable as "having autonomy." Unfortunately, a simple binary measure, as AUTON2 of MAR, does not capture everything so important to minorities: whether the autonomous region is large enough to contain all of them, or is too large to feel in control of it, the depth of the autonomy (the competences typifying it), and also the share of these regions from the national or federal budget.

10. The three pseudo-R2-s given by SPSS suggest quite different values. The Nagelkerke is generous and the McFadden very thrifty. In cases when there is possible to run OLS models as well, such as in the case of the model with political grievances, the OLS "real" R-squared comes closest to the Cox & Snell Pseudo-R2-s (in the case of this particular model, for instance, it is 0.236).

11. They are negatively correlated at –0.211. In the imputed datasets they mutually impede each other to reach significance – this is the single most important difference between the original and the imputed models explaining political grievance.

12. I have studied the OLS models for 2005 with the same independent variables, and they are absolutely dominated by two predictors, the measures for past violence and regional concentration. Of the oppression and inequality variables, Economic discrimination and Cultural restriction are significant above Alpha = 0.05, while INEQ is significant at 0.1 only, with a p-value of 0.082. (For 2004, INEQ is also significant above 0.05.)

13. Technically, the logarithmic form was used in the regressions.

14. Year was designated as the time-series variable, and group name as cross-sectional variable. The country name remained an unhandled factor. For all variables in need of imputation, I asked the software to consider past and future values of it (otherwise, I set "lags" and "leads," as Amelia calls these), and limited the values to their logical bounds (such as percentages between 0 and 100, the ordinal scale values between the lower and upper threshold values).

15. The originally five-level political grievance variable, which has already been studied with OLS, produced decent residual plots, and so did the economic grievance

variable. Yet, the originally three-level cultural grievance did not lead to convincingly healthy OLS models, and subsequently the detailed presentation of the results confines to the economic grievance and political grievance. The alternative solution would have been to allocate the closest integer value to the "replacements" produced by Amelia, and keep working with ordinal scales. Yet ordinal models are not good at handling covariates, anyway, which reduced the temptation to revert to them.

16. In the imputed models, the p-values for the unemployed young males measure oscillate widely between 0.967 and 0.019. Unfortunately, there are no good covariates for this measure, and Amelia seems to have assigned it widely scattered random values.

17. For instance, what justifies that the economic and the cultural grievance variables have three levels, while the political grievance variable has five levels? In addition, strangely, the political grievance variable is practically unrelated to political discrimination, but related to autonomy status and separatist movements. POLDIS is defined with regard to the group's representation in the national government (as EPR's power rank scale), while POLGR is defined with regard to the group's demands for separatism, which makes good sense only in conditions of the existence of a regional base containing most of the group members.

Chapter 7

A Country-Level Analysis

PRESENTING THE COUNTRY-LEVEL DATASET

The EPR_MAR_EXT and MAR_EPR_MI datasets, previously introduced and analyzed, contain a number of variables measured on country level, but the analyses in Chapter 5 and 6 relied on groups as units of study. Unfortunately, the amalgamating of group-level and country-level measurements is not without all methodological risks. When we do not address the fact that the groups are nested in their countries, we are likely to lose explanatory power, while the comparative magnitudes of the group-level variables, on the one hand, and the country-level variables, on the other, may turn out to be distorted.

The alternative is to have pure one-level analyses, in this case, for instance, a pure group-level and a pure country-level study. This project faces, however, some problems of its own. The toolbox of available measurements and indicators is not rich enough to allow for running the same regressions, with the same variables, on both levels. For instance, we cannot really imagine a democracy measurement on group level; and some measurements that we can imagine, such as data on employment disaggregated along communal groups, have not been implemented thus far. Though a handful of countries may have these measures, most of them do not. There is a lot of uncertainty about whether the country-level and the group-level measurements of seemingly identical things are the same things, indeed.[1] As for the association among phenomena, there are clear examples for their divergence on different levels of analysis, and all methodology textbooks include warnings about the "ecological fallacy."

Yet, another century-old methodological endeavor is to build bridges between different levels of study, find the causes of any divergence experienced, and formulate laws that explain the transformation of lower-level phenomena into upper-level features, sometimes referred to as "bridge laws."[2]

Within the limits of the feasible, I intend to carry out a pure country-level analysis in this chapter, and confront these results with the findings obtained from the group-level analysis.

I will proceed by presenting my country-level dataset, and then I operationalize the hypotheses with the available country-level measurements. As the research questions for this country level analysis are identical with those targeted in the group-level analysis, I set out to collect data on similar phenomena, able to serve as good operationalization of my dependent and independent variables. I aimed at obtaining information about domestic turbulence, the country's group structure, development level, international environment, institutions, and issues of social justice. I have used four large-scale compilations (1) and several primary data sources (2). In the codebook attached to my replication data, the source of every variable is marked.

The four compilations are:

1.1 Quality of Government (QOG).[3] This collection specializes in institutional data, such as democracy and good governance, but also contains information on development levels, group structure, and history of the countries. It contains all widely used democracy indicators, such as the Freedom House, Cingranelli-Richards (CIRI), and political terror scale ratings, as well as the World Bank Institute's Worldwide Governance Indicators initiated by Kaufmann et al. in the early 2000s.[4]

1.2 Database of Political Institutions (DPI).[5] This database is more narrowly focused on formal institutions, and I consulted it for detailed institutional variables such as decentralization measures and electoral proportionality.

1.3 Pippa Norris's Democracy Data (Norris).[6] These have a very broad inventory including institutions as well as development and conflict indicators, besides country averages of opinion survey results.

1.4 The World Factbook maintained by the CIA. This source was consulted mainly for information on unemployment and vertical inequality.

I begin the list of original sources with statistical data from the United Nations [2.1], but actually these can be regarded as, and partly certainly are, compilations, as well. The data provided by the UN are collections of official national data, but they also harmonize and systematize those, while specialized UN organizations, such as the World Bank and the UN University, produce datasets that go beyond the national statistics. I relied on the World Development Indicators (UN WDI 2011) for population numbers, migration and refugee data, and development indicators. For the Gini measures, I consulted the UNU-Wider dataset, and two other UN publications.[7] The UN's World Development Report of 2009 also includes two variables of the UCDP-PRIO database, relating to the type and intensity of armed conflicts in 171 countries.[8]

Other direct sources of data included in my data collection sheet are listed in the following text. Some of them have been included in the compilations mentioned earlier, as well, but I consulted the original source so that I obtain the freshest data available and occasionally, to make better sense of how those data were obtained, such as in the case of the Institutional Profiles Database (IPD) data.

2.2 KOF Globalization Indicators.[9] The set of globalization indicators consists of three indexes for economic, social, and political globalization, plus a summative index including information of all three. The economic indicator was missing for the largest number of countries, a total of 32, and I created a duplicate of it by imputing 27 values from its regression on the overall globalization index, which has had only 5 countries missing (Iraq, North Korea, Somalia, Taiwan, and Timor-L'este).
2.3 IPD.[10] This is a database maintained by the French government, offering expert coded indicators. The experts collected and rated information along nine dimensions of social life, one of them being "Social cohesion and mobility," which includes three ordinal variables of high importance for my project: (i) respect for minorities (ethnic, religious, linguistic, etc); (ii) conflicts of an ethnic, religious, or regional nature; and (iii) violent social conflicts of not communal nature.[11] As of 2012, values were available for years 2006–2009, but for 121 countries only. The IPD conflict measures were incorporated in the World Governance Indicators (WGI), or otherwise, IPD is one of the sources of WGI.
2.4 The GPI.[12] This measure of peacefulness and/or bellicosity was launched by the Vision of Humanity think tank. It relies on 23 component indicators,[13] which include the military conflict levels together with potential for terrorism, violent demonstrations, and violent crime. Some indicators measure the consequences or the remedies against violence, such as the number of displaced people, and funding for UN peacekeeping missions. Though called "peace index," it is coded toward increasing violence levels: the highest value is the least peaceful. The index, initiated by Steve Killelea, has been endorsed by Kofi Annan, the Dalai Lama, Desmond Tutu, Martti Ahtisaari, Muhammad Yunus, Jeffery Sachs, Mary Robinson, and Jimmy Carter, and the specialist teams serving the project are coordinated by the Economist Intelligence Unit.
2.5 The FSI series, which has recently been rebaptized "Fragile States Index," is the work of a Washington-based think tank called Fund for Peace.[14] Though the organization was founded in 1957, the indexes have been published since 2005 only. Technical advancement has been crucial for the elaboration of this index set: it is mainly based on a gigantic content analytic endeavor, involving millions of media feeds each year,

carried out by a software dubbed Conflict Assessment Software Tool (CAST). In its early years, the project was led by Pauline H. Baker. The methodological concept behind the creation of the yearly FSI is to add up scores obtained along 12 dimensions deemed to be the most consequential for state failure. For my project, two dimensions are of special importance, called "uneven development" and "(vengeance-seeking) group grievances."

The data collection effort resulted in much more variables than I effectively used in subsequent analyses. I gave up considering variables that turned out to have limited geographic coverage, and opted for alternative measurements, when they were available. For instance, of several fractionalization indexes, I chose those of Alesina, because they were missing for a smaller number of countries (3 to 8), than those of Fearon, or of Annett. The *lacunae* in the Alesina data were filled in by calculating the corresponding indexes based on my own group composition data.

All my imputations (calculations, extra- and interpolations) are thoroughly documented in the codebook's "Notes" column. Other changes that I had to make to the imported data are also marked in the codebook, for instance, the recoding of a variable.[15] Beyond imputations and recoding, though, I have also created new variables, mainly with mathematical, sometimes with more intuitive methods, for instance:

- Data on the number of internally displaced persons, as well as of net migration have been divided by the population number in order to get comparable percentages.
- A federalism and a decentralization indicator, both designed as ordinal scales, were created as averages of preexisting measures. QOG includes four measures of federalism (gtm_unitary, no_ufs, h_f, and iaep_ufs), while Norris includes two (watts2, geering). By also consulting Blume & Lorenz's (2008) summary of previous trials to quantify federalism, I chose the values that were congruent with the largest number of previous measurements possible. With the decentralization index, I could rely on pure mathematics to a larger extent, my values are averages of four decentralization measures included in DPI.
- With the vertical inequality (Gini) and unemployment data, I faced the double challenge of missing values and diverse sources working with different methodologies. The UNU-WIDER World Income Inequality Database (WIID) of 2008 highlights the complexities around measuring vertical inequality. Equally legitimate Gini indexes may be calculated from income data and from consumption data, for individuals and for households, from market revenues and from after-state-redistribution revenues. I chose to

rely on two Gini index series used by the UN experts in their own calculi, and used further sources in order to fill in values for 26 countries missing from the UN accounts.[16] The unemployment data were even more lacunar. The main and practically single data collector in this domain is the International Labour Organization (ILO). Of the countries included in my sample, there are 58 for which the 2011 edition of the WDIs does not have any measurement of the unemployed young males between 2001 and 2010. Where there have been any, I extended the value on all years between 2005 and 2010. Unfortunately, the countries without these indicators cannot be taken for a random sample—they are all in the less developed country group.[17]

- I have also created a variable to measure minority autonomy in countries, but in ways that incorporate the necessity for this autonomy, too, in the measure. As already revealed in Chapter 4, I started out from a variable meant to measure the regional concentration of communal groups in each country. Its long-form descriptive name is "administrative subdivisions fall along communal lines," and the technical label is "Communal_sub_divisions." Because of its novelty, this proxy for regional concentration is rough enough, it was designed as a 5-point ordinal scale. The minimum value of 0 is for countries in which the administrative divisions are practically completely blind toward the ethnic (communal) composition of the population, and there are no minority-majority territorial units beyond a few villages (for instance, Algeria, Slovenia, Sweden). The maximum value of 1 is for countries where there are extended areas in which the minority is a majority, and the subdivisions are defined with respect to this (e.g., Belgium and Switzerland). Three in-between values have been allocated to transitional forms, such as 0.25 for Slovakia,[18] 0.5 for Chad and Sri Lanka, and 0.75 for Nigeria and Spain. The bulk of the work was carried out by comparing the administrative maps of the countries with the language maps retrieved from the Ethnologue website, while trying to place all groups included in my EPR_MAR_EXT on these maps.[19] In a next step, the Communal_sub_divisions variable was used to create a measure capturing minority autonomy by interacting it with the Decentralization index.

With all variables considered, including identifier variables, such as year and country name, the country-level data collection datasheet stretches to 252 variables, and includes 169 countries, all for the time interval 1999–2010. A selection of these variables has been used to add country-level information to the 155 countries included in the EPR_MAR_EXT dataset. For country-level analyses, I also shortened the variable list. The operational dataset to be introduced in the statistical software does not contain, for instance:

- the "raw" variables from which a more synthetic was calculated, such as alternative federalism, decentralization, and Gini measures.
- measurements that were dropped on behalf of alternatives with larger geographical coverage (such as Fearon's ethnic fractionalization on behalf of Alesina's, and "Employment in agriculture" on behalf of "Rural population").
- measurements that were omitted from the final analyses, such as variables pertinent to country history and consciousness values measured with the WVS.

The operative dataset used for this chapter contains 100 variables. The size of the dataset counts for the application of multiple imputation techniques. Softwares like Amelia calculate the missing values with reference to all variables existing in the dataset. In general, the more interconnected variables there are, the better are the estimations, but too many variables may exceed the capacity of the software. Ultimately, though, the dataset introduced in Amelia II had to be cut back to 57 variables, and it took three hours to be processed.[20]

OPERATIONALIZING THE ASSUMPTIONS WITH COUNTRY-LEVEL DATA

The primary analysis level of a study focused on the relationships among groups should be, obviously, group level. Yet the group interactions, such as cooperation versus overt hostility, emerge as the "peacefulness" versus "bellicosity" of the domestic realm. These may seem to be elusive features, but actually, there have been several measurements of them, scientifically sanctioned and effectively used for decision-making. Most variables to be dealt with in this chapter have been designed as country-level measurements, without much concern about how they would look on the group level. Inversely, however, when we try to derive country-level measurements from group-level measurements, certain validity issues emerge. Some "translations" are more straightforward than others. I would call a valid transposition, for instance, the EPR variable for the proportion of the population excluded from power ("Excluded"). The country-level version of my INEQ_1, derived as the standard deviation of the WQI values in each country, captures some of the magnitude of horizontal inequalities, but does not address the group structure issues of fractionalization and polarization, which shape the political impact of economic inequality.

A number of group-level variables used in Chapters 5 and 6, such as group grievance and intergroup conflict, intergroup inequality, and group power rank, here are replaced with country-level indicators. Others, unfortunately, have no adequate "translations," only proxy measurements. For instance, group proportions are approximated with fractionalization and polarization indicators; and past intergroup violence may be approximated with lagged values of the conflict indicators. My selections of measurements are listed below by using some numbering to facilitate the overview. Dependent variables make up the first big group, and the explanatory variables come next.

1. The dependent variables are meant to capture intergroup animosity and hostility of varying magnitude. There are at least four synthetic indicators created to measure the peacefulness or bellicosity (or conflict-proneness) of societies, all four with the advantage that they include and quantify smaller conflicts, as well, which may not result in battle deaths, but involve violence and cause human suffering.
   1.1 The GPI of the Vision of Humanity is available for a large number of countries, but only after 2007. It is coded toward decreasing peacefulness, thus it is, actually, a measure of bellicosity, rather than of peacefulness.
   1.2 Among the WGIs, which we may attribute either to the World Bank Institute, or more concretely to Kaufmann, Kraay, and Mastruzzi, there is one called "Political stability and lack of violence" (WGI Political Stability), meant to measure the extent to which the central authority has a legitimate monopoly on the use of force. It is coded toward increasing peacefulness, or, more generally, toward more virtuousness of the government.
   1.3 The Weighted Conflict Index of Banks is a composite measure including assassinations, *coups d'état*, purges, riots, and guerilla warfare, along with demonstrations and strikes. The Norris compilation contains values for the years 1999–2007, but there are several missing entries, mainly for the last year (2007).
   1.4 The FSI is supposed to measure the attributes of a failing state, such as loss of the monopoly on the legitimate use of force. Since I intended to use a part-measure of this index as an explanatory variable, I could not include it as a dependent variable. Yet this index has one more part-measure of interest, which may serve as an intermediary dependent variable, or mediating variable, as listed below.
   1.5 The FSI series component called "(Vengeance-Seeking) Group Grievance," which was elaborated it in order to measure the:

   > history of aggrieved communal groups citing injustices of the past, sometimes going back centuries; pattern of atrocities committed with impunity against communal groups; specific groups singled out by state authorities, or by dominant groups, for persecution or repression;

> institutionalized political exclusion; public scapegoating of groups believed to have acquired wealth, status or power as evidenced in the emergence of 'hate' radio, pamphleteering, and stereotypical or nationalistic political rhetoric; groups aggrieved because they are denied autonomy, self-determination or political independence.[21]

There are several direct measurements of conflict available, such as the number of battle deaths, of refugees and of internally displaced people. Table 7.1 sheds light on my reasons to select the first two on the above list as my dependent variables. Both are more strongly correlated with the direct measurements (battle deaths, refugees, displaced persons), than these three are associated among themselves. And they have more common cases with the Failed States indicators, than the Banks Conflict measure. The comprehensive Failed States indicator was included in the table in order to check on its validity, and I think that its performance ($r > 0.80$ with both WGI Political Stability and the GPI) may convince us about the capacities of content analytic data collection.

Table 7.1 includes two variables that we owe to the group of French experts working for their government, who produce the IPD, and distinguish between conflicts of a communal nature (such as ethnic, regional, and religious), on the one hand, and conflicts not involving communal groups (and dubbed "social," for simplicity), on the other. To date, we have no better measurement to distinguish between these two types of conflict. The UCDP-PRIO classification into "conflict over government" and "conflict over territory" is pertinent to very severe conflicts only, and may miss the communal nature of certain conflicts not involving territory, such as caste emancipation issues, for instance. As for the GPI and the WGI Political Stability, they are both more strongly related to communal conflicts than to social conflicts. The empirical problem is that the two types of conflict are quite strongly correlated between themselves, at 0.504 across the 121 cases. There are, in addition, conceptual problems, as well, around distinguishing between communal and noncommunal social conflicts. I would adopt the working definition that communal conflicts are those induced and fueled by group grievances.[22]

2. My explanatory variables cluster in six groups.
   2.1 Intergroup economic inequality has only one country-level measure of wide geographical coverage, the FSI series' component called "Uneven Economic Development" (FS_inequality). It is supposed to measure "ethnic, religious, or regional disparities"[23]. Because this is a relatively new indicator, not really tested in the literature yet, I compared it to (i) the vertical inequality measure Gini; (ii) the country-level measure generated from my INEQ_1 variable by calculating the

Table 7.1 Correlation Matrix of Main Country-Level Measurements of Conflict

	Failed States Index	*Global Peace Index*	*WGI political stability*	*IPD communal conflict*	*IPD social conflict*	*Banks Conflict Index*	*Refugees*	*Internally displaced*	*Battle deaths*
Global Peace Index	.801 (684)								
WGI political stability & lack of violence	–.804 (726)	–.885 (542)							
IPD communal conflicts	–.625 (475)	–.662 (454)	.739 (484)						
IPD (noncommunal) social conflicts	–.665 (475)	–.577 (454)	.663 (484)	.504 (484)					
Banks Conflict Index	.311 (382)	.497 (253)	–.481 (1155)	–.466 (238)	–.194 (238)				
Refugee population	.250 (735)	.239 (548)	–.223 (1516)	–.287 (484)	–.237 (484)	.148 (1493)			
Internally displaced persons	.288 (724)	.418 (540)	–.353 (1345)	–.376 (481)	–.173 (481)	.272 (1158)	.267 (1517)		
Battle-related deaths	.181 (560)	.377 (399)	–.277 (1349)	–.326 (365)	–.111 (365)	.313 (1492)	.119 (1692)	.160 (1353)	
UCDP-PRIO Conflict intensity	.343 (558)	.635 (395)	–.542 (1347)	–.501 (363)	–.246 (363)	.557 (1492)	.196 (1689)	.285 (1351)	.471 (1688)

Note: All Pearson correlation coefficients are significant above 0.001, except for two that feature p-values of 0.003 and 0.035, respectively. Numbers in parentheses are case numbers, the correlations were calculated across all cases available (from all years available).

standard deviations; and (iii) the inequality measure used by Baldwin & Huber (2010), which exists, unfortunately, for only 46 countries. Table 7.2 shows these correlations. In addition, the extended correlation matrix highlights that the group grievance and group conflict indicators display much higher correlations with the horizontal inequality indicators than with the vertical inequality measure Gini.

Table 7.2 shows the values for year 2006. The year selection is important because of the Failed States inequality measure. Other measures in the table are invariant or close to invariant for the period 2005–2010, but the Failed States measures' coverage expanded from 76 countries in 2005 to 146 countries in 2006, surging up to 168 countries in 2010. In addition, the data collection method is likely to have undergone a major software overhaul after 2005, as well.[24]

Table 7.2 reveals decent, reasonably high correlation values among the five horizontal economic inequality measures. Further, the associations of the horizontal inequality measures with the Gini indexes show the same interesting pattern. None of them is significantly associated with the market income–based Gini, but they are significantly associated with the Gini measure after state redistribution took place. Since people are effectively left with the after-redistribution income, group relationships are more likely to be influenced, indeed, by Gini_net, than by Gini_market. Further, the least associated with Gini is my own variable, and this may suggest that it is the least likely to be associated with conflicts other than communal. This conjecture has been borne out by the IPD data of the French experts. Table 7.3 shows that the vertical inequality indexes are stronger associated with noncommunal violence than with communal conflict. The Baldwin & Huber measures are also strongly related to noncommunal violence, while the Fund for Peace measure is almost evenly related to the two types. My variable, or more exactly, its country-level manifestation, is maximally selective: it is only related to conflicts of communal nature.

The Fund for Peace's group inequality indicator seems to get enough support to serve as a country-level measure of intergroup inequality, mainly for the years after 2005. Indeed, the only thing we may reproach it for is that it incorporates too much of vertical inequality. But so does the only competitor, the Baldwin & Huber measure, as well.

2.2 The country's group structure is an unavoidable control in a study focused on group relationships. Unfortunately, the country-level toolkit to measure these features is more limited than what we have had in EPR_MAR_EXT and MAR_EPR_MI. There are the fractionalization indexes, and the variables pertinent to polarization (the proportion

Table 7.2 Correlations of the Failed States Inequality Scale with Other Economic Inequality Measures (2006)

	Failed States Inequality	*Standard dev. of Ineq_1*	*Baldwin & Huber v1*	*Baldwin & Huber v2*	*Baldwin & Huber v3*
Standard deviation of Ineq_1 values	.269				
(significance)	.001				
(number of cases)	142				
Baldwin & Huber horizontal inequality v1	.562	.450			
(significance)	.000	.002			
(number of cases)	45	46			
Baldwin & Huber horizontal inequality v2	.547	.426			
(significance)	.000	.003			
(number of cases)	45	46			
Baldwin & Huber horizontal inequality v3	.559	.405			
(significance)	.000	.012			
(number of cases)	37	38			
My_Gini (based on two UN series)	.452	.126	.520	.478	.579
(significance)	.000	.119	.000	.001	.000
(number of cases)	146	155	46	46	38
Gini after state redistribution (Solt)	.545	.395	.580	.579	.639
(significance)	.000	.000	.000	.000	.000
(number of cases)	84	84	35	35	29
Gini without state redistribution (Solt)	–.046	.045	–.028	–.065	–.048
(significance)	.681	.684	.874	.710	.803
(number of cases)	84	84	35	35	29

Table 7.3 The Inequality Measures' Correlation with Types of Conflict (2006)

	Failed States Inequality	*Standard deviation of Ineq_1*	*Baldwin & Huber v1*	*Baldwin & Huber v2*	*Baldwin & Huber v3*	*Gini (UN based)*	*Gini Net (Solt)*	*Gini Market (Solt)*
IPD communal conflicts	–.538	–.241	–.359	–.354	–.388	–.246	–.332	.051
(significance)	.000	.008	.020	.022	.021	.007	.004	.671
(number of cases)	115	120	42	42	35	121	72	72
IPD social conflicts	–.593	–.130	–.486	–.424	–.458	–.505	–.583	–.026
(significance)	.000	.157	.001	.005	.006	.000	.000	.827
(number of cases)	115	120	42	42	35	121	72	72

of the largest minority group and of the plurality), to serve as basic measurements. I could not venture to obtain certain finer-grained variables, such as the nature of group markers, and distances on them, for my whole sample. The lack of group history variables was the most painful, as past violent conflict has been proven to make conflicts more likely in the future. This concern was partly answered by adding lagged values of two conflict variables to the dataset. In addition, I have used my indicator "Administrative subdivisions fall along communal lines" (labeled "Communal sub-divisions") as a proxy for group concentration.

2.3 My basic assumption related to the country developmental level is that violent conflicts are less likely in economically more advanced countries. Yet, this inhibiting effect is probably mostly mediated, mainly through the institutions of democracy, and partly through urbanism affecting geographical concentration, occupational structure, and education. Democracy creates possibilities to express more grievances, but the developmental level is likely to influence the *severity* of grievances and their *salience* for the groups. The Third World's ethnic conflicts are typically clashes about the necessary means of living (either land, or control of state revenues, or both), issues that have a deep existential impact on the participants. Though the claim that groups in more developed countries are less likely to engage in violent conflicts is not controversial in the literature, development level is a very important control for all other potential explanatory factors. Fortunately we have a number of available indicators with wide geographical coverage, such as GDP, HDI, urbanism, education, life expectancy, and Internet use.

2.4 There are several assumptions related to the impacts of the international environment, but in general this is not taken for the main factor, or a very strong factor determining the relationships among domestic groups. The strongest impacts are expected by those who claim that

- International support to minorities, either from kin states or from the international community, will encourage them to articulate grievances and engage in mobilization. (This is a widely endorsed belief, shared by MAR theorists and advocates of the opportunity for insurrection hypothesis alike.)
- Western-imposed global norms of solving group conflicts, and mainly the Western ideal of nation-state, induce group conflict in the global South. As a special case we may think of Amy Chua's (2002) argument that the Westerners' blindspot toward group-asymmetrical distribution of wealth

may lead to underestimating the risk of ethnic hatred and violence, when they promote free-market policies in the less fortunate parts of the world.

Even in these cases, the international effects add to, or trigger, preexisting internal problems, and are not causes in themselves. Other, more moderate impacts on group relations are expected from the spread of modernist and postmaterial values, which reduce parochialism and majority exclusivism, as well as from the norms and power of the international community, which work to smooth away intergroup conflicts.

The country-level dataset addresses these concerns with the set of KOF globalization indicators. Political and social globalization may be deemed to reduce intergroup conflict, while the expectations related to economic globalization are mixed. Sadly, any test involving the economic globalization indicator, such as a test of Amy Chua's claim that importation of neoliberal economic policies by states with market-advantaged minorities undermines internal peace, is obfuscated by the fact that the most developed countries are both the most globalized and the less diverse.

2.5 Within the variable group of country institutions, I have targeted accounting for both the effectiveness of the state apparatus and the inclusiveness of the political system. Effectiveness has a very convincing measure, the WGIs' "Government Effectiveness" component. Indicators of inclusiveness toward minorities should tap on two main venues in which minorities may be politically successful: (i) having representation in the national government, and (ii) self-governing. The first venue is best served by democracy, and mainly by proportional representation electoral systems. Arrangements supportive of self-governing are federalism along group lines, decentralization along group lines, group territorial autonomy, and functional autonomy (pillarization). The inclusion measurements contained by the dataset are the Freedom House/imputed Polity democracy indicator, the political terror scales, electoral family scale, and a dummy for a proportional electoral system. Ethnic self-government is operationalized with an interaction term of the decentralization indicator and my "administrative subdivisions fall along communal lines" variable. Since a measurement of functional autonomy keeps missing from the cross-national research's toolbox, I considered introducing a variable that measures the outcome of all institutional arrangements, the political empowerment of minorities. From EPR, we may derive two pertinent country-level indicators, the number of excluded groups, and the proportion of the population excluded from political power. These measures exist for 149 countries in my sample, and are missing for 20, while the ordinal variable for "Respect for minorities"; originated by IDP, exists for 121 countries, and is missing for 48.

Unfortunately, work with these institutional indicators is complicated by both collinearity issues and missing data. There is a very high correlation between state effectiveness and of democracy, and further, between the democracy indicators and the ordinal measure for proportional representation. The interaction term between the degree of federalism and "federalism along ethnic lines" indicator is also too much correlated with the degree of federalism indicator itself.

2.6 Finally, the opportunity for insurrection hypothesis forwarded by Fearon and Laitin in 2003, claiming that decisions about military action are taken in function of the likelihood of success, and/or of the benefits of insurgency for the organizing political entrepreneurs, may be addressed with variables such as the WGI government effectiveness, the group concentration proxy ("administrative subdivisions fall along communal lines"), proportion of rural population, and the proportion of unemployed young males. Substantively, these variables may be classified with the development, group structure, and institutional clusters, as well.

DATA ANALYSIS AND RESULTS

Exploratory Analysis

I checked on the bivariate relationships between the dependent variables, on the one hand, and the explanatory variables, on the other, with simple Pearson correlation coefficients. The correlation matrices are summarized in Appendix 6. I have included in analyses all cases available, from all years.

As in the previous chapters, as well, I looked at the bivariate association of the outcome variables with the predictors grouped in the five large explanatory groups.

The first group included the economic inequality measures. With the exception of the preredistribution Gini index, all inequality measures are convincingly correlated with the conflict indicators, and all in the expected direction: more inequality means more conflict. The horizontal economic inequality measures are more strongly associated with conflict than the vertical inequality measures. Meaningfully, vertical inequality has more impact on IPD's noncommunal social conflict, than on communal conflict.

Of the predictors belonging to the group structure cluster, it is only the religious fractionalization indicator that fails to emerge as significant in relation to the conflict measures. Larger plurality group reduces the likelihood of conflict, while larger minority group, regional concentration, and past violence, as measured with lagged conflict indicators, increase it.

Ethnic and linguistic fractionalization show strong positive association with the incidence of violence. Since the relationship between fractionalization and conflict is deemed to be curvilinear, I studied their scatterplots. We may capture the real nature of this relationship only when we control for a confounding factor, the development level. In developed countries violent conflict is rarer than in the less developed, since a part of communal issues gets solved with peaceful political means. Against this background, the fact that developed countries have less fractionalization than the less developed, leads to an overestimation of the pacifying impact of less fractionalization. If we split the countries in two large groups along the development indicator "Female life expectancy above 70 years," we get two convincingly inverse U-shaped regression lines in the developed group, as Figures 7.1 and 7.2 show it. (The WGI Political Stability measure was coded inversely than the GPI.)

The development indicators themselves are associated, as generally expected by previous scholarship, with lack of violence. The associations

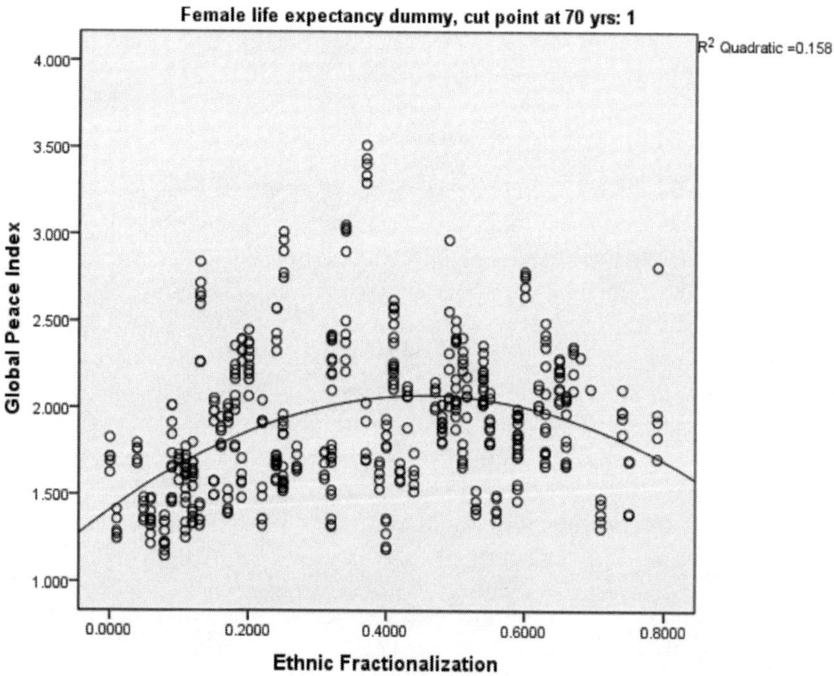

Figure 7.1 Relationship between Ethnic Fractionalization and Conflict I.

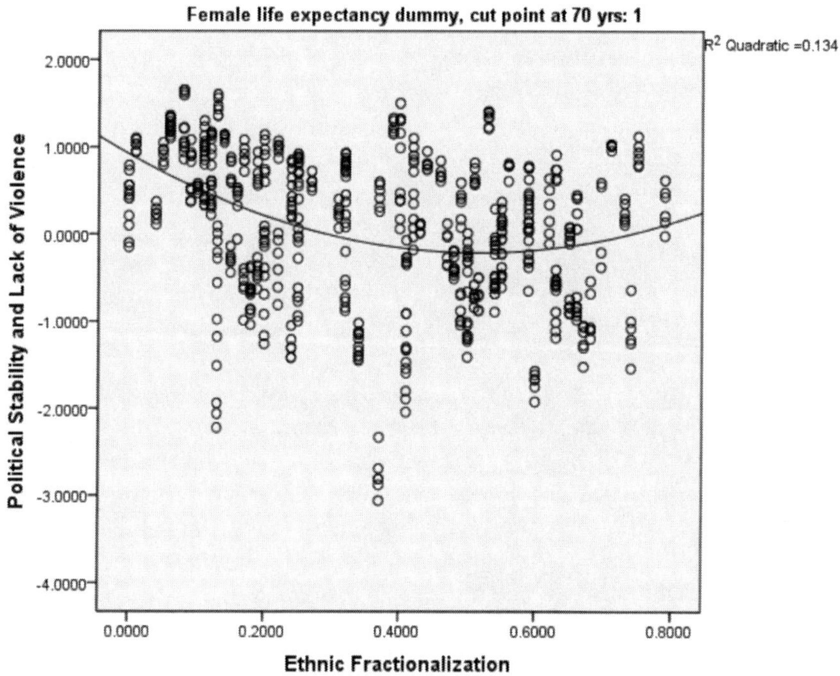

Figure 7.2 Relationship between Ethnic Fractionalization and Conflict II.

are higher in the case of the noncommunal social conflict, than in the case of the communal conflict. Also, the developmental indicators tend to show lower coefficients with the Group Grievance indicator, than with the conflict indicators. As for globalization, we may assume that the correlation coefficients between the KOF indicators and conflict are magnified by the connection between development level and globalization. Partial correlations, calculated with controlling for female life expectancy, are 100–300 points lower than the simple bivariate globalization*conflict coefficients, and political globalization fails to reach significance in relation with three conflict indicators.

Further, I studied the relationships between conflict and institutions, or, more broadly stated, the factors that express and shape political inequality issues among groups. Unfortunately, some of these, such as EPR's "Excluded groups" variable, and two indicators showing whether ethnicity and religion-based parties are banned, cover only earlier years in my dataset, and have little if any common cases with most dependent variables. Their correlation coefficients with the WGI Political Stability measure convey the idea that prohibiting communal politicizing increases the likelihood of violent conflict. Congruently, the associations displayed by the IPD

"Respect for minorities (ethnic, linguistic, religious, etc)" variable can be read in the sense that minority-friendly policies reduce the probability of violence. These findings do justice to those who believe that the best way to prevent communal animosities from escalating into violence is to channel them into the molds of everyday politicizing. Yet, association of two phenomena, without accounting for complex circumstances, is not yet a conclusive argument. A defender of the ban on ethnic and religious parties would argue that it was the already exacerbated communal hostility that led to banning the parties. Unfortunately, I cannot pursue the inclusion of these variables in my regression models, because of time span and case number limitations.

The narrow-sense institutional variables, such as the democracy, proportional representation, and decentralization measures, cover a larger range of countries. Both democracy measures are strongly associated with more peacefulness. The measures of proportional representation are also associated with less violence, if not very strongly, but at least persistently across several measures, doing justice to Reynal-Querol (2005), for instance. The study of the impact of autonomy arrangements is less common in the previous literature, and I had to use my own measurement of minority autonomy, conceived as an interaction term. Findings show that while the regional concentration of minorities increases the risk of conflict, decentralization reduces it, and their interaction term becomes insignificant several times. Unfortunately, this is a simplified version of the story. In a more comprehensive approach, we have to account for the country development level, as both regional concentration, and decentralization are associated with it.

A matrix of partial correlations (summarized in Appendix 6) shows that the relationship between regional concentration and conflict is smaller, when we discount the development effects. Most surprisingly, decentralization in itself cannot be claimed to reduce violence. When we control for development level, decentralization is mostly insignificant. Yet, my minority autonomy measure suggests that regional concentration paired with decentralization is always less dangerous than regional concentration not allowing for regional and local governance.

The indicator of regional concentration may also be taken for an "opportunity for insurrection" variable, and it is a quite potent one, even when we control for the development level. Lack of both urbanism and of government effectiveness have strong impact on the likelihood of violence; yet they are strongly associated with development indicators, as well. The unemployed young males variable is not convincingly correlated either with the FSI or with the IPD Social Conflicts scale. This may be the artifact of the missing data; in the case of the other four conflict measures, the percentage of young unemployed males increases the risk of conflict, as predicted.

Regression Models with the Original (Collected) Data

The regression analysis includes three types of models. In cross-national studies, the traditional way to engage in the explanation of violent conflict are the omnibus models including all available explanatory variables promoted in the literature. This type of model-building is unavoidable for my results to be comparable with previous achievements. Yet, since I hypothesized a two-stage model, in which the causes of intergroup conflict lead to grievances first, and the grievances lead to violent conflict only in cases when the ways for peaceful solutions are blocked, I will have to test these steps with the corresponding models. These involve models in which the Group Grievance indicator becomes the dependent variable, and then models in which the Group Grievance indicator functions as explanatory variable along a number of institutional measures.

I have had fewer reasons to test the impact of my main explanatory variable against the country factor (or alternately, against country dummies), than in the case of the group-level dataset. I ran, however, a model to explain conflict as measured by WGI Political Stability, with only two explanatory variables: the country factor and the FSI's Uneven Development component (FS_inequality). This fourth type of regression, run in SPSS's GENLIN models procedure, returned the p-value of 0.000 for the horizontal inequality measure. Intergroup economic inequality is therefore an undeniably strong determinant of intrastate conflict, but in order to compare its power with those of other predictors promoted in the literature, I had to experiment with different kinds of models, Type I, II and III.

Type I Of the three types of models on which I report here, logically first is the regression explaining group grievance. Unfortunately, the country-level dataset is much less equipped for testing the determinants of grievances, than for explaining conflict. We have only one measure of group grievance, the Fund for Peace's indicator. And the best country-level measure of intergroup inequality, of relatively extended coverage, also belongs to the Fund for Peace indicator series. The two are so highly correlated, at r=0.754, that we cannot completely reject the idea that the content-analytic method of the Fund for Peace leads to some blurring together of the two phenomena. Thus, at the price of seriously reducing the number of cases, I built these models with the Baldwin & Huber horizontal inequality measures, and tested my own "standard deviation" variable, as well. As a further complication, there has been a scarcity of measures for the political status of minorities.

Tables 7.4 and 7.5 summarize findings obtained with the variables at hand. The three models in Table 7.4 achieve considerably high adjusted R-squared values, but the case numbers are low. By replacing the IPD's "Respect for

Table 7.4 Explaining Group Grievances with the Baldwin & Huber Inequality Measure

	Model 1		Model 2		Model 3	
Dependent Variable	FS Group Grievances		FS Group Grievances		FS Group Grievances	
Adjusted R-squared	0.587		0.572		0.526	
Case number	229		167		45	
	St.Coeff.	Sig.	St.Coeff.	Sig.	St.Coeff.	Sig.
Baldwin & Huber 2010 v1	.156	.005	.201	.003	.159	.234
Ethnic fractionalization	-.393	.000	-.431	.000	-.400	.035
Religious fractionalization	.196	.000	.164	.007	.149	.229
Proportion of largest minority	.073	.175	.073	.266	.022	.874
Regional concentration proxy	.193	.000	.199	.001	.172	.187
Lagged Banks Conflict Index	.352	.000	.316	.000	.350	.008
GDP per capita (PPP)	-.565	.000	-.438	.000	-.488	.061
KOF overall globalization index	-.183	.070	-.229	.064	-.276	.285
IPD Respect for minorities			-.116	.082		
EPR Excluded Population (lag)					.032	.801

Note: Here and in all following regressions presented, I will use the same pattern (and color) coding as in previous chapters. The cells of the p-values significant above alpha=0.05 have a (green) trellis pattern, and p-values between 0.05 and 0.01 are highlighted with (yellow) vertical lines. The insignificant coefficients are not marked, (pink) dot pattern is reserved for coefficients that turn up as significant with the theoretically unexpected sign.

Table 7.5 Explaining Group Grievances with My Inequality Measure Adapted to Country Level

	Model 4		Model 5		Model 6	
Dependent Variable	FS Group Grievances		FS Group Grievances		FS Group Grievances	
Adjusted R-squared	0.574		0.623		0.604	
Case number	748		471		134	
	St.Coeff.	Sig.	St.Coeff.	Sig.	St.Coeff.	Sig.
Standard deviation of Ineq_1 (ln)	.179	.000	.121	.001	.142	.020
Ethnic fractionalization	-.226	.000	-.207	.000	-.244	.004
Religious fractionalization	.067	.009	.088	.005	.070	.236
Proportion of largest minority	.216	.000	.185	.000	.138	.055
Regional concentration proxy	.114	.000	.102	.001	.111	.053
Lagged Banks Conflict Index	.264	.000	.233	.000	.273	.000
GDP per capita (PPP)	-.303	.000	-.268	.000	-.407	.000
KOF overall globalization index	-.374	.000	-.351	.000	-.274	.007
IPD Respect for minorities			-.182	.000		
EPR Excluded Population (lag)					.107	.088

Trellis pattern shows significance above alpha=0.05; vertical lines show significance between alpha = 0.05 and 0.1.

Minorities" with the alternate measurement of "Population excluded from power" (a lagged measure from EPR) the case number sinks even deeper, to 45, and the residuals look problematic. The horizontal economic inequality measure scores convincing coefficients in the first two models, and fails to reach significance in Model 3 only. The change can be attributed to the loss of so many cases, rather than to the overriding effect of the last added variable, which also fails to turn up as significant.

Though my group-level INEQ variable was not meant to explain country-level phenomena, I tested its explanatory power in a series of models analogous with the triad above.

Using my own horizontal inequality measure preserves a higher number of cases, and results in slightly higher adjusted R-squared values. In these models only the religious fractionalization measure sinks below the significance level of alpha = 0.1, once, and all other predictors perform as theoretically expected. The standard deviation of INEQ_1 turns out to be a consistent, if not very strong predictor of group grievance. These models may really foster our belief that the knowledge about intra-state conflict is cumulative! Yet given the curvilinear impact of the fractionalization indexes, we cannot have very clear expectations with regard to how they behave in linear models. The impact of the institutions here was meant to be measured with the political standing of the minorities, a fact for which we have reasonably good measurements, with the only problem that they are deficient in covering the area and the time for which these models were built.

Type II Table 7.6 presents four models that aim at explaining the occurrence of conflict when we control for group grievances. I assume that grievances may have several outcomes, essentially depending on a balance of inhibiting and stimulating factors. There are, on the one hand, institutions that may avert violence, and on the other, factors that facilitate the choice of violent ways, impersonated by a total of five predictors in the regressions. The sixth opportunity variable of interest, the proportion of unemployed young males measure was included in separate models, not reported here, because it reduced the case numbers quite considerably. In those models it emerged significant once, in the model analogous with Model 1 of Table 7.6.[25]

The four models explain two different dependent variables, and the models with the same dependent variable differ from each other with regard to the democracy measure used. There are two powerful predictors in these models, along which others may or may not emerge as significant depending on their correlations with these two and other *explanans* included in the model. The two dominant predictors are Group Grievance and Political Terror. A group of development-related indicators, including, but not confining to, GDP, globalization index, rural population, and government effectiveness, which are strongly associated, impede each other to reach significance, and their rivalry is mostly solved on behalf of the government effectiveness.[26] An analogous phenomenon happens with the political inclusiveness indicators.

Table 7.6 Explaining Conflict with Group Grievance and Opportunity Variables

	Model 1		Model 2		Model 3		Model 4	
Dependent variable	Global Peace Index		Global Peace Index		WGI Political Stability		WGI Political Stability	
Adjusted R-squared	.766		.676		.794		.730	
Number of cases	379		518		543		703	
	St.Cf.	Sig.	St.Cf.	Sig.	St.Cf.	Sig.	St.Cf.	Sig.
FS Group Grievance	.407	.000	.646	.000	-.407	.000	-.591	.000
Regional concentration proxy	.161	.014	.242	.000	-.044	.355	-.152	.001
GDP per capita (PPP)	-.008	.854	-.033	.481	.017	.625	.031	.397
KOF globalization index	-.022	.694	-.098	.101	-.065	.139	-.039	.378
Political Terror Scale (US)	.499	.000			-.396	.000		
Freedom H./imputed Polity			.057	.173			-.033	.280
Electoral family	.030	.295	.000	.993	.008	.719	.045	.052
Decentralization index	.039	.348	.131	.002	-.046	.165	-.131	.000
Minority autonomy proxy	-.164	.030	-.231	.003	-.003	.963	.096	.089
Rural population	-.126	.001	-.148	.000	.035	.225	.026	.381
WGI governm.t effectiveness	-.073	.220	-.219	.000	.264	.000	.366	.000

Trellis pattern shows significance above alpha=0.05; vertical lines show significance between alpha = 0.05 and 0.1.

The Political Terror scale is such a strong predictor, that in its presence all other institutional measurements tend to remain insignificant. By contrast, in models with the Freedom House/Imputed Polity democracy measure, the two inclusiveness measures, Electoral Family and the minority autonomy proxy (Decentralization Index * Communal_sub_divisions), get a chance to show their impact. The positive sign on Electoral Family, when it turns up as significant, means that proportional electoral systems are more successful in averting violent conflict, than plurality systems are.

With regard to regional autonomies, the models show that both the regional concentration of communal groups, and administrative decentralization in itself tend to increase the likelihood of conflict once there are group grievances around. Yet, when decentralization means more autonomy for the communal groups, the accumulating group tensions are slightly less likely to result in violent conflict.

Taken together, the models do justice to a number of assumptions about the impact of institutions: democracy in itself, and inclusive democracy in particular, may smooth away violent conflicts. They also do justice to the "opportunity for insurrection" hypotheses; government effectiveness, rural population, and regional concentration of the communal groups have shown a consistent, if not perfect performance across the models. The unemployed young male measure has been less convincing, but, unfortunately, this variable is far from perfect.

Type III Last, but not least, I ran 14 "omnibus" regression models with my dataset containing collected data, labeled the "original dataset," as a difference from the five datasets obtained with multiple imputation later. The first and probably most important models are included in Table 7.7, while the following Tables 7.8 and 7.9 add additional information to these.

Table 7.7 contains two models with each of the two main dependent variables, the GPI and the WGI Political Stability and Lack of Violence component. First of all, these models fully support the substantively important impact of the horizontal inequality variable. The control variables were chosen with the intent to maximally represent each predictor group, but within the safety limits dictated by the need to reduce collinearity. In addition, models with the measure of unemployed young males were run separately, again, and presented in Table 7.9. With all these precautions, Model 1 and Model 3 were built with 14 predictors each, and the highest VIF value of the predictors did not exceed 9.47 (with a tolerance of 0.106). The models have

Table 7.7 Explaining Violent Conflict with Inter-Group Inequality and Controls

	Model 1		Model 2		Model 3		Model 4	
Dependent variable	Global Peace Index		Global Peace Index		WGI Political Stability		WGI Political Stability	
Adjusted R-squared	.677		.678		.736		.735	
Number of cases	529		529		637		637	
	St.Cf.	Sig.	St.Cf.	Sig.	St.Cf.	Sig.	St.Cf.	Sig.
Failed States Inequality (Uneven Development)	.270	.000	.270	.000	-.144	.000	-.145	.000
Linguistic fractionalization	-.050	.158	-.038	.249	.045	.116	.066	.015
Religious fractionalization	.062	.033	.067	.020	-.007	.759	.002	.936
Proportion of largest minority	-.016	.569	-.015	.597	-.057	.014	-.055	.018
Regional concentration proxy	.375	.000	.378	.000	-.286	.000	-.281	.000
Lagged Banks Conflict Index	.352	.000	.352	.000	-.375	.000	-.373	.000
Life expectancy (female)	-.043	.365			-.082	.030		
KOF political globalization	.037	.268	.039	.240	-.225	.000	-.220	.000
Freedom H./imputed Polity	-.111	.006	-.109	.007	.104	.001	.109	.001
Electoral family	-.019	.520	-.022	.457	.065	.007	.062	.010
Decentralization index	.044	.316	.038	.379	.041	.259	.025	.474
Minority autonomy proxy	-.310	.000	-.315	.000	.181	.003	.174	.004
Proportion of rural population	-.089	.017	-.074	.026	-.114	.000	-.085	.002
WGI governm.t effectiveness	-.312	.000	-.328	.000	.473	.000	.442	.000

Trellis pattern shows significance above alpha=0.05; vertical lines show significance between alpha=0.05 and 0.1; dots highlight coefficients that turn up as significant with the theoretically unexpected sign

Table 7.8 Explaining Violent Conflict with Inter-Group Inequality and Controls—Distinguishing between Communal and Social Conflicts

	Model 7		Model 8		Model 9		Model 10	
Dependent variable	IPD Communal Conflict		IPD Communal Conflict		IPD Social Conflict		IPD Social Conflict	
Adjusted R-squared	.497		.479		.555		.535	
Number of cases	472		472		472		472	
	St.Cf.	Sig.	St.Cf.	Sig.	St.Cf.	Sig.	St.Cf.	Sig.
Failed States Inequality (Uneven Development)	-.406	.000	-.394	.000	-.105	.067	-.118	.043
Linguistic fractionalization	-.258	.000	-.175	.000	.062	.195	-.029	.517
Religious fractionalization	.032	.431	.077	.056	-.004	.910	-.053	.165
Proportion of largest minority	-.046	.239	-.036	.375	.004	.907	-.008	.842
Regional concentration proxy	-.166	.046	-.152	.072	-.358	.000	-.373	.000
Lagged Banks Conflict Index	-.296	.000	-.303	.000	-.237	.000	-.229	.000
Life expectancy (female)	-.282	.000			.306	.000		
KOF political globalization	-.035	.424	-.023	.613	-.042	.314	-.056	.190
Freedom H./imputed Polity	-.016	.753	.010	.841	-.079	.105	-.108	.029
Electoral family	-.012	.758	-.027	.506	.073	.052	.089	.021
Decentralization index	.241	.000	.201	.001	-.085	.128	-.042	.457
Minority autonomy proxy	-.007	.942	-.026	.789	.337	.000	.358	.000
Proportion of rural population	-.236	.000	-.156	.001	-.118	.014	-.206	.000
WGI governm.t effectiveness	-.082	.264	-.196	.005	.232	.001	.356	.000

Trellis pattern shows significance above alpha=0.05; vertical lines show significance between alpha=0.05 and 0.1; dots highlight coefficients that turn up as significant with the theoretically unexpected sign. A new (color) pattern used in this table to highlight the findings is (blue) horizontal stripes. Non-communal social conflict is not expected to be seriously affected by inter-group economic inequality, and the small coefficients do justice to this expectation. Similarly, we do not expect fractionalization to have an impact on social conflict.

high explanatory value, and do justice to most hypotheses promoted in the literature, but also suffer from two sign reversals: on the one hand, political globalization,[27] and on the other, two development indicators turn up with the theoretically unexpected sign, in different models.[28]

In order to probe the depth to which the relationships in the models are influenced by development level, I ran a split-sample analysis of Model 4, with a developed and a less developed country group. The impact of the inter-group inequality variable is considerably higher in the developed country group. It happened that some predictors significant in one development group failed to emerge as significant in the other, but there was only one case of complete reversal of the impact. The interaction variable with which I measured communal autonomy, turns up with negative sign in the less developed group (meaning it induces conflict potential), and with positive sign in the developed group (meaning it reduces conflict potential). I do not have a full explanation for the phenomenon, but it seems that the uneven and antithetical

Table 7.9 Explaining Violent Conflict with Inter-Group Inequality and Controls—Adding the Unemployment Variable

	Model 11		Model 12		Model 13		Model 14	
Dependent variable	Global Peace Index		WGI Political Stability		IPD Communal Conflict		IPD Social Conflict	
Adjusted R-squared	.677		.758		.532		.541	
Number of cases	384		427		353		353	
	St.Cf.	Sig.	St.Cf.	Sig.	St.Cf.	Sig.	St.Cf.	Sig.
Failed States Inequality (Uneven Development)	.478	.000	-.264	.000	-.499	.000	-.007	.921
Linguistic fractionalization	-.016	.676	-.022	.493	-.297	.000	.013	.788
Religious fractionalization	.140	.000	-.050	.086	.035	.452	.019	.683
Proportion of largest minority	-.088	.012	.000	.996	-.035	.434	.071	.113
Regional concentration proxy	.344	.000	-.229	.001	.055	.599	-.235	.023
Lagged Banks Conflict Index	.331	.000	-.346	.000	-.241	.000	-.287	.000
Life expectancy (female)	-.042	.397	-.097	.023	-.247	.000	.485	.000
KOF political globalization	.091	.016	-.217	.000	-.056	.262	.052	.295
Freedom H./imputed Polity	-.130	.005	.119	.001	-.053	.361	-.174	.003
Electoral family	-.003	.940	.087	.003	-.068	.147	.056	.228
Decentralization index	-.075	.137	.108	.009	.361	.000	-.029	.651
Minority autonomy proxy	-.219	.023	.085	.267	-.262	.027	.255	.030
Proportion of rural population	-.117	.004	-.040	.240	-.213	.000	.053	.341
WGI governm.t effectiveness	-.163	.006	.443	.000	-.063	.426	.305	.000
Unemployed young males	.068	.027	-.065	.009	-.064	.108	.146	.000

Trellis pattern shows significance above alpha=0.05; vertical lines show significance between alpha=0.05 and 0.1; dots highlight coefficients that turn up as significant with the theoretically unexpected sign.

distribution of the two component variables making up the interaction term is responsible for the difference found. In the less developed group we have a lot of regional concentration and little decentralization, while in the developed group, it is inversely: there is less regional concentration and considerable levels of decentralization.

Table 7.8 presents work with the two additional dependent variables, which allow for distinguishing between communal conflict and non-communal social conflict. The most important fact about these models is the obviously different impact of a number of explanatory variables. Communal conflict and non-communal social conflict have different causes, for instance, the horizontal inequality measure and the linguistic fractionalization index, fairly strong in models explaining communal conflict, weaken to insignificance in models explaining social conflict. Despite the 0.5 correlation between communal and social conflict, as measured by the IPD indicators, the differences of the impact of predictors are fairly visible. Of 13 indicators it is only the measure of past conflict that affects both types in very similar way, and three variables do not have really significant impact in either case (political globalization, largest minority, and religious fractionalization). Electoral Family counts for social conflict, and does not count for communal conflict, while the configuration of the triad of regional concentration/decentralization/interaction-of-the-two is different in communal and social conflict models.[29]

Finally, Table 7.9 reports on omnibus models that include the predictor for the proportion of unemployed young males. This variable substantially reduces the case numbers, and the omissions are not completely random—the least developed countries are overrepresented among those with missing data. Models 11 through 14 do not contradict findings obtained from the models without the unemployment variable, but there is a larger percentage of unexpected coefficient signs.[30]

The regression models presented in sections 2.1 through 2.3 have all supported the impact of intergroup economic inequality on the likelihood of conflict, both in direct "omnibus" models, and in the two-stage modeling, through the articulation of group grievances. In addition, most predictors promoted in the literature have also received some empirical support.

Sadly, all regression models presented in sections 2.1 through 2.3 suffered from two issues: (i) high association between the explanatory variables, and (ii) missing cases. While our response to collinearity cannot be but casuistic, for missing cases there is a generally recommended cure: multiple imputation. The next section will put it to work.

Multiple Imputation

I cut back the dataset to 57 variables and introduced it in the Amelia II multiple imputation software. I obtained five imputed datasets, each containing 2,028 cases (169 countries along 12 years, from 1999 to 2010). Since the FSI exists from 2006 only, and the GPI from 2007, I ran my "omnibus" models on shorter time frames, to maximize the number of original values of the main dependent variable and the main explanatory variable. The five imputed datasets returned surprisingly similar regression models, which essentially resemble the models based on original data, as well. Out of 116 regression coefficients from the original models only one that was significant above alpha = 0.05 in the right direction did not receive confirmation from any imputed model.[31] It has never happened that all 15 predictors have been significant in the same model, but across all models, 14 out of 15 predictors received empirical support. The exception is a control for the impact of the international environment, the KOF Political Globalization index.[32]

Tables 7.10 through 7.13 present the pooled results from the five imputed models side by side with the originals. The pooling algorithm does not give R-squared value and standardized coefficients. Thus I included, on the one

Table 7.10 Explaining Conflict as Measured by the Global Peace Index

	Model 1		Model 11		POOLED Model	
Dependent variable	Global Peace Index		Global Peace Index		Global Peace Index	
Adjusted R-squared	0.677		0.677		0.652 (average)	
Number of cases	529		384		676*5 (>2006)	
	St.Cf.	Sig.	St.Cf.	Sig.	Coeff.	Sig.
Failed States Inequality (Uneven Development)	0.270	0.000	0.478	0.000	.063	.000
Linguistic fractionalization	-0.050	0.158	-0.016	0.676	-.168	.001
Religious fractionalization	0.062	0.033	0.140	0.000	.082	.105
Proportion of largest minority	-0.016	0.569	-0.088	0.012	-.058	.546
Regional concentration proxy	0.375	0.000	0.344	0.000	.645	.000
Lagged Banks Conflict Index	0.352	0.000	0.331	0.000	.000	.000
Life expectancy (female)	-0.043	0.365	-0.042	0.397	-.003	.116
KOF political globalization	0.037	0.268	0.091	0.016	.001	.093
Freedom H./imputed Polity	-0.111	0.006	-0.130	0.005	-.024	.000
Electoral family	-0.019	0.520	-0.003	0.940	-.018	.171
Decentralization index	0.044	0.316	-0.075	0.137	.082	.102
Minority autonomy proxy	-0.310	0.000	-0.219	0.023	-.535	.000
Proportion of rural population	-0.089	0.017	-0.117	0.004	-.001	.044
WGI government effectiveness	-0.312	0.000	-0.163	0.006	-.123	.000
Unemployed young males			0.068	0.027	.003	.015

Trellis pattern shows significance above alpha=0.05; vertical lines show significance between alpha=0.05 and 0.1; dots highlight coefficients that turn up as significant with the theoretically unexpected sign.

hand, the average of the five adjusted R-squared values from the individual imputed models, and the simple slope estimates given for each predictor, displayed near its significance (p-) value. The standardized coefficients for the imputed datasets one by one come closer to the values obtained for the original models without the unemployed young males variable than to the coefficients from the unimputed models containing it. They may be studied in Appendix 7, where the five individual imputed models are described with their standardized coefficients and p-values.[33]

DISCUSSION AND CONCLUSIONS

I hoped that my models would speak for themselves, and would be convincing. They show that we are able to explain large proportions of the variation of violent conflict across states. At a closer look, however, even if we have a grip on a number of determinants, the concrete measures used in regression models may falter either because of the complexities of measuring the phenomenon, or because of the dense association network among social phenomena.

Table 7.11 Explaining Conflict as Measured by the WGI Political Stability and Lack of Violence Scale

	Model 3		Model 12		POOLED Model	
Dependent variable	WGI Political Stability		WGI Political Stability		WGI Political Stability	
Adjusted R-squared	0.736		0.758		0.733 (average)	
Number of cases	637		427		845*5 (>2005)	
	St.Cf.	Sig.	St.Cf.	Sig.	Coeff.	Sig.
Failed States Inequality (Uneven Development)	-0.144	0.000	-0.264	0.000	-.080	.000
Linguistic fractionalization	0.045	0.116	-0.022	0.493	.137	.105
Religious fractionalization	-0.007	0.759	-0.050	0.086	.011	.895
Proportion of largest minority	-0.057	0.014	0.000	0.996	-.420	.009
Regional concentration proxy	-0.286	0.000	-0.229	0.001	-1.231	.000
Lagged Banks Conflict Index	-0.375	0.000	-0.346	0.000	.000	.000
Life expectancy (female)	-0.082	0.030	-0.097	0.023	-.005	.084
KOF political globalization	-0.225	0.000	-0.217	0.000	-.012	.000
Freedom H./imputed Polity	0.104	0.001	0.119	0.001	.036	.000
Electoral family	0.065	0.007	0.087	0.003	.057	.015
Decentralization index	0.041	0.259	0.108	0.009	.052	.525
Minority autonomy proxy	0.181	0.003	0.085	0.267	.827	.000
Proportion of rural population	-0.114	0.000	-0.040	0.240	-.004	.000
WGI government effectiveness	0.473	0.000	0.443	0.000	.431	.000
Unemployed young males			-0.065	0.009	-.004	.120

Trellis pattern shows significance above alpha=0.05; vertical lines show significance between alpha=0.05 and 0.1; dots highlight coefficients that turn up as significant with the theoretically unexpected sign.

In these circumstances, the consistency achieved across models is reasonably high. My main explanatory variable, the intergroup economic inequality, performed flawlessly in all "omnibus" models, run on both the original and the imputed datasets. I think that it undoubtedly established itself as a serious predictor of intrastate conflict, primarily of conflicts of communal nature. Unfortunately, this is not good news for practice. Intergroup inequality is hard to alleviate. Usually it takes a strong redistributive state and a benevolent majority/plurality to redress the relative poverty of minority groups. The emancipation of poorer majorities, on the other hand, takes market-contrary measures. In addition, serious results cannot be expected within the near future, the economic equalizing may take decades and generations.

This fact directs attention to the institutional solutions. What can politics do to alleviate the condition of disadvantaged groups, and channel their political action toward less violent, democratic and parliamentary means? Fortunately, my models have supported the importance of democracy, proportional

Table 7.12 Explaining Conflict as Measured by the IPD Communal Conflict Measure

	Model 7		Model 13		POOLED Model	
Dependent variable	IPD Communal Conflict		IPD Communal Conflict		IPD Communal Conflict	
Adjusted R-squared	0.497		0.532		0.465 (average)	
Number of cases	472		353		845*5 (>2005)	
	St.Cf.	Sig.	St.Cf.	Sig.	Coeff.	Sig.
Failed States Inequality (Uneven Development)	-0.406	0.000	-0.499	0.000	-0.154	0.000
Linguistic fractionalization	-0.258	0.000	-0.297	0.000	-0.585	0.000
Religious fractionalization	0.032	0.431	0.035	0.452	0.188	0.120
Proportion of largest minority	-0.046	0.239	-0.035	0.434	-0.584	0.023
Regional concentration proxy	-0.166	0.046	0.055	0.599	-0.503	0.072
Lagged Banks Conflict Index	-0.296	0.000	-0.241	0.000	0.000	0.000
Life expectancy (female)	-0.282	0.000	-0.247	0.000	-0.018	0.000
KOF political globalization	-0.035	0.424	-0.056	0.262	-0.002	0.272
Freedom H./imputed Polity	-0.016	0.753	-0.053	0.361	-0.005	0.662
Electoral family	-0.012	0.758	-0.068	0.147	-0.034	0.240
Decentralization index	0.241	0.000	0.361	0.000	0.502	0.000
Minority autonomy proxy	-0.007	0.942	-0.262	0.027	-0.078	0.794
Proportion of rural population	-0.236	0.000	-0.213	0.000	-0.011	0.000
WGI government effectiveness	-0.082	0.264	-0.063	0.426	-0.027	0.612
Unemployed young males			-0.064	0.108	-0.007	0.010

Trellis pattern shows significance above alpha=0.05; vertical lines show significance between alpha=0.05 and 0.1; dots highlight coefficients that turn up as significant with the theoretically unexpected sign.

representation, and communal autonomy, measured as decentralization in conditions of regional concentration of the communal groups. They also supported the hypotheses related to the opportunity of insurrection, of which some, such as government effectiveness, and the proportion of young males, can be classified among the things easier to master than intergroup economic inequality.

Compared to results from the group-level analysis (Chapters 5 and 6), this country-level analysis is more convincing in two important regards: the overall explanatory power (as measured by the adjusted R^2-s), and the impact of the horizontal inequality variable. I think that the difference is mainly attributable to the ways in which we measure conflict. The country-level measurements used here are much more sensitive than the UCDP-PRIO, and even than the CONIS conflict data. On the flipside, the GPI and the WGI Political Stability mix communal and social conflict in an undistinguishable amalgamate. This does not weaken the validity of the impact of the horizontal inequality measure, on the contrary. Yet, the fusion of the two types of conflict may

Table 7.13 Explaining Conflict as Measured by the IPD Social Conflict Measure

	Model 9		Model 14		POOLED Model	
Dependent variable	IPD Social Conflict		IPD Social Conflict		IPD Social Conflict	
Adjusted R-squared	0.555		0.541		0.557 (average)	
Number of cases	472		353		845*5 (>2005)	
	St.Cf.	Sig.	St.Cf.	Sig.	Coeff.	Sig.
Failed States Inequality (Uneven Development)	-0.105	0.067	-0.007	0.921	-0.044	0.017
Linguistic fractionalization	0.062	0.195	0.013	0.788	0.113	0.323
Religious fractionalization	-0.004	0.910	0.019	0.683	0.156	0.136
Proportion of largest minority	0.004	0.907	0.071	0.113	0.225	0.261
Regional concentration proxy	-0.358	0.000	-0.235	0.023	-0.949	0.000
Lagged Banks Conflict Index	-0.237	0.000	-0.287	0.000	0.000	0.000
Life expectancy (female)	0.306	0.000	0.485	0.000	0.023	0.000
KOF political globalization	-0.042	0.314	0.052	0.295	-0.001	0.655
Freedom H./imputed Polity	-0.079	0.105	-0.174	0.003	-0.020	0.055
Electoral family	0.073	0.052	0.056	0.228	0.039	0.101
Decentralization index	-0.085	0.128	-0.029	0.651	-0.125	0.174
Minority autonomy proxy	0.337	0.000	0.255	0.030	0.775	0.001
Proportion of rural population	-0.118	0.014	0.053	0.341	-0.003	0.038
WGI government effectiveness	0.232	0.001	0.305	0.000	0.191	0.000
Unemployed young males			0.146	0.000	0.010	0.000

Trellis pattern shows significance above alpha=0.05; vertical lines show significance between alpha=0.05 and 0.1; dots highlight coefficients that turn up as significant with the theoretically unexpected sign.

leave undetected the fact that they have distinct sets of predictors, or more likely, the strength of the individual predictors in the same set is different in the two cases. The variables provided by the IPD are very helpful in this regard. Unfortunately, the French experts coded only 121 countries, thus we have to rely on artificial imputations to get the picture for all countries.

With all the weakness of the economic inequality and intrastate conflict measures that we have, it is still possible to obtain a consistent story of the relationship between the two phenomena. The key to clear-sightedness is to distinguish between communal conflict and noncommunal social conflict, on the one hand, and intergroup inequality and interindividual inequality, on the other. In virtue of the analytical clarity of these distinctions we may sharpen our hypotheses in order to achieve models with higher explanatory power. We should expect horizontal economic inequality to have an impact on communal conflict, and vertical inequality to affect social conflict. The imputed datasets made possible to study this connection on 676 cases (for years above

2006). I ran 20 (4*5) models similar to those reported in Tables 7.10–7.13 on two imputed datasets. (With a random choice, on the first and the fourth imputed dataset.) All models included 14 predictors identical with those in the previous tables, while the Failed States horizontal inequality variable was exchanged, in turn, with two alternative intergroups, and three vertical inequality measures. Table 7.14 reports the standardized coefficient value and the significance of the inequality measures across the four dependent variables, based on the fourth imputed dataset.[34]

The main pattern is common to the two imputations: the vertical inequality measures are highly significant for the explanation of noncommunal social conflict, while the horizontal inequality measures are the strongest for the explanation of communal conflict, but also contribute seriously to the strength of the models explaining conflict in general. The failure of the Gini indexes to reach significance in models with "general" conflict measures may have—at least—two plausible explanations. First, it may be that both variables, GPI as well as WGI Political Stability, measure communal, rather than social conflicts. (This, in its turn, may also accommodate two explanations. First, that our world contains, effectively, more communal, than social conflicts; and second, that our data collection tools are biased toward noticing communal, rather than social conflicts.) The second reason for the failure of the Gini measures in explaining "general" conflict is that they are much more correlated with other predictors than the horizontal inequality measures. Thus

Table 7.14 The Impact of Vertical and Horizontal Inequality in Models with 15 Predictors—Results Based on Imputed Dataset #4, and 676 Cases

Dependent variable	Global Peace Index		WGI Political Stability		IPD Communal Conflict		IPD Social Conflict	
	St.Cff.	Sig	St.Cff.	Sig	St.Cff.	Sig	St.Cff.	Sig
Inter-group (horizontal) inequality measures								
Baldwin & Huber 2010 v.1	0.242	0.000	-0.122	0.000	-0.174	0.000	-0.095	0.007
Standard deviation of Ineq_1	0.030	0.288	-0.042	0.068	-0.091	0.007	0.040	0.191
Failed States Inequality	0.252	0.000	-0.147	0.000	-0.303	0.000	-0.109	0.005
Inter-individual (vertical) inequality measures								
My_Gini (based on UN series)	0.005	0.855	0.025	0.306	-0.046	0.215	-0.284	0.000
Gini after redistribution (Solt)	-0.001	0.960	0.001	0.844	-0.042	0.261	-0.299	0.000
Gini w/out redistribution (Solt)	0.013	0.639	-0.016	0.489	0.063	0.061	-0.184	0.000

Trellis pattern shows significance above alpha=0.05; vertical lines show significance between alpha=0.05 and 0.1; dots highlight coefficients that turn up as significant with the theoretically unexpected sign.

the vertical inequality's impact is lost in multivariate models to collinearity. And obviously, any combination of the two explanations is plausible, as well.

Of all variable clusters considered in the models, it is the group structure cluster of which assessment is the most elusive in this country level analysis. Instead of the actual group size and history of conflict, as well as instead of the group's actual position on the power ladder, we have to be contented with proxies such as fractionalization, proportion of largest minority, lagged conflict indexes, and excluded population. Still, the lagged conflict index and the variable used for measuring regional concentration (communal subdivisions), performed very consistently and convincingly across models. The fractionalization and polarization measures were much more capricious, but given their strong association with the development level, we could not reasonably expect them to show consistent patterns in models overstuffed with development-related predictors.

The choice of the political globalization measure to account for the impact of the international environment does not seem to have been very inspired. It obviously does not measure some important features of this environment, such as support to rebel groups, which was shown to be a very potent predictor in Chapter 6. Yet in these models the main disturbing issue with political globalization is its association with other variables, primarily with government effectiveness. It is hard to reasonably and convincingly account for the impact of colinearity on results. But collinearity may be, and is likely to be, the cause of the most intriguing anti-intuitive findings, including the theoretically unexpected sign on political globalization.

At the end of this chapter focused on country-level phenomena, we may wonder how the findings from the two different levels of analysis - and from the three different datasets - relate to each other. Since the commonalities from the three analytical chapters (5 through 7) are also the general and generalizable results of the project, this comparative overview of the findings is included in Chapter 8, as its first, technical section.

NOTES

1. An example that brings home the argument is my measurement of intergroup economic inequality. I created a country-level indicator out of my group-level measurement of the groups' Wealth Quintile Index (WQI) values by calculating the standard errors of INEQ_1 for each country. Though this country-level measurement expresses the dispersion of the groups on the WQI scale, it does not address my assumption that it is the difference between pluralities and minorities (in both directions), which is highly consequential to social hostility levels, while the minority-minority horizontal relationships are much less likely to have politically relevant

outcomes. Important group structure features, such as size of the largest minority, are also missing from the country-level indicator.

2. The term may be attributed to Ernst Nagel (1961), and it frequently occurs in studies on reductionism and emergence (or supervenience).

3. Teorell, J., M. Samanni, S. Holmberg, and Rothstein (2011) The Quality of Government Dataset, version 6 April 2011, University of Gothenburg: The Quality of Government Institute, http://www.qog.pol.gu.se.

4. The first year for which these indicators were measured is 1996, but the pre-2000 measurements are not commonly included in newer versions of the dataset.

5. Users of the database are requested to cite it as: "Thorsten Beck, George Clarke, Alberto Groff, Philip Keefer, and Patrick Walsh, 2001. 'New tools in comparative political economy: The Database of Political Institutions.' 15:1, 165–176 (September), *World Bank Economic Review.*" Actually, the database was updated in 2010, and it is available at http://econ.worldbank.org/WBSITE/EXTERNAL/EXTDEC/EXTRESEARCH/0,,contentMDK:20649465~pagePK:64214825~piPK:64214943~theSitePK:469382,00.html.

6. These data have a cross-national and a time-series version, both at their third edition in 2009, available at http://www.hks.harvard.edu/fs/pnorris/Data/Data.htm

7. Human Development Report of 2009, and the Gini values used by the UN to correct previous HDI values by incorporating vertical inequality data.

8. In the UCDP-PRIO dataset there are 45 countries out of 171 that have values different from zero for any year of the 12 included in the dataset, and several countries experienced high violence in a shorter timespan only. Since the explanatory variables, such as GDP, fractionalization, state repressiveness, and intergroup inequality show only small-scale, slow changes over the years taken into consideration, relating them to sudden bursts of violence cannot be expected to accurately capture the relationship between *explanans* and *explanandum*. The UCDP-PRIO data is embedded into the GPI of the Vision of Humanity think tank.

9. The authors ask for referring to these data as: "Dreher, Axel (2006): Does Globalization Affect Growth? Evidence from a new Index of Globalization, *Applied Economics 38*, 10: 1091–1110. Updated in: Dreher, Axel, Noel Gaston and Pim Martens (2008), *Measuring Globalisation—Gauging its Consequences* (New York: Springer)." They are freely downloadable from http://globalization.kof.ethz.ch/.

10. Available at: http://www.cepii.fr/anglaisgraph/bdd/institutions.htm.

11. For brevity, I will refer to the latter two as "communal conflict measure" versus "social conflict measure," which does not mean, obviously, that communal conflicts are NOT social.

12. Information and data are available at http://www.visionofhumanity.org/.

13. Number of external and internal conflicts fought; estimated number of deaths from organized conflict (external); number of deaths from organized conflict (internal); level of organized conflict (internal); relations with neighboring countries; level of perceived criminality in society; number of displaced people as a percentage of the population; political instability; level of disrespect for human rights; potential for terrorist acts; number of homicides per 100,000 people; level of violent crime; likelihood of violent demonstrations; number of jailed population per 100,000 people; number

of internal security officers and police per 100,000 people; military expenditure as a percentage of GDP; number of armed services personnel per 100,000 people; exports of major conventional weapons per 100,000 people; imports of major conventional weapons per 100,000 people; funding for UN peacekeeping missions; aggregate weighted number of heavy weapons per 100,000 people; ease of access to small arms and light weapons; military capability/sophistication.

14. Their web address is http://www.fundforpeace.org.

15. Norris used her Electoral_family variable with four levels called 1= majoritarian, 2=mixed, 3=proportional, 4=no competitive elections. I recoded "no competitive elections" into 0, in order to use the variable as an ordinal, rather than nominal measurement.

16. The resulting Gini indexes are correlated at 0.93 with the Solt Gini_net values, which seem to be the most harmonized Gini index series to date, based on the UNU-Wider VIID. Yet, they are also missing for 19 countries in my sample. (http://dvn.iq.harvard.edu/dvn/dv/fsolt/faces/study/StudyPage.xhtml?studyId=36908).

17. The countries without unemployment data for young males are Afghanistan, Angola, Belarus, Botswana, Burkina Faso, Burundi, Cambodia, Cameroon, Cape Verde, Central African Republic, Chad, China, Comoros, Congo DR, Congo Rep, Cote d'Ivoire, Djibouti, Equatorial Guinea, Eritrea, Fiji, Gabon, Gambia, Ghana, Guatemala, Guinea, Guinea-Bissau, Haiti, Iraq, Kenya, Korea (North), Laos, Lesotho, Libya, Malawi, Mali, Mauritania, Montenegro, Mozambique, Myanmar, Nepal, Nigeria, Oman, Papua New Guinea, Rwanda, Sao Tome & Principe, Solomon Islands, Somalia, Sudan, Swaziland, Taiwan, Tajikistan, Timor-Leste, Togo, Turkmenistan, Uganda, Uzbekistan, Yemen, and Zambia.

18. Hungarians tend to live in a certain area of the country, except for those in the capital city and other large cities, but their region of concentration is divided into several counties. Romas of Slovakia do not have a region of concentration.

19. The idea of checking on the congruence of settlement patterns and administrative units originally emerged with regard to federalism and federal units (states or provinces). I have created the corresponding 5-point ordinal variable (named Communal_divisions), with values between 0 to 1, for federal states. Unfortunately, it turned out not to be very useful in a research whose design involves maximizing the number of cases (states) for analyses. The problem is the large number of unitary states. These either become missing cases, or a composite variable has to be defined, in which unitary states take a value clearly distinguishable from all values that federal states may take on. I have experimented with this solution, but the resulting variable is highly correlated with the federalism indicator itself, and the interaction term of federalism with Communal_division is virtually identical with the federalism component.

20. In the light of the large-scale multiple imputation performed with Amelia, my small-scale imputations may seem unnecessary. Yet I needed these filled-in values for the analysis of the original dataset, as I have been reluctant to rely on the imputed datasets only.

21. Fund for Peace webpage, description of the Failed States indicators, as accessed in 2010–2012. The currently (2013) available label and explanatory text is

shorter. Group Grievance includes "pressures and measures related to discrimination, powerlessness, ethnic violence, communal violence, sectarian violence, religious violence."

22. The FS Group Grievance indicator is associated with IPD Communal Conflict at –0.71, and with IPD Social Conflict at –.58. This latter is only slightly higher than the correlation of the two conflict types (.504).

23. Fund for Peace webpage description of FS indicators as displayed in February 2013. The previously posted information (available in 2010–2012) specified that "Group-based inequality, or perceived inequality, in education and economic status; group-based impoverishment as measured by poverty levels, infant mortality rates, educational levels, etc.; rise of communal nationalism based on real or perceived group inequalities."

24. It seems that in the first year of its existence, the FSI was produced with a less perfect algorithm, which led to results little correlated with the indexes obtained in the following years. Results from 2006 through 2010 are highly correlated among themselves, and give convincing correlations with other conflict indicators, as well.

25. The other predictors were affected in the sense that their significance values decreased, but the strongest ones, mainly the group grievance and the political terror measures, kept highly significant.

26. The WGI Government Effectiveness measure is especially strong in models with the dependent variable taken from the same series of indexes (WGI Political Stability). A special affinity between measures belonging to the same battery generally emerges not only because the authors tend to see the respective phenomena as interconnected, but also because of technical issues such as similar scales.

27. Political globalization is expected to have a moderating effect on conflict, and this is what it shows in bivariate correlations. Yet, in partial correlations controlling for development indicators, the association dissipates completely. This seems to express the fact that there are several less developed countries with dense international political connections, but with high communal heterogeneity, weak economy and weak state institutions—all which contribute to their conflict-torn-ness. In these models, in which development levels are over-controlled, political globalization seems to be pushed in the role of an "antidevelopment" indicator.

28. In Model 1, the Rural Population, while in Model 3, the Life Expectancy variable turns up as significant with the wrong sign. Since the most plausible explanation was multiple collinearity, I re-ran the models without "Life Expectancy." The resulting models (Models 2 and 4) are equally strong, but in Model 2 the wrong sign on the Rural Population persists, even if in a mitigated form, that is, the variable came closer to insignificance. Unfortunately, there are further variables in the model that are highly associated with Rural Population, as well.

29. Unfortunately, the VIF value of the interaction term in these models rises to above 8.7, and that of the regional concentration above 6.4, thus we cannot draw far reaching conclusions from these configurations.

30. The measure for the unemployment of young males turns up as significant in the predicted sense in the models with the main dependent variables, and it is not significant for explaining communal conflict. Yet, in the models with the IPD Social

Conflict, the unemployment measure produces an unexpected positive coefficient. It cannot be ruled out that the anomaly is due to the truncated sample.

31. It involved the Decentralization index, highly associated with the interaction term between decentralization and regional concentration.

32. Unfortunately, it is highly correlated ($r = 0.535$) with the Government Effectiveness variable, besides its correlations above 0.4 with Life Expectancy and Rural Population. Thus it happens that the political globalization measure reaches significance with the wrong sign. I am inclined to believe that this is an artifact of collinearity and the fact that large numbers of poor countries with high heterogeneity and internal strife are members in several international organizations. But we cannot exclude the possibility that this KOF measure focuses too much on formal criteria of political globalization, and less on the real commitments of the leaders to a peaceful world.

33. At very strict standards, each model should have been tested for collinearity, heteroskedacity, and autoregression in order to stay with the ordinary least squares (the only method that produces standardized coefficients) and not to switch to models with robust errors. I routinely tested for collinearity, and obtained the diagnostic residual plots with each model. The VIF values went high, but not above 10. The residuals were decent; and heteroskedacity and autoregression do not normally occur in really large samples. Models with robust standard errors, which are recommended in cases of untreatable heteroskedacity or autoregression, make it harder for any predictor to reach significance. Yet, having the standardized coefficients displayed, we may decide ourselves whether a coefficient of 0.086, with a p-value of 0.035, for instance, is a substantively convincing finding or not.

34. If I had used the pooled models, I would not have obtained standardized coefficients for easy comparison. The imputed models have shown in the previous trials that they are reasonably similar. Here the main difference between results from the two datasets is that my standard deviation of INEQ_1 has a little stronger showing in the first imputation (significant at 0.045 in the model with WGI Political Stability, and at 0.000 in the IPD Communal Conflict), while the Gini_market approaches significance with a p-value of 0.091 in the model with WGI Political Stability.

Chapter 8

Conclusions and Questions for Further Research

OVERVIEW OF THE FINDINGS

My simple research design has become so complex in the process of implementation that a synthesis of the findings and conclusions from the three empirical chapters seems unavoidable. Thus, I will compare and contrast results from the group-level and country-level analysis, on the one hand, and from the two-stage explanations and the "omnibus" modeling, on the other hand. This synthesis, the "Overview of the Findings," is meant to contextualize the final conclusions and caveats formulated in the second part of the chapter, the "Epilogue."

Since the single most important research task of this project has been to establish the consequentiality of intergroup economic inequality on the evolution of hostility and occurrence of violence, I begin by referring to some findings obtained with the simplest tests of the horizontal inequality measures. In bivariate relationships, measured with Pearson correlations, all of the intergroup inequality measures used, including my own INEQ series, MAR's economic discrimination, and the Fund for Peace Uneven Development indicator, showed significant coefficients, in the expected direction, with either the grievance or the conflict indicators used as dependent variables. Further, the effect of the horizontal economic inequality measures may be shown to persist against the effect of the most serious challenger, the idiosyncrasies of the countries sampled. I have built a few unorthodox models including only an inequality measure and the country factor, which in generalized linear models is the functional equivalent of incorporating scores of country dummies in ordinary least squares models. The intergroup economic inequality variable turned up as statistically significant against the effect of all country features, or otherwise, against all features characterizing the more than 150 countries included in the samples.

This test of the horizontal inequality confirmed the significance of my INEQ variable with regard to the EPR_MAR_EXT dataset (composed of 155 countries), and of the Fund for Peace Uneven Development (FS_inequality) indicator with regard to the country-level dataset (composed of 169 countries). The significance of the inequality variable in these special models is an argument on behalf of a methodology in pursuit of covering laws, even if these laws are only of a statistical-probabilistic nature, *versus* succumbing to the temptation of more idiographic methods. From the perspective of a social ontology, the measurable causal effect of certain group-level features, of economic inequality as well as of political inequality, and of past intergroup violence, buttresses the importance of communal groups, and their consequentiality for the sub-, supra-, and national environments. As for horizontal economic inequality's rivalry with a number of country-level variables promoted in the literature, such as democratic institutions, and proportion of unemployed young males, its keeping significant against the country dummies means that the horizontal economic inequality should keep its significance in models that would replace ALL country effects with the corresponding variables. It does not mean, however, that the inequality measure surely keeps significant against any group of variables describing a specific selection of country features.[1]

The models with the country factor (or with country dummies) do not answer our interest in the impact of certain phenomena over which we may have some practical degree of political control, and which may, thus, be consciously altered in order to achieve more peaceful group relations. Political institutions are the first to come to mind as subject to change, but a country's globalization and urbanization parameters may also be influenced over time through policy change. Figure 8.1, which is technically an image, but content-wise a table, recapitulates the main "omnibus" models from the three empirical sections of the work (Chapters 5 through 7).

The dependent variable in these omnibus models is conflict turning violent. This is clearer in the case of the group-level datasets than in the case of the country-level data. The dependent variable for the group-level analysis (Intensity index) was specially formulated to include cases of hostility exceeding a certain threshold, high enough so that only a relatively small percentage of the cases score a value different from zero on it. The small variance on the dependent variable (actually used in its logarithmic form in models, to smooth out its tilt to some extent) results in models with significantly lower explanatory power than the country-level models, which have different types of dependent variables. The Global Peace Index (GPI) and the Political Stability and Lack of Violence measure (WGI Political Stability) are more sensitive to lower intensity conflicts within countries, which means that there is virtually no country coded as completely, absolutely peaceful. By taking into account a larger scale of manifestations of intergroup hostility, the explanatory power of the models has increased substantially, up to above 70 percent of the variation explained with the predictors at hand. As a drawback, these conflict measures did not allow us to distinguish between communal and social conflict; thus, two conflict measures from the Institutional Profile Database (IPD) are included in the table. These show that intergroup economic inequality increases communal conflict very substantially, but has a smaller effect on noncommunal social conflict. (Other models, which are not reproduced here, showed that vertical inequality, as measured by the Gini index, has an inverse impact pattern: it increases social conflicts substantially, and the communal conflicts to a lesser degree.)

As for the performance of the intergroup economic inequality variables in these basic models, six of seven turned up as statistically significant above alpha = 0.05, and the seventh is an example par excellence for the exception reinforcing the rule. The model in which the horizontal inequality measure scores a p-value of only 0.067, is the model explaining noncommunal social conflict—in which it has not been expected to perform well, because no theory sanctions that. I must admit, however, that the substantive impact of the intergroup inequality measures in the group-level datasets does not appear strong: the highest standardized coefficient is 0.100. Fortunately, the country-level results present the horizontal inequality variable as not only significant, but also powerful, with a standardized coefficient reaching –0.406, and becoming the single most powerful predictor in the model explaining communal conflict. The discrepancy may be explained with the already referred to difference between the dependent variables used in group-level analysis, as compared to the country-level study. The group-level conflict measures have a high threshold for a conflict to be accounted for, while the country-level conflict measures are more sensitive toward lower intensity hostilities, as well.

Figure 8.1 lists the predictors of these omnibus models grouped in the categories of explanatory factors specified in my flowchart-models presented in Chapter 3. Of the number of available measurements, I used the ones most appropriate to the level of analysis, and attempted to minimize the covariance of the predictors. The association between pairs of explanatory variables, and actually, among whole clusters of them, made the analysis more difficult and accounts for a number of anomalies, that is, predictors turning up as significant with the unexpected sign. By reducing the number of variables of the same kind selected for inclusion in models, such as using only two of three fractionalization indexes, or of four globalization indexes, respectively, I prevented a few anomalies, but could not avoid others related to the broad sense development-modernization complex.[2]

	EPR_MAR_ext		MAR_EPR_mi (robust ml 1)		MAR_EPR_mi (robust ml 2)		Country-level Model_1		Country-level Model_3		Country-level Model_7		Country-level Model_9	
Dependent variable	Intensity index		Intensity index		Intensity index		Global Peace Index		WGI Political Stability		IPD Communal Conflict		IPD Social Conflict	
Adjusted R2	.245		[apprx. 0.277]		[apprx. 0.279]		.677		.736		.497		.555	
# cases	1848		491		491		529		637		472		472	
	St.Cf	Sig.	Est.	Sig.	Est.	Sig.	St.Cf	Sig.	St.Cf	Sig.	St.Cf	Sig.	St.Cf	Sig.
Inter-group economic inequality														
Ineq_3_In	.052	.015												
Ineq_4_In			.045	.014										
MAR economic discrimination					.051	.041								
FS_Inequality							.270	.000	-.144	.000	-.406	.000	-.105	.067
Group/ group structure														
Group proportion	.034	.139	-.177	.573	-.392	.202								
Ethnic fractionalization	-.015	.709												
Linguistic fractionalization			.257	.078	.254	.092	-.050	.158	.045	.116	-.258	.000	.062	.195
Religious fractionalization	-.046	.058	-.258	.088	-.224	.138	.062	.033	-.007	.759	.032	.431	-.004	.910
Proportion of plurality	.014	.727												
Diff. plurality-largest minority			.322	.022	.287	.044								
Largest minority							-.016	.569	-.057	.014	-.046	.239	.004	.907
Communal_sub_divisions	.230	.000					.375	.000	-.286	.000	-.166	.046	-.358	.000
Proportion in regional base			.072	.013	.080	.007								
Past violence (2)	.381	.000	.006	.000	.005	.000								
Lagged Banks Conflict Index							.352	.000	-.375	.000	-.296	.000	-.237	.000

	EPR_MAR_ext		MAR_EPR_mi (robust ml 1)		MAR_EPR_mi (robust ml 2)		Country-level Model_1		Country-level Model_3		Country-level Model_7		Country-level Model_9	
Dependent variable	Intensity index		Intensity index		Intensity index		Global Peace Index		WGI Political Stability		IPD Communal Conflict		IPD Social Conflict	
	St.Cf	Sig.	Est.	Sig.	Est.	Sig.	St.Cf	Sig.	St.Cf	Sig.	St.Cf	Sig.	St.Cf	Sig.
Development														
Life expectancy (female)	.231	.000					-.043	.365	-.082	.030	-.282	.000	.306	.000
GDP per capita, PPP			-.013	.036	-.014	.021								
International environment														
Political globalization index	.078	.005					.037	.268	-.225	.000	-.035	.424	-.042	.314
Economic globalization index	.078	.136												
External military support			.823	.014	.826	.016								
Institutions														
Power rank ordinal scale	.015	.512												
Political Terror Scale	.181	.000	.101	.018	.100	.021								
Freedom House/iPolity							-.111	.006	.104	.001	-.016	.753	-.079	.105
Electoral family (PR)	-.007	.773					-.019	.520	.065	.007	-.012	.758	.073	.052
Decentralization index							.044	.316	.041	.259	.241	.000	-.085	.128
Decentraliz*Communal_s_div	-.270	.000					-.310	.000	.181	.003	-.007	.942	.337	.000
Opportunity for insurrection														
Country's rural population	.156	.000					-.089	.017	-.114	.000	-.236	.000	-.118	.014
Group's urbanism			-.041	.091	-.034	.170								
WGI government effectiveness	.038	.392	.276	.000	.294	.000	-.312	.000	.473	.000	-.082	.264	.232	.001

Figure 8.1 Summary of Seven "Omnibus" Models from Chapters 5 through 7.

The patterning (and coloring) technique used in the figures, identical with the technique used in the previous chapters, may facilitate the observation that, aside from intergroup inequality, two factors always turn up as significant: group concentration and a past marred by serious conflicts. Past violence and its country-level correspondent, the lagged version of the Banks Conflict Index, are the strongest predictors across all models. The effect of the group concentration is also strong, as measured by both MAR's "proportion in regional base" and my country-level "administrative subdivisions fall along communal settlements" (Communal_sub_divisions) variables.

The next pair of predictors with convincing performance is decentralization and decentralization that follows the communal settlement patterns (Decentralization* Communal_sub_divisions). In models containing this pair of variables,[3] at least one of them turned up as significant, in the sense of reducing conflict. This is to be assessed against the backdrop of the persistently significant conflict-increasing effect of regional concentration. My reading of these models is that institutional arrangements that allow for more territorial autonomy of the regionally concentrated groups reduce the probability and/or intensity of serious conflict. This does justice to a Lijphartian vision, rather than to that of Horowitz. However, I could not test the effect of federalism along or crosscutting ethnic lines; and my measure for proportional electoral systems performed weakly, though sometimes it turned up as significant with the sign predicted by the Lijphartian theory and by previous tests by Reynal-Querol (2005). In both cases, there were collinearity issues, mainly the association of the available measurements with the Modernization indicator-cluster that prevented adequate testing without significant changes to the basic research design.[4]

One more predictor that performs convincingly in my models is democracy. I have used two measures of it, the Freedom House/Imputed Polity scale, and the Political Terror scale of the US State Department. Five of seven models in Figure 8.1 indicate that democracy reduces the likelihood of conflict escalation.[5]

Nothing conclusive can be said about the group- and group-structure features beyond the already mentioned effect of past violence and group concentration. On the one hand, fractionalization has a curvilinear relationship with conflict, which does not come across accurately in linear regression models, and on the other, the proportion of the plurality group is too much associated with the development level. I think that the inclusion of these measures in models was necessary, but I could not fine-tune my models to gain more information about the effect of these variables. The other marginally addressed effect was that of the international environment. Only MAR has variables that measure foreign assistance to communal groups. Several tests showed that the military assistance affects conflicts more than the overall assistance levels; thus, I included the former measure in the models run on the MAR_EPR_MI dataset. The social and economic globalization measures, unfortunately, turned out to be too closely related to the development indicators, and I refrained from adding them to a number of models. This also means that I had to give up plans for testing, within the frames of this book, Chua's (2002) claim that too hasty importation of liberal economic policies harms democracy in countries with market-dominant minorities.[6]

As a final remark concerning Figure 8.1, the predictor group of "opportunity for insurrection" is actually larger than the three variables listed there, and it is exactly the variables listed off-category that performed convincingly. External aid, mainly military aid to groups, increases the chances and/or intensity of conflict. Group concentration, which makes organization easier, is one of the strongest explanatory variables in these models. The effect of the proportion of unemployed young males, addressed in the individual chapters, and proven to be oscillating between significance and insignificance, cannot be seen in the models in Figure 8.1, as I had to run separate, smaller-number models with this variable. Unfortunately, there are no good unemployment indicators available to cover all countries in my sample, and the multiple imputation procedure left this effect in limbo; in some imputed models, the proportion of unemployed young males is significant, in others, it is not.

The "omnibus" models were constructed in order to make my findings comparable with those commonly reported in the literature in which violent conflict is the dependent variable. I have been, however, very interested in building models along the two-step process in order to answer my intuition about the evolution of intergroup hostility. Unfortunately, the task turned out to be a little less straightforward than originally anticipated, and was hindered by some technical challenges. As a result, the two-stage resolution did not lead to convincingly stronger explanatory models than the omnibus single-step approach. Nonetheless, and importantly for my overall argument, the effect of intergroup inequality amasses additional support from these models. Figures 8.2 and 8.3 reiterate a few models explaining grievances from Chapters 5 through 7.

One of the two theoretically most challenging questions in my analysis was how to distinguish between institutional features that affect grievances themselves, and institutional features that affect the choice of strategy. For instance, lack of democracy may be a cause of political discontentment, on the one hand, while it also means lack of opportunity for peaceful promotion of group cultural goals, on the other hand. As a compromise solution, these models were built with institutional features that affect communal groups in the most direct ways (i.e., their power rank, and autonomy status), and with the Political Terror Scale, rather than the Freedom House/Imputed Polity measure of democracy. The other difficult decision was related to the

	EPR_MAR_ext (2005)				MAR_EPR_mi (2004-2005)							
Dependent variable	Political grievance (ordinal)		Political grievance (OLS)		Political grievance (robust ml)		Political grievance (robust ml)		Political grievance (robust ml)		Political grievance (ordinal)	
Number of cases	623		623		541		541		543		273 (2005)	
Log Likelihood					-917.132		-917.617		-923.888			
Adjusted R-squared			0.215		[approx. 0.243]		[approx. 0.246]		[approx. 0.237]			
Cox & Snell Pseudo-R^2	.242										.281	
Nagelkerke Pseudo-R^2	.271										.295	
	Est.	Sig.	St.Cf.	Sig.	Est.	Sig.	Est.	Sig.	Est.	Sig.	Est.	Sig.
Horizontal inequality measures												
Ineq_3_ln	.409	.024	.091	.014	.334	.003						
MAR economic discrimination							.135	.002				
MAR political discrimination									.071	.096	.157	.070
Group- and group structure												
Group proportion	3.677	.001	.111	.005	-.432	.340	-.789	.081	-.876	.048	-1.299	.208
Past violent episodes	.034	.000	.393	.000	.007	.000	.007	.000	.007	.000	.018	.000
Ethnic fractionalization	.142	.825	.093	.163								
Linguistic fractionalization					.224	.349	.215	.362	.140	.551	-.031	.958
Religious fractionalization	-.245	.586	-.009	.831	-.634	.016	-.530	.045	-.580	.031	-.662	.250
Proportion of plurality	1.592	.015	.226	.000								
Difference plurality--minority					.810	.000	.743	.001	.695	.001	.764	.168
Proportion in regional base					.277	.000	.271	.000	.266	.000	.331	.001
Communal_sub_divisions	-.186	.661	.019	.640								

	EPR_MAR_ext (2005)				MAR_EPR_mi (2004-2005)							
Dependent variable	Political grievance (ordinal)		Political grievance (OLS)		Political grievance (robust ml)		Political grievance (robust ml)		Political grievance (robust ml)		Political grievance (ordinal)	
	Est.	Sig.	St.Cf.	Sig.	Est.	Sig.	Est.	Sig.	Est.	Sig.	Est.	Sig.
Development & International environment												
GDP per capita, PPP					.016	.025	.017	.017	.017	.019	.000	.219
Life expectancy (female)	.037	.011	.153	.025								
KOF economic globalization	-.034	.086	-.158	.211								
KOF political globalization	.005	.370	.046	.278								
KOF social globalization	.016	.339	.089	.536								
Institutions												
EPR power_rank	-.221	.009	-.032	.426								
Political Terror Scale (US)					.093	.152	.094	.154	.082	.213	.020	.881
MAR group polit.representation					.226	.200	.318	.085	.269	.151	.313	.419
MAR group autonomy					.858	.000	.971	.000	.933	.000	1.539	.000

Figure 8.2 Summary of Six Models Explaining Political Grievances.

	EPR_MAR_ext (2005)				MAR_EPR_mi (2005)		Country level (after 2005)			
Dependent variable	Any grievance (binary)		Economic grievance (ordinal)		Economic grievance (ordinal)		FS Group Grievance		FS Group Grievance	
Number of cases	624		624		273		471		167	
Adjusted R-squared							0.623		0.572	
Cox & Snell Pseudo-R^2	.203		.152		.199					
Nagelkerke Pseudo-R^2	.273		.196		.224					
Predicted %	72.1									
	Est.	Sig.	Est.	Sig.	Est.	Sig.	St.Cf.	Sig.	St.Cf.	Sig.
Inequality measures										
H. economic inequality Ineq_3_ln	.563	.003	.741	.000						
MAR economic discrimination					.625	.000				
Standard deviation of Ineq (ln)							.121	.001		
Baldwin & Huber (2010, 1st v.)									.201	.003
Development & international environment										
GDP per capita, PPP					.000	.208	-.268	.000	-.438	.000
Life expectancy (female)	.029	.058	.042	.014						
KOF globalization index							-.351	.000	-.229	.064
KOF economic globalization index	-.044	.030	.002	.942						
KOF political globalization index	.007	.221	.028	.000						
KOF social globalization index	.028	.105	-.013	.464						

	EPR_MAR_ext (2005)				MAR_EPR_mi (2005)		Country level (after 2005)			
Dependent variable	Any grievance (binary)		Economic grievance (ordinal)		Economic grievance (ordinal)		FS Group Grievance		FS Group Grievance	
	Est.	Sig.	Est.	Sig.	Est.	Sig.	St.Cf.	Sig.	St.Cf.	Sig.
Group- & group structure										
Group proportion	4.351	.001	3.192	.010	-3.942	.001				
Past violent episodes	.045	.000	.012	.000	.001	.678				
Lagged Banks Conflict Index							.233	.000	.316	.000
Ethnic fractionalization	-.138	.840	1.189	.103			-.207	.000	-.431	.000
Linguistic fractionalization					-.007	.991				
Religious fractionalization	-.104	.826	-.169	.736	.013	.982	.088	.005	.164	.007
Proportion of plurality	.816	.229	1.120	.129						
Largest minority							.185	.000	.073	.266
Difference plurality—lg. minority					-.503	.384				
Proportion in regional base					.228	.025				
Communal_sub_divisions	-.837	.069	-.526	.260			.102	.001	.199	.001
Institutions										
EPR power rank scale	-.386	.000	-.272	.005						
Political Terror Scale (US)					-.080	.565				
MAR group polit. representation					1.351	.001				
MAR group autonomy					-.247	.479				
IPD respect for minorities							-.182	.000	-.116	.082

Figure 8.3 Summary of Five Models Explaining Grievances at Group Level and Country Level.

country-level analysis. The only country-level measure of group grievance is part of the Fund for Peace FSI indicator group, to which my main country-level measurement of intergroup economic inequality (i.e., FS uneven development or FS_inequality) also belongs. They are correlated above 0.8, and obviously, FS_inequality would have made a very strong predictor of FS grievance. So strong, that I did not consider it fair to include in my models, and replaced it with less effective, but still potent, intergroup inequality measures, such as the country-level measurement derived from my group-level inequality indicators, and a country-level measurement that exists for 46 countries only, taken from Baldwin and Huber (2010).

Technical hurdles emerged because of the ordinal nature of MAR's grievance indicators. There is some consensus in the literature about the fact that ordinal models do not work well with covariates only; they are better suited for use with factors, that is, other ordinal, or binary and nominal variables. Yet here the software had to handle 11–14 covariates, and regularly complained about the high percentage of "empty cells." In the case of the five-level political grievance variable, I usually repeated the models with the ordinary least square procedure, as well, and the results showed some slight discrepancies, as displayed in Figure 8.2, where the first two and the last two models are identical, but one predictor (the EPR power rank, and the political grievance, respectively), is significant above alpha = 0.05 in one model and not in the other.

Despite these technical challenges, however, all four versions of the horizontal economic inequality measures used in models explaining grievance showed their ability to have an effect on grievances on both the group level and the country level. Of the controls, past conflict and political inequality showed the same constancy across levels of measurement. The country-level measure of past conflict (Lagged Banks Conflict Index) is significant in both models; while the group-level measure (Past violence) is significant eight times out of nine, the exception being the explanation of economic, not of political grievance.[7] In order to reveal the impact of relative political status of the communal groups on political conflict, I used EPR's power rank variable with the EPR_MAR_EXT dataset, and the French experts' coding of state policies toward minorities ("Respect for minorities") with the country-level dataset. Both performed convincingly, even if not impeccably. As for the MAR_EPR_MI data, I wanted to use MAR's own variables, and I included MAR's autonomy dummy together with an indicator of political representation from MAR, and the US State Department's political terror scale. In hindsight, it seems that I should have created a more articulated variable for autonomy as a group-level variable. The models in Figure 8.2 show autonomy as increasing the amount of political grievances. Fortunately, it is easy to notice that the main boosting effect comes from group concentration

("Proportion in the regional base").[8] Without group concentration, there is no need for territorial autonomy. However, in the presence of group concentration and in case of a poorly designed autonomy, requests for more comprehensive or deeper autonomy arrangements will not cease. In addition, some countries are more generous with autonomies than with granting effective and potent political representation to their minorities, and often, autonomy does not exclude political terror.[9]

As for other controls, we cannot really say anything conclusive about the effect of the group proportion and group structure, such as fractionalization and polarization measures. Since they are not linearly related to outcomes, their performance in models built on linear associations is capricious enough. There is, however, an important influence of the development level to be highlighted. In group-level analysis, the development indicators (and a number of factors associated with them, such as democracy and globalization) show a positive effect on grievances: there are more minority complaints in developed countries than in the less developed. At the country level, on the contrary, the development indicator's regression coefficient is negative; it reduces the amount and/or severity of grievances. We may explain this difference by relying on the fact that violent conflict is rarer in developed settings, a finding that has repeatedly been confirmed in group-level bivariate and group means analyses. MAR's grievance indicators used for group-level analysis, and the Fund for Peace's grievance indicator, used in the country-level analysis, are slightly differently formulated. The latter speaks about "vengeance-seeking groups." Thus, higher values on this variable imply a tendency towards violent political activity. MAR's economic and cultural grievance variables are coded toward "seeking remedies" for disadvantages, which leaves open the option for democratic solutions. Actually, the idea of asking for state-provided remedies already assumes a certain development level—such as redistributive capabilities of the state. Moreover, those who target more education, or better jobs, or more representation in the national government, prepare for peace, not for war.[10]

The second step of my two-stage solution features models with a higher explanatory power than that of the omnibus models—not spectacularly, but convincingly higher. A selection of such models, presented in Figure 8.4, has adjusted R-squared values between 0.288 and 0.358 in the case of the group-level models, and between 0.766 and 0.794 in the case of the country-level models. This indicates that grievances are very powerful predictors at both the group level and country level. Their standardized coefficients show them to be among the three most powerful predictors in each model, being occasionally eclipsed by the magnitude of the coefficients for past violence, development, and political terror indicators.[11] The strength of the grievances in explaining conflict does justice to the MAR theorists and followers, or

	EPR_MAR_ext (2005)				MAR_EPR_mi (2004-2005)				Country level (after 2006)			
Dependent variable	Intensity index		Intensity index		Intensity index		Intensity index		Global Peace Index		WGI Political Stability	
Number of cases	620		619		493		491		379		543	
Log Likelihood					-507.81		-489.811					
Adjusted R-squared	0.292		0.358		[appx. 0.288]		[appx. 0.333]		.766		.794	
	St.Cff.	Sig.	St.Cff.	Sig.	Est.	Sig.	Est.	Sig.	St.Cff.	Sig.	St.Cff.	Sig.
Grievances												
Any grievance in MAR	.464	.000			.355	.000						
MAR political grievance			.531	.000			.154	.000				
FS Group Grievance									.407	.000	-.407	.000
Group- and group structure												
Group proportion	.001	.979	-.012	.727	-.441	.148	-.292	.321				
Past violent episodes					.006	.000	.005	.000				
Ethnic fractionalization	-.085	.194	-.099	.114								
Linguistic fractionalization					.245	.103	.235	.097				
Religious fractionalization	-.058	.151	-.058	.134	-.265	.074	-.177	.221				
Proportion of plurality	-.108	.092	-.148	.016								
Difference plurality-lg. minority					.227	.106	.135	.322				
Communal_sub_divisions	.238	.001	.207	.002					.161	.014	-.044	.355
MAR Proportion in regional base					.065	.022	.012	.666				

	EPR_MAR_ext (2005)				MAR_EPR_mi (2004-2005)				Country level (after 2006)			
Dependent variable	Intensity index		Intensity index		Intensity index		Intensity index		Global Peace Index		WGI Political Stability	
	St.Cff.	Sig.	St.Cff.	Sig.	Est.	Sig.	Est.	Sig.	St.Cff.	Sig.	St.Cff.	Sig.
Development and international environment												
GDP/capita, PPP					-.014	.018	-.015	.017	-.008	.854	.017	.625
Life expectancy (female)	.080	.229	.099	.117								
KOF globalization index									-.022	.694	-.065	.139
KOF economic globalization	-.001	.994	.067	.417								
KOF political globalization	-.031	.503	-.007	.866								
MAR External military support					.712	.038	.573	.064				
Institutions												
Political Terror Scale (US)	.169	.001	.185	.000	.096	.024	.102	.012	.499	.000	-.396	.000
Electoral family (PR)	-.005	.911	-.006	.876					.030	.295	.008	.719
Decentralization index									.039	.348	-.046	.165
Decentraliz*Communal_s_divisions	-.180	.020	-.223	.002					-.164	.030	-.003	.963
Opportunity for insurrection												
MAR group urbanism					-.034	.162	-.038	.118				
Country's rural population	.108	.040	.141	.005					-.126	.001	.035	.225
WGI government effectiveness	.133	.068	.102	.142	.273	.000	.261	.000	-.073	.220	.264	.000

Figure 8.4 Summary of Six Models Explaining Conflict, with Grievances Included.

more generally, to a communitarian vision, versus individualistic and rational choice-rooted visions. Grievances, as objective ordeals, affect people as members of a group; the articulation of grievances needs a collective group consciousness, while making it known inside and outside of a country, needs collective action. In addition, the other group-level variable scoring the strongest coefficients in my models is the measure of past conflict, which, as a predictor of impending conflict, is also strongly related to the collective selves of people. My hypotheses about the importance of intergroup inequality have been rooted in a belief in the power of social identities; indeed, if we allow for the causal consequentiality of these identities, we cannot spare questions about their formation and about what hardens the group boundaries.

The weakness of these models consists, again, in some theoretical and technical issues. Theoretically, it is difficult to decide how to handle the variables that from the perspective of this project are neutral controls. No specific hypotheses have been formulated with regard to them, and they are neutral in the debate between communitarian (grievance-supporting) and individualistic (opportunity supporting) visions as well. In the models included in Figure 8.4, these are the group- and group-structure-related variables, included in the group-level analyses rather than than in the country-level tests. It was only the measure of regional concentration included in all models, because it is also a type of opportunity measure; it facilitates the organization of the groups. The technical hurdle consisted in high collinearity (VIF) values in the country-level models, as most institutional and opportunity variables are related to the development measures. Occasionally, this also led to the emergence of a predictor with the unexpected sign, such as of the rural population in the model explaining conflict as measured by the GPI.

The testing of the "opportunity for insurrection" hypotheses suffered from a double hindrance in my analyses. On the one hand, I lacked a good measure of the proportion of unemployed young males; on the other hand, two prominent variables, urbanism and government effectiveness, have been too closely related to the Modernization cluster. The regressions confirmed the serious impact of external aid onto communal group behavior, especially of the military aid, and that of the group concentration.[12] As for the rival hypothesis, the effect of grievances on conflict is indisputably strong, as is the effect of political terror. Together, they suggest that on the ground of existing grievances, terror does not deter minority political action, but rather pushes it toward violent solutions, as it removes the possibility of democratic problem solving. Of other institutional features, decentralization along communal lines showed its positive, conflict-reducing effect, and it did more convincingly, than "pure" decentralization. This, again, does justice to a Lijphartian, rather than a Horowitzian vision of how to pacify ethnically divided societies.

EPILOGUE

I hope that the presentation of the regression results from the three parts of the work, based on Figures 8.1 through 8.4, has managed to give a good summary of the most essential findings. My research design was geared toward supporting the effect of horizontal economic inequality on the evolution of intergroup hostility. The regression models developed for this analysis show horizontal economic inequality to be a consistently significant predictor of intergroup hostility, both grievance and violent conflict, and in country-level analysis it may become a really strong determinant.

I worked with three types of models, of which only those labeled "omnibus" may be rightly compared with previous scholarly work on explaining violent conflict. In these, I endeavored to include all predictors advocated in the literature, and my models support the belief that intergroup conflict is a multicausal phenomenon. The concrete ways in which certain factors have been operationalized have obviously affected the results, and the concrete selections of variables in each model led to idiosyncratic collinearity effects, which resulted in some predictors displaying uneven performance. My omnibus models, however, consistently confirmed the effect of a number of controls taken from diverse categories of predictors, such as clusters operationalizing features of group structure, development level, and institutional opportunities for either peaceful resolution or rebellion.

However, if the omnibus models support the effect of intergroup inequality on violent conflict, they also support that omnibus modeling is not the only way to explain the violent outcome. Intergroup inequality, either economic, political, cultural, or all three combined, may be causally efficient when a group consciousness exists, and group collective action is possible. That is, we must admit to the existence of groups as social entities with a history of their own and a history of their interaction with other groups in society. This warrants a diachronic approach to the explanation of conflict, and further, when the diachronic approach meets congruent macro-level statistical data, such as the observation that in developed countries there are more grievances, but less violent conflict (or rebellion) than in the less developed countries, we cannot help thinking about intergroup relations in terms of stages or steps.[13]

I believe that the two-step modeling of conflict should lead to more variance explained, and I regret that some adverse circumstances rendered the country-level test of this belief inconclusive. Because of validity issues, to avoid putting together two variables belonging to the same index battery, I could not use my best country-level economic inequality variable as a predictor of grievance. There are no simple techniques available to compare the explanatory potential of a one-step modeling with a multiple-step modeling. What I hoped to be able to show was that both models in the two-stage resolution have higher explanatory power than models in the one-stage resolution. Yet, because of the use of the less-performing horizontal economic inequality measures, the R^2-s of the country-level models explaining grievance remained below the R^2-s of the country-level models explaining conflict. The other three comparisons support my methodological vision.

Two additional findings from the regressions concern two debates in the literature. The models show that certain policy arrangements, which substantiate Lijphart's proposal of power sharing along ethnic lines, lower the risk and intensity of violent conflict, while decentralization on its own (while disregarding the ethnic or other communal settlement patterns) does not have the same effect. Lijphart's vision of inclusive democracy gained further validation through the significance of the proportional representation-type electoral arrangements, the conflict-averting effect of which was first shown by Reynal-Querol in 2005. The other controversial issue is whether group grievances are stronger predictors of violent conflict than certain circumstances appealing to Machiavellian elites, either as opportunity for insurrection, or as opportunity for looting. This latter hypothesis (of "greed," as suggested by Collier and Hoeffler 1999, 2004) has not been directly addressed in this book, because (i) certain economically motivated intergroup issues are "Robin Hood-ism," rather than outright robbery; and (ii) larger groups of people cannot be beguiled into violence without creating a discourse that legitimizes the greedy action. Thus, in order to actualize, greed has to surface as economic grievance. My models showed economic grievances, legitimate and illegitimate all together, to have a smaller effect on violent conflict than political grievances.[14] The opportunity for insurrection hypothesis has been tested through a number of variables, and, although I admit to having had some technical issues with its testing, the opportunity for insurrection indicators turned out to be weaker determinants of conflict than the grievance indicators. This finding supports those who have advocated the causal power of grievances, such as the MAR theorists. However, it is not really good news for practitioners intending to avert violent conflict. Group grievances seem to be less influenceable than a number of institutional features that we may deem to be causally consequential for the decision of greedy elites.

I designed my models to test two kinds of "opportunity" factors: on the one hand, those facilitating militarized action, and on the other, those facilitating the peaceful democratic settlement of the issues. These opportunities for "protest" to curb the attraction of "rebellion" have been measured as the country's democracy level, proportional representation system, and minority territorial autonomy. Two of these, democracy (mainly as absence of terror) and autonomy (mainly as decentralization along communal lines) had a convincingly, if not impeccably, consistent performance in the models; proportional representation turned up as significant very rarely. Yet, all institutional variables had a difficult time to manifest their potential because of the high association among them, and also between the institutional cluster and the development measures. Despite a number of technical hurdles, the models allow for the conclusion that grievances count a lot, but the concrete circumstances within which they emerge may shape the outcomes, directing minority political action either toward peaceful or violent-militarized action.

My datasets allowed for obtaining some information in which we may rightly be interested, but have not had the means to gain dependable estimates of them thus far. First, the size and proportion of minorities worldwide is surprisingly high, and in a large number of countries, the boundaries between plurality and minority groups are very fluid. The EPR_MAR_EXT dataset contains data about communal groups comprising 97.5 percent of the world's population, 34.9 percent of whom do not belong to the country's plurality communal (e.g., ethnic, linguistic, or religious) group. Yet, another 10.7 percent of the population included in EPR_MAR_EXT belongs to plurality groups smaller than 50 percent of their country's population, which, in principle, may be rendered a minority by a coalition of other groups. Compared to their large share of the world's population, minorities, as minorities, do not seem to have received their fair share of academic interest. I think there are many benefits from this dataset compiled from scattered previous research; for instance, it allows for:

- an overview of the size and proportion of the communal groups worldwide;
- creating typologies of communal groups;
- taking stock of what we have, in terms of measurements;
- comparing similar variables from different research projects;
- contextualizing (framing) any communal group–related project;
- facilitating the testing of a few older hypotheses, such as the curvilinear association between fractionalization and peacefulness;[15] and
- facilitating the articulation of new approaches and hypotheses.

As for this latest possibility, my idea that the effect of background conditions on violent conflict should be studied in two steps, received early support from the statistical fact that in developed countries there are more grievances, but less violent conflict than in the less developed countries. If a country's group is better at averting low-to-medium level hostility from breeding violent clashes than the other, we should search for country features that are responsible for this variation. More generally, this suggests that with the right data at hand, a simple cross-tabulation may lead to meaningful new research questions. The pacifying effect of development must be assessed against unexpectedly adverse circumstances. Data show that Modernization, as such, is not as favorable for minorities as for pluralities: the relative disadvantage of minorities increases in advanced states. This pattern may be explained, though only partly, with structural issues, such as that developed states have larger pluralities and more new immigrant groups. Unfortunately, we fail to detect any large-scale worldwide trend that would suggest that the economic, political, and cultural gaps between minorities and pluralities would shrink with Modernization.

Once again, I assert my gratitude to the authors of the data on which I relied and endeavored to put to their best use. Nonetheless, faced with the oft-asked question that if I started it all over, what I would change, I have a long list.

First, assuming that I would continue with the large-N quantitative design, I might consider either changing individual variables, or changing the flow-chart-defined variable clusters, or both.

Two disturbing issues with my variables (beyond collinearity, which has no safe antidote, to date[16]), were related to the country-level measurement of conflict, on the one hand, and the measurement of minority political empowerment, on the other. The country-level dependent variable that best suited my research was provided by the IPD, which distinguished between communal and noncommunal social conflict. Yet, the French experts worked out their indicators for only 121 countries, and I had to rely on the less specific GPI and the WGI Political Stability and lack of violence measure, to avoid the sin of list-wise deletion of 48 countries from my sample. A further welcome distinction among types of conflict is between "protest" and "rebellion," as MAR carried it out for group-level. The country level measures that expressly focus on "rebellion," that is, on violent conflict, confine their interest to large-scale violence, mainly, militarized violence. UCDP-PRIO makes its choices based on battle deaths; yet, battle deaths may not be well associated with the number of refugees, internally displaced people, or victims of pogroms, hate crime, and assassinations. The GPI and the WGI Political Stability measure factor in all of these, but, on the other hand, they include nonviolent forms of social unrest, such as demonstrations and strikes, as well.

As for the political participation of minorities, there are three main venues through which they feel empowered: (i) representation in the national government[17]; (ii) territorial autonomy; and (iii) functional autonomy ("pillarization"). Most data are available for the first type, and less—or less adequate—for the second type, while about the third type we do not have cross-national data at all. Yet, none of the available measures addresses the conceptual problem of incorporating in the measure the minority's need for it. Most obviously, the demands for territorial autonomy and functional autonomy tend to be antithetical: regionally concentrated minorities want territorial autonomy, and are relatively indifferent toward functional autonomy, such as a hierarchy of cultural institutions ("pillars") in their language. Regionally dispersed minorities, inversely, want pillarization, not autonomous regions.

The problem that I confronted during data analysis was related to the territorial autonomy dummies. Table 8.1 shows why I think that the autonomy dummies, the only measures available in the scholarly literature, have not been suitable for my purposes.

The problem is aggravated by the lack of group concentration measures. Only MAR has two measures for it, for the 283 groups included in its 2004–2006 version. For the country level, I worked out a more nuanced (interval) variable to capture the autonomy level that the states allow for, and used it in models together with my proxy for regional concentration. With a preference for unique synthetic measures, however, I believe that we should create a group level autonomy measure that fuses the level of need for autonomy with the level of *de facto* autonomy obtained. The same should be done for a functional autonomy measure, while even the measure of representation in the national government could be better adjusted to the need for this representation.[18] Further problems arise if we contemplate the possibility of merging the three types of empowerment measures into one; and if we think about seriously addressing the fact that some minorities may be split along the ideological left-right scale or some more idiosyncratic issue. Unfortunately, there are many respects in which we may plan to improve our tools for measuring minority political status.

Another enticing way to improve the explanatory power of our models is to factor in socioterritorial consciousness(es), either minority or plurality group consciousness, or both. On the minority side, the most important question may be the extent to which the members share the belief in a "linked fate." The corresponding survey question became well known as a strong predictor of African American political behavior.[19] With the multiplication of the international survey projects, the same or similar questions can be asked in a large number of countries. Yet, as of 2013, this has not been implemented, and cross-national survey data on socioterritorial consciousness is very rare. The 2003 edition of the International Social Survey Program (ISSP) on National Identities included an item inquiring about the respondent's attachment to his/her ethnic group, but it was not asked in all participating countries. The WVS inquire about

Table 8.1 Territorial Autonomy Coding and Expectable Minority Attitude

Fact	*MAR and EPR coding*	*Expected minority attitude*
No regional concentration, no autonomy	No autonomy	No grievance
There is regional concentration, no autonomy	No autonomy	Grievance
Regional concentration, some autonomy, not sufficient	Autonomy	Grievance
Regional concentration, some autonomy, felt satisficing	Autonomy	No grievance

attachment to nation, and Pippa Norris (2009) built a cosmopolitanism index from it. Further information, such as about the dominant type of nationalism (typically ethnic or civic) might be a very useful addition to our regression models, but their use strictly hinges on their availability for most countries—and there is not enough survey data to cover all countries of interest.

This question of "How much data is enough?" is vexing. How many countries are necessary and sufficient in order to draw worldwide conclusions from the findings? My choice for the EPR_MAR_EXT was the most conservative, as I aimed at including all countries above 500,000 people that have at least one minority larger than 1 percent. MAR and EPR set up their selection criteria in functional response to their research purposes, which highlights the fact that the necessary sample size is not the same for all projects. In general, a scientifically sanctioned method is to draw random samples from the totality of independent states, or of states and jurisdictions. A really random sample, from which we do not lose cases because of missing data, should allow for conclusions that are generally valid. Yet, my intuition is that with countries, the standard ways in which statistics calculates the minimum samples necessary for reaching given confidence levels, lead to underestimation. Countries differ from each other to a much larger extent than anything else we normally sample, such as bars of chocolate, fish from a pond, and even human beings for an opinion survey. Thus, if I were to pursue a new large-N research project, with improved variables, I would strive to have them for at least a random half of all independent states, to optimize validity. Yet, in order to address collinearity, I would probably opt for near-completeness again. I think that the single most effective improvement to the ways I built my models would have been to create two country groups, split along a development variable. This speculation about sample size may also suggest that I am not very confident about the possibilities of multiple imputation. Actually, in one regard, I completely share the attitude of King and colleagues: use of educated guesses is superior to list-wise deletion. In addition, I am confident about smaller numbers of statistical imputation. However, where the correlation between the variables to be imputed and those with which we predict the missing values is low, the software may depart from the real values too much. The underlying ontological reason here is the complexity of the countries, and the idiosyncratic large differences among them. This latter *caveat* is highly justified with regard to communal groups, as well, though they are less complex structures than countries. Unfortunately, in the case of my groups, a specific limitation of the otherwise very useful Amelia software has come into play: it was not designed to accommodate nested data,[20] while my group-level data does not make perfect sense without acknowledging that the groups are nested in their countries.

The level of analysis is one more problem that I must mention in a series of technical issues with my quantitative research. I am very pleased to have had the opportunity to test my hypotheses on both the group level and country level. Yet, an important challenge remained in suspension. We often have, and I also had in Chapters 5 and 6, mixed models that include both group-level and country-level variables. In Chapter 5, I experimented with multilevel models, and I am convinced that addressing the groups' nestedness in their country leads to models with higher explanatory power than simply adding the effects of the variables from the two levels. The nested models, on the other hand, are more difficult to interpret and diagnose, and, mainly, they exacerbate the collinearity issues, which are, anyway, very severe in a large proportion of social science models.

At the end of this work we may wonder whether we have been equipped enough to address my research question—or similar questions, for instance, about the effect of group concentration, or of the cultural distance between groups—with cross-national quantitative methods. Alternatively, are we better off applying more qualitative methods, such as a multiple case study design? From the point of view of research, as a political science project, my hypothesis has been more suitable for large-N testing than for qualitative tests. The causal links to be traced between intergroup economic inequality and hostility levels are the terrain of social psychology, rather than of political science, even if they have common areas, such as political psychology.

Practically, as of today, it is only politics that may undertake any therapeutic action in this domain. At times, the social psychology advice of Allport to desegregate schools managed to amass the political momentum to make a difference. The advice corroborated by sociology to reduce intergroup economic differences in order to prevent violent communal conflict has not made its way into political decision-making yet. More painfully, however, it is a slow and costly preventive measure. What may make it more attractive, is the moral satisfaction we draw from our society becoming more egalitarian—when we do. On the therapeutic side, we seem to have faster and simpler remedies, truly inherent to politics, which are pertinent to the institutional design. This really brings the argument back to the field of political science, but can we trust that the profession gives the best advice to decision-makers? While there is no agreement about the value of power sharing versus that of Horowitzian constitutional engineering, or the role of group consciousness versus that of political entrepreneurs, or the importance of representation in central power versus that of autonomy, political science cannot really help the practitioners. I would suggest that there is at least one piece of advice that political scientists of all traditions may endorse in their quest for pacifying solutions, even if it is in need of fine-tuning and warnings about possible side effects. Democracy, as such, has convincingly shown its potential to channel group hostilities in the molds of nonviolent "protest," as opposed to violent "rebellion." Yet, as democracy is often associated with unbridled market liberalization, and primarily in the ethnically more complex less developed countries, it may facilitate the economic polarization of the population, increase the distances among groups, and foster animosities. In new democracies, the suddenly emerging minority demands may take majorities by surprise, and the intergroup relations may actually become worse for the duration of the "learning curve."

The discouraging balance is that there are a really small number of generally advocated institutional solutions to prevent deadly conflicts, at least when we think in terms of formal institutions of power-holding, state administration, and electoral systems. When we think in terms of larger written social institutions, we have a few more options, such as reducing the number of unemployed young males, fostering urbanization, building infrastructure, and improving communication. I hope, at least the conflict mediation and conflict resolution knowledge base, which has not been addressed in this work, is less controversial and, thus, more useful for addressing the continuously emerging hot issues around the world.

Personally, I am biased toward the importance of preventive measures, and it was this interest that motivated and powered the book. International relations liberals and many other traditions in the field—with the sole exception of realists—believe that humanity managed to curb the plague of interstate war in virtue of its finding the right principles, the right solutions, and acting upon them—such as bringing about the United Nations system. We are still looking for the right principles and right solutions to curb violent domestic conflicts, as well; but this is a quest that we cannot afford to give up. The more we believe in democracy, the less comfortable we may feel about leaving hostile groups to fight each other until they find their own ways of coexistence in a world replete with arbitrarily drawn state boundaries and increasing numbers of transnationals and migrants.

The logic of the situation is that the games among nonranked groups sharing the state are not zero-sum, and most of the time they are not perceived as zero-sum, which leads to smooth coexistence and cooperation, such as among the tribes in Botswana (except for the Bushmen) and Mali (except for the nomadic Moors). Redressing cultural and political inequalities is a mixed bag with regard to zero-sumness. Pluralities may be convinced that mitigating the minority disadvantages have some positives for them, not only negatives. Allowing for minority cultural advancement is advantageous for the country's international embedding and reputation, and may also be attractive for tourism. Democracy, proportional representation system, and decentralization may also be valued by majorities for their own sake.

Economic inequalities, however, have widely been regarded as zero-sum games, mainly by those who are in the position to implement equalizing policies. For instance, US conservatives as well as West European anti-immigrationist crusaders, both anchor their arguments in the perception of the economy reduced to a tax cycle: money is being taken from "people" to be given to "those lazy minorities" or "those dangerous strangers." This simplifying vision of the world has been promoted by the currently most influential economic doctrine, the Washington consensus-sense neoliberalism. Keynesianism makes the point that putting money in the pockets of the poor is the best investment to keep the economy moving forward. Marxism and brands of radical developmental economics deny both the ability and right of the market to single-handedly allocate all wealth in the society. The neoliberal view of the market is that it lifts all boats, and wealth, even if occasionally it concentrates in the hand of the few, will ultimately trickle down. All other economic visions warn that market allocations are neither efficient nor just, and that unbridled markets are not the right choice for humanity.[21] For nonorthodox economic visions, taxation is not "taking away" from citizens, but rather "taking back" from market-advantaged groups to serve legitimate social purposes, including some assistance to those who are disadvantaged in the marketplace. (Actually, there is only a small fraction of all tax money going to the welfare of the poor.)

Yet, large proportions of the plurality groups have diversity-related reasons to endorse the "taking back" vision only when they face a market-advantaged minority, such as Chinese in East Asia, whites in Africa, and Jews in Eastern Europe. In the more typical cases when a country has minorities poorer than their majority, as in most of the OECD countries, the diversity-related egoist motivation is to endorse the neoliberal view.

My emphasis on "reasons" or "motivations" questions the expectation that people are able to overcome egoism and sincerely commit to ideals such as equality. All great religions and most modern ideologies promote egalitarianism, but humanity has always been inventive enough to find reasons for making exceptions. The contemporary forms of succumbing to nonegalitarianism include the naive naturalness with which people in rich countries accept both the fact that someone in the Third World does his or her job for a fraction of the OECD wages, and the fact that bankers and CEOs deserve more than 200 times as much per hour as a blue-collar worker. These come in addition to the traditional inequalities (e.g., caste and gender) which are still with us. One of the typical ways in which people strike compromises between the egalitarian ideals and the deeply unequal reality is to morally denigrate those who are below them on the social ladder.[22] This is probably most obvious in the case of the communal disparities, but ostensibly typifies other inequalities, as well.

This book has distinguished between intercommunal and interindividual economic inequality within countries, and repeatedly tried to depict their relationships. Unfortunately, our world is torn by one more type of economic inequality, that among countries. It is important to factor in this type, as well, when we try to reflect on the attitudes of the developed countries' pluralities, who also set—more or less successfully—the tone of discourse on equality for the less fortunate parts of the world. Currently, wealthy countries feel threatened both by large influxes of immigrants from developing countries and by "outsourcing" of jobs. Both phenomena encounter bitter resistance; yet, the populations of all developed countries agree that developing countries should keep their markets largely open to the products of the advanced. In this sense, the free-marketeer element of the neoliberal imagery is nicely compatible with the perceived interests.[23]

Based on the OECD plurality population's attitudes toward the developing countries' population and their own—predominantly disadvantaged—minorities, we seem to be able to identify some selfish reasons that explain their enduring attachment to the neoliberal doctrine. The third type of inequality, the vertical one, is generally expected to divide populations, including pluralities, along the "market-advantaged" and "market-disadvantaged" line. Since wage earners are always on the "market-disadvantaged" side as compared to capital owners, support for labor, socialist, social-democratic, and communist parties may be expected to be above half of the plurality population, and in the Nordic countries, it was much higher for decades. In certain cases, and primarily in the United States, however, a vast majority of the white population cannot break free from the spell of Reaganomics. I am not the first and only observer who cannot stop wondering how certain elements of the neocons' agenda, such as destroying trade unions, privatizing and corporatizing the education system, resisting socialized medicine, and making pensions dependent on stock market vagaries could take hold of the minds of the US population to the extent that wages have been declining for several decades and the world hegemon sank to the 23rd position for the median wealth of its population? Yet, I find much less merit in explanations with the antiabortionist Christianity of the Americans than in explanations with a certain perception of their "best interests," as articulated in the context of an increasingly colorful country that wants to dump its products on developing countries. That is, masses of economically disadvantaged minorities and the developing world's disadvantaged billions make American whites believe that they are better off by siding with their national capital than by committing themselves to greater social justice.

While the free-marketeer ideology has such a tough hold on the minds of those who may do something for a fairer world, plans for narrowing the economic gaps are severely constrained. The poverty of a minority actually may be redressed without specific policies targeting minorities; as such, it can be solved within the frames of general poverty alleviation and equalizing the opportunities for all. This is how Roma in East Europe and Blacks in Cuba almost reached parity during communism. Yet, since the fall of communism, there is no country in the world that would venture in that amount of general ("color-blind") redistribution that suffices to emancipate seriously disadvantaged groups.[24] In a neoliberal world, these groups' only chance is to benefit from targeted, group-specific policies, often fueled by some remorse rather than the sense of justice of the plurality population, such as Western Europe's policies toward guest workers, and the US policies toward Blacks.

The baseline condition for redressing minority disadvantages is suppressing all discrimination, legal and economic alike. Nominally, most countries enshrine this ideal, but practically discriminative practices from the part of the population abound, and they are often committed by state institutions, as well, such as with "racial profiling" by police.

Beyond eradicating discrimination, the positive measures favoring the disadvantaged may take two basic forms: targeting regions or targeting groups. Geographically concentrated minorities may greatly benefit from "Affirmative Action" on behalf of their region of residence, such as building infrastructure, improving telecommunications, extending education and health care, and creating jobs in their area. The European Union's cohesion policies, for instance, pursue the development of the disadvantaged areas.

The other venue to help groups emancipate are policies that offer some advantage to the disadvantaged in education, employment, health care, housing, and contracting.

Previously, in Chapter 2, I mentioned the initiative called "Decade of Roma inclusion 2005–2015," involving 11 Eastern European countries and Spain. The participating governments submit periodic reports about what they achieved on behalf of the Roma, share their best practices, and account for the money spent. We may expect a general evaluation of the Decade after it comes to an end in 2015, but currently we have only the individual country reports and a number of civil society reports, to get a hint about its scope and achievements. First, the participating countries and the European Union have already agreed that the program must be continued after 2015, which underscores both its necessity and the fact that it could not attain its goals within the previous decade. We may gain a sense of how much is spent from the 2013 report of Hungary and Slovakia. The Hungarian report claims 239 billion HUF have been spent on Roma integration projects over 3 years, which means slightly less than $500 per year for each of Hungary's approximately 700,000 Roma. As the programs affiliated with the Decade are 50–50 percent financed by the EU and the Hungarian state, this also means an investment of $250 per person of the Hungarian state. The report refers to a number of educational programs, of which the pre-school ability development and types of vocational education seem to be the most emphatic, special health care measures, such as screenings, housing assistance, and employment within public work projects. The Slovakian report sums up the amounts that the Slovakian government invested in projects of the Decade, and the amount, divided by the country's approximately 400,000 Roma, totals about $125 per person in 2013.

The whole concept of the Decade seems to follow the logic of making Roma more competitive in the given environment, by direct investment in their education, healthcare, housing, and sometimes creating jobs for them.[25] This is somehow at variance with the US Affirmative Action programs, which were geared toward regulating the environment to become more hospitable toward minorities. Colleges and workplaces have been expected to feature a representative proportion of minority students and employees, while the concrete ways of achieving more diversity have been left to the individual institutions. Since many of these, mainly colleges, adopted the method to choose, from two equally qualified candidates, the minority applicant, Affirmative Action attracted so much resentment that conservatives have attained its rollback in several aspects by now. Worldwide, individuals and countries are divided on the issue of positive discrimination, its concept and its implementation methods. Some countries set up quotas (India, Finland), others outlaw them (United States); some countries target the promotion of ethnic or racial groups, others prohibit communal trait-based action but offer Affirmative Action based on neighborhood (France); some countries try to subsume all of the gender, race, ethnicity and disability-related positive actions under the same policy patterns, others pursue different goals for different categories of disadvantages.

This book aimed at supporting the need for policies that equalize the economic standing of the communal groups making up the state. Arguing for one or another type of policy would take another research project and another book. Yet, I have a strong intuition that policies that do not make absolutely transparent the amount of common resources that go into assisting a disadvantaged group are not viable. That is, within the Affirmative Action–type policies clear quota systems are preferable to a system that blurs the advantages it offers to minorities, and subsequently remains open to grossly overstated accusations about the extent to which it subordinated efficiency and meritocracy to what is sometimes ridiculed as "political correctness" and other times hated as selfish political allotment to own supporters. Quotas may also highlight the nature of the goals served, whether the policy is about positive discrimination (as offering an advantage) or about the prevention of negative discrimination.[26]

Even better than quota systems in education and employment, is preparing the new generations of minorities to be really competitive in college admissions and job interviews. The European Union's Roma Decade has pursued this, but with the exception of some rare and small-scale experiments, the initiative does not promise the suppression, but only some alleviation of the Roma disadvantage. Of the really radical approaches, a Bulgarian project of establishing medical and social centers for work in Roma communities, to offer nutritional and health care assistance to Roma children since their birth and even earlier, during the pregnancy of their mother, as well as projects that target the preschool education of children, are the most promising. Since in poor communities the disadvantage of children starts as early as their lives, efficient assistance must start balancing those concomitantly. There are not enough data in to make conclusions yet, but it seems that the provision of baby food is cheaper than maintaining special schools for those who fail to cope with the general educational standards, and schooling is cheaper than struggling with crime and maintaining prisons. That is, small well-targeted investments into the welfare of disadvantaged groups may go a long way to narrow gaps. Odds are that society pays much more when hostile myopia blocks the way of small assistance.

Policies targeting vulnerable groups tend to be an issue of the developed world, while in developing countries, where communal groups live in concentration, the agenda is dominated by regional allocation issues. It is not easier to reach agreements in this regard than with regard to allocations to groups, but at least nominally, the ideal of equalizing regional disparities is not seriously challenged. Yet, an increasingly difficult task for policy-makers in many countries, primarily in Africa, is to address the damages done by climate change, which happens to completely destroy resources in places. The affected communal groups may experience dramatic decline of their life standards and become dependent on the sense of solidarity and social justice of others. Unfortunately, we cannot claim either that the developed world offers high moral standards about how to handle these cases, or that the developed countries' dominant discourse could integrate economic and moral considerations into one efficient policy recommendation package. Neoliberalism is programmatically dissociated from all considerations of solidarity and social justice; unfortunately, it has been taking a long time for a critical mass of people to realize that it is dissociated from long-term economic efficiency and welfare increase for the 99 percent, as well.

NOTES

1. In models accounting for all country effects with really adequate variables, the strong effect of some predictors that could interfere with, and reduce the effect of intergroup inequality would be counterbalanced by crosscutting effects, exactly as they are in the reality represented by the totality of country dummies. For instance, the effect of democracy is offset by the "modernization paradox effect," because in

more developed settings, where democracy levels are higher, minorities are smaller, relatively poorer, and less powerful.

2. In each model, I used only one of the two preferred development measures, GDP/capita and life expectancy. Yet, democracy, economic and social globalization, percentage of rural population, and government effectiveness, are highly correlated with both of them; additionally, they are related among themselves, as well. Fractionalization and the size of plurality, and further, group concentration and decentralization, are also significantly associated with the development complex, in both the group-level and the country-level dataset.

3. These are country-level variables, and were not introduced in models with the MAR_ EPR_MI dataset, since this had its own autonomy and political discrimination variables to test.

4. Federalism is related to development, and in addition, the number of federal states is relatively small, which leads to a very high correlation between the federalism indicator and the variable of interest "federalism along ethnic lines." The proportional representation measure includes nondemocracies as the lowest value of the scale, which makes the variable highly correlated with other democracy measures. The only way to fix this would have been to have all autocracies deleted from the sample when using the proportionality measure, and I was reluctant to do this.

5. We may wonder why it has not turned up as significant in the IPD models. It seems that the Freedom House/imputed Polity scale is weaker where the rural population, and/or the life expectancy development measures are stronger. Unfortunately for the model-building activity, development and democracy are intricately interwoven.

6. This test can be designed as predicting intergroup hostility with economic globalization on a sample of countries with advantaged minority groups, which is a relatively small sample, small enough to prevent the application of my models with 12–15 control variables.

7. The predictors of different types of grievance are not exactly the same, a point that was made in chapters five and six. Cultural grievance and cultural restrictions, as a measure of cultural inequality, addressed in Chapter 6, have not been included in this summary, as there is no possibility of comparison with other chapters.

8. MAR's own, group-level group concentration measure is highly significant in all models. My country-level proxy for group concentration ("administrative subdivisions fall along communal lines") is also highly significant in the country-level models, but fails to reach significance in the group-level model.

9. Most typically, the communist states have allowed for autonomous areas of their minorities, while deeply interfering with the actual workings of the government there. However, in the case of complicatedly interspersed settlement patterns, not even a reasonably benevolent central government can impose subdivision boundaries to satisfy all groups involved, such as in the case of the tribal communities in Northeast India.

10. Obviously, these reasons contributed to my option to model the road from minority discontentment to violence as a process with stages. Plenty of evidence shows that the visibility of minorities and their demands on their majorities increase with the advancement of modernization and of democracy. Yet, on the other hand,

considerable evidence indicates that communal violence is becoming rarer in more developed settings.

11. At the country level, I have had only one grievance measure, from the Fund for Peace. Yet, at the group-level, I had the three MAR grievances and the synthetic grievance measure. For a comparison across levels; this latter is the best choice. Further, I included in the sample two models with political grievance, which was the strongest determinant of the three MAR grievance types, followed by the economic grievances.

12. This latter, however, may be conceptualized as a factor affecting grievances, as well. Geographically concentrated minorities tend to develop autonomy demands.

13. In international relations, Diehl and Goertz managed to account for the effect of long-term rivalries on the likelihood of war without admitting to the effect of the interaction between countries, in a theory that challenges the liberal views involving this latter explanatory principle. On the subnational level, though, the existence of the groups (the salience of the group markers for both in-group and out-group) needs to be explained, as well, which is not an issue in the case of countries. There is no convincing utilitarian explanation for the persistence of minorities.

14. Also, my models show that *de facto* horizontal economic inequality, as well as the economic discrimination coded by the MAR group, have a strong effect on both economic and political grievances. In addition, even cultural inequality, that is, cultural restrictions on a minority, lead to (cultural) grievances that may also be consequential for violent conflict.

15. The association between group structure and conflict-proneness has two aspects. We may look at either the impact of fractionalization or that of polarization on intergroup hostility. In both cases, distinguishing between minorities and pluralities, and types of minorities, may evince much more plausible behavioral patterns than we may have without these distinctions.

16. At least not within the frames of classic regression modeling. Other techniques, such as classification and regression tree (CART) modeling may cope with collinearity and point out the most effective predictors irrespective to their association among themselves; however, we have to learn yet about the significance of CART model results for practical purposes.

17. This may be extended onto supra-national and international representation, such as in the European Union and the United Nations.

18. EPR had a value of the political status variable specifying the lack of interest in having communal group-based representation (labeled "Irrelevant"), which has been an inspired addition to their categories. Yet, it was a rarely assigned value, since EPR included only groups that have had some political organization representing them. A perfect dataset on minorities should be able to account for facts such as small minorities tend to have collective political representation and umbrella cultural institutions, while others—mainly larger ones—may pursue representation for multiple ideological factions. If the minority is divided, but the national representatives come from one faction only, the grievance levels cannot be expected to subside.

19. The importance of the belief in "linked fate" (i.e., of group consciousness and group solidarity) has been advocated by Katherine Tate, in a number of successive publications on African American politicizing.

20. Amelia II considers only two string (noninterval) variables, one for the time (in this case, the year measure), and one cross-sectional variable. Other string variables remain "unhandled factors." Thus, when the group names are the cross-sectional variable, the country names are completely disregarded by the software.

21. Yet certain forms of market regulation are defended by arch-supporters of "market freedom," and are bitterly opposed by supporters of a socialized market. As Stieglitz wrote in a New York Times article on June 27, 2014: "Congress maintains subsidies for rich farmers as we cut back on nutritional support for the needy. Drug companies have been given hundreds of billions of dollars as we limit Medicaid benefits. The banks that brought on the global financial crisis got billions while a pittance went to the homeowners and victims of the same banks' predatory lending practices."

22. President Lyndon Baines Johnson is attributed the observation that "If you can convince the lowest white man he's better than the best colored man, he won't notice you're picking his pocket. Hell, give him somebody to look down on, and he'll empty his pockets for you." In Bill Moyers: "What a Real President Was Like; To Lyndon Johnson, the Great Society Meant Hope and Dignity," The Washington Post, Nov. 13, 1988.

23. The neoliberal "Austrian economics" conquered the US academia when the First World lenders became anxious over the Third World's debt crisis; we cannot deny that global issues have had a tremendous effect on doctrinal positions.

24. In developed settings, this takes at least Sweden-like extent of state redistribution. In a developing country, it also involves a whole development package, such as creating jobs, fostering urbanization, improving infrastructure and communication, and expanding state services such as education, health care, and policing, always equally across all regions of a country, maybe with the exception of positive discrimination of the least advantaged.

25. Actually, the public work programs in Hungary are a very controversial issue. Legally, they were not created to employ Roma only, but Roma are heavily overrepresented among people who cannot find any other work and must take these low-status, low-paying jobs. The government propaganda says that, on the one hand, they are not necessarily low-status, low-paying jobs (it depends on the local governments to make them more attractive), and on the other hand, they keep the employees in contact with the world of work, making it easier to them to find new employment. The opposition is highly skeptical about these claims, but indeed, public work projects are not doomed to be slavery; they may be upgraded to become "normal" work.

26. Finland, for instance, maintains a quota system in higher education for Swedish-speaking students, with the declared goal to assure the continuation of native language services in areas populated by Swedes. This is a fairly unambiguous example for positive discrimination serving a legitimate social cause. On the other side, quotas reserved for women in politics and business leadership are fairly clear examples of combatting prejudices. In the developed world, women's educational and work credentials are incontestably at parity with those of men; yet, their salaries and statuses are inferior.

Appendix 1

Group Consciousness (Chapter 3.a)

Group consciousness is an important explanatory variable of group relationships and occurrence of violence. The literature has elaborated on several aspects of these impacts, and many of them have also received empirical support. I would refer here to four ways in which group consciousness has been shown to be consequential for my dependent variables.

(a) First and most pertinent to the topic, the strength of the minority identity has been included in analyses conducted by the MAR theorists, and shown to have an impact on the likelihood of violence.
(b) Psychological studies of ethnicity depicted the negative consequences of "barricaded" (exclusivist, impermeable, antisyncretism) identities on intergroup relations.[1]
(c) Majority nationalism is a special type of group consciousness, and the most studied type of all socioterritorial identity forms. Yet, it rarely happens that the researchers contrast it with the minority group consciousness. The refreshing exception is Elke Winter's 2007 paper, which highlights the difference between the constitution of majority *versus* minority group consciousness, as compared to the constitution of two unranked groups' consciousness (in Sherif's and Tajfel's experiments). The majority group tends to construct its own features as universal,[2] and the nation-state as the closest proxy for the unified human society, which leaves minorities without ideological weapons to protect their specificity. I think that this tendency was paramount for the eighteenth century pioneers of nation-state building (the Americas, France, maybe United Kingdom), and dominant in the nineteenth century, but claims to universality have seriously been limited for later followers in East European and postcolonial states. A further welcome contribution to the study of

majority group consciousness is the distinction between two kinds of nationalism, ethnic and civic, sometimes referred to as "Eastern" and 'Western." The prevalence of one or the other in a state affects the policies toward minorities, as Roger Brubaker's *Citizenship and Nationhood in France and Germany* (1992) argues.

(d) Last, but not least, there are concerns with regard to the future of nationalism, and the possibilities of achieving postnational socioterritorial identities. While conceptions about nationalism tend to converge on a few basic features, the image of postnationalist consciousness varies across different ideologies and traditions, and actually, it is constructed under a number of brand names, of which cosmopolitanism is the most widespread, though transnational has also been in ascension lately. Marxists tend to take postnational for international, while those socialized to the European Union believe in the formation of a supranational identity.

The modernist/developmentalist school predicts the gradual effacement of all parochial ties, and the WVS asked about the respondents' loyalty toward the nation-state as opposed to their loyalty toward smaller and larger geographical units, such as region, continents, and the whole of the humanity. Based on these WVS measurements of nationalism, Norris (2009) calculated the "cosmopolitanism index" of the countries that have participated in the WVS series, and these are decently associated with objective measurements of the countries' globalization.[3]

I think that group consciousness would make a very useful control variable, but its inclusion may not be absolutely necessary. Constructivists claim, and I concur, that the strength and nature of group consciousness is a function of social facts. Actually, the works cited in this section also tend to suggest some farther causes beyond the features of and changes in group consciousness. Most obviously, for developmentalists, the cosmopolitan mentality is result of modernization and globalization. MAR also traces a causal arrow from group disadvantage to group identity, and a feedback loop from a group's mobilization to its strength of identity. A nation's preference for civic or ethnic type of nationalism can be related to the task that the nation had to accomplish in order to achieve the normative ideal of nationalism, the nation state, that is, to make ethnicity and state congruent.[4]

If I had had any of these group consciousness indicators available for the whole sample with which I want to work, I would have been happy to include them. Yet I do not think that their absence has resulted in an omitted variable bias of the models that I was able to build.

NOTES

1. A theorist of ethnicity, Ken Jowitt, forwarded a historical picture of collective identities, in which ideologically barricaded identities are the most exclusivist. Ethnically barricaded identities may also lead to horrific violence, but they "have a rationale and source of discipline that are more chosen and less derived, more instrumental and strategic, and less metaphysical," and hopefully they are easier to dismantle by changing the payoff from them.

2. "Majority group members. . . remain imagined as 'individuals': as neither determined nor even marked by 'race', sex/gender, culture, ethnicity, or. . .'nature'. . . Indeed, the cultural specificity of the dominant group is masked, as it is conceived as incarnating the social norm. It is, therefore, represented in universal terms (Guillaumin, 1972; Juteau, 1999)."

3. I calculated the correlation coefficients between these "subjective" measures of cosmopolitanism and the KOF globalization indexes. Further, the WVSs provide measures of state secularism, as well, and these also can be shown to covary with the objective modernization indicators. These associations do justice to those who believe in the power of institutions to shape human attitudes.

4. France had to assimilate various minorities to a unique—so-called universal—culture to fill up existing state boundaries with a unitary *demos*. Germany had to unify separate small states to get the boundaries including most ethnic Germans.

Appendix 2

Checklist of Hypotheses to Be Tested in the Analytical Parts (Chapter 3.b)

INTERGROUP ECONOMIC INEQUALITY

H1a Economic inequality between groups increases the likelihood and intensity of violent conflict between them; and

H1b Intergroup economic inequality increases the number and severity of the grievances forwarded by minorities.

DEVELOPMENT

H2.a More well-being in a country reduces the likelihood of violent conflict.

H2.b More well-being in a country does not reduce the amount of grievances voiced by minorities.

GROUP STRUCTURE

H3.1a The likelihood of violent conflict increases with the relative size of the minority.

H3.1b Larger minorities have more grievances.

H3.2a A history of violent conflicts makes further conflicts more likely.

H3.2b A history of violent conflicts makes minority grievances more likely.

INSTITUTIONS

H4.2a Political arrangements that allow for more autonomy of the minority and/or more success of the minority parties lead to less intergroup violence.
H4.2b Political arrangements that allow for more autonomy of the minority and/or more success of the minority parties mitigate the severity of minority grievances.

INTERNATIONAL ENVIRONMENT

H5.1 Higher social globalization of a country reduces intergroup hostility.
H5.2 Higher political globalization of a country reduces intergroup hostility.

OPPORTUNITY FOR INSURRECTION

H6 A group's opportunities to launch an insurrection increase the likelihood and intensity of intergroup violence.

Appendix 3

Sources of Information on Inter-Group Inequality (Chapter 4.a)

Table A3.1 Sources of Information on Intergroup Inequality (1)

States (Not in EPR are starred)	*MAR data available*	*Information status*	*UNESCO DME based on*	*MICS3 availability*	*DHS other than in DME*	*Statistics, national & international*	*UNDP Roma*	*ILO/ ACHPR2009*
Afghanistan	Y	Y		not	not			
Albania	Y	Y	MICS	y	y		y	
Algeria	Y	Y		not				y
Angola	Y	n/quant.		not	not			
Antigua & B.		small						
Argentina	Y	Y						
Armenia		no groups	DHS					
Australia	Y	Y				y		
Austria		Y				y		
Azerbaijan	Y	Y	DHS	not				
**Bahamas		small						
**Bahrain	Y	n/quant.						
Bangladesh	Y	Y	MICS	y	y			
**Barbados		small						
Belarus	Y	Y		y				
Belgium		Y				y		
**Belize		small	MICS	y				
Benin		Y	DHS					
**Bhutan	Y	n/quant.						
Bolivia	Y	Y	DHS	not				
Bosnia & H.	Y	Y	MICS	y			y	
Botswana	Y	Y			not [?]			y
Brazil	Y	Y			1996			
**Brunei		small						
Bulgaria	Y	Y				y	y	

Table A3.1 Sources of Information on Intergroup Inequality (1) (continued)

States (Not in EPR are starred)	*MAR data available*	*Information status*	*UNESCO DME based on*	*MICS3 availability*	*DHS other than in DME*	*Statistics, national & international*	*UNDP Roma*	*ILO/ ACHPR2009*
**Burkina Faso		Y	DHS	y				y
Burundi	Y	n/quant.	MICS	y	y			y
Cambodia	Y	Y	DHS					
Cameroon	Y	Y	DHS	y				y
Canada	Y	Y				y		
**Cape Verde		no groups			y			
Central African R.		Y	MICS	y	y			y
Chad	Y	Y	DHS					y
Chile	Y	Y						
China	Y	n/quant.		not		y		
Colombia	Y	Y	DHS					
**Comoros		no groups			y			
Congo Dem.Rep.	Y	Y	DHS	not				y
Congo Rep.	Y	Y	DHS					y
Costa Rica	Y	Y						
Cote d'Ivoire		Y	DHS	y				
Croatia	Y	Y				y	y	
Cuba		Y	MICS	y				
**Cyprus	Y	Y						
Czech Republic	Y	Y					y	
**Denmark		Y				y		
**Djibouti	Y	Y		y				
**Dominica		small						
Dominican Rep.	Y	Y	DHS	not				
Ecuador	Y	Y			y			
Egypt	Y	Y	DHS	not				y
El Salvador	Y	Y			1985			
**Eq. Guinea		Boobi		not				
Eritrea	Y	n/quant.			not [?]			y
Estonia	Y?	Y				y		
Ethiopia	Y	Y	DHS	not				y
**Fiji	Y	Y				y		
Finland		Y						
France	Y	Y				y		
Gabon		Y	DHS	not				y
Gambia		Y	MICS	y				
Georgia	Y	Y	MICS	y				
**Germany	Y	Y						
Ghana	Y	Y	DHS	y				
Greece	Y	Y				y		
**Grenada		small						
Guatemala	Y	Y	DHS					
Guinea	Y	Y	DHS	not				

States (Not in EPR are starred)	MAR data available	Information status	UNESCO DME based on	MICS3 availability	DHS other than in DME	Statistics, national & international	UNDP Roma	ILO/ ACHPR2009
Guinea-Bissau		Y	MICS	y				
**Guyana	Y	Y		y	y			
Haiti		Mulattos	DHS					
Honduras	Y	Y	DHS					
Hungary	Y	Y					y	
**Iceland		Y				y		
India	Y	Y	DHS	not		y		
Indonesia	Y	Y	DHS	not		y		
Iran	Y	Y		not				
Iraq	Y	Y	MICS	y				
**Ireland		Y				y		
Israel	Y	Y				y		
Israel-Occupied Palestine T.s	Y	Y		not		y		
**Italy	Y	Roma				y		
**Jamaica		no groups	MICS	y				
Japan	Y	Y				y		
Jordan	Y	Y	DHS			y		
Kazakhstan	Y	Y	MICS	y	1999	y		
Kenya	Y	Y	DHS	partly				y
**Kiribati		small						
**Korea, North		no groups		not				
**Korea, South	Y	Y						
**Kosovo		too young				y		
Kuwait		n/quant.				y		
Kyrgyzstan	Y	Y	MICS	y	1997			
Laos	Y	Y	MICS	y				
Latvia	Y	Y						
Lebanon	Y	Y		not				
**Lesotho		no groups	DHS	not				
Liberia		Amer.-Lib.	DHS	not				
**Libya		n/quant.						
Lithuania	Y	Y				y		
**Luxembourg		small						
Macedonia	Y	Y	MICS	y			y	
Madagascar	Y	Y	DHS	not				
Malawi		Y	DHS	y				
Malaysia	Y	Y						
**Maldives		no groups			y			
Mali	Y	Y	DHS					y
**Malta		small						
**Marshall Islands		small						
Mauritania	Y	Y		y	y			

Table A3.1 Sources of Information on Intergroup Inequality (1) (continued)

States (Not in EPR are starred)	*MAR data available*	*Information status*	*UNESCO DME based on*	*MICS3 availability*	*DHS other than in DME*	*Statistics, national & international*	*UNDP Roma*	*ILO/ ACHPR2009*
**Mauritius		Y				y		
Mexico	Y	Y			1987			
**Micronesia		small						
Moldova	Y	Y			2005	y		
Mongolia		Y	MICS	y				
**Montenegro		Y	MICS	y			y	
Morocco	Y	Y	DHS	not				y
Mozambique		Y	DHS	not				
Myanmar	Y	Indians	MICS					
Namibia	Y	Y	DHS			y		
**Nauru		small						
Nepal		Y	DHS	not		y		
Netherlands		Y				y		
New Zealand	Y	Y				y		
Nicaragua	Y	Y	DHS					
Niger	Y	Y	DHS	not				y
Nigeria	Y	Y	DHS	y				y
**Norway		Y				y		
**Oman		n/quant.		not		y		
Pakistan	Y	n/quant.	DHS	not		y		
**Palau		small						
Panama	Y	Y		not				
**Papua N.Guinea	Y	Y				y		
Paraguay	Y	Y			y			
Peru	Y	Asians	DHS					
Philippines	Y	Y	DHS	not				
Poland		Germans				y		
**Portugal		Y				y		
**Quatar		Y				y		
Romania	Y	Y				y	y	
Russia	Y	Roma,Jews				y		
Rwanda	Y	n/quant.	DHS					y
**SaintKitts&N.s		small						
**Saint Lucia		small						
**Saint Vincent& G.		small						
**Samoa		no groups			y			
**SaoTome &Pr.		no groups	MICS	not	y			
Saudi Arabia	Y	Y				y		
Senegal	Y	Y	DHS	not				
Sierra Leone	Y	Y	MICS	y	y			
**Singapore		Y				y		
Slovakia	Y	Y					y	
Slovenia		Y				y		

States (Not in EPR are starred)	MAR data available	Information status	UNESCO DME based on	MICS3 availability	DHS other than in DME	Statistics, national & international	UNDP Roma	ILO/ ACHPR2009
**Solomon Islands		small				y		
**Somalia	Y	Y	MICS	y				
South Africa	Y	Y			1998			y
Spain	Y	Roma				y		
Sri Lanka	Y	Y			1987			
Sudan	Y	Y		not	1990			y
**Suriname		Y	MICS	y				
**Swaziland		Y	DHS	not				
**Sweden		Y				y		
Switzerland	Y	Y				y		
Syria	Y	Christians	MICS	y		y		
Taiwan	Y	Y						
Tajikistan	Y	Y	MICS	y				
**Tanzania	Y	Y	DHS					y
Thailand	Y	Y		y	y			
**Timor-Leste		no groups			y			
Togo	Y	Y	MICS	y	y			
**Tonga		small						
Trinidad & T.		Y	MICS	y	y			
**Tunisia		no groups			y			
Turkey	Y	Y	DHS	not		y		
Turkmenistan	Y	n/quant.		not	not [?]	y		
**Tuvalu		small						
Uganda	Y	Y	DHS					y
Ukraine	Y	Y	DHS	y		y		
**United Arab E.s		n/quant.				y		
United Kingdom	Y	Y				y		
United States	Y	Y				y		
**Uruguay		Y						
Uzbekistan	Y	Y		y	2002			
**Vanuatu		no groups		y				
Venezuela	Y	Y	MICS					
Vietnam	Y	Y	DHS	y				
Yemen		Y	MICS	y	1992	y		
Yu Serbia	Y	Y	MICS	y			y	
Zambia	Y	Y	DHS	not				
Zimbabwe	Y	Y	DHS					

**Note*: Not all countries listed in this table are included in EPR_MAR_EXT. They might have been excluded either because of a population below 500,000 people ("small") or because lacking any relevant communal group larger than 1% of the population ("no groups"). Some other remarks in the column of "information status" refer to issues with the quality of data I could obtain. "N/quantit" means my sources did not give numeric values of the economic standing of the groups, but only comparison (e.g. "poorer than."). When a group name is specified, it refers to one about which I could not obtain solid numeric values. "Y" in this column means reasonably satisfactory data have been obtained.

Table A3.2 Sources of Information on Inter-Group Inequality (2)

States (Not in EPR are starred)	UN ESA SOWIP 2009	ISSP 2003	WVS 2005 wave	Afrobarometer third Round	Arab Barometer	Asian Barometer	Latinobarometro 2007	Other survey/ source (abbreviated)
Afghanistan								AsiaFoundat. survey
Albania								
Algeria								
Angola								HR Watch
**Antigua & B.								
Argentina	y		y				y	R.Weiner
Armenia								
Australia		y	y					
Austria		y						
Azerbaijan								
**Bahamas								
**Bahrain								OHCHR R.'08
Bangladesh						2005		M.Rahman 2003
**Barbados							y	
Belarus								
Belgium								
**Belize								
Benin				y				
**Bhutan								UNHCR
Bolivia	y						y	
Bosnia & H.								
Botswana				y				
Brazil	y		y				y	
**Brunei								
Bulgaria		y	y					
**Burkina Faso			y	y(R4)				
Burundi								
Cambodia						2008		RR Ross 1987
Cameroon								
Canada		y	y					
**Cape_Verde				y				
Central African R.								
Chad								
Chile	y		y				y	
China			y			2002,08		

States (Not in EPR are starred)	*UN ESA SOWIP 2009*	*ISSP 2003*	*WVS 2005 wave*	*Afrobarometer third Round*	*Arab Barometer*	*Asian Barometer*	*Latinobarometro 2007*	*Other survey/ source (abbreviated)*
Colombia	y		y				y	
**Comoros								
Congo Dem.Rep.								
Congo Rep.								
Costa Rica	y						y	
Cote d'Ivoire								
Croatia								
Cuba								J.Meerman 2009, Prieto & Ruiz
**Cyprus			y					
Czech Republic		y						
**Denmark		y						
**Djibouti								
**Dominica								
Dominican Rep.	y						y	
Ecuador	y						y	
Egypt			y					
El Salvador	y						y	
**Eq. Guinea								OHCHR Report.
Eritrea								ILO/ACHPR
Estonia								
Ethiopia			y					
**Fiji								
Finland		y	y					
France		y	y					
Gabon								
Gambia								
Georgia			y					
**Germany		y	y					
Ghana			y	y				
Greece								
**Grenada								
Guatemala	y		y				y	
Guinea								
Guinea-Bissau								

Table A3.2 Sources of Information on Inter-Group Inequality (2) (continued)

States (Not in EPR are starred)	*UN ESA SOWIP 2009*	*ISSP 2003*	*WVS 2005 wave*	*Afrobarometer third Round*	*Arab Barometer*	*Asian Barometer*	*Latinobarometro 2007*	*Other survey/ source (abbreviated)*
**Guyana	y						y	
Haiti								
Honduras	y						y	
Hungary		y						
**Iceland								
India			y			2005		NFHS-3
Indonesia			y			2006		
Iran			y					Dom advocacy gr.
Iraq			y					
**Ireland		y						
Israel		y						Naim Aridi
Israel-Occupied Palestine T.s								UNDP
**Italy			y					
**Jamaica								
Japan		y	y			2003,07		Buraku advocacy gr.
Jordan			y		y			
Kazakhstan								
Kenya				y				
**Kiribati								
**Korea, North								
**Korea, South		y	y			2003,06		
**Kosovo								
Kuwait					y			J.Crystal 1993
Kyrgyzstan								
Laos								
Latvia		y						
Lebanon					y			UNRWA 2006
**Lesotho				y				
Liberia				y(R4)				
**Libya								ACHPR/IWGIA
Lithuania								
**Luxembourg								
Macedonia								
Madagascar				y				

States (Not in EPR are starred)	*UN ESA SOWIP 2009*	*ISSP 2003*	*WVS 2005 wave*	*Afrobarometer third Round*	*Arab Barometer*	*Asian Barometer*	*Latinobarometro 2007*	*Other survey/ source (abbreviated)*
Malawi				y				
Malaysia			y			2007		
**Maldives								
Mali			y	y				
**Malta								
**Marshall Islands								
Mauritania								
**Mauritius								
Mexico	y		y				y	
**Micronesia								
Moldova			y					
Mongolia						2002,06		
**Montenegro								
Morocco			y					
Mozambique				y				
Myanmar								Amy Chua 2002
Namibia				y				
**Nauru								
Nepal						2005		L.Bennett, UNHCR
Netherlands		y	y					
New Zealand		y	y					
Nicaragua							y	
Niger								
Nigeria				y				
**Norway		y	y					
**Oman								F.Mohamedi 1993
Pakistan						2005		ACHR 2007
**Palau								
Panama	y						y	
**Papua N.Guinea								Bougainv.Copper Ltd
Paraguay	y						y	
Peru			y				y	
Philippines		y				2002,05		Amy Chua 2002
Poland		y	y					
**Portugal		y						

Table A3.2 Sources of Information on Inter-Group Inequality (2) (continued)

States (Not in EPR are starred)	*UN ESA SOWIP 2009*	*ISSP 2003*	*WVS 2005 wave*	*Afrobarometer third Round*	*Arab Barometer*	*Asian Barometer*	*Latinobarometro 2007*	*Other survey/ source (abbreviated)*
**Quatar								
Romania			y					
Russia		y	y					
Rwanda			y					
**Saint Kitts & N.s								
**Saint Lucia								
**Saint Vincent& G.								
**Samoa								
**Sao Tome &Pr.								
Saudi Arabia								E.A.Doumato 1992
Senegal				y				
Sierra Leone								
**Singapore						2006		
Slovakia		y						
Slovenia		y	y					
**Solomon Islands								
**Somalia								V.Lehman&Eno'02
South Africa		y	y	y				
Spain		y	y					
Sri Lanka						2005		
Sudan								
**Suriname								
**Swaziland								Encycl.Britannica
**Sweden		y	y					
Switzerland		y	y					
Syria								
Taiwan		y	y			2001,06		
Tajikistan								
**Tanzania				y				
Thailand			y			2001,06		
**Timor-Leste								
Togo								
**Tonga								
Trinidad & T.			y					
**Tunisia								

States (Not in EPR are starred)	UN ESA SOWIP 2009	ISSP 2003	WVS 2005 wave	Afrobarometer third Round	Arab Barometer	Asian Barometer	Latinobarometro 2007	Other survey/ source (abbreviated)
Turkey			y					
Turkmenistan								
**Tuvalu								
Uganda				y				
Ukraine			y					
**United Arab Emirates								Hooglund &Toth'94
United Kingdom			y					
United States		y	y					
**Uruguay		y	y				y	
Uzbekistan								
**Vanuatu								
Venezuela		y					y	
Vietnam			y			2005		
Yemen					y			
Yu_Serbia			y					
Zambia			y	y				
Zimbabwe				y				

Appendix 4

The Country-Level Data (Chapter 4.b)

Table A4.1 List of the Country-Level Variables Included in the Country-Level Dataset*

Source	*Variable name*	*Label*
	General	
QOG	year	
QOG	cname	
QOG	ccodealp_year	3-letter Country Code and Year
	Population	
UN WDI 2011 May	population2011	Population, total
UN WDI 2011 May	pop_rural	Rural population (% of total population)
UN WDI 2011 May	pop_urban	Urban population (% of total)
QOG	al_ethnic	Ethnic Fractionalization (Alesina)
QOG	al_language	Linguistic Fractionalization (Alesina)
QOG	al_religion	Religious Fractionalization (Alesina)
WDR 2009	Official_Language	Nr. of nation-wide official languages (regional not included)
UN WDI 2011 May	net_migration	Net migration
Calculated	net_migr_%1yr	Net migration as % population, for 1 year
UN WDI 2011 May	migrant_stock	International migrant stock (% of population)
	Conflict/ Stateness	
UN WDI 2011 May	refugee_out	Refugee population by country/ territory of origin, 1999–2009

Table A4.1 List of the Country-Level Variables Included in the Country-Level Dataset* (continued)

Source	*Variable name*	*Label*
UN WDI 2011 May clc.	refug_out/1000	Refugee population as/1000 of country of origin, 1999–2009
UN WDI 2011 May	int_displ_high	Internally displaced persons (number, high estimate)
QOG	wdi_idp	Internally displaced persons
WDR 2009	IntDispl	WDR/UN
UN WDI 2011 May	int_displ_low	Internally displaced persons (number, low estimate)
Calculated	int_displ_av	Internally displaced persons, average of available 4 estimates
Calculated	int_displ_av%	Internally displaced persons (int_displ_av) as % of population
UN WDI 2011 May	battle_deaths	Battle-related deaths (number of people), 1999–2008
Norris/Banks	conflict_idx	Norris/Weighted Conflict Index (Banks CNTS 2007)
Vision for Humanity	Global_Peace_index	Global Peace Index
Fund for Peace	FS_Index	Failed States Index (1–120, highest the worst)
Fund for Peace	FS_inequality	Failed States Uneven Development
Fund for Peace	FS_group_grievance	Failed States Group Grievance
WGI (bis)	wbgi_pse	Political Stability—Estimate
	Federalism/Centralization	
QOG	gtm_unitary	Unitarism
QOG	no_ufs	Unitary or Federal State (Norris)
QOG	h_f	Independent Subfederal Unit
QOG	iaep_ufs	Unitary or Federal State
Norris	watts2	Type of unitary or federal constitution
Norris	geering	Federalism index (Gerring-Thacker)
Compiled	my_fed_letter	My federalism index, from the six above, letter notation
Compiled	my_fed_nr	My federalism index, number notation
My code	communal_division	Federalism is along communal division
Norris/Schneider	fiscal_dc	Fiscal decentralization; 68 nations (Schneider)
Norris/Schneider	admin_dc	Administrative decentralization; 68 nations (Schneider)
Norris/Schneider	politic_dc	Political decentralization; 68 nations (Schneider)
DPI2010	author	Local authorities' authority over taxing, spending, and legislating
DPI2010	auton	Any contiguous autonomous regions?
DPI2010	muni	Are municipal governments locally elected?

Source	*Variable name*	*Label*
DPI2010	state	Are state/provincial governments locally elected?
DPI2010	stconst	Are the senate constituencies the states or provinces?
Compilation	decntralization_index	Decentralization Idx (auton, muni, state, stconst average)
My code	communal_sb_divisions	Administrative subdivisions fall along communal lines
Calculated	Decentr*commnal_s_div	Interaction term of the two above
	Democracy Level	
QOG	fh_cl	Civil Liberties, 1999–2009
QOG	fh_pr	Political Rights, 1999–2009
QOG	fh_ipolity2	Democracy (Freedom House/Imputed Polity), 1999–2009
QOG	gd_ptsa	Political Terror Scale – Amnesty International, 1999–2008
QOG	gd_ptss	Political Terror Scale – US State Department, 1999–2008
	Good Governance and Repressiveness	
QOG	wbgi_cce	Control of Corruption
QOG	wbgi_gee	Government Effectiveness
QOG	wbgi_pse	Political Stability
QOG	wbgi_rle	Rule of Law
QOG	wbgi_rqe	Regulatory Quality
QOG	wbgi_vae	Voice and Accountability
Prison studies	PP_rate	Prison population per 100,000 population
	Proportionality	
QOG	checks_dpi	Number of veto players, from DPI 2010 directly
Norris (Modified)	elecfam	Electoral family (after 2005, based on DPI values)
QOG	no_elecfam	Electoral family (Norris)
DPI2010	pluralty_dpi	Plurality electoral system
DPI2010	pr_dpi	Proportional electoral system
DPI2010	housesys_dpi	In combined systems, majority of house seats is governed by
	Development Indicators	
UN HDR 2010	hdi_HDR2010	HDI from HDR 2010 (Table 2)
UN WDI 2011 May	gdp_ppp_cap2	GDP per capita, PPP (constant 2005 international $)
UN WDI 2011 May	gdp_ppp_cap1	GDP per capita, PPP (current international $)
UN WDI 2011 May	lifeexp_total	Life expectancy at birth, total (years)

Table A4.1 List of the Country-Level Variables Included in the Country-Level Dataset* (continued)

Source	*Variable name*	*Label*
UN WDI 2011 May	lifeexp_female	Life expectancy at birth, female (years)(r>.93 with HDI)
UN WDI 2011 May	lifeexp_male	Life expectancy at birth, male (years)
UN WDI 2011 May	web_users	Internet users (per 100 people) (r>.75 with GDP)
	Other Economic	
KOF 2011 (Long v.)	glob_idx	overall globalization index
KOF 2011 (Long v.)	glob_ec	economic globalization index
KOF 2011 (modified)	glob_ec_regr	economic globalization with imputations from regression
KOF 2011 (Long v.)	glob_pol	political globalization index
KOF 2011 (Long v.)	glob_soc	social globalization index
UN WDI 2011 May	milit_exp	Military expenditure (% of GDP)
UN WDI 2011 May	soldiers	Armed forces personnel (% of total labor force)
CIA WFctBook 2011	cia_unempl	Total unemployed %
CIA WFctBook 2011	cia_y_unempl	Unemployed total youth of 15–24 yrs %
CIA WFctBook 2011	cia_y_male_unemp	Unemployed young males of 15–24 yrs
CIA WFctBook 2011	cia_y_fem_uneml	Unemployed young females of 15–24 yrs
Compilation	y_male_unempl	Unemployed young males (with extra- & intrapolations)
UN WDI 2011 May	unemp_y_male	Unemployed young males of 15–24 yrs
UN WDI 2011 May	unempl_male	Unemployed, males (% of male labor force)
UN WDI 2011 May	unempl_total	Unemployed, total (% of total labor force)
QOG	wdi_tdebt_s	Total debt service (% of GNI)
QOG	wdi_cgdebt	Central government debt (% of GDP)
	Inequality	
Compilation	My_GINI	Most likely Gini index based on the below two UN-series
UN	Gini 1992–2007	UN Human Development Report 2009
UN	Gini 2000–2010	UN Gini from the HDI adjustment
UNU-WIDER	Unu_wider_gini	Gini calculated from abbreviated UNU-WIDER
QOG	uw_gini	Gini (mean)
QOG	uw_quality	Quality (mean)
QOG	wdi_gini	Gini index

Source	Variable name	Label
QOG	utip_ehii	University of Texas – estimated household income inequality
CIA WFctBook	CIA_Gini	CIA World Factbook Gini indexes
GPI	GPI_Gini07_10	Vision of Humanity/Global Peace Index – Gini index
QOG	wdi_isl20	Income share of Lowest 20%
CIA WFctBook	CIA R/P 10%	CIA rich/poor 10% ratio based on their D1 and D10
CIA WFctBook	Lowest 10%	Lowest decile's share of GDP
CIA WFctBook	Highest 10%	Highest decile's share of GDP

**Note*: Both EPR_MAR_EXT and MAR_EPR_MI have been completed with variables from this list. The full codebooks, with more detailed information on variables, exist as Excel files.

Appendix 5

Details of the Imputed Models (Chapter 6)

Table A5.1 Conflict Intensity with Economic Inequality (ECDIS) and Controls: Imputed Models # 1, 2, and 3

	IMP_1		IMP_2		IMP_3	
Dependent Variable	Intensity index		Intensity index		Intensity index	
Case number	727		727		727	
Adjusted R-square	.264		.267		.264	
	St.Cff.	Sig	St.Cff.	Sig	St.Cff.	Sig
Economic discrimination	.091	.008	.103	.002	.102	.003
Group proportion	-.002	.961	-.005	.898	.004	.907
Past violent episodes	.403	.000	.409	.000	.415	.000
Linguistic Fractionalization	.053	.278	.056	.242	.067	.165
Religious Fractionalization	-.081	.018	-.070	.040	-.075	.029
Difference plurality-largest minority	.068	.159	.071	.139	.074	.120
Prop. in regional base	.107	.003	.137	.000	.082	.021
GDP per capita, PPP	-.025	.676	-.043	.463	-.017	.770
Political Terror Scale	.174	.000	.167	.000	.168	.000
Group urbanism	-.090	.019	-.050	.179	-.085	.025
WGI Gov.t Effectiveness	.171	.005	.182	.002	.164	.006
External military support	-.050	.143	-.059	.078	-.056	.098
Young male unemployed	.098	.004	.052	.117	.066	.052

Table A5.2 Conflict Intensity with Economic Inequality (ECDIS) and Controls: Imputed Models # 4, 5, and 6

	IMP_4		IMP_5		IMP_6	
Dependent Variable	Intensity index		Intensity index		Intensity index	
Case number	727		727		727	
Adjusted R-square	.256		.263		.262	
	St.Cff.	Sig	St.Cff.	Sig	St.Cff.	Sig
Economic discrimination	.066	.054	.070	.040	.099	.004
Group proportion	-.002	.958	-.006	.877	.004	.904
Past violent episodes	.416	.000	.413	.000	.417	.000
Linguistic Fractionalization	.057	.240	.051	.291	.067	.167
Religious Fractionalization	-.079	.021	-.074	.032	-.071	.040
Difference plurality-largest minority	.073	.133	.077	.110	.084	.079
Prop. in regional base	.103	.004	.121	.001	.104	.004
GDP per capita, PPP	-.038	.515	-.033	.569	-.034	.560
Political Terror Scale	.168	.000	.160	.000	.166	.000
Group urbanism	-.072	.055	-.070	.065	-.036	.333
WGI Govt .Effectiveness	.179	.003	.170	.005	.162	.007
External military support	-.048	.150	-.059	.079	-.042	.207
Young male unemployed	.049	.147	.060	.071	.054	.109

Table A5.3 Conflict Intensity with Economic Inequality (INEQ) and Controls: Imputed Models # 1, 2, and 3

	IMP_1		IMP_2		IMP_3	
Dependent Variable	Intensity index		Intensity index		Intensity index	
Case number	727		727		727	
Adjusted R-square	.260		.261		.258	
	St.Cff.	Sig	St.Cff.	Sig	St.Cff.	Sig
Ineq_3_ln	.061	.076	.065	.058	.064	.062
Group proportion	.006	.877	.007	.841	.010	.789
Past violent episodes	.411	.000	.416	.000	.424	.000
Linguistic Fractionalization	.049	.318	.050	.304	.055	.254
Religious Fractionalization	-.093	.007	-.082	.015	-.080	.019
Difference plurality-largest minority	.066	.175	.069	.148	.073	.131
Prop. in regional base	.097	.007	.125	.000	.072	.043
GDP per capita, PPP	-.023	.692	-.036	.542	-.025	.667
Political Terror Scale	.171	.000	.166	.000	.167	.000
Group urbanism	-.095	.014	-.056	.129	-.089	.019
WGI Govt .Effectiveness	.161	.008	.172	.005	.155	.011
External military support	-.053	.122	-.061	.071	-.059	.080
Young male unemployed	.099	.004	.048	.154	.064	.060

Table A5.4 Conflict Intensity with Economic Inequality (INEQ) and Controls: Imputed Models # 4, 5, and 6

	IMP_4		IMP_5		IMP_6	
Dependent Variable	Intensity index		Intensity index		Intensity index	
Case number	727		727		727	
Adjusted R-square	.256		.263		.257	
	St.Cff.	Sig	St.Cff.	Sig	St.Cff.	Sig
Ineq_3_ln	.064	.061	.069	.043	.066	.054
Group proportion	.011	.764	.009	.813	.017	.656
Past violent episodes	.417	.000	.415	.000	.424	.000
Linguistic Fractionalization	.054	.265	.052	.285	.059	.224
Religious Fractionalization	-.081	.017	-.083	.015	-.080	.019
Difference plurality-largest minority	.075	.121	.080	.097	.084	.081
Prop. in regional base	.099	.006	.118	.001	.094	.008
GDP per capita, PPP	-.033	.575	-.026	.653	-.030	.605
Political Terror Scale	.164	.000	.160	.000	.166	.000
Group urbanism	-.074	.047	-.071	.061	-.043	.244
WGI Govt .Effectiveness	.164	.007	.156	.010	.148	.014
External military support	-.049	.144	-.057	.092	-.043	.207
Young male unemployed	.048	.156	.061	.069	.058	.090

Appendix 6

Details of the Bivariate Relationships (Chapter 7.a)

Table A6.1 Bivariate Relationships between Dependent Variables and the Economic Inequality Predictor Group (All Available Years)

	Failed States (FS) Index	*Global Peace Index*	*WGI Political Stability*	*IPD Communal Conflicts*	*IPD Social Conflicts*	*FS Group Grievance*
Failed States Inequality ("Uneven Development")	.862	.708	−.680	−.557	−.614	.754
Number of cases	894	684	726	475	475	894
Standard deviation of INEQ_1 (ln)	.220	.215	−.178	−.259	−.142	.247
Number of cases	832	674	931	480	480	832
Baldwin & Huber 2010 v.1	.468	.536	−.437	−.359	−.486	.376
Number of cases	242	220	276	168	168	242
My_Gini, based on 2 UN series	.369	.341	−.276	−.246	−.505	.227
Number of cases	894	694	1516	484	484	894
Gini after redistribution (Solt)	.551	.636	−.397	−.284	−.603	.436
Number of cases	353	282	925	235	235	353
Gini without redistribution (Solt)	−.141	.012	.139	.095	−.061	−.085
significance	.008	.847	.000	.146	.352	.111
Number of cases	353	282	925	235	235	353

Note: Where significance is not marked, it was given by SPSS as 0.000, with only 2 exceptions (of alpha=0.002 and alpha=0.003).

Table A6.2 Bivariate Relationships between Dependent Variables and the Group Structure Predictor Group (All Available Years)

	Failed States (FS) Index	*Global Peace Index*	*WGI Political Stability*	*IPD Communal Conflicts*	*IPD Social Conflicts*	*FS Group Grievance*
Ethnic fractionalization (Alesina)	.446	.338	−.398	−.289	−.357	.329
Linguistic fractionalization (Alesina)	.363	.255	−.326	−.400	−.356	.303
Number of cases	894	694	1516	484	484	894
Religious fractionalization (Alesina)	−.005	−.031	.048	.040	−.034	−.007
significance	.880	.411	.063	.374	.450	.826
Number of cases	894	694	1516	484	484	894
Proportion of plurality group	−.403	−.377	.391	.396	.293	−.358
Number of cases	890	694	1010	484	484	890
Proportion of largest minority	.248	.183	−.213	−.231	−.136	.266
Number of cases	890	694	1010	484	484	890
Difference Plurality – Largest minority	−.384	−.341	.362	.376	.266	−.357
Number of cases	890	694	1010	484	484	890
Regional concentration proxy ("Communal_sub_ divisions")	.162 894	.253 694	−.277 1514	−.307 484	−.246 484	.261 894
Lagged average of Battle Death between 1999 and 2005	.235 818	.393 694	−.346 676	−.251 484	−.188 484	.257 818
Lagged average of Banks Conflict Index between 1999 and 2005	.359 810	.516 694	−.541 668	−.434 484	−.329 484	.446 810

Note: Where significance is not marked, it was given by SPSS as 0.000, with only 2 exceptions (of alpha = 0.002 and alpha = 0.003). The number of cases for the 2 fractionalization indexes is the same.

Table A6.3 Bivariate Relationships between Dependent Variables and Development, Plus Globalization Measures

	Failed States Index	*Global Peace Index*	*WGI Political Stability*	*IPD Communal Conflicts*	*IPD Social Conflicts*	*Failed States Group Grievance*
GDP per capita, PPP2	–.780	–.562	.597	.432	.618	–.575
Number of Cases	894	694	1516	484	484	894
Life expectancy (female)	–.677	–.500	.511	.366	.625	–.449
Number of Cases	894	694	1516	484	484	894
Internet users	–.834	–.610	.571	.445	.618	–.598
Number of Cases	894	694	1516	484	484	894
KOF overall globalization index	–.826	–.602	.602	.418	.661	–.578
Number of Cases	872	676	1471	480	480	872
KOF economic globalization	–.822	–.613	.662	.439	.691	–.612
Number of Cases	872	676	1471	480	480	872
KOF political globalization	–.501	–.355	.235	.146	.238	–.280
Number of Cases	894	689	1507	480	480	894
KOF social globalization	–.833	–.621	.666	.425	.690	–.600
Number of Cases	888	685	1498	480	480	888

Note: In all cases where significance is not marked, it was given by SPSS as 0.000, with only one exception, the coefficient between the KOF political globalization and IPD Communal conflicts is significant at alpha = 0.001 only.

Table A6.4 Partial Correlations between Dependent Variables and Three Explanatory Variables, While Controlling for Female Life Expectancy

	Failed States Index	Global Peace Index	WGI Political Stability	IPD Commnal conflicts	IPD Social conflicts	Failed States Group Grievance
Regional concentration proxy ("Communal_sub_divisions")	.071	.201	-.229	-.270	-.187	.214
significance	.033	.000	.000	.000	.000	.000
Decentralization Index	-.154	.037	.061	.016	-.113	-.063
significance	.000	.333	.019	.727	.013	.060
Minority autonomy proxy (Decentraliz._idx*Commnl_s_div)	-.022	.127	-.146	-.201	-.125	.123
significance	.516	.001	.000	.000	.006	.000

Note: Cases of coefficients turning up as significant with the unexpected sign are patterned with horizontal lines (and bright pink color).

Table A6.5 Bivariate Relationships between Dependent Variables and Institutional Explanatory Variables (All Years Available)

	Failed States Index	*Global Peace Index*	*WGI Political Stability*	*IPD Commnal conflicts*	*IPD Social conflicts*	*Failed States Group Grievance*
Population excluded from pol. power	.182		−.381			.133
Significance	.126		.000			.264
Number of cases	72		734			72
Ethnicity Based Banning of Parties	.079		−.107			.094
Significance	.499		.003			.418
Number of cases	76		803			76
Religion Based Banning of Parties	−.126		−.074			−.126
Significance	.278		.035			.277
Number of cases	76		803			76
IPD Respect for minorities	−.554	−.493	.487	.522	.417	−.536
Number of cases	475	454	484	484	484	475
Freedom House/ Imputed Polity	−.647	−.487	.498	.261	.313	−.525
Number of cases	721	538	1511	481	481	721
Political Terror Scale (US St.D)	.729	.829	−.817	−.594	−.577	.685
Number of cases	557	394	1342	362	362	557
Electoral family (based on Norris)	−.288	−.233	.227	.062	.195	−.231
Significance	.000	.000	.000	.176	.000	.000
Number of cases	894	694	1512	484	484	894
Plurality system indicator (DPI)	.148	.095	−.123	−.060	−.150	.116
Significance	.000	.016	.000	.209	.001	.001
Number of cases	798	637	1326	447	447	798
Proportional system indicator (DPI)	−.264	−.198	.199	.163	.186	−.197
Number of cases	786	632	1290	443	443	786
House seats rule (0=PR, l=plurality)	.204	.134	−.145	−.112	−.236	.142
Significance	.000	.001	.000	.018	.000	.000
Number of cases	792	632	1312	443	443	792
Regional concentration proxy	.162	.253	−.277	−.307	−.246	.261
Number of cases	894	694	1514	484	484	894

	Failed States Index	*Global Peace Index*	*WGI Political Stability*	*IPD Commnal conflicts*	*IPD Social conflicts*	*Failed States Group Grievance*
Decentralization Index	–.390	–.183	.170	.169	.186	–.242
Number of cases	894	694	1514	484	484	894
Minority autonomy proxy	–.100	.047	–.061	–.141	–.019	.053
Significance	.003	.213	.017	.002	.671	.111
Number of cases	894	694	1515	484	484	894

Note: In all cases where significance is not marked, it was given by SPSS as 0 .000. The err pty cells me; m that there are no common cases of the respective variables in ı ny dataset. ("rhe p-valuesof the insignificant coefficients arehighlighted with pink.)

Table A6.6 Association between Dependent Variables and the Explanatory Variables Expressing Opportunity for Insurgence

	Failed States Index	Global Peace Index	WGI Political Stability	IPD Commnal conflicts	IPD Social conflicts	Failed States Group Grievance
Proportion of Rural Population	.605	.368	-.431	-.416	-.535	.451
Significance	.000	.000	.000	.000	.000	.000
Number of cases	894	694	1516	484	484	894
WGI Government Effectiveness	-.893	-.706	.743	.430	.632	-.682
Significance	.000	.000	.000	.000	.000	.000
Number of cases	726	542	1515	484	484	726
Proportion of Unemployed Young Males	.065	.146	-.149	-.136	.068	.120
Significance	.114	.001	.000	.010	.199	.004
Number of cases	586	497	556	360	360	586

Appendix 7

Details of the Imputed Models (Chapter 7.b)

Table A7.1 Explaining Conflict as Measured by the Global Peace Index

	Imputed 1		Imputed 2		Imputed 3		Imputed 4		Imputed 5	
Dependent variable	Global Peace I.		Global Peace I.		Global Peace I.		Global Peace I.		Global Peace I.	
Adjusted R-Square	.653		.650		.650		.660		.646	
Case number	676 (>2006)		676 (>2006)		676 (>2006)		676 (>2006)		676 (>2006)	
	St.Cf	Sig.	St.Cf	Sig.	St.Cf	Sig.	St.Cf	Sig.	St.Cf	Sig.
Failed States Inequality	.256	.000	.267	.000	.265	.000	.252	.000	.262	.000
Linguistic Fractionalization	-.107	.001	-.117	.000	-.104	.001	-.117	.000	-.103	.001
Religious Fractionalization	.037	.167	.053	.049	.044	.098	.048	.070	.041	.125
Prop. of Largest Minority	-.016	.519	-.022	.401	-.008	.767	-.012	.634	-.022	.386
Reg.l Concentration proxy	.341	.000	.362	.000	.363	.000	.359	.000	.337	.000
Banks Conflict Index (lag.)	.325	.000	.327	.000	.323	.000	.332	.000	.319	.000
Life expectancy (female)	-.081	.052	-.081	.049	-.072	.085	-.049	.231	-.063	.130
KOF Political Globalization	.047	.131	.078	.011	.052	.092	.063	.038	.048	.120
Freedom H./ imputed Polity	-.169	.000	-.177	.000	-.183	.000	-.173	.000	-.158	.000
Electoral family (Norris-b.)	-.040	.143	-.042	.131	-.032	.247	-.045	.098	-.034	.220
Decentralization Index	.068	.088	.076	.054	.090	.023	.052	.180	.062	.121
Minority Autonomy proxy	-.290	.000	-.313	.000	-.316	.000	-.301	.000	-.278	.000
Prop. of Rural Population	-.058	.084	-.076	.024	-.068	.043	-.069	.035	-.074	.028
WGI Gov.t Effectiveness	-.274	.000	-.278	.000	-.266	.000	-.299	.000	-.294	.000
Unemployed young males	.075	.001	.050	.034	.064	.006	.086	.000	.074	.002

Table A7.2 Explaining Conflict as Measured by the WGI Political Stability Scale

	Imputed 1		Imputed 2		Imputed 3		Imputed 4		Imputed 5	
Dependent variable	WGI Polit. Stability		WGI Polit. Stability		WGI Polit. Stability		WGI Polit. Stability		WGI Polit. Stability	
Adjusted R-Square	.726		.726		.744		.741		.726	
Case number	845 (>2005)		845 (>2005)		845 (>2005)		845 (>2005)		845 (>2005)	
	St.Cf	Sig.	St.Cf	Sig.	St.Cf	Sig.	St.Cf	Sig.	St.Cf	Sig.
Failed States Inequality	-.162	.000	-.155	.000	-.146	.000	-.147	.000	-.139	.000
Linguistic Fractionalization	.039	.119	.039	.116	.049	.045	.041	.095	.037	.146
Religious Fractionalization	.009	.677	.000	.987	.006	.778	-.003	.870	.003	.900
Prop. of Largest Minority	-.054	.007	-.051	.012	-.050	.011	-.054	.006	-.055	.007
Reg.l Concentration proxy	-.317	.000	-.313	.000	-.293	.000	-.303	.000	-.308	.000
Banks Conflict Index (lag.)	-.350	.000	-.363	.000	-.369	.000	-.367	.000	-.367	.000
Life expectancy (female)	-.062	.058	-.054	.099	-.047	.144	-.062	.051	-.066	.045
KOF Political Globalization	-.240	.000	-.235	.000	-.233	.000	-.237	.000	-.240	.000
Freedom H./ imputed Polity	.113	.000	.128	.000	.116	.000	.119	.000	.107	.000
Electoral family (Norris-b.)	.063	.004	.044	.041	.061	.004	.054	.011	.059	.007
Decentralization Index	.016	.609	.012	.702	.026	.392	.025	.416	.022	.489
Minority Autonomy proxy	.220	.000	.227	.000	.188	.000	.208	.000	.212	.000
Prop. of Rural Population	-.110	.000	-.094	.000	-.098	.000	-.107	.000	-.100	.000
WGI Gov.t Effectiveness	.439	.000	.443	.000	.456	.000	.454	.000	.464	.000
Unemployed young males	-.060	.001	-.031	.094	-.039	.029	-.043	.018	-.022	.240

Table A7.3 Explaining Conflict as Measured by the IPD Communal Conflict Measure

	Imputed 1		Imputed 2		Imputed 3		Imputed 4		Imputed 5	
Dependent variable	IPD Communal Conflict		IPD Communal Conflict		IPD Communal Conflict		IPD Communal Conflict		IPD Communal Conflict	
Adjusted R-Square	.464		.452		.470		.462		.479	
Case number	845 (>2005)		845 (>2005)		845 (>2005)		845 (>2005)		845 (>2005)	
	St.Cf	Sig.	St.Cf	Sig.	St.Cf	Sig.	St.Cf	Sig.	St.Cf	Sig.
Failed States Inequality	-.307	.000	-.319	.000	-.309	.000	-.303	.000	-.342	.000
Linguistic Fractionalization	-.201	.000	-.185	.000	-.191	.000	-.192	.000	-.184	.000
Religious Fractionalization	.065	.028	.053	.078	.055	.062	.051	.087	.031	.292
Prop. of Largest Minority	-.101	.000	-.088	.002	-.089	.002	-.064	.025	-.061	.031
Reg.l Concentration proxy	-.106	.104	-.196	.003	-.131	.043	-.126	.053	-.127	.047
Banks Conflict Index (lag.)	-.277	.000	-.296	.000	-.273	.000	-.287	.000	-.316	.000
Life expectancy (female)	-.222	.000	-.223	.000	-.227	.000	-.213	.000	-.237	.000
KOF Political Globalization	-.055	.104	-.099	.004	-.043	.198	-.037	.278	-.026	.443
Freedom H./ imputed Polity	-.043	.255	-.035	.360	-.007	.842	.004	.919	-.013	.721
Electoral family (Norris-b.)	-.035	.245	-.032	.301	-.033	.276	-.044	.147	-.037	.222
Decentralization Index	.218	.000	.194	.000	.204	.000	.225	.000	.223	.000
Minority Autonomy proxy	-.049	.509	.038	.611	-.045	.538	-.035	.636	-.018	.801
Prop. of Rural Population	-.283	.000	-.252	.000	-.320	.000	-.273	.000	-.285	.000
WGI Gov.t Effectiveness	-.001	.984	-.017	.757	-.053	.319	-.025	.647	-.056	.297
Unemployed young males	-.074	.005	-.080	.002	-.106	.000	-.064	.015	St.Cf	Sig.

Table A7.4 Explaining Conflict as Measured by the IPD Social Conflict Measure

	Imputed 1		Imputed 2		Imputed 3		Imputed 4		Imputed 5	
Dependent variable	IPD Social Conflict		IPD Social Conflict		IPD Social Conflict		IPD Social Conflict		IPD Social Conflict	
Adjusted R-Square	.542		.547		.565		.560		.573	
Case number	845 (>2005)		845 (>2005)		845 (>2005)		845 (>2005)		845 (>2005)	
	St.Cf	Sig.	St.Cf	Sig.	St.Cf	Sig.	St.Cf	Sig.	St.Cf	Sig.
Failed States Inequality	-.114	.004	-.120	.003	-.076	.052	-.109	.005	-.099	.011
Linguistic Fractionalization	.004	.908	.041	.202	.067	.034	.042	.190	.055	.081
Religious Fractionalization	.050	.068	.034	.215	.057	.031	.068	.012	.032	.222
Prop. of Largest Minority	.041	.119	.025	.330	.014	.576	.054	.035	.042	.102
Reg.l Concentration proxy	-.297	.000	-.268	.000	-.276	.000	-.311	.000	-.322	.000
Banks Conflict Index (lag.)	-.183	.000	-.186	.000	-.190	.000	-.167	.000	-.201	.000
Life expectancy (female)	.307	.000	.313	.000	.359	.000	.329	.000	.334	.000
KOF Political Globalization	-.047	.138	-.088	.005	.024	.426	-.023	.458	.000	.989
Freedom H./ imputed Polity	-.093	.008	-.074	.034	-.096	.005	-.091	.008	-.048	.154
Electoral family (Norris-b.)	.035	.207	.058	.040	.052	.057	.050	.070	.044	.109
Decentralization Index	-.042	.296	-.050	.212	-.053	.181	-.075	.059	-.082	.037
Minority Autonomy proxy	.240	.000	.220	.001	.228	.001	.271	.000	.272	.000
Prop. of Rural Population	-.068	.047	-.109	.001	-.136	.000	-.082	.015	-.101	.002
WGI Gov.t Effectiveness	.262	.000	.253	.000	.223	.000	.273	.000	.233	.000
Unemployed young males	.136	.000	.142	.000	.117	.000	.143	.000	.120	.000

Appendix 8

Checklist of the Findings (Chapter 8)

A. RESULTS OF HYPOTHESIS TESTING, ACROSS ALL THREE DATASETS

Table A8.1 Support for the Impact of Various Predictors of Inter-Group Hostility

	Supported by regression models
INTERGROUP ECONOMIC INEQUALITY	
H1.a Economic inequality between groups increases the likelihood and intensity of violent conflict between them.	Yes
H1.b Intergroup economic inequality increases the number and severity of the grievances forwarded by minorities.	Yes
DEVELOPMENT	
H2.a More well-being in a country reduces the likelihood of violent conflict.	Yes (not 100%)
H2.b More well-being in a country does not reduce the amount of grievances voiced by minorities.	Yes
GROUP STRUCTURE	
H3.1a The likelihood of violent conflict increases with the relative size of the minority.	Ambiguous
H3.1b Larger minorities have more grievances.	Ambiguous
H3.2a A history of violent conflicts makes further conflicts more likely.	Yes
H3.2b A history of violent conflicts makes minority grievances more likely.	Yes
INSTITUTIONS	
H4.2a Political arrangements that allow for more autonomy of the minority and/or more success of the minority parties lead to less intergroup violence.	Yes

Table A8.1 Support for the Impact of Various Predictors of Inter-Group Hostility (Continued)

	Supported by regression models
H4.2b Political arrangements that allow for more autonomy of the minority and/or more success of the minority parties mitigate the severity of minority grievances.	Yes
INTERNATIONAL ENVIRONMENT	
H5.1 Higher social globalization of a country reduces intergroup hostility.	Ambiguous
H5.2 Higher political globalization of a country reduces intergroup hostility.	Ambiguous
OPPORTUNITY FOR INSURRECTION	
H6 A group's opportunities to launch an insurrection increase the likelihood and intensity of intergroup violence.	Partial

B. BENEFITS FROM THE DATASETS COMPILED FROM SCATTERED PREVIOUS RESEARCH

The EPR_MAR_EXT dataset contains data on communal groups comprising 97.5 percent of the world's population, the most extensive list of communal groups thus far, and it allows for:

- an overview of the size and proportion of communal groups worldwide.[1]
- creating typologies of communal groups.
- taking stock of what we have, in terms of measurements.
- comparing similar variables from different research projects.
- contextualizing (framing) any communal group–related project.
- facilitating the testing of a few older hypotheses, such as the curvilinear association between fractionalization and peacefulness, and
- facilitating the articulation of new approaches and hypotheses.

I have also contributed two new measurements of group features, a variable(group) addressing intergroup economic inequality, and a variable(group) addressing minority territorial autonomy.

C. OTHER METHODOLOGICAL AND THEORETICAL PROCEEDS

(i) Support for a multicausal approach to intergroup conflict. My models have consistently confirmed the impact of a number of controls taken from diverse categories of predictors, such as clusters operationalizing inequality, grievance, features of group structure, development level, and institutional opportunities for either peaceful resolution or rebellion.
(ii) Support for a diachronic approach to the explanation of conflict. There is, on the one hand, a well-supported impact of the past violent episodes, and on the other hand, there is a proven possibility to study the unfolding of intergroup hostility as a process in stages.
(iii) Support for policy arrangements that substantiate Lijphart's suggestion of power sharing in order to defuse communal hostility. I have designed variables that may clearly distinguish between the policies promoted by Lijphart *versus* the liberal-integrative proposals of Horowitz. The regression models supported Lijphart's vision.

NOTE

1. A surprising 34.9 percent of the world's population do not belong to their country's plurality communal group, and 45.6 percent belong to groups that are smaller than 50 percent of their country's population.

Appendix 9

Note on the Supplementary Data Files

All tables and bibliographical data included in this volume do not contain all information for a reader who would like to reconstruct the whole trail from "raw data" to findings and conclusions. There are additional data related to this project that have been made public. The dissertation at the basis of this book is retrievable from Simon Fraser University's library along with a CD containing essential tables and analytic results, called Supplementary Data Files. Part of the data stored on that CD, primarily the replication material, is available via http://www.agneskkoos.net/Pages/Data.aspx, as well.

More detailedly, the Supplementary Data Files contain the replication datasets for the three analytic chapters, that is, they include the EPR_MAR_EXT, MAR_EPR_MI, and the Country-Level data files. Yet the electronic appendix goes beyond providing the strictly necessary replication data.

For instance, it includes the multiply imputed files that I happened to obtain from the Amelia II software, as the multiple imputation procedure works with randomness, and does not produce the same imputed file twice. It also includes a number of Excel files with copies of the SPSS outputs of some correlation matrices and regressions, many of which are not or are only marginally mentioned in the book.

Most importantly, I think in terms of improving my datasets, and if future researchers pursued correcting my data on Gabon or Myanmar, they should be able to trace my information to their origins, and confront those sources with alternate information. Traditional replication datasets contain only scarce information about the origins of the information included, typically in their (separate) codebook. My replication datasets also come with codebooks, but in addition, they are doubled with "data collection" versions, which give *in situ* explanation for most datapoints of interest.

Last, but not least, a number of supplementary files document the preparatory work through which certain indicators were made suitable for inclusion into my datasets, for instance, the selection of country Gini indexes and the derivation of the group-level conflict measures from CONIS and UCDP-PRIO data. These preparatory data files cluster in "group-level" and "country-level" folders. The two basic datasets, on which I relied extensively, EPR and MAR, have an almost unchanged version copied there. The reason for including these "raw" formats is that these older versions may become unavailable as their authors work out improved versions of them.

Practically, the CD has three big folders, one for replication data and basic information, one for summarizing data analytic steps, and one for the details of data collection.

Bibliography

Ahmed, Patricia; Cynthia Feliciano, and Rebecca Jean Emigh. 2007. "Internal and External Ethnic Assessments in Eastern Europe." *Social Forces* 86(1): 231–255.

Alcoff, Linda Martín; Michael Hames-García, Satya P. Mohanty, and Paula M. L. Moya, eds. 2006. *Identity politics reconsidered.* New York: Palgrave Macmillan.

Alesina, Alberto, and Eliana La Ferrara. 2000. "Participation in Heterogeneous Communities." *The Quarterly Journal of Economics* 115(3): 847–904.

Alesina, Alberto; A. Devleeschauwer, W. Easterly, S. Kurlat, and R. Wacziarg. 2003. "Fractionalization." *Journal of Economic Growth* Boston: 8: 155–194.

Allport, Gordon W. [1954] 1979. *The Nature of Prejudice.* Reading, MA: Addison-Wesley Pub. Co.

Amiot, Catherine E; Roxane de la Sablonnière, Deborah J. Terry, and Joanne R. Smith. 2007. "Integration of Social Identities in the Self: Toward a Cognitive-Developmental Model." *Personality & Social Psychology Review* 11(4): 364–388.

Anagnostou, Dia, and Anna Triandafyllidou. 2007. "Regions, minorities and European integration." *Romanian Journal of Political Science* 7(1): 100–125.

Anderson, Benedict. 1983. *Imagined Communities: Reflections on the Origin and Spread of Nationalism.* New York: Verso.

Annett, Anthony. 2001. "Social Fractionalization, Political Instability, and the Size of Government." *IMF Staff Papers* Vol. 48, No. 3.

Arutiunian, Iu V. 2009. "On the Symptoms of Interethnic Integration in Post-Soviet Society." *Sociological Research* 48(1): 3–19.

Baldwin, Kate, and John D. Huber. 2010. "Economic versus Cultural Differences: Forms of Ethnic Diversity and Public Goods Provision." *American Political Science Review* 104(04): 644–62.

Banton, Michael. 2005. "Three Current Issues in Ethnic and Racial Studies." *British Journal of Sociology* 56(4): 621–633.

———. 2008. "The Sociology of Ethnic Relations." *Ethnic & Racial Studies* 31(7): 1267–1285.

Barany, Zoltan D. 2002. The East European Gypsies: Regime Change, Marginality, and Ethnopolitics. Cambridge University Press.

Bargal, David, and Charles Garvin. 2008. "Summary and Implications for the Next Stage, An Epilogue." *Small Group Research* 39(1): 104–110.

Beck, Thorsten; George Clarke, Alberto Groff, Philip Keefer, and Patrick Walsh. 2001. "New Tools in Comparative Political Economy: The Database of Political Institutions." *World Bank Economic Review* 15(1): 165–176.

Behar, Moshe. 2009. "Across Nationalisms: Nascent Conceptualisation, Rudimentary Cross-Regional Historicisation." *Politics* 29(2): 83–92.

Bellamy, Richard, and Dario Castiglione. 2004. "Lacroix's European Constitutional Patriotism: A Response." Political Studies 52(1): 187–193.

Bendix, Reinhard. 1964. *Nation-Building and Citizenship: Studies in Our Changing Political Order*. New York: Wiley.

Berberoglu, Berch. 2004. *Nationalism and Ethnic Conflict: Class, State, and Nation in the Age of Globalization*. Rowman & Littlefield Publishers, Inc.

Best, Shaun. 2005. *Understanding Social Divisions*. London; Thousand Oaks, Calif.: SAGE.

Bhalla, Ajit S, and Shufang Qiu. 2006. *Poverty and Inequality among Chinese Minorities*, Milton Park, Abingdon, Oxon; New York: Routledge.

Bhavnani, Ravi. 2006. "Ethnic Norms and Interethnic Violence: Accounting for Mass Participation in the Rwandan Genocide." *Journal of Peace Research* 43(6): 651–669.

Bigler, Rebecca S, and Meagan M. Patterson. 2007. "When and Why Social Categorization Produces Inequality (and Vice Versa)." *Human Development* (0018716X) 50(6): 328–332.

Birnir, Jóhanna Kristín. 2007. *Ethnicity and electoral politics*. New York; Cambridge: Cambridge University Press.

Birnir, Jóhanna Kristín, and Donna Lee Van Cott. 2007. "Disunity in Diversity." *Latin American Research Review* 42(1): 99–125.

Blimes, Randall J. 2006. "The Indirect Effect of Ethnic Heterogeneity on the Likelihood of Civil War Onset. *Journal of Conflict Resolution* 50(4): 536–547.

Bloch, Alice, and John Solomos, eds. 2010. *Race and Ethnicity in the 21st Century*. Houndmills, Basingstoke, Hampshire: New York, NY: Palgrave Macmillan.

Blume, Lorenz, and Voigt, Stefan. 2008. "Federalism and Decentralization - A Critical Survey of Frequently Used Indicators." Available at *Social Science Research Network*: http://ssrn.com/abstract=1263995 or http://dx.doi.org/10.2139/ssrn.1263995

Bobo, Lawrence, and Vincent L. Hutchings. 1996. "Perceptions of Racial Group Competition: Extending Blumer's Theory of Group Position to a Multiracial Social Context." *American Sociological Review* 61: 951–972.

Bobo, Lawrence. 2000. "Reclaiming a Du Boisian Perspective on Racial Attitudes." *Annals of the American Academy of Political and Social Science* 568: 186–202.

Boix, Carles. 2008. "Economic Roots of Civil Wars and Revolutions in the Contemporary World." *World Politics* 60(3): 390–437.

Bowler, Shaun; Todd Donovan, and David Brockington. 2003. *Electoral Reform and Minority Representation: Local Experiments with Alternative Elections*. Columbus: Ohio State University Press.

Bramadat, Paul A. 2005. "Toward a New Politics of Authenticity: Ethno-Cultural Representation in Theory and Practice." *Canadian Ethnic Studies* 37(1): 1–20.

Brewer, Marilynn. 1999. "The Psychology of Prejudice: Ingroup Love or Outgroup Hate?" *Journal of Social Issues* 55(3): 429–444.

———. 2007. "The Importance of Being We: Human Nature and Intergroup Relations." *American Psychologist* 62(8): 728–738.

Brown, David. 2000. *Contemporary Nationalism: Civic, Ethnocultural, and Multicultural Politics*. Routledge.

Brown, Rupert; Anja Eller, Sarah Leeds, and Kim Stace. 2007. "Intergroup Contact and Intergroup Attitudes: A Longitudinal Study." *European Journal of Social Psychology* 37(4): 692–703.

Brubaker, Roger. 1992. *Citizenship and Nationhood in France and Germany*. Harvard University Press.

Buhaug, Halvard; Lars-Erik Cederman, and Jan Ketil Rød. 2008. "Disaggregating Ethno-Nationalist Civil Wars: A Dyadic Test of Exclusion Theory." *International Organization* 62(3): 531–551.

Burguière, André, and Raymond Grew, eds. 2001. *The Construction of Minorities: Cases for Comparison across Time and around the World*. Ann Arbor: University of Michigan Press.

Cairns, Ed, and Micheál D. Roe, eds. 2003. *The Role of Memory in Ethnic Conflict*. New York: Palgrave Macmillan.

Cargile, Aaron Castelan; James J. Bradac, and Tim Cole. 2006. "Theories of Intergroup Conflict: A Report of Lay Attributions." *Journal of Language & Social Psychology* 25(1): 47–63.

Carment, David. 2007. "Exploiting Ethnicity." *Harvard International Review* 28(4): 62–66.

Carment, David, and Patrick James, eds. 1997. *The International Politics of Ethnic Conflict*. Ottawa: Carleton University.

Castles, Stephen. 2000. *Ethnicity and Globalization: From Migrant Worker to Transnational Citizen*. Sage Publications.

Castles, Stephen, and Mark J. Miller 2009. *The Age of Migration: International Population Movements in the Modern World*. Basingstoke [England]; New York : Palgrave Macmillan.

Catt, Helena, and Michael Murphy. 2002. *Sub-state Nationalism: A Comparative Analysis of Institutional Design*. London; New York: Routledge.

Cederman, Lars-Erik, and Luc Girardin. 2007. "Beyond Fractionalization: Mapping Ethnicity onto Nationalist Insurgencies." *American Political Science Review* 101: 173–185.

Cederman, Lars-Erik, Luc Girardin, and Kristian S. Gleditsch. 2009. "Ethno-Nationalist Triads: Assessing the Influence of Kin Groups on Civil Wars." *World Politics* 61: 403–437.

Cederman, Lars-Erik, Andreas Wimmer, and Brian Min. 2010. "Why Do Ethnic Groups Rebel? New Data and Analysis." *World Politics* 62(1): 87–119.

Cederman, Lars-Erik; Nils Weidmann & Kristian S. Gleditsch. 2011. "Horizontal Inequalities and Ethno-nationalist Civil War: A Global Comparison." *American Political Science Review* 105(3): 478–495.

Cernat, Vasile. 2010. "Intergroup Contact in Romania: When Minority Size is Positively Related to Intergroup Conflict." *Journal of Community & Applied Social Psychology* 20(1): 15–29.

Chandra, Kanchan. 2001. "Introduction: Constructivist Findings and Their Non-Incorporation." In *Symposium: Cumulative Findings in the Study of Ethnic Politics*, APSA-CP.

———. 2004. *Why Ethnic Parties Succeed: Patronage and Ethnic Headcounts in India*. Cambridge, UK; New York: Cambridge University Press.

———. 2006. "What is ethnic identity and does it matter?" *Annual Review of Political Science* 9: 397–424.

Chirot, Daniel, and Martin E.P. Seligman, eds. 2001. *Ethnopolitical Warfare: Causes, Consequences, and Possible Solutions*. Washington, DC: American Psychological Association.

Chua, Amy. 2002. *World on Fire: How Exporting Free Market Democracy Breeds Ethnic Hatred*. Doubleday.

Cohrs, J. Christopher, and Frank Asbrock. 2009. "Right-Wing Authoritarianism, Social Dominance Orientation and Prejudice against Threatening and Competitive Ethnic Groups." *European Journal of Social Psychology* 39(2): 270–289.

Collier, Paul. 2001. "Implications of Ethnic Diversity." *Economic Policy* 16(32): 127–155.

Collier, Paul, and Nicholas Sambanis. 2002. "Understanding Civil War: A New Agenda," *Journal of Conflict Resolution* 46(1): 3–12.

Collier, Paul, and Anke Hoeffler. 2004. "Greed and Grievance in Civil War." *Oxford Economic Papers* 56(4): 563–595.

Cordell, Karl, and Andrzej Dybczynski. 2005. "Poland's Indigenous Ethnic Minorities and the Census of 2002." *Perspectives on European Politics & Society* 6(1): 79–102.

Cornell, Stephen, and Douglas Hartmann. 2007. Ethnicity and race: making identities in a changing world. Thousand Oaks, Calif.: Pine Forge Press, an Imprint of Sage Publication.

Côté, Rochelle R, and Bonnie H. Erickson. 2009. "Untangling the Roots of Tolerance: How Forms of Social Capital Shape Attitudes toward Ethnic Minorities and Immigrants." *American Behavioral Scientist* 52(12): 1664–1689.

Cross, Sharyl, and Pauline Komnenich. 2005. "Ethnonational Identity, Security and the Implosion of Yugoslavia: The Case of Montenegro and the Relationship with Serbia." *Nationalities Papers* 33(1): 1–27.

Cunningham, Emily, and Michael J. Platow. 2007. "On Helping Lower Status Out-Groups: The Nature of the Help and the Stability of the Intergroup Status Hierarchy." *Asian Journal of Social Psychology* 10(4): 258–264.

David, Clarissa C. 2009. "Intergroup Attitudes and Policy Support: How Prejudice against Minority Groups Affects Support for Public Policies." *International Journal of Public Opinion Research* 21(1): 85–97.

de Moura, Georgina Randsley; Tirza Leader. Joseph Pelletier, and Dominic Abrams. 2008. "Prospects for Group Processes and Intergroup Relations Research: A Review of 70 Years' Progress." *Group Processes & Intergroup Relations*. 11(4): 575–596.

de Zavala, Agnieszka Golec; Roy Eidelson, Aleksandra Cichocka, and Nuwan Jayawickreme. 2009. "Collective Narcissism and Its Social Consequences." *Journal of Personality & Social Psychology* 97(6): 1074–1096.

Delamater, John, ed. 2006. Handbook of social psychology. New York: Springer.

Delanty, Gerard. 2002. "Models of European Identity: Reconciling Universalism and Particularism." *Perspectives on European Politics & Society* 3(3): 345–360.

Demoulin, Stéphanie; Jacques-Philippe Leyens, and John F. Dovidio, eds. 2009. Intergroup Misunderstandings: Impact of Divergent Social Realities. New York: Psychology Press.

Deutsch, Karl W. 1953. *Nationalism and Social Communication: An Inquiry into the Foundations of Nationality*. Cambridge, MA: MIT Technology Press; John Wiley & Sons.

Deutscher, Irwin. 2005. *Preventing Ethnic Conflict: Successful Cross-National Strategies*. Lanham, Md.: Lexington Books.

DeVotta, Neil. 2005. "From Ethnic Outbidding to Ethnic Conflict: The Institutional Bases for Sri Lanka's Separatist War." *Nations & Nationalism* 11(1): 141–159.

Domínguez, Esteban Morales. 2008. *Challenges of the Racial Problem in Cuba*. Casa de la Fundación Don Fernando Ortiz, the Introduction is posted at http://etnocuba.ucr.edu/?p=143.

Dovidio, John F; Peter Glick, and Laurie A. Rudman. eds. 2005. On the Nature of Prejudice: Fifty Years after Allport. Oxford, UK; Malden, MA: Blackwell Pub.

Dovidio, John F; Samuel L. Gaertner, and Tamar Saguy. 2009. "Commonality and the Complexity of 'We': Social Attitudes and Social Change." *Personality & Social Psychology Review* (Sage Publications Inc.) 13(1): 3–20.

Dreher, Axel. 2006. "Does Globalization Affect Growth? Evidence from a new Index of Globalization." *Applied Economics* 38(10): 1091–1110.

Dreher, Axel, Noel Gaston, and Pim Martens. 2008. *Measuring Globalisation – Gauging its Consequences*. New York: Springer.

Drzewicki, Krzysztof. 2005. "The Lund Recommendations on the Effective Participation of National Minorities in Public Life – Five Years After and More Years Ahead," *International Journal on Minority & Group Rights* 12(2–3): 123–131.

Dumont, Kitty, and Johann Louw. 2009. "A Citation Analysis of Henri Tajfel's Work on Intergroup Relations." *International Journal of Psychology* 44(1): 46–59.

Edmonds, David. 2006. Caste wars: a philosophy of discrimination. London; New York: Routledge.

Edwards, Aaron. 2008. "'Accuracy' versus 'Utility' in the 'Ethnic Conflict' Paradigm: A Rejoinder to Sean Swan." *Politics* 28(3): 215–219.

Elkins, Zachary, and John Sides. 2007. "Can Institutions Build Unity in Multiethnic States?" *American Political Science Review*, 101(4): 693–708.

Espina Prieto, Rodrigo. 2007. "The Racial Perspective in Equity Studies in Cuba." Seminar paper, *UNDP/IPC*, Brasilia, January 2007. (Not meant for circulation)

Espina Prieto, Rodrigo, and Pablo Rodríguez Ruiz. 2010. "Race and Inequality in Cuba Today." *Socialism and Democracy* 24(1): 161–177, DOI: 10.1080/08854301003619600.

Esses, Victoria M, and Gordon Hodson. 2006. "The Role of Lay Perceptions of Ethnic Prejudice in the Maintenance and Perpetuation of Ethnic Bias." *Journal of Social Issues* 62(3): 453–468.

Fearon, James D. 2003. "Ethnic and Cultural Diversity by Country." *Journal of Economic Growth* 8: 195–222.

Fearon, James D, and David D. Laitin, 1996. "Explaining Interethnic Cooperation." *American Political Science Review* 90(4): 715–35.

———. 2003. "Ethnicity, Insurgency, and Civil War." *American Political Science Review* 97 (1): 75–91.

Feldman, Gregory. 2005. "Essential Crises: A Performative Approach to Migrants, Minorities, and the European Nation-state." *Anthropological Quarterly* 78(1): 213–246.

Fossum, John Erik. 2003. "The European Charter – Between Deep Diversity and Constitutional Patriotism?" *ARENA Working Papers* 5/03.

Fox, Jonathan. 2002. *Ethnoreligious Conflict in the Late 20th Century: A General Theory*, Lexington Books.

———. 2004. *Religion, Civilization and Civil War: 1945 Through the New Millennium*, Lexington Books.

Fox, Jonathan, and Shmuel Sandler. 2006. *Bringing Religion into International Relations*, Palgrave Macmillan.

Fozdar, Farida; Raelene Wilding, and Mary Hawkins. 2009. *Race and Ethnic Relations*. South Melbourne, Vic.: Oxford University Press.

Ganguly, Rajat. 2005. "Poverty, Malgovernance and Ethnopolitical Mobilization: Gorkha Nationalism and the Gorkhaland Agitation in India." *Nationalism & Ethnic Politics* 11(4): 467–502.

Garcia-Montalvo, José, and Marta Reynal-Querol. 2005a: "Ethnic Polarization, Potential Conflict and Civil War." *American Economic Review* 95(3): 796–816.

———. 2005b. "Ethnic Diversity and Economic Development." *Journal of Development Economics* 76(1): 293–323.

Garry, John. 2009. "Consociationalism and Its Critics: Evidence from the Historic Northern Ireland Assembly Election 2007." *Electoral Studies* 28(3): 458–466.

Gellner, Ernest. 1983. *Nations and Nationalism,* Ithaca: Cornell University Press

———. 1997. *Nationalism*. New York University Press.

Ghebali, Victor-Yves. 2009. "The High Commissioner on National Minorities after 15 Years: Achievements, Challenges and Promises." *Security & Human Rights* 20(2): 111–122.

Gibson, James L. 2006. "Do Strong Group Identities Fuel Intolerance? Evidence From the South African Case." *Political Psychology* 27(5): 665–705.

Glazer, Nathan. 1997. *We Are All Multiculturalists Now*. Cambridge, Mass.: Harvard University Press.

Gleditsch, Kristian S, and Michael D. Ward. 1997. "Double Take: A Reexamination of Democracy and Autocracy in Modern Polities." *The Journal of Conflict Resolution* 41(3): 361–383.

Glick, Peter. 2005. "The Choice of Scapegoats." In On the nature of prejudice: fifty years after Allport, edited by John F. Dovidio, Peter Glick, and Laurie A. Rudman, 244–262. Oxford, UK; Malden, MA: Blackwell Pub.

Golebiowska, Ewa. 2009. "Ethnic and Religious Tolerance in Poland." *East European Politics & Societies* 23(3): 371–391.

Gould, Carol C, and Pasquale Pasquino, eds. 2001. *Cultural Identity and the Nation-State*. Lanham, MD: Rowman & Littlefield Publishers.

Greenfeld, Liah. 1992. *Nationalism: Five Roads to Modernity*. Harvard University Press.

Greenfeld, Liah, and Jonathan Eastwood. 2007. "National Identity." In *The Oxford Handbook of Comparative Politics, edited by* Carles Boix and Susan Stokes. New York: Oxford.

Guinote, Ana; Megan Brown, and Susan T. Fiske. 2006. "Minority Status Decreases Sense of Control and Increases Interpretive Processing." *Social Cognition* 24(2): 169–186.

Gurr, Ted Robert. 1993. *Minorities at Risk: A Global View of Ethnopolitical Conflict*. United States Institute of Peace.

———. 2000. *Peoples Versus States: Minorities at Risk in the New Century*. United States Institute of Peace.

Gurr, Ted Robert, and Barbara Harff. 1994. *Ethnic Conflict in World Politics*. Westview Press.

Haas, Ernest. 1986. "What is Nationalism and Why Should We Study It?" *International Organization* 40(3): 707–744.

Habermas, Jürgen, and Jacques Derrida. 2003. "February 15, or What Binds Europeans Together: A Plea for a Common Foreign Policy, Beginning in the Core of Europe." *Constellations: An International Journal of Critical & Democratic Theory* 10(3): 291–298.

Hagendoorn, Louk; Hub Linssen, and Sergei Tumanov. 2001. *Intergroup Relations in States of the Former Soviet Union : The Perception of Russians*. London: Psychology Press; New York: Taylor & Francis, 2001.

Hagmann, Tobias. 2005. "Beyond Clannishness and Colonialism: Understanding Political Disorder in Ethiopia's Somali Region, 1991–2004." *Journal of Modern African Studies* 43(4): 509–536.

Halabi, Samer; John F. Dovidio, and Arie Nadler. 2008. "When and How Do High Status Group Members Offer Help: Effects of Social Dominance Orientation and Status Threat." *Political Psychology* 29(6): 841–858.

Halevy, Nir; Gary Bornstein, and Lilach Sagiv. 2008. "'In-Group Love' and 'Out-Group Hate' as Motives for Individual Participation in Intergroup Conflict: A New Game Paradigm." *Psychological Science* 19(4): 405–411.

Hancock, Ange-Marie. 2007. "When Multiplication Doesn't Equal Quick Addition: Examining Intersectionality as a Research Paradigm." *Perspectives on Politics* 5(1): 63–79, DOI: 10.1017/S1537592707070065.

Hansen, Holley E, and Vicki L. Hesli. 2009. "National Identity: Civic, Ethnic, Hybrid, and Atomised Individuals." *Europe-Asia Studies* 61(1): 1–28.

Hello, Evelyn; Peer Scheepers, and Peter Sleegers. 2006. "Why the More Educated Are Less Inclined to Keep Ethnic Distance: An Empirical Test of Four Explanations." *Ethnic & Racial Studies* 29(5): 959–985.

Herbst, Jeffrey. 2000. *States and Power in Africa*. Princeton University Press.
Herrmann, Richard K, Thomas Risse, and Marilyn B. Brewer, eds. 2004. *Transnational Identities: Becoming European in the EU*. Rowman & Littlefield.
Hobsbawm, Eric J. 1992. *Nations and Nationalism since 1780: Programme, Myth, Reality*. 2nd edition, Cambridge University Press.
Hoeffler, Anke. 2011. "'Greed' versus 'Grievance': A Useful Conceptual Distinction in the Study of Civil War?" *Studies in Ethnicity and Nationalism* 11(2): 274–285.
Hogg, Michael A. 2006. "Intergroup relations," in Handbook of social psychology, edited by John Delamater, New York: Springer, pp. 479–502.
Hogg, Michael A.; Janice R. Adelman, and Robert D. Blagg. 2010. "Religion in the Face of Uncertainty: An Uncertainty-Identity Theory Account of Religiousness." *Personality & Social Psychology Review* (Sage Publications Inc.) 14(1): 72–83.
Hong, Ying-yi; Melody Manchi Chao, and Sun No. 2009. "Dynamic Interracial/Intercultural Processes: The Role of Lay Theories of Race." *Journal of Personality* 77(5): 1283–1310.
Hooker, Juliet. 2005. "Indigenous Inclusion/Black Exclusion: Race, Ethnicity and Multicultural Citizenship in Latin America." *Journal of Latin American Studies*. 37(2): 285–310.
Horowitz, Donald L. 1985. *Ethnic Groups in Conflict: Theories, Patterns, and Policies*. University of California Press.
———. 1991. *A Democratic South Africa? Constitutional Engineering in a Divided Society*. University of California Press.
Howard, Michael C. 2011. *Transnationalism and Society: An Introduction*. Jefferson, NC: McFarland
Howe, Philip. 2010. "Voting across Ethnic Lines in Late Imperial Austria." *Nations & Nationalism* 16(2): 308–334.
Hunter, John A.; Kerry O'Brien, and Maurice Stringer. 2007. "Threats to Identity, Self-Esteem and Intergroup Discrimination." *Social Behavior & Personality: An International Journal* 35(7): 937–941.
Inglehart, Ronald, and Christian Welzel. 2005. *Modernization, Cultural Change, and Democracy: The Human Development Sequence*. Cambridge: Cambridge University Press.
———. 2009. *Development and Democracy: What We Know about Modernization Today*, http://www.worldvaluessurvey.org/wvs/articles/folder_published/publication_593
Ishiyama, John. 2009. "Do Ethnic Parties Promote Minority Ethnic Conflict?" *Nationalism & Ethnic Politics* 15(1): 56–83.
Jackman, Mary R. 1996. *The Velvet Glove: Paternalism and Conflict in Gender, Class, and Race Relations*. University of California Press.
Jackson Preece, Jennifer. 1998. *National Minorities and the European Nation-States System*. Clarendon Press, Oxford.
Jansen, Thomas, ed. 1999. *Reflections on European Identity*. European Commission Working Paper, europa.eu.int/comm/cdp/working-paper/european_identity_en.pdf
Jasiewicz, Krzysztof. 2007. "National and Pan-European Identity in the New EU Member States: The Case of Poland." Paper presented at the *12th Annual*

Convention of the Association for the Study of Nationalities, Harriman Institute, Columbia University, New York, 12–14 April 2007.

Joppke, Christian. 2004. "Ethnic Diversity and the State." British Journal of Sociology. 55(3): 451–463.

Kahn, Kimberly; Arnold K. Ho, Jim Sidanius, and Felicia Pratto. 2009. "The Space between Us and Them: Perceptions of Status Differences." *Group Processes & Intergroup Relations* 12(5): 591–604.

Kaldor, Mary. 2004. "Nationalism and Globalisation." *Nations & Nationalism* 10(1–2): 161–178.

Kalyvas, Stahtis. 2006. *The Logic of Violence in Civil War,* Cambridge: Cambridge University Press.

Kaufman, Stuart J. 2006. "Escaping the Symbolic Politics Trap: Reconciliation Initiatives and Conflict Resolution in Ethnic Wars," *Journal of Peace Research* 43(2): 201–218.

Keating, Michael, and John McGarry, eds. 2001. *Minority Nationalism and the Changing International Order*. Oxford; New York: Oxford University Press.

King, Ryan D. 2008. "Conservatism, Institutionalism, and the Social Control of Intergroup Conflict." *American Journal of Sociology* 113(5): 1351–1393.

Klandermans, Bert; Jojanneke van der Toorn, and Jacquelien van Stekelenburg. 2008. "Embeddedness and Identity: How Immigrants Turn Grievances into Action." *American Sociological Review* 73(6): 992–1012.

Koinova, Maria. 2009. "Why Do Ethnonational Conflicts Reach Different Degrees of Violence? Insights from Kosovo, Macedonia, and Bulgaria during the 1990s." *Nationalism & Ethnic Politics* 15(1): 84–108.

Korf, Benedikt. 2006. "Functions of Violence Revisited: Greed, Pride and Grievance in Sri Lanka's Civil War." *Progress in Development Studies* 6 (2): 109–122.

Kourvetaris, Andrew G. 2009. "Perspectives on Ethnicity, Gender and Race and Their Empirical Referents: A Four-sided Paradigm and Critical Review." *International Review of Sociology* 19(1): 127–146.

Kunovich, Robert M. 2009. "The Sources and Consequences of National Identification." *American Sociological Review* 74(4): 573–593.

Kymlicka, Will. 1995. *Multicultural Citizenship: A Liberal Theory of Minority Rights*. Oxford: Oxford University Press.

———. *Multicultural Odysseys: Navigating the New International Politics of Diversity*. Oxford; New York: Oxford University Press.

Kymlicka, Will, and Magda Opalski, eds. 2001. *Can Liberal Pluralism be Exported?: Western Political Theory and Ethnic Relations in Eastern Europe*. Oxford; New York: Oxford University Press.

Ladányi, János, and Iván Szelényi. 2002. "Roma and Poor in Hungary, Romania, and Bulgaria", *Szociológiai Szemle* [Sociological Review] 12(4): 72–94.

Laitin, David D. 1998. *Identity in Formation: The Russian-Speaking Populations in the Near Abroad*. Ithaca, NY: Cornell University Press.

Leach, Cohn Wayne, and Russell Spears. 2008. "'A Vengefulness of the Impotent': The Pain of In-Group Inferiority and Schadenfreude Toward Successful Out-Groups." *Journal of Personality & Social Psychology* 95(6): 1383–1396.

Lecours, Andre. 2005. "Structuring Nationalism." In *New Institutionalism: Theory and Analysis,* edited by Andre Lecours, Chapter 9.

Lee, Yueh-Ting; Clark McCauley, Fathali M. Moghaddam, and Stephen Worchel, eds. 2004. The Psychology of Ethnic and Cultural Conflict. Westport, Conn.: Praeger.

Lehmiller, Justin J, and Michael T. Schmitt. 2007. "Group Domination and Inequality in Context: Evidence for the Unstable Meanings of Social Dominance and Authoritarianism." *European Journal of Social Psychology* 37(4): 704–724.

Lemarchand, René. 2007. "Consociationalism and Power Sharing in Africa: Rwanda, Burundi, and the Democratic Republic of the Congo." *African Affairs* 106(422): 1–20.

Letschert, Rianne M. 2005. *The impact of minority rights mechanisms*. The Hague: T.M.C. Asser.

———. 2007. "Successful Integration while Respecting Diversity; 'Old' Minorities versus 'New' Minorities." *Helsinki Monitor* 18(1): 46–56.

Levy, Sheri R; Chi-Yue Chiu, and Ying-Yi Hong. 2006. "Lay Theories and Intergroup Relations." *Group Processes & Intergroup Relations* 9(1): 5–24.

Lichbach, Mark Irving. 1989. "An Evaluation of 'Does Economic Inequality Breed Political Conflict' Studies." *World Politics* 41(July): 431–470.

Liebkind, Karmela; Anna Henning-Lindblom, and Erling Solheim. 2008. "Group Size, Group Status and Trait Valence as Determinants of Intergroup Bias: Stereotyping in Finland and Sweden." *European Journal of Social Psychology* 38(4): 637–651.

Lijphart, Arend. 1968. *The Politics of Accommodation. Pluralism and Democracy in the Netherlands*. Berkeley: University of California Press.

———. 1977. *Democracy in Plural Societies: A Comparative Exploration.* New Haven: Yale University Press.

———. 1999. *Patterns of Democracy: Government Forms and Performance in Thirty-Six Countries*. New Haven, Yale University Press.

Livingstone, Andrew G; Russell Spears, Antony S. R. Manstead, and Martin Bruder. 2009. "Illegitimacy and Identity Threat in (Inter)action: Predicting Intergroup Orientations among Minority Group Members." *British Journal of Social Psychology* 48 (4): 755–775.

Louis, Winnifred R. 2009. "Collective Action—and Then What?" *Journal of Social Issues* 65(4): 727–748.

Madrid, Raúl L. 2005. "Indigenous Voters and Party System Fragmentation in Latin America." *Electoral Studies* 24 (4): 689–707.

Mahon, Patrice C. 2005. "Managing Ethnicity." *Problems of Post-Communism* 52(1): 15–27.

Marc, Alexandre. 2010. *Delivering Services in Multicultural Societies*. Washington, D.C.: World Bank.

Marx, Anthony W. 1998. *Making Race and Nation: A Comparison of South Africa, the US, and Brazil.* New York: Cambridge University Press.

Mason, Thomas David. 2004. *Caught in the Crossfire: Revolutions, Repression, and the Rational Peasant*. Rowman & Littlefield.

Masuoka, Natalie. 2006. "Together They Become One: Examining the Predictors of Panethnic Group Consciousness among Asian Americans and Latinos." *Social Science Quarterly* (Dec 2006 Supplement) 87: 993–1011.

Matser, Carine; Jan Pieter van Oudenhoven, Françoise Askevis-Leherpeux, Arnd Florack, Bettina Hannover, and Jerôme Rossier. 2010. "Impact of Relative Size and Language on the Attitudes between Nations and Linguistic Groups: The Case of Switzerland." *Applied Psychology: An International Review* 59(1): 143–158.

McClain, Paula D. 2006. "Racial Intergroup Relations in a Set of Cities: A Twenty-Year Perspective (Presidential Address)." *Journal of Politics* 68(4): 757–770.

McMillan, Joyce. 1996. "Scotland's Quiet Nationalism." In *Europe's New Nationalism: States and Minorities in Conflict*, edited by Richard Caplan and John Feffer, 75–84. New York: Oxford University Press.

Medrano, Juan Díez, and Paula Gutiérrez. 2001. "Nested Identities: National and European Identity in Spain." *Ethnic & Racial Studies* 24(5): 753–780.

Meerman, Jacob. 2009. *Socio-Economic Mobility and Low-Status Minorities: Slow Roads to Progress.* London; New York: Routledge.

Mendoza-Denton, Rodolfo, and Michelle Goldman-Flythe. 2009. "Personality and Racial/Ethnic Relations: A Perspective from Cognitive–Affective Personality System (CAPS) Theory." *Journal of Personality* 77(5): 1261–1282.

Migdal, Joel. 1997. "Studying the State." In *Comparative Politics: Rationality, Culture and Structure,* edited by Mark I. Lichbach and Alan S. Zuckerman, 208–237. New York: Cambridge University Press.

Mihailescu, Mihaela. 2008. "The Politics of Minimal 'Consensus'." *East European Politics & Societies* 22(3): 553–594.

Minority Rights Group International. 1997. *World Directory of Minorities*. London: Minority Rights Group International.

Mischel, Walter; Rodolfo Mendoza-Denton, and Ying-yi Hong. 2009. "Toward an Integrative CAPS Approach to Racial/Ethnic Relations." *Journal of Personality* 77(5): 1365–1380.

Moghaddam, Fathali M. 2008. *Multiculturalism and Intergroup Relations: Psychological Implications for Democracy in Global Context*. Washington, DC: American Psychological Association.

———. 2010. *The New Global Insecurity: How Terrorism, Environmental Collapse, Economic Inequalities, and Resource Shortages Are Changing Our World.* Praeger.

Moghaddam, Fathali M, Donald M. Taylor, and Stephen C. Wright. 1993. *Social Psychology in Cross-cultural Perspective*. New York: W.H. Freeman.

Moore, Margaret. 2001. *The Ethics of Nationalism*. Oxford University Press.

Moscovici, Serge, and Juan A. Pérez. 2007. "A Study of Minorities as Victims." *European Journal of Social Psychology* 37(4): 725–746.

Moshman, David. 2007. "Us and Them: Identity and Genocide." *Identity* 7(2): 115–135.

Nagda, Biren (Ratnesh) A; Linda R. Tropp, and Elizabeth Levy Paluck. 2006. "Looking Back as We Look Ahead: Integrating Research, Theory, and Practice on Intergroup Relations." *Journal of Social Issues* 62(3): 439–451.

Nagel, Ernst. 1961. *The Structure of Science: Problems in the Logic of Scientific Explanation*. New York, Harcourt, Brace & World.

Nakao, Keisuke. 2009. "Creation of Social Order in Ethnic Conflict." *Journal of Theoretical Politics* 21(3): 365–394.

Norris, Pippa. 2008. *Driving Democracy: Do Power-Sharing Institutions Work?* Cambridge University Press.

Norris, Pippa, and Ronald Inglehart. 2009. *Cosmopolitan Communications: Cultural Diversity in a Globalized World.* Cambridge University Press.

O'Flynn, Ian, and David Russell, eds. 2005. *Power Sharing: New Challenges for Divided Societies*. London: Pluto.

O'Leary, Brendan. 2001. "Nationalism and Ethnicity: Research Agendas on Theories of Their Sources and Their Regulation." In *Ethnopolitical Warfare: Causes, Consequences, and Possible Solutions*, edited by Daniel Chirot and Martin E.P. Seligman, 37–48. Washington, DC: American Psychological Association.

O'Loughlin, John, and Gearoid O Tuathail (Gerard Toal). 2009. "Accounting for Separatist Sentiment in Bosnia-Herzegovina and the North Caucasus of Russia: A Comparative Analysis of Survey Responses." *Ethnic & Racial Studies* 32(4): 591–615.

Olsen, Johan P. 2005. *"Unity and diversity - European style." ARENA Working Paper* No. 24, https://www.sv.uio.no/arena/english/research/publications/arena-publications/workingpapers/working-papers2005/wp05_24.pdf.

Oommen, T.K. 1997. *Citizenship, Nationality and Ethnicity: Reconciling Competing Identities*. Polity Press.

Organista, Pamela Balls; Gerardo Marin, and Kevin M. Chun. 2010. *The Psychology of Ethnic Groups in the United States*. Thousand Oaks: Sage.

Özcan, Ali Kemal. 2005. "Nationalism: Distilling the Cultural and the Political." *Nationalism & Ethnic Politics* 11(2): 163–193.

Parrillo, Vincent N, and Christopher Donoghue. 2005. "Updating the Bogardus Social Distance Studies: A New National Survey." *Social Science Journal* 42(2): 257–271.

Pettigrew, Thomas F, and Linda R. Tropp. 2006. "A Meta-Analytic Test of Intergroup Contact Theory." *Journal of Personality & Social Psychology* 90(5): 751–783.

Phinney, Jean S, and Anthony D. Ong. 2007. "Conceptualization and Measurement of Ethnic Identity: Current Status and Future Directions." *Journal of Counseling Psychology* 54(3): 271–281.

Phinney, Jean S; Brian Jacoby, and Charissa Silva. 2007. "Positive Intergroup Attitudes: The Role of Ethnic Identity." *International Journal of Behavioral Development* 31(5): 478–490.

Poggi, Gianfranco. 1978. *The Development of the Modern State: A Sociological Introduction*. Stanford University Press.

Ponterotto, Joseph G, and Jennie Park-Taylor. 2007. "Racial and Ethnic Identity Theory, Measurement, and Research in Counseling Psychology: Present Status and Future Directions." *Journal of Counseling Psychology* 54(3): 282–294.

Posner, Daniel N. 2004. "The Political Salience of Cultural Difference: Why Chewas and Tumbukas are Allies in Zambia and Adversaries in Malawi." *American Political Science Review* 98(4): 529–45.

———. 2006. *Institutions and Ethnic Politics in Africa.* New York: Cambridge University Press.

———. 2007. "Regime Change and Ethnic Cleavages in Africa," *Comparative Political Studies* 40(11): 1302–1327.

Pratt, Jeff. 2003. *Class, Nation and Identity: The Anthropology of Political Movements*. Pluto Press.

Pratto, Felicia, and Demis E. Glasford. 2008. "Ethnocentrism and the Value of a Human Life." *Journal of Personality & Social Psychology* 95(6): 1411–1428.

Prentice, Deborah A, and Dale T. Miller, eds. 1999. Cultural Divides: Understanding and Overcoming Group Conflict. New York: Russell Sage Foundation.

Primoratz, Igor, and Aleksandar Pavković, eds. 2006. *Identity, Self-Determination and Secession*. Aldershot, Hants, England; Burlington, VT: Ashgate.

Prügl, Elisabeth, and Markus Thiel, eds. 2009. *Diversity in the European Union*. New York: Palgrave Macmillan.

Przeworski, Adam; Michael E. Alvarez, Jose Antonio Cheibub, and Fernando Limongi. 2000. *Democracy and Development: Political Institutions and Well-Being in the World, 1950–1990.* Cambridge University Press.

Rabushka, Alvin, and Kenneth Shepsle. 1972. *Politics in Plural Societies: A Theory of Democratic Instability.* Columbus, Ohio, Charles E. Merrill Publishing.

Radnitz, Scott. 2004. "The Tyranny of Small Differences: The Relationship between Ethnic Diversity and Democracy in the Former Socialist Bloc." Demokratizatsiya 12(4): 575–606.

Ratner, Steven R. 2000. "Does International Law Matter in Preventing Ethnic Conflict*?" New York University Journal of International Law and Politics*. 32(3): 591–698.

Reynal-Querol, Marta. 2002. "Ethnicity, Political Systems, and Civil Wars." *Journal of Conflict Resolution* 46(1): 29–54.

———. 2005. "Does Democracy Preempt Civil Wars?" *European Journal of Political Economy* 21: 445–465.

Riek, Blake M; Eric W. Mania, and Samuel L. Gaertner. 2006. "Intergroup Threat and Outgroup Attitudes: A Meta-Analytic Review." *Personality & Social Psychology Review* (Lawrence Erlbaum Associates) 10(4): 336–353.

Risse, Thomas. 2005. "Neofunctionalism, European Identity, and the Puzzles of European Integration." Journal of European Public Policy 12(2): 291–309.

Ross, Marc Howard. 2007. *Cultural Contestation in Ethnic Conflict*. Cambridge University Press.

———. 2011. "Reflections on the Strengths and Limitations to Cross-Cultural Evidence in the Study of Conflict and Its Mitigation." *Cross-Cultural Research* 45(1): 82–96.

Rumford, Chris, ed. 2009. *The SAGE Handbook of European Studies*. Los Angeles; London: SAGE.

Rutter, Michael, and Marta Tienda, eds. 2005. *Ethnicity and Causal Mechanisms*. Cambridge, UK; New York: Cambridge University Press.

Rydgren, Jens. 2007. "The Power of the Past: A Contribution to a Cognitive Sociology of Ethnic Conflict." *Sociological Theory* 25(3): 225–244.

Saguy, Tamar; Nicole Tausch, John F. Dovidio, and Felicia Pratto. 2009. "The Irony of Harmony: Intergroup Contact Can Produce False Expectations for Equality." *Psychological Science* 20(1): 114–121.

Salomon, Gavriel, and Edward Cairns, eds. 2010. Handbook on Peace Education. New York: Psychology Press.

Saxton, Gregory, and Michelle Benson. 2008. "Means, Motives and Opportunities in Ethno-Nationalist Mobilization." *International Interactions* 34(1): 53–83.

Scott, James. 1999. *Seeing Like a State.* New Haven: Yale University Press.

Sears, David O. 1993. "Symbolic Politics: A socio-Psychological Theory." In *Explorations in Political Psychology*, edited by Shanto Iyengar and William J. McGuire, 113–150. Durham, NC: Duke University Press.

Segura, Gary M, and Helena Alves Rodrigues. 2006. "Comparative Ethnic Politics in The United States: Beyond Black and White." *Annual Review of Political Science* 9(1): 375–395.

Sekuli, Duško; Garth Massey, and Randy Hodson. 2006. "Ethnic Intolerance and Ethnic Conflict in the Dissolution of Yugoslavia." *Ethnic & Racial Studies* 29(5): 797–827.

Shapiro, Jenessa R, and Steven L. Neuberg. 2008. "When Do the Stigmatized Stigmatize? The Ironic Effects of Being Accountable to (Perceived) Majority Group Prejudice-Expression Norms." *Journal of Personality & Social Psychology* 95(4): 877–898.

Sibley, Chris G, and Marc S. Wilson. 2007. "Political Attitudes and the Ideology of Equality: Differentiating Support for Liberal and Conservative Political Parties in New Zealand." *New Zealand Journal of Psychology* 36(2): 72–84.

Sidanius, Jim, and Felicia Pratto. 1999. *Social Dominance: An Intergroup Theory of Social Hierarchy and Oppression.* Cambridge, U.K.; New York: Cambridge University Press.

Sidanius, Jim; Hillary Haley, Ludwin Molina, and Felicia Pratto. 2007. "Vladimir's Choice and the Distribution of Social Resources: A Group Dominance Perspective." *Group Processes & Intergroup Relations* 10(2): 257–265.

Skutsch, Carl, and Martin Ryle, eds. 2005. *Encyclopedia of the world's minorities.* New York: Routledge.

Slocum-Bradley, Nikki. 2007. "Constructing and De-constructing the ACP Group: Actors, Strategies and Consequences for Development." *Geopolitics* 12(4): 635–655.

Smith, Anthony D. 1996. "Culture, Community, and Territory: The Politics of Ethnicity and Nationalism." *International Affairs* 72(3): 445–458.

———. 1998. *Nationalism and Modernism: A Critical Survey of Recent Theories of Nations and Nationalism.* Routledge.

Solt, Frederick. 2009. *The Standardized World Income Inequality Database*, http://hdl.handle.net/1902.1/11992 V4 [Version].

Sorens, Jason. 2005. "The Cross-sectional Determinants of Secessionism in Advanced Democracies." *Comparative Political Studies* 38(3): 304–326.

Spruyt, Hendrik. 2007. "War, Trade, and State Formation." In *The Oxford Handbook of Comparative Politics,* edited by Carles Boix and Susan Stokes, 211–236. New York: Oxford.

Squires, Judith. 2002. "Terms of Inclusion: Citizenship and the Shaping of Ethnonational Identities." In *Ethnonational Identities*, edited by Steve Fenton and Stephen May, 227–252. Palgrave Macmillan.

St. Louis, Gemima R, and Joan H. Liem. 2005. "Ego Identity, Ethnic Identity, and the Psychosocial Well-Being of Ethnic Minority and Majority College Students." *Identity* 5(3): 227–246.

Staub, Ervin. 1992. *The Roots of Evil: The Origins of Genocide and other Group Violence*. Cambridge University Press.

Steinberg, David A, and Stephen M. Saideman. 2008. "Laissez Fear: Assessing the Impact of Government Involvement in the Economy on Ethnic Violence." *International Studies Quarterly* 52(2): 235–259.

Stewart, Frances, ed. 2008. Horizontal Inequalities and Conflict: Understanding Group Violence in Multiethnic Societies. Basingstoke [England]; New York: Palgrave Macmillan.

Stokes, Gale. 2005. "From Nation to Minority: Serbs in Croatia and Bosnia at the Outbreak of the Yugoslav Wars." *Problems of Post-Communism* 52(6): 3–20.

Stolzenberg, Lisa; David Eitle, and Stewart J. D'Alessio. 2006. "Race, Economic Inequality, and Violent Crime." *Journal of Criminal Justice* 34(3): 303–316.

Stroschein, Sherrill. 2001. "Measuring Ethnic Party Success in Romania, Slovakia, and Ukraine." *Problems of Post-Communism* 48(4): 59–69.

Subaši, Emina, and Katherine J. Reynolds. 2009. "Beyond 'Practical' Reconciliation: Intergroup Inequality and the Meaning of Non-Indigenous Identity." *Political Psychology* 30(2): 243–267.

Tajfel, Henri. 1974. "Social Identity and Intergroup Behaviour." *Social Science Information,* 13: 65–93.

———. 1982: "Social Psychology of Intergroup Relations." *Annual Review of Psychology* 33: 1–39.

Tajfel, Henri, and John C. Turner. 1979. "An Integrative Theory of Intergroup Conflict." In *The Social Psychology of Intergroup Relations,* edited by William G. Austin and Stephen Worchel. Monterey, CA: Brooks-Cole.

Tarling, Nicholas, and Edmund Terence Gomez, eds. 2008. *The State, Development and Identity in Multi-Ethnic Societies: Ethnicity, Equity and the Nation*. London; New York: Routledge.

Tarr, G. Alan; Robert F. Williams, and Josef Marko, eds. 2004. *Federalism, Subnational Constitutions, and Minority Rights*. Westport, CT: Praeger.

Tausch, Nicole; Miles Hewstone, and Ravneeta Roy. 2009. "The Relationships between Contact, Status and Prejudice: An Integrated Threat Theory Analysis of Hindu–Muslim Relations in India." *Journal of Community & Applied Social Psychology* 19(2): 83–94.

Teorell, Jan; Marcus Samanni, Soren Holmberg, and Bo Rothstein. 2011. *The Quality of Government Dataset*, version 6 April 2011. University of Gothenburg: The Quality of Government Institute, http://www.qog.pol.gu.se.

Tesser, Abraham, and Norbert Schwarz, eds. 2001. *Blackwell Handbook of Social Psychology: Intraindividual Processes.* Malden, MA; Oxford: Blackwell Publishers.

Tilly, Charles. 1990. *Coercion, Capital, and European States, AD 990–1990.* Wiley-Blackwell.

Tir, Jaroslav, and Michael Jasinski. 2008. "Domestic-Level Diversionary Theory of War: Targeting Ethnic Minorities." *Journal of Conflict Resolution* 52(5): 641–664.

Transue, John E. 2007. "Identity Salience, Identity Acceptance, and Racial Policy Attitudes: American National Identity as a Uniting Force." *American Journal of Political Science* 51(1): 78–91.

Tredoux, Colin, and Gillian Finchilescu. 2007. "The Contact Hypothesis and Intergroup Relations 50 Years On: Introduction to the Special Issue." *South African Journal of Psychology* 37(4): 667–678.

Tyler, Tom R. 2006. "Psychological Perspectives on Legitimacy and Legitimation." *Annual Review of Psychology* 57(1): 375–400.

Ukiwo, Ukoha. 2007. "Education, Horizontal Inequalities and Ethnic Relations in Nigeria." *International Journal of Educational Development* 27(3): 266–281.

van Evera, Stephen. 1994. "Hypotheses on Nationalism and War." *International Security* 18(4): 5–39.

———. 2001. "Primordialism Lives!" I *Symposium: Cumulative Findings in the Study of Ethnic Politics*, APSA-CP Newsletter, 12(1): 20–22.

Verkuyten, Maykel. 2005. "Ethnic Group Identification and Group Evaluation among Minority and Majority Groups: Testing the Multiculturalism Hypothesis." *Journal of Personality & Social Psychology* 88(1): 121–138.

———. 2007. "Ethnic In-Group Favoritism among Minority and Majority Groups: Testing the Self-Esteem Hypothesis Among Preadolescents." *Journal of Applied Social Psychology* 37(3): 486–500.

Vorrath, Judith, and Lutz F. Krebs. 2009. "Democratisation and Conflict in Ethnically Divided Societies." *Living Reviews in Democracy* http://democracy.livingreviews.org/index.php/lrd/article/view/lrd-2009–1/3.

Wagner, Ulrich; Oliver Christ, Thomas F. Pettigrew, Jost Stellmacher, and Carina Wolf. 2006. "Prejudice and Minority Proportion: Contact instead of Threat Effects." *Social Psychology Quarterly* 69(4): 380–390.

Weaver, Charles N. 2008. "Social Distance as a Measure of Prejudice among Ethnic Groups in the United States." *Journal of Applied Social Psychology* 38(3): 779–795.

Weldon, Steven A. 2006. "The Institutional Context of Tolerance for Ethnic Minorities: A Comparative, Multilevel Analysis of Western Europe." *American Journal of Political Science* 50(2): 331–349.

Weller, Marc, and Katherine Nobbs, eds. 2010. *Political Participation of Minorities: A Commentary on International Standards and Practice*. Oxford: New York: Oxford University Press.

Willms, J. Douglas, and Marie-Andre Somers. 2001. "Family, Classroom, and School Effects on Children's Educational Outcomes in Latin America." *School Effectiveness and School Improvement* 12(4): 409–445. DOI: 10.1076/sesi.12.4.409.3445.

Wimmer, Andreas. 2002. *Nationalist Exclusion and Ethnic Conflict: Shadows of Modernity*. Cambridge, UK; New York, NY, USA: Cambridge University Press.

Wimmer, Andreas; Lars-Erik Cederman, and Brian Min. 2009. "Ethnic Politics and Armed Conflict: A Configurational Analysis of a New Global Data Set." *American Sociological Review* 74(2): 316–337.

Winter, Elke. 2007. "How Does the Nation Become Pluralist?" *Ethnicities* 7(4): 483–515.

Wright, Stephen C; Donald M. Taylor, and Fathali M. Moghaddam. 1990. "Responding to Membership in a Disadvantaged Group: From Acceptance to Collective Protest." *Journal of Personality and Social Psychology* 58(6): 994–1003.

Wright, Stephen C, and Donald M. Taylor. 2003. "The Social Psychology of Cultural Diversity: Social Stereotyping, Prejudice and Discrimination." In *Sage Handbook of Social Psychology*, edited by Michael A. Hogg and Joel M. Cooper, 432–458. New York: Sage.

Wu, Da. 2006. "Rational Choice and Primordialism: A Case Study of Ethnic Identities among the Ersu of Sichuan, China." *Taiwan Journal of Anthropology* 4(1): 113–147.

Wyer, Natalie A. 2010. "Salient Egalitarian Norms Moderate Activation of Outgroup Approach and Avoidance." *Group Processes & Intergroup Relations* 13(2): 151–165.

Yashar, Deborah J. 2005. *Contesting Citizenship in Latin America: Indigenous Movements and the Postliberal Challenge*. Oxford University Press.

Young, Crawford. 1983. "The Temple of Ethnicity." *World Politics* 35(4): 652–656.

Ysseldyk, Renate; Kimberly Matheson, and Hymie Anisman. 2010. "Religiosity as Identity: Toward an Understanding of Religion from a Social Identity Perspective." *Personality & Social Psychology Review* (Sage) 14(1): 60–71.

Zhu, Yuchao, and Dongyan Blachford. 2006. "Ethnic Disputes in International Politics: Manifestations and Conceptualizations." *Nationalism & Ethnic Politics* 12(1): 25–51.

Sources of Information for the Datasets

SOURCES OF GROUP-LEVEL DATA

Datasets and Databases

CONIS: Conflict Information System. Previously Cosimo or Kosimo, maintained by the Heidelberg Institute for International Conflict Research (HIIK) in the Department of Political Science, University of Heidelberg. They publish annual "Conflict Barometers" since 1992. http://www.hiik.de/en/kosimo/kosimo2.html.

DHS: Demographic and Health Survey series, by USAID. http://www.dhsprogram.com/

EPR: Ethnic Power Relations. Lars-Erik Cederman; Brian Min; Andreas Wimmer, 2009-05-01, "Ethnic Power Relations dataset", http://hdl.handle.net/1902.1/11796 UNF:5:k4xxXC2ASI204QZ4jqvUrQ==V1 [Version]

MAR: Minorities at Risk. http://www.cidcm.umd.edu/mar.

MICS: Multiple Indicator Cluster Survey series, by UNICEF. http://www.unicef.org/statistics/index_24302.html

MRG: Minority Rights Group International, author of the World Directory of Minorities. http://www.minorityrights.org/

UCDP/ PRIO: Armed Conflict Dataset. http://www.prio.no/CSCW/Datasets/Armed-Conflict/UCDP-PRIO.

UNDP Roma Survey. http://vulnerability.undp.sk/

UNESCO DME: UNESCO's Deprivation and Marginalization in Education dataset, http://www.unesco.org/new/fileadmin/MULTIMEDIA/HQ/ED/GMR/html/dme-1.html (Downloaded in summer 2010.)

Opinion Survey Series

Afrobarometer: Third round, implemented in 2005–2006.

Arab Barometer: Lebanon 2007.

Asia Foundation: Survey of the Afghan People series, 2006–2010.
Asian Barometer: Selected countries and years.
ISSP 2003: International Social Survey Programme 2003 Round on National Identities.
Latinobarometro: 2007.
WVS 2005: World Value Survey series 2005–2006 wave.

Publications by International Organizations and Governments

ACHPR/ IWGIA. 2009. Report of the African Commission's Working Group on Indigenous Populations/Communities. Research and information visit to Libya 11–25 August 2005.

Asian Centre for Human Rights (ACHR). 2007. "Pakistan: The Land of Religious Apartheid and Jackboot Justice," Executive summary and recommendations, http://www.achrweb.org/Review/2007/179-07.htm

Bennett, Lynn. 2005. "Gender, Caste and Ethnic Exclusion in Nepal." World Bank conference paper, http://siteresources.worldbank.org/INTRANETSOCIALDEVELOPMENT/ Re-sources/Bennett.rev.pdf

Human Rights Watch. 2004. "Angola: Between War and Peace in Cabinda." A Human Rights Watch Briefing Paper.

ILO/ACHPR. 2009. Country Report of the Research Project by the International Labour Organization and the African Commission on Human and Peoples' Rights on the Constitutional and Legislative Protection of the Rights of Indigenous Peoples: Eritrea. Geneva: ILO.

ILO/ACHPR. 2009. Overview Report of the Research Project by the International Labour Organization and the African Commission on Human and Peoples' Rights on the Constitutional and Legislative Protection of the Rights of Indigenous Peoples in 24 African countries. Geneva: ILO.

Ministry of Health and Family Welfare, Government of India. Nutrition in India, National Family Health Survey 3rd Round 2005–06 Report. International Institute for Population Sciences, Deonar, Mumbai – 400 088.

Oduori, S; R. Vargas, and Alim, M. 2007. "Land Use Characterisation of the Juba and Shabelle Riverine Areas in Southern Somalia." FAO-SWALIM. Project Report No. L-07. Nairobi, Kenya.

OHCHR. 2004. Concluding Observations on the Situation of Civil and Political Rights: Equatorial Guinea. 07/30/2004.

Programme of Assistance to the Palestinian People, United Nations Development Programme, http://www.papp.undp.org/en/index.html

UN_DESA SOWIP. 2009. State of the World's Indigenous Peoples. http://www.un.org/esa/socdev/unpfii/documents/SOWIP_web.pdf.

United States Department of State. 2010. Report on International Religious Freedom – Bhutan. 17 November 2010, available at: http://www.unhcr.org/refworld/docid/4cf2d0b16e.html.

UNRWA 2006: The Situation of Palestine Refugees in South Lebanon.

Library of Congress Country Studies

Collelo, Thomas, ed. 1991. *Angola: A Country Study*. Washington: GPO for the Library of Congress.

Crystal, Jill. 1993. "Kuwait." In *A Country Study: Kuwait*. Washington: GPO for the Library of Congress.

Doumato, Eleanor Abdella. 1992. "Chapter 2 – The Society and Its Environment." In *A Country Study: Saudi Arabia*. Washington: GPO for the Library of Congress.

Fareed Mohamedi. 1993. "Chapter 6." In *A Country Study: Oman*. Washington: GPO for the Library of Congress.

Hooglund, Eric, and Anthony Toth. 1993. "Chapter 5." In *A Country Study: United Arab Emirates*. Washington: GPO for the Library of Congress.

Ross, Russell R, ed. 1987. *Cambodia: A Country Study*. Washington: GPO for the Library of Congress.

Other

Aridi, Naim. "The Druze." http://www.jewishvirtuallibrary.org/jsource/Society_&_Culture/druze.html, Accessed March 2011.

Bougainville Copper Limited. http://www.bougainvillecopper.com.pg/.

Buraku Liberation and Human Rights Research Institute. 2007. Fact-Finding Survey of Minority Women in Japan. 1st Quarterly, 2007(143). http://blhrri.org/blhrri_e/news/new143/new143-4.htm

Ishikida, Miki Y. 2005: Living Together: Minority People and Disadvantaged Groups in Japan. iUniverse, Inc.

Mizanur Rahman. 2003. A Community in Transition: The Biharis in Bangladesh. Publisher: Empowerment Through Law of the Common People (ELCOP).

Van Lehman, Dan, and Omar Eno. 2002. "The Somali Bantu: Their History and Culture." Center for Applied Linguistics, Cultural Orientation Resource Center, Boston, MA.

Williams, G.A. 2000. "Dom of the Middle East – An Overview." http://www.domresearchcenter.com/journal/11/dom.html, accessed March 2011.

MAIN SOURCES OF COUNTRY-LEVEL DATA

QOG: Teorell, Jan, Marcus Samanni, Soren Holmberg, and Bo Rothstein. 2011. *The Quality of Government Dataset*, Version 6 April 2011. University of Gothenburg: The Quality of Government Institute, http://www.qog.pol.gu.se.

DPI: Beck, Thorsten; George Clarke, Alberto Groff, Philip Keefer, and Patrick Walsh. 2001. "New Tools in Comparative Political Economy: The Database of Political Institutions." *World Bank Economic Review* 15 (1):165–176. The database was updated in 2010, and it is available at http://econ.worldbank.org/WBSITE/EXTERNAL/EXTDEC/EXTRESEARCH/0,,contentMDK:20649465~pagePK:64214825~piPK:64214943~theSitePK: 469382,00.html.

Norris: Pippa Norris's Democracy dataset, which has a Crossnational and a Time-series version, both at their third edition in 2009. http://www.hks.harvard.edu/fs/pnorris/Data/Data.htm.

WGI: Worldwide Governance Indicators. http://data.worldbank.org/data-catalog/worldwide-governance-indicators.

IPD: Institutional Profiles Database. http://www.cepii.fr/IPD.asp.

FSI: Failed States Index. First launched in 2005; on May 28, 2014, the Fund for Peace changed the name of the index into Fragile States Index. http://ffp.statesindex.org/.

GPI: Global Peace Index. http://www.visionofhumanity.org/#/page/indexes/global-peace-index.

KOF: Dreher, Axel. 2006. "Does Globalization Affect Growth? Evidence from a new Index of Globalization." *Applied Economics* 38(10): 1091–1110. Updated in: Dreher, Axel; Noel Gaston, and Pim Martens. 2008. *Measuring Globalisation – Gauging its Consequences*. New York: Springer.

SOLT GINI: Solt, Frederick. 2009. "The Standardized World Income Inequality Database." http://hdl.handle.net/1902.1/11992. V10.

Index

About the Author

Agnes Katalin Koós was born as a Hungarian in Romania, immigrated to Hungary, then to the United States, and earned her PhD in political science in Canada. Her embracing of topics related to communal relations and socioterritorial identities is a very logical outcome of life experiences. Her personal world has always challenged the notion of a homogeneous nation-state, and has been premised on communal diversity.